MICHIGAN'S UPPER PENINSULA

PAUL VACHON

May 2018

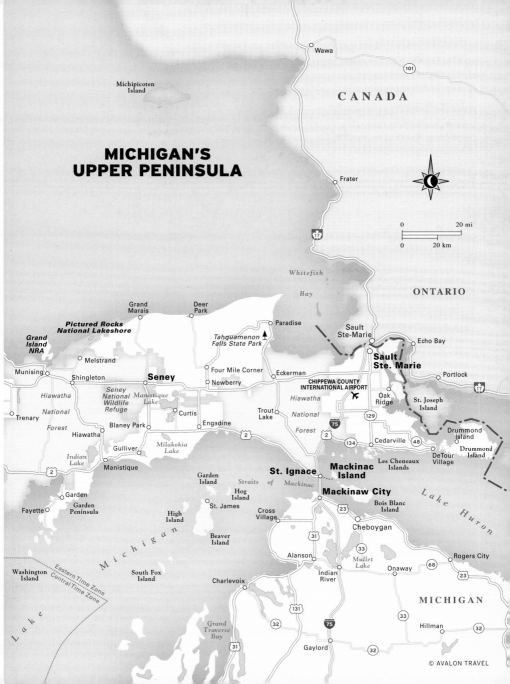

Contents

PRAYER OF THE WOODS

"I AM THE HEAT OF YOUR HEARTH ON THE COLD WINTER NIGHTS, THE FRIENDLY SHADE SCREENING YOU FROM THE SUMMER SUN, AND MY FRUITS ARE REFRESHING DRAUGHTS QUENCH- ING YOUR THIRST AS YOU JOURNEY ON." "I AM THE BEAM THAT HOLDS YOUR HOUSE, THE BOARD OF YOUR TABLE, THE BED ON WHICH YOU LIE, AND THE TIMBER THAT BUILDS YOUR BOAT." "I AM THE HANDLE OF YOUR HOE, THE DOOR OF YOUR HOMESTEAD, THE WOOD OF YOUR CRADLE, AND THE SHELL OF YOUR COFFIN." "I AM THE BREAD OF KINDNESS AND THE FLOWER OF BEAUTY." YE WHO PASS BY, LISTEN TO MY PRAYER: HARM ME NOT."

DISCOVER

Michigan's
Upper Peninsula

Locals call Michigan's Upper Peninsula the world *above* the bridge. Here you'll discover miles of freshwater coastline, hundreds of picturesque trails, and countless inland lakes, rivers, and waterfalls.

Sporting a rustic, even austere terrain, the U.P.'s sparse population provides peace and solitude. The eastern portion, part of the Great Lakes plain, contrasts sharply with the rocky western half. Each offers idyllic settings for camping, boating, and fishing. There's a good chance you'll see moose, black bears, red foxes, and white-tailed deer. Around these parts, packing a camera is an absolute necessity.

In many U.P. towns, descendants of European immigrants maintain the traditions of their ancestors from Scandinavia, Cornwall, Germany, or Italy. The blend of heritage and warm hospitality in the region can

Clockwise from top left: the bridge between Houghton and Hancock; a sign at Tahquamenon Falls; Crisp Point Light near Whitefish Point; the mining office at Lakenenland near Marquette; Whitefish Bay in winter; Point Iroquois Light in Sault Ste. Marie.

be absorbed through the food: Enjoy meatballs at a Swedish café, homemade ravioli at an Italian eatery, or try a Cornish pasty (a bread turnover filled with pork, chicken, or venison), a local favorite.

So, what *doesn't* the U.P. have? Crowds and congestion. Even the larger population centers have a small-town feel, exemplified by the absence of parking meters. With a population density of just 19 people per square mile, Michigan's extreme north offers plenty of room to explore.

Welcome to America's northern paradise.

Clockwise from top left: Little Girl's Point in Ironwood; Pictured Rocks National Lakeshore; Menominee River near Piers Gorge; Cornish pasty served with gravy.

Planning Your Trip

Where to Go

The Straits of Mackinac

As the only physical connection between the two peninsulas, all the traffic from the Lower Peninsula funnels onto the five-mile-long Mackinac Bridge and into the great northern counterpart. The photogenic span prompts many travelers to stop with their cameras. Uniquely charming **Mackinac Island** endures as one of America's perfect getaways, while historic sites and state parks both on and off the island bring the region's bountiful history to life. For some fascinating exposure to this history, visit **Colonial Michilimackinac** in Mackinaw City and **Fort Mackinac** on Mackinac Island.

Escanaba and the Lake Michigan Shore

The Lake Michigan shoreline makes for a pleasant drive, with waterfront stops and sandy beaches awaiting off U.S. 2. The Garden Peninsula, which juts out into Lake Michigan, is home to **Fayette Historic State Park,** which memorializes the region's mining history. Continuing to the southwest, **Escanaba** and **Menominee** each offer their special appeal. An old mining town, Escanaba is experiencing a rebirth. Be sure not to overlook the city's waterfront, where you can tour the **Sand Point Lighthouse** and spend time in **Ludington Park.**

The Superior Upland

The western U.P. is known for fantastic recreation at **Porcupine Mountains Wilderness State Park** (a.k.a. "the Porkies"). In summer, miles and miles of **hiking trails** lure visitors; in winter, the area's relatively mountainous terrain and extreme levels of snowfall combine to make **Ironwood** and its environs the top downhill destination in

the Mackinac Bridge

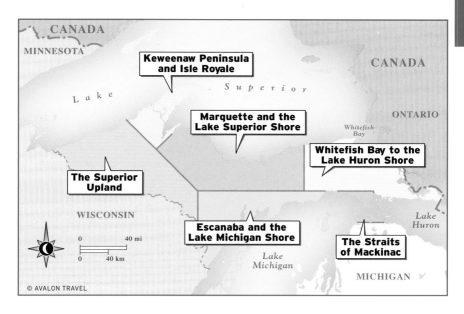

the Midwest, with many noteworthy **ski resorts** to choose from.

Keweenaw Peninsula and Isle Royale

Copper Harbor, at the top of the Keweenaw Peninsula, is mainland Michigan's "end of the road." But along the journey, the twin cities of **Houghton** and **Hancock** offer a cosmopolitan experience characteristic of college towns. Continuing north you'll find the historic town of **Calumet,** perhaps the most telling remnant of the glory days of Michigan copper mining.

Sequestered by Lake Superior, the rugged **Isle Royale National Park** can be reached only by boat or plane. The quiet isolation of the island park offers the best recreation in the U.P. as well as a chance to see reclusive **moose** and **wolves.**

Marquette and the Lake Superior Shore

Lake Superior's southern shore offers some of the nation's most beautiful scenery: tough pine, stony beaches, and craggy rocks. Rent a **sea kayak** or

view of Copper Harbor

Pictured Rocks National Lakeshore

take a boat tour to see the wonderful pallet of colors on the formations at **Pictured Rocks National Lakeshore. Marquette** boasts a vibrant arts scene, a historic downtown, and tranquil **Presque Isle Park.** Situated on a picturesque bay, **Munising** is flanked by **Grand Island,** an offshore recreation area with unique hiking and camping options.

Whitefish Bay to the Lake Huron Shore

Whitefish Bay offers boaters welcome protection from Lake Superior's wildly unpredictable weather. The bay drains south into the St. Mary's River like a giant funnel, guiding ships through the **Soo Locks** that connect Lakes Superior and Huron, providing the Great Lakes with an essential shipping lane. Be sure to visit the famous locks when visiting **Sault Ste. Marie.** On the shore of Lake Huron, the **Les Cheneaux Islands** and **Drummond Island** remain remote, quiet destinations that are perfect for visitors seeking seclusion.

Know Before You Go

When to Go

Summer is when nature is at its most vibrant. It can get very hot and humid this time of year, with July being the warmest and most bug-infested month. Try to time a camping trip before the mosquitoes and blackflies hatch, generally in mid-June, or go after mid-August. Hotel rates tend to spike around July 4 and Labor Day.

Autumn may be the very best time to visit—temperatures are mild, the bugs are gone, and fall colors put on a show that rivals New England's. Predicting the period of peak color is an inexact science, but it generally occurs around the first or second week of September. Late October starts to get somewhat cold.

Winter arrives in early December and usually lingers through March. For winter sports, February is the likeliest to ensure good snow

Tahquamenon Falls in autumn

cover. Planning a winter trip does require special attention to detail, as some businesses close for the winter. For more on winter in the U.P., see page 268.

If you're able, avoid November and April, both of which are characterized by unpleasant gray skies and rain-snow-sleet mixtures. **Spring** usually doesn't begin until about mid-May, and the shady pine forests of the U.P. can hold snow until Memorial Day or even later. Spring can be wonderful, with moderate temperatures, blossoming trees, and gushing waterfalls.

Transportation

The Upper Peninsula is accessible by any manner of transportation, but for travel within the U.P., a **car** is an absolute necessity. **Public transportation** is scarce and rarely operates outside larger cities. The U.P. is much larger than many people assume, and it takes hours to drive from one city to the next. Secondary roads are pretty rugged, so if you plan on venturing off the major routes, make sure your vehicle has **four-wheel-drive** and high clearance.

What to Pack

For many travelers to the Upper Peninsula, camping is the lodging of choice. In this case, it is essential to pack a **tent** and other necessities for traveling from campsite to campsite across the peninsula. Required outdoors staples include **bug spray with DEET,** sturdy shoes, and clothing for inclement weather. A small backpack for day trips or short hikes is also a good idea.

For other visitors, seasonal casual clothing and basic essentials are all that's necessary. Unless you plan to dine at one of Marquette's finer restaurants or to enjoy a formal dinner at the Grand Hotel (several places on Mackinac Island have dress codes), dress clothing is unnecessary.

A good idea is to purchase a Michigan Recreation Passport ahead of time through the state's **Passport Perks** program. The annual pass allows you to access any Michigan state park and offers savings at participating restaurants and stores. If you decide to cross the International Bridge into Canada, you'll need a **passport** or other suitable travel document.

Best of Michigan's Upper Peninsula

The Charming East

On a map, the enormity of the Upper Peninsula can be deceptive. The unique qualities that give the U.P. its appeal are scattered over 30,000 square miles, 14 counties, and two times zones. If you only have a week and want to experience a bit of everything—without having to work too hard to do so—stick to the eastern half. Rustic hiking trails, breathtaking lake views, and charming small towns await you.

Day 1

Chances are you'll be arriving in **Mackinaw City,** the gateway to the U.P., after a very long drive from home. Check into a comfortable hotel room, enjoy a meal at one of the local restaurants, and take a bit of time to explore downtown. A

respite like this is the perfect tonic for early vacation fatigue—one you'll thank yourself for later.

Day 2

Catch an early ferry to **Mackinac Island** (7:30am is the first). If you plan on spending just one day on the island, it's best to be a commuter visitor and return to your Mackinaw City lodgings at day's end. Visit **Fort Mackinac,** take a captivating carriage ride past the lovely Victorian cottages, and visit the **Governor's Residence** and the magnificent veranda at the **Grand Hotel.** Yes, they charge $15 per person for the veranda privilege, but the experience is truly unforgettable. After lunch, take in a relaxing round of golf at **The Jewel** or spend some time at **Mackinac**

the ferry to Mackinac Island

Bond Falls

Scattered around the U.P. are no less than 300 sites of cascading water that punctuate its vast network of rivers and streams. Most require at least a short walk to reach, but the beauty awaiting at the end of your hike will make the effort worthwhile. While their sizes vary in terms of width and drop (the vertical height), virtually all are in idyllic tree-lined settings.

Spring is when the flow of water tends to be the strongest, as the runoff from the winter's snow and ice swell the rivers, allowing gravity to work its magic. In **summer,** trees that are in full bloom combined with the warm temperatures can make waterfall viewing an ideal daylong activity. But **autumn** is without question the most satisfying time to see waterfalls—watching the cascading stream amidst patches of yellow, orange, and crimson is endlessly engaging. **Winter** is for the more intrepid visitor, but they'll be rewarded with solitude and unique beauty.

Be sure not to miss these beauties:

- **Tahquamenon Falls,** Paradise (page 236)

- **Bond Falls,** Paulding (page 120)

- **Presque Isle Falls,** Porcupine Mountains Wilderness State Park (page 135)

Island Butterfly House. If you have a sweet tooth—and who doesn't?—pick up a wedge or two of world-famous Mackinac Island fudge at either **Murdick's Fudge** or **Ryba's.** Enjoy dinner on the island at the **Woods Restaurant** before returning to your lodgings on the mainland.

Day 3

Get an early breakfast at Darrow's Family Restaurant; you have a bit of a drive ahead of you. Cross the bridge, turn right and make a brief stop at **Straits State Park.** Here you can enjoy a breathtaking bridge view on the Upper Peninsula side. Head west along U.S. 2. As you begin your trip from St. Ignace to Naubinway, you'll be treated with a pleasing panorama of the Lake Michigan shore, with St. Helena Island in the distance. There are many turnouts along

trail near Tahquamenon Falls State Park

this route, and with a good zoom lens and clear weather, you can get a shot of the island's lighthouse. Continue on toward **Manistique** and stop for lunch at **Clyde's Drive-In No. 2** for a great burger and malt. After lunch, turn off onto M-149 and head to **Palms Book State Park** to see Kitch-Iti-Kipi, better known as "Big Spring." Continue on U.S. 2, ending your day's sojourn in **Escanaba.** Have dinner and stay the night at the historic **House of Ludington.**

Day 4

After breakfast in Escanaba at the authentic **Swedish Pantry,** head up M-35 toward Marquette, the Upper Peninsula's largest and most cosmopolitan city. Once you arrive, a stroll along the waterfront will be invigorating after time behind the wheel. Bring your camera so you can get some great shots of **Marquette Harbor Lighthouse,** a photogenic lighthouse on rocks located offshore. Grab lunch and spend the rest of the afternoon exploring the area,

perhaps perusing junkyard art at **Lakenenland Sculpture Park** or viewing the sunset at **Presque Isle Park.** Choose from one of several excellent downtown dining spots for dinner before spending the night in Marquette.

Day 5

Grab breakfast at the **Sweet Water Café** before setting course on M-28 for **Munising** and **Pictured Rocks National Lakeshore.** Since the colorful rocks can only be seen from the water, either book a three-hour **boat tour** with Pictured Rocks Cruises or a six-hour **kayak tour** (departing at 9am) with Paddling Michigan. Enjoy dinner at **Lake Superior Brewing Company** and stay the night in **Grand Marais;** renting one of the **Hilltop Cabins** will offer a great waterfront view.

Day 6

Grab a convenient breakfast at **West Bay Diner and Deli,** then hit the road for **Tahquamenon**

Planning a fall color tour of Michigan's Upper Peninsula can be tricky, as the timing of peak colors is often unpredictable. The risk is that you'll arrive a week early and be met with a landscape of midsummer green, or you'll come too late and be greeted by a sea of bare trees. But the fortunate traveler is in for a real treat. If your timing is right, all you need to enjoy the glory of countless trees in their peak color is the will to get outside, whether it's on a hiking trail, in a kayak along the shoreline, or in a car on one of the main highways. Visit **The Fall Color Blog** (www.fallcolorblog.com) for updates during the fall color season.

- One of the finest routes in the U.P. is the circle formed between **Eagle River** and **Copper Harbor** by U.S. 41 and M-26, an hour-long 45-mile loop. The scene is truly breathtaking, especially the section along U.S. 41/Copper Country Trail Scenic Byway.

- The **Keweenaw** from mid-September to early October showcases the best colors.

- The **Marquette-Negaunee-Au Train tour** will take you into the Huron Mountains on the way to Big Bay and back, as well as on a wider loop south and east of the city along M-35, U.S. 41, M-94, and M-28.

- Pure Michigan's website (www.michigan.org) lists ten U.P. **fall foliage driving routes,** including stops along the way and detailed maps for each tour.

fall colors near Manistique

Falls State Park, where you'll find the most magnificent waterfall in the U.P. You can see the Upper Falls from the observation deck, which is only a short trail walk from the parking area. Four miles downstream, the Lower Falls produce a similar spectacle. The awe-inspiring power of the falls is hard to overstate. As much as 50,000 gallons of water per second cascade over Upper Tahquamenon, the second most powerful waterfall in the eastern United States, exceeded only by Niagara. Enjoy lunch at the **Tahquamenon Falls Brewery and Pub** before setting out for **Sault Ste. Marie.** Sail through the always fascinating **Soo Locks** with Soo Locks Boat Tours and marvel at how gargantuan ships can transit though the locks with just inches to spare. Cap off your adventure with a special dinner at **Freighters.** Check in at the **Ojibway Hotel** for the night before departing for home the next morning.

Day 7

Enjoy one last breakfast at **Cup of the Day** before heading back to Mackinaw. Start planning your next trip on the drive home!

Best Hikes

hiking in Porcupine Mountains Wilderness State Park

What better way to experience the abundance of natural beauty in the UP than with a hike? Here are a few winners:

PORCUPINE MOUNTAINS WILDERNESS STATE PARK

Escarpment Trail

8.8 miles round-trip

This fairly short trail is a wonderfully scenic hike. The relatively high elevation offers a view of the Lake of the Clouds to the south, where summer greenery resembles a vast, lush carpet. Lake Superior is visible to the north.

PICTURED ROCKS NATIONAL LAKESHORE

Miners Falls Trail

2.4 miles round-trip

A delightful option for those unable to undertake a longer trek, this trail is an easy, flat, and well-maintained walk through sparse maple forest. Its low density allows for excellent viewing of deer and an occasional moose. The big payoff, however, comes at the end—the roaring, majestic Miners Falls.

TAHQUAMENON FALLS STATE PARK

Tahquamenon River Trail

8 miles round-trip

This great trail hugs the shore of the Tahquamenon River between the Upper and Lower Falls—you're never more than about twenty feet from the roaring river. This is an especially nice walk in the springtime, when the current is strongest due to the melting of the winter snow and ice.

ISLE ROYALE NATIONAL PARK

Greenstone Trail

42.2 miles one-way

Intended for the serious hiker/backpacker, this is perhaps the least ventured trail in the least visited park in the National Park system. Talk about experiencing nature in solitude! This four-day, three-night adventure will take you along the spine of the main island of the park. Seeing moose is not uncommon; if you're lucky, you may even see a gray wolf.

KEWEENAW PENINSULA

Keweenaw State Trail

51.7 miles one-way

This challenging trail makes for an interesting backpacking trip. The trail follows U.S. 41 at widely varying elevations, with portions consisting of old railroad beds that pierce through both pine and hardwood forests. It's especially enjoyable during the fall for leaf-peepers.

The Wild West

Adventure awaits in the western half of Michigan's Upper Peninsula. Take your time to really examine the scenery—it's much more rustic than in the east, and nothing like what you'll find in the big city!

Day 1

Start your trip on the U.S. 2 going west toward Iron River. Along the way you'll cross into the central time zone and begin to see some of the rough terrain the U.P. is known for. This area was the heart of iron country during the heyday of mining. To learn about this historic period, visit the **Iron Mountain Iron Mine** near Vulcan. Afterward, get back on U.S. 2 and stop in **Iron Mountain** for lunch; try either **Bimbo's Wine Press** on East Main Street if you appreciate good Italian fare (owing to the area's Italian heritage), or **Famers** on Pine Mountain Road if you'd prefer a sports bar

atmosphere. Continue west on U.S. 2, taking a brief detour into a corner of Wisconsin on the way to **Crystal Falls.** You're entering the Superior Upland, the area of rough beauty known as iron country. Stop in Crystal Falls just long enough to admire the spectacular view looking down Main Street and take a picture of the highlands in the distance. Continue west along U.S. 2 until you come to Watersmeet. Book a room at the **Lac Vieux Desert Resort Casino** for a well-deserved rest. After dinner at the Thunderbird Sports Lounge, make the short trek up U.S. 45 to view the baffling **Paulding Mystery Light.**

Day 2

The most picturesque wilderness of the Upper Peninsula awaits you! After breakfast at the hotel, take U.S. 45 north toward **Ontonagon,** where you'll find the eastern end of **Porcupine**

Lake of the Clouds

Mountains Wilderness State Park. Pick up picnic supplies in town before taking M-107 up the large hill to **Lake of the Clouds Overlook.** Park your car and make the very short hike up to the top of the cliff to take in the breathtaking view. Follow M-107 through the park, being careful of the frequent turns in the road. After exiting the park near Union Bay you'll find a series of scenic turnouts along the Lake Superior shore. Most have tables, so stop here to enjoy your picnic lunch and chat with some of your fellow travelers. After lunch, head to **Ontonagon** to take in the **Ontonagon County Historical Museum,** which offers a fascinating look at the community's past, with an emphasis on the logging and mining industries. The historical society also offers tours of the **Ontonagon Lighthouse,** an 1853 structure gradually being restored. Grab dinner at **Syl's Cafe** and get a cabin for the night at the **Mountain View Lodges** on M-64, featuring a waterfront view and a sandy beach.

Day 3

Today you'll be heading into the **Keweenaw Peninsula,** as north as you can go and still be in mainland Michigan. From Ontonagon, take U.S. 45 to M-26 and head north. As you progress, you'll see more pine and spruce trees mixed in with maples and elms. When you come to **Houghton,** a college town that's home to Michigan Technological University, stop and take a leisurely break, possibly at **Cyberia Café.** Stop to view the unusual "lift bridge" linking the city to Hancock across the Keweenaw Waterway. Continue north on U.S. 41 until you come to **Calumet,** considered by some to be the capital of the once-dominant copper industry. Take some time to look around at the magnificent if somewhat neglected architecture flanked by abandoned mines. Continue until you get to **Copper Harbor** and the end

of U.S. 41. Take a tour of the **Copper Harbor Lighthouse,** which involves a fun 15-minute boat ride from the marina. Book a room at the **Keweenaw Mountain Lodge.**

Day 4

Shift into nautical mode and board the *Isle Royale Queen IV* for the three-hour trip to **Isle Royale National Park,** the least-visited property in the National Park system. Although the park is very rugged and most visitors choose to camp, indoor accommodations are available at the **Rock Harbor Lodge** at Rock Harbor at the far eastern tip. Either way, you'll have virtually unlimited opportunities to commune with nature.

Hiking, fishing, observing wildlife, and kayaking are some of the activities you can enjoy. Spend two to three days exploring Isle Royale—a truly unforgettable experience.

Days 5-6

Take a few **day hikes** along some of the shorter trails into the island—**Scoville Point** and **Lookout Louise** are good choices, and the view from **Ojibway Tower** is phenomenal. Look into a National Park Service boat tour or rent a sea kayak and explore the shoreline yourself. Pack lunches and take them with you, but note that dinners at the lodge are satisfying.

Backwoods campers and hikers will have 165 miles of trails to explore. There's no way to hike it all in a few days, but a well-planned trip will have you walking from campsite to campsite while you keep a lookout for moose.

Day 7

Make sure you're back at the ferry dock by 2:45pm for the ride back to **Copper Harbor.** You'll get into town a little before 6pm, just in time for dinner at the **Harbor Haus.** Make your way back home in the morning.

Fort Wilkins Historic State Park

The region's prolific history is quite noticeable throughout the Upper Peninsula, with virtually every community boasting a local history museum and a variety of state-recognized sites. The state's Michigan History Center operates the Michigan Historical Marker Program, which has designated 128 noteworthy sites scattered among the U.P.'s 15 counties.

MINING HISTORY

- **Fayette Historic State Park** (page 79): Perhaps the best preserved "ghost town" in America, Fayette serves as a three-dimensional window to the nineteenth century, when belching blast furnaces turned raw iron ore into pig iron.

- **Keweenaw National Historic Park** (page 147): This park is made up of sites throughout the Keweenaw seminal to the area's copper mining heritage. Don't miss the Quincy Mine!

- **Iron County Heritage Trail** (page 114): This complex of attractions is a great destination for history buffs. The Iron County Historical Museum is its centerpiece (page).

- **Downtown Calumet** (page 147): This town offers a dynamic reminder of the once prosperous copper industry.

MARINE HISTORY

- **Great Lakes Shipwreck Museum** (page 235): This haunting yet intriguing museum pays tribute to those lost while working in commercial shipping on the Great Lakes.

- **Marquette Maritime Museum and Lighthouse** (page 186): This fascinating nautical museum emphasizes the role lighthouses have played in Great Lakes shipping.

MILITARY HISTORY

- **Colonial Michilimackinac State Park** (page 58): The site of the original fort, built in 1715, is the location of a 50-year-long archaeological dig, summertime reenactments, and a big wooden replica fort.

- **Fort Wilkins Historic State Park** (page 159): An example of excessive nineteenth century military spending, Fort Wilkins was built to combat trouble that never occurred. Today it's a historically accurate display of military life during the era, complete with costumed interpreters.

- **Fort Mackinac** (page 36): A massive fortress perched on a bluff overlooking the Straits of Mackinac and the village below, Ft. Mackinac best exemplifies the quintessential nineteenth century military fort. Interesting programing featuring interpreters in period dress make this a "must visit" destination.

campsite at Indian Lake State Park

For those with a more rustic spirit, the Upper Peninsula is a truly quintessential camping destination. Campers usually arrive at their site of choice, set up camp, and venture off on day hikes or fishing adventures.

- **Tahquamenon Falls State Park:** Take I-75 from the Mackinac Bridge to M-123 and head to Tahquamenon Falls State Park. Choose either the modern campground or its rustic counterpart, both located near the Lower Falls.

- **Mead Creek Campground:** Located off W-77 near the town of Germfask and right on the edge of the Seney National Wildlife Refuge, this campground is a true paradise for wildlife photographers and nature lovers. From the National Wildlife Refuge Visitors Center near the entrance road, choose from several nature trails, where you can see and hear loons, nesting bald eagles, beavers, river otters, and perhaps an occasional bear or moose—all of which thrive in this protected habitat.

- **Indian Lake State Park:** Just a short drive down U.S. 2, you can experience a classic U.P. camping experience. Fish, swim, or rent a boat to venture out on crystal clear Indian Lake. While you're in the area, don't forget to check out Kitch-Iti-Kipi, the fascinating natural spring in nearby Palms Book State Park.

- **Porcupine Mountains Wilderness State Park:** This is where you'll get the quintessential U.P. camping experience. The park offers backcountry camping, hiking trails of various lengths, and stunning views of the majestic landscape. You'll also find over 35,000 acres of old growth hardwood forest.

- **Straits State Park:** For those interested in a less primitive camping experience, Straits offers a spectacular view of the Mackinac Bridge as well as fully or partly serviced sites. There's also a one-mile-long nature trail.

a carriage outside of the Grand Hotel

Mackinac Island Getaway

If you're looking for a long, romantic weekend away with your partner, look no further than Mackinac Island. You'll find plenty of Victorian charm, picturesque views, and recreational opportunities to enjoy with your significant other.

Day 1

After a long day of driving, take Shepler's ferry from St. Ignace to **Mackinac Island** for a relaxing evening. If you're splurging, spend the night at the **Grand Hotel.** If you're on a budget, try the **Inn at Stonecliffe.**

Day 2

Start your day leisurely with breakfast at the hotel and a **carriage tour** to get the lay of the land. Stops include the Butterfly House, Fort Mackinac, and Arch Rock. Be sure to also visit the Governor's Residence and stop for some fudge at Murdick's. If you're more athletically inclined, skip the carriage tour and rent **bicycles** from Ryba's and ride along **Lake Shore Drive** (M-185), which rings the island's perimeter. Pack a picnic to enjoy in between visiting the island's highlights. Regardless of how you spend your day, end it by watching the sunset at the aptly named **Sunset Rock** before heading to **Woods** at the Grand Hotel for a decadent dinner.

Day 3

In the morning, return to the mainland for your last day of adventure. Take I-75 north to M-123, continuing for about an hour to reach **Tahquamenon Falls State Park,** home to one of the most beautiful waterfalls in North America. Plan on experiencing the falls up close—either by **hiking** the nearby trails or **canoeing** the Tahquamenon River. It's an experience you won't soon forget. From the park, check into the **Paradise Inn,** located in its namesake town. Spend an afternoon unwinding, and have a delightful meal at the **Tahquamenon Falls Brewery and Pub** before retiring. Return home in the morning.

More Ideas

- Take a sunset cruise at Pictured Rocks National Lakeshore.

- Go wine-tasting in southern UP.

- Rent a rustic cabin in the Porcupine Mountains Wilderness State Park for some privacy.

icy Munising Bay

Although the allure of summer is what attracts most visitors to the Upper Peninsula, the cold weather months reveal a different—and equally diverse—set of recreational opportunities. Thanks to an abundance of lake effect snow (over 200 inches annually), temperatures that, while cold, seldom descend to subzero levels, and the region's rugged topography, the Upper Peninsula is tailor-made for almost any winter pastime.

SKIING

Downhill skiing can only be enjoyed at destination resorts. Here are a few of the best:

- Big Powderhorn, Bessemer
- Pine Mountain Resort, Iron Mountain
- Blackjack Ski Resort, Bessemer

Cross-country skiers are welcome on any of the dozens of designated trails throughout the Upper Peninsula. Try one of the following:

- Black River Trails, Ironwood
- Mt. Zion, Ironwood
- Bear Track Back Country, Ironwood
- Miljevich Cross Country Ski Trail, Wakefield

SNOWSHOEING

Certain trails throughout the UP are dedicated exclusively to snowshoeing. Here are a few:

- Bruno's Run, Schoolcraft
- Michigan Tech Trails, Houghton

- ABR Trails, Gogebic
- Fumee Lake Natural Area, Dickinson

SNOWMOBILING

Snowmobiling trails are plentiful in the entire Upper Peninsula. Visit www.michigan.gov/dnr and search for "Snowmobile Trail Maps" to find downloadable maps of trails that run throughout the state. Always be careful to respect private property rights and avoid trespassing.

ICE FISHING

Anglers well versed in summer fishing may want to try the quite different art of winter ice fishing. Venturing out onto a thoroughly frozen lake, setting up a shanty, and lowering a line through a small hole can be a challenging way to spend an afternoon.

- Lake Gogebic, Gogebic County
- Big Manistique Lake, Curtis
- Munising Bay, Lake Superior
- Little Bay de Noc, Lake Michigan

FESTIVALS AND EVENTS

A major festival is the annual **Winter Carnival** at Michigan Technological University. Held in early February, the event includes snow statues, ice sculptures, a queen contest, and nighttime fireworks.

The Straits of Mackinac

Look for ★ to find recommended sights, activities, dining, and lodging.

Highlights

★ **Mackinac Island Butterfly House:** See a wide array of geraniums while being entertained by hundreds of butterflies (page 33).

★ **Grand Hotel:** This 1887 hotel lives up to its name with 385 rooms, the world's longest front porch, and a history of Hollywood glamor (page 33).

★ **Fort Mackinac:** British and American troops fought here during the War of 1812. Today, Fort Mackinac's costumed interpreters bring its glory days to life (page 36).

★ **Lilac Festival:** This 10-day festival in early June showcases Mackinac Island at its best, with music, food, horses, and a parade (page 38).

★ **Mackinac Bridge:** Drive across the five-mile-long "Mighty Mac" or stop at Mackinac Bridge View Park to take pictures of this amazing feat of engineering (page 45).

★ **Colonial Michilimackinac State Park:** The site of the original fort, built in 1715, is the location of a 50-year-long archaeological dig, summertime reenactments, and a big wooden replica fort (page 58).

★ **McGulpin Point Lighthouse:** This late-19th century lighthouse has been excellently

restored. Climb the stairs to get a panoramic view of the Straits (page 60).

The Straits of Mackinac have long separated the "Yoopers" from the "Trolls." Yoopers get their nickname from the U.P., as in, "U.P.-ers," while "Trolls" is their good-natured name for Michiganders who live to the south, "under the bridge."

A particular curiosity is the locale's variant spellings. The city on the south side of the Straits is Mackinaw City, but the bridge, resort island, and the Straits themselves are all identified as Mackinac. Fortunately, the pronunciation is universal. Both are pronounced "MACK-i-*naw*," and never "MACK-i-*nack*."

Five miles wide at the narrowest point, the Straits are largely responsible for the Upper Peninsula's profound isolation. Before the completion of the Mackinac Bridge in 1957, passenger cars waited in miles-long lines for a spot on one of the ferries that crossed the Straits each day. Now, thanks to the bridge, the only ferries are headed for Mackinac Island, occasionally offering a side trip to the bridge for travelers to catch a glimpse of its underside.

But the slender gap between the two Michigans is also home to one of the nation's most incomparable travel destinations: Mackinac Island. Resting strategically between Lake Michigan and Lake Huron, and between the Upper and Lower Peninsulas, the island's 19th-century charm has welcomed visitors since it became Mackinac National Park in 1875—the United States' second national park after Yellowstone. The park, which has since been transferred to state control, covers some 80 percent of the island.

You'll instantly notice the absence of automobiles, banned since the 1920s. As a result, Mackinac Island really does seem frozen *Somewhere in Time*, which just happens to be the name of a semi-famous movie, starring Christopher Reeve and Jane Seymour, which was filmed on the island. The Victorian atmosphere draws families, romantics, history buffs—and those simply looking for a good old-fashioned horse-and-buggy ride.

Try not to be offended when you hear locals refer to you as a "Fudgie," probably under their breath, but usually in good humor. While fudge wasn't invented on Mackinac, the

Previous: streamers over Mackinac Island; bicycles and horses on Main Street . **Above:** Round Island Light.

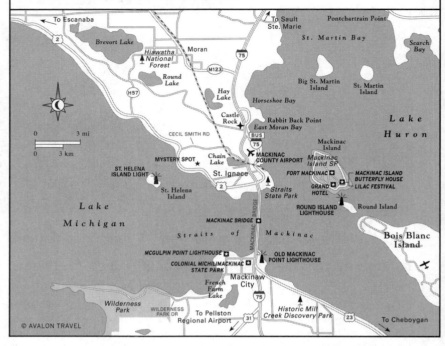

The Straits of Mackinac

island has since become famous for it—and then some. Odds are you'll be buying at least one sliver of it while you're here, which is why residents have dubbed you and the millions of other visitors with the endearing nickname. You might say it comes with the territory.

St. Ignace in the U.P. and Mackinaw City in the Lower Peninsula bookend the bridge, and each possesses its own distinct personality. Stop in Mackinaw for the fudge, St. Ignace for the auto shows, and in both for the history. Museums in each city retell the region's past from the original inhabitants through today. A noteworthy difference is the all too noticeable cultural divide. Despite being small, Mackinaw City gives off a slightly urban, if still northerly, atmosphere. St. Ignace feels much more rustic.

If you're looking for a good base for day trips to other U.P. locations, you can take advantage of the area's plentiful lodgings and restaurants.

PLANNING YOUR TIME

If you're entering the U.P. from the south by crossing the bridge, you'll be passing through both Mackinaw City and St. Ignace—situated at opposite ends of the five-mile stretch. You may be on the way to Copper Harbor for some kayaking or driving west for Ironwood's downhill skiing, but in any event it's worth your time to get off the highway and spend some time in the Straits, one of the most picturesque locations in Michigan.

Although two days will be enough time to see the best of the region, the Straits' natural beauty and Mackinac Island's unique atmosphere often entice people to stay longer. It's best to plan on spending a full day on the island. Lodging tends to be more expensive

Pedaling M-185

biking along Highway 185

For most visitors, their exposure to Mackinac Island is limited to the few blocks near the boat docks, Fort Mackinac, and maybe the Governor's Residence and the veranda of the Grand Hotel. But for the slightly more adventurous, a compelling alternative is available.

To see the island from a different perspective, rent a bicycle from any of the rental shops along Main Street and set off on a ride along M-185, better known as Lakeshore Road. This idyllic route hugs the shoreline along the entire circumference of Mackinac Island and offers a bevy of scenic views—and a few challenging hills.

Despite its unique oddity—the absence of motor vehicles—M-185 is an official Michigan state highway and is maintained by the Michigan Department of Transportation. Other than the noticeably narrower lanes, the road otherwise resembles any other highway: two lanes of paved asphalt complete with mileposts and directional signs.

The total length of the route is approximately eight miles. If you choose to start out at Mission Street and pedal east, you'll find the first few miles the toughest, with several points where you'll be riding uphill.

But the reward is the notable sights you'll see—Arch Rock, the site of the British Landing, and Devil's Kitchen. Bring along your camera, as you'll find some very photo-worthy spots. When you get to British Landing (about two-thirds of the way if you ride counterclockwise) you'll find a pleasant rest stop with a concession stand and benches.

Most people take 1.5 to 2 hours to complete the eight miles. After finishing, head to one of the Main Street pubs and toast your adventure!

(particularly at the palatial Grand Hotel), but if you don't mind spending a little more, a stay on Mackinac Island is certainly worth it. Mackinaw City and St. Ignace can both be seen in a single day.

Summers are the busiest (and the best) season for visiting, with Mackinac Island drawing the largest crowds. St. Ignace tends to be

best for outdoor activities. If you're interested in the area's history, you'll want to make an afternoon of Mackinaw City's numerous historical sites.

HISTORY

Native Americans knew of the abundant hunting and fishing in the Straits area long before the French or British arrived. Originally called Michilimackinac (Land of the Great Turtle), the island was considered sacred by the Anishinaabe-Ojibwe, who thought it was populated by the first people and home of the Great Spirit Gitchie Manitou. In addition to using the island as a gathering place, the Ojibwa, Ottawa, and other nations hunted on Mackinac Island and neighboring Bois Blanc Island. Their success allowed them to trade some of their catch to nations farther south in exchange for vegetables and grain.

Europeans arrived in the 17th century. The first were French Jesuits who arrived in the 1670s both to take advantage of the fur trade and to convert Native Americans to Christianity. Jacques Marquette, a priest and an explorer, founded a town and a mission at St. Ignace in 1671, naming it after the founder of the Society of Jesus, Saint Ignatius of Loyola. It was quickly followed by a trading post and later by Fort Michilimackinac.

The British and French skirmished over the land, with the fort periodically changing hands until the Treaty of Paris, signed at the conclusion of the French and Indian War, gave it—and all French land east of the Mississippi—to the British in 1763. Seven years later, the British commander abandoned the fort for a more easily defendable position on Mackinac Island, where the British would overstay their welcome even after the land was given to the United States following the American Revolution.

American soldiers took possession of Fort Mackinac in 1796 and held it for almost 20 years. During the War of 1812, the British retook the fort by invading the island under cover of night and surprising the Americans, who surrendered without a fight. The British ran the fortification for two years, despite repeated American assaults aimed at retaking it. In 1814 the Treaty of Ghent returned the island to the United States.

Throughout it all, the fur trade formed the foundation of the area's economy. Europeans traded canoe-loads of goods for pelts from beavers and other animals that had been trapped by the Native Americans. Mackinac Island became one of the country's most valuable trading posts during the 1820s, making way for the country's first millionaire, John Jacob Astor. His American Fur Company was the leader in Mackinac's thriving fur trade. However, overhunting eventually ended the industry, which was replaced by commercial fishing.

After the military conflicts ended, the island began earning a reputation as one of the Victorian era's most popular and fashionable resort areas. An American soldier wrote, "The air up here is so healthy, you have to go somewhere else to die." The vacation spot grew more and more famous, drawing vacationers from the Midwest and beyond. A growing interest during the second half of the 19th century culminated in the 1890s as lumber barons, railroad magnates, and other wealthy Americans began building large, sumptuous cottages on the island, many of which still stand today and can be viewed on one of the many carriage tours available.

When cars first arrived on the island, their presence proved highly controversial. These "mechanical monsters," as they came to be known, were loathed for their noise and emissions and also because they frightened horses. Many communities around the country decided to ban automobiles around this time, but virtually all eventually succumbed to the inevitable. Mackinac Island remains perhaps the last vestige of this era, and cars (and most other forms of motorized transportation) have been prohibited here since 1898. Some 600 horses serve visitors during the summer months—a number that dwindles to just a few dozen in the winter. The horses, carriages, carts, and well-kept Victorian homes and hotels all combine to give Mackinac its timeless charm, and continue to make it one of the most popular vacation destinations in the Midwest.

Mackinac Island

During its peak tourism season, Mackinac Island draws some 15,000 people each day, reflecting its status as one of the Upper Peninsula's quintessential destinations. This little island sports a rich history: Native Americans, French fur traders, and British soldiers eventually gave way to Victorian resorts. By design, the island today displays little evidence of the contemporary world. Fort Mackinac stands above a town that really does seem frozen in time.

Despite this faithfulness to history, much of the downtown area can feel overly touristy and is often packed with visitors, but there are plenty of treasures here for those willing to look. Most of the island—80 percent of it—is undeveloped state land, much of which adjoins commercial areas within just a block or two of downtown. Fortunately, getting away from the showy commercialism is easy.

SIGHTS
Downtown

After disembarking from the ferry, you may decide to linger a while so you can get a glimpse of the necessary "heavy lifting" that keeps Mackinac Island running. Workers unload cartons of vegetables from ferries and reload them by hand onto drays (horse-drawn wagons) for delivery to local restaurants. Another horse-drawn wagon pulls huge bales of hay to feed the island's numerous equines. Even the USPS and UPS carriers do their routes on bicycle, pulling a cart loaded with letters or packages.

After spending a little time at the four blocks of shops and restaurants on **Main Street,** make the most of your visit by getting off the main drag. For an overview of what the island has to offer, take a carriage tour with **Mackinac Island Carriage Tours** (906/847-3307, www.mict.com, $29 adults, $11 children, hours vary mid-May-late Oct.), located across from the Arnold Line ferry dock next to the Chamber of Commerce. The pleasant narrated tour takes about 1 hour and 45 minutes, rambling along at a relaxing pace past the Grand Hotel, Arch Rock, Skull Cave, Fort Mackinac, and most of the island's other key sites. This locally owned business is the

Mackinac Island retains its 19th-century charm.

Mackinac Island

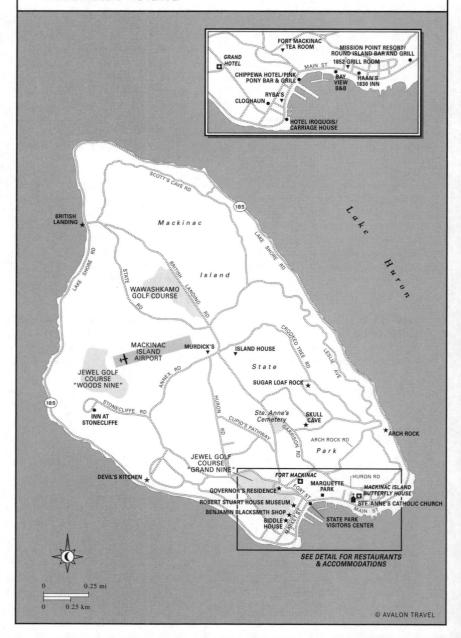

FORT MACKINAC TEA ROOM

MISSION POINT RESORT/
ROUND ISLAND BAR AND GRILL

GRAND HOTEL

1852 GRILL ROOM

MAIN ST

CHIPPEWA HOTEL/PINK PONY BAR & GRILL

BAY VIEW B&B

HAAN'S 1830 INN

RYBA'S

CLOGHAUN

HOTEL IROQUOIS/
CARRIAGE HOUSE

SCOTT'S CAVE RD

185

Lake

BRITISH LANDING

Mackinac

LAKE SHORE RD

Huron

LAKE SHORE RD

STATE RD

BRITISH LANDING RD

Island

WAWASHKAMO GOLF COURSE

MACKINAC ISLAND AIRPORT

MURDICK'S

ISLAND HOUSE

CROOKED TREE RD

JEWEL GOLF COURSE "WOODS NINE"

ANNEX RD

State

SUGAR LOAF ROCK

LESLIE AVE

185

STONECLIFFE RD

INN AT STONECLIFFE

HURON RD

Ste. Anne's Cemetery

CUPID'S PATHWAY

SKULL CAVE

GARRISON RD

ARCH ROCK

ARCH ROCK RD

JEWEL GOLF COURSE "GRAND NINE"

Park

DEVIL'S KITCHEN

FORT MACKINAC

HURON RD

GOVERNOR'S RESIDENCE

FORT ST

MARQUETTE PARK

MACKINAC ISLAND BUTTERFLY HOUSE

ROBERT STUART HOUSE MUSEUM

STE. ANNE'S CATHOLIC CHURCH

BENJAMIN BLACKSMITH SHOP

MARKET ST

MAIN ST

BIDDLE HOUSE

STATE PARK VISITORS CENTER

SEE DETAIL FOR RESTAURANTS & ACCOMMODATIONS

0   0.25 mi

0   0.25 km

world's largest horse-and-buggy livery, with more than 300 horses, mostly crosses of beefy Percherons, Belgians, and Clydesdales. Seasonal peak hours (mid-June through Labor Day) are 9am-5pm (weather permitting), with slightly shorter hours from early May to mid-June and after Labor Day through the end of October.

MARKET STREET

One block inland from Main Street, some of Mackinac's original residences line up along **Market Street.** Much quieter than Main, Market Street has several interesting stops for visitors. At 34 Market Street, the headquarters of John Jacob Astor's American Fur Company is now the **Robert Stuart House Museum** (906/847-3307, 11am-6pm daily May-Oct., donation). The 1817 building is named for the man who was once Astor's resident agent on the island. It retains many of its original furnishings, including fur company ledgers, fur weighing scales, and other artifacts.

One block west, knowledgeable interpreters demonstrate spinning at **Biddle House** and iron smithing at the **Benjamin Blacksmith Shop.** These and other historic buildings are part of Mackinac Island State Park, and are included with the admission ticket to Fort Mackinac, although they have shorter hours than the fort, 11am-6pm daily, $13 adults, $7.50 ages 5-17. A discount is offered for online ticket purchases. For current information, stop by the park visitors center across from Marquette Park on Huron Street, or contact **Mackinac State Historic Parks** (231/436-4100, www.mackinacparks.com).

★ MACKINAC ISLAND BUTTERFLY HOUSE

Tucked away on McGulpin Street is the **Mackinac Island Butterfly House** (906/847-3972, www.originalbutterflyhouse.com, daily 10am-7pm daily summer, 10am-6pm daily Labor Day-Memorial Day, hours vary, $9 adults, $4.50 children). Owner Doug Beardsley used to use his greenhouses to grow thousands of geraniums for the Grand Hotel

and other clients. He relied on biodynamic growing methods, releasing beneficial insects to care for his plants instead of using chemical sprays. When economics made his small greenhouse less viable, he stuck with his insects. After hearing about a butterfly house in Europe, Beardsley added some different plants and began ordering pupae from around the world. Now hundreds of butterflies flutter freely in his greenhouse atrium, some nearly six inches long. You can observe them up close on walls and plants, or sit still long enough and they'll land on your knee—both an unusual and delightful experience.

STE. ANNE'S CATHOLIC CHURCH

You'll find **Ste. Anne's Catholic Church** (906/847-3507, www.steanneschurch.org), the oldest church on Mackinac Island, near the butterfly house. It's worth even a brief visit to take in its architecture and history. Ste. Anne's is a testimony to the island's long history of Roman Catholicism, with Jesuits being the first nonnatives to arrive here. The parish has served the island community since the 1740s.

In addition to weekend masses, you'll find a community square dance on the spacious front porch once a week. The basement hosts a small **museum** (10am-4pm Mon.-Fri., 10am-5:30pm Sat., 9am-3pm Sun., free) that preserves and interprets the religious history of Mackinac Island. A number of religious articles and church documents (baptismal, marriage, and burial records) date as far back as 1695.

Ste. Anne's gift shop has a number of souvenirs and collectibles, plus standard religious items. If you're interested in old cemeteries you'll want to check out Ste. Anne's Cemetery, up the hill behind Fort Mackinac on the way to Fort Holmes.

★ Grand Hotel

The iconic **Grand Hotel** (286 Grand Ave., 800/334-7263, www.grandhotel.com), a gracious edifice built on a scale appropriate to its name, has become practically synonymous with Mackinac Island. It is one of the largest summer resorts in the world, operating each year from early April through late October. Its famous 660-foot-long covered front porch gets decked out each spring with 2,500 geraniums planted in seven tons of potting soil. Its 12 restaurants and bars serve as many as 4,000 meals a day. The resort's impeccable grounds offer guests every amenity, from saddle horses to designer golf to bocce ball to swimming in the outdoor pool made famous by 1940s actress Esther Williams, who filmed *This Time for Keeps* here.

But opulence and refinement were the goals of the railroads and steamship companies when they formed a consortium to build the Grand Hotel in 1887, dragging construction materials across the frozen water by horse and mule. The wealthiest Mackinac Island visitors stayed here, on a hill with a commanding view of the Straits.

Yet unlike other resorts from the Gilded Age that burned to the ground or faded, the Grand Hotel has managed to maintain its grace and dignity. It still hosts all manner of celebrities and politicians—five U.S. presidents to date—and still offers a sip of a truly bygone era with high tea in the parlor each afternoon and demitasse served after dinner each evening. Room rates still include a five-course dinner in the soaring main dining room. For men, the evening (6pm) dress code calls for jackets and ties, and for women, skirts, dresses, or formal pantsuits.

The Grand Hotel's time-capsule setting prompted director Jeannot Szwarc to choose it as the location for the 1980 film *Somewhere in Time*, starring Christopher Reeve, Jane Seymour, and Christopher Plummer. For whatever reason, the movie has developed a huge following; its fan club reunites at the hotel each year in late October.

While room rates can get outright absurd (from $563, with doubles from $319 pp—plus a 19.5% added fee), they include breakfast, lunch, and dinner, and perhaps can be considered a worthwhile splurge if you'd like to experience a level of hospitality reminiscent of the Gilded Age. Each of the 385 rooms is decorated differently, and since 2007, for the first time in its history, the entire hotel is air-conditioned. A more affordable option is to stay just one night for the experience and then book less expensive lodging on or off the island for the rest of your visit.

Enjoy this moment in time—take tea, loll in the beautifully landscaped pool, or dance to the swing orchestra in the Terrace Room.

Ste. Anne's Catholic Church

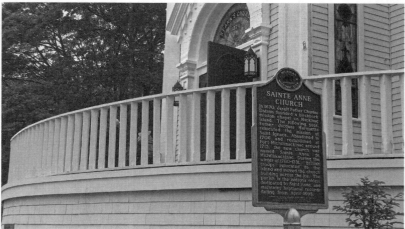

Somewhere in Time

the Grand Hotel

> Beyond fantasy. Beyond obsession. Beyond time itself … he will find her.
>
> *Somewhere in Time*

Your reaction to the tagline for *Somewhere in Time,* a 1980 movie starring Christopher Reeve and Jane Seymour filmed at the Grand Hotel, is a pretty good indication of whether you'll love or hate the movie. If you find it hopelessly romantic, a bit old fashioned, and somewhat endearing—go rent the movie now. But if you thought it was too sweet and you shuddered a little, you might want to make another choice.

The film tells the story of Richard Collier, a writer who, after a strange encounter with an old woman who pleads "Come back to me," tries to figure out who she was. While staying at the Grand Hotel, he learns she was a turn-of-the-20th-century actress named Elise McKenna, and quickly becomes enamored with her. He soon travels back in time, where he meets her and the two fall in love. But will Richard be able to stay in 1912?

Mackinac Island's Victorian setting, and in particular the Grand Hotel, made it a natural location for the film. Unfortunately, when the movie was released it was much maligned by film critics, and its only Oscar nod was for Best Costume Design. Still, it has found a passionate following among people who are enthralled by its story of timeless love and old-fashioned values. In fact, the *Somewhere in Time* fan club has met at the Grand Hotel for a weekend each October since 1991.

It really is a good, if affected, movie that's perfect for Valentine's Day or a first date, and it's a great way to relive your Grand Hotel stay or just to peek inside.

Nonguests can sneak a peek at the hotel's public areas and grounds for a mildly unreasonable fee ($10 adults, $5 children, free under age 4), which is redeemable for the Grand Luncheon Buffett. More than anything, it's used to thin the sightseers. Highly recommended are a stroll through the grounds, which are filled with Victorian gardens, with 25,000 tulips in spring; and a visit to the snazzy Cupola Bar, with views halfway to Wisconsin.

Governor's Residence

From Marquette Park, follow Fort Street up the hill to the **Governor's Residence** at the corner of Fort Street and East Bluff Road. The state purchased the "cottage" (the fact that it lacks central heat qualifies it as such) in 1945. It's the official summer residence of Michigan's chief executive, though different governors spend varying amounts of time here. The house is open for free tours (Wed. morning June-Aug.), except when the governor is in residence. Photography is not permitted inside the house. For more information, contact **Mackinac State Historic Parks** (231/436-4100, www.mackinacparks.com).

★ Fort Mackinac

Located at the crest of the bluff, whitewashed **Fort Mackinac** (Huron Rd., 231/436-4100, www.mackinacparks.com, 9am-4:30pm daily May 6-June 6, 9:30am-6pm daily June 7-Aug. 23, 9:30am-4:30pm daily Aug. 24-Oct. 12, $13 adults, $7.50 ages 5-17) is worth a visit for the views alone, presiding over—as forts often do—the downtown, the marina, and Lake Huron. But there's also plenty to see at this military outpost, which the British and Americans haggled over for nearly 40 years.

Along with peering over the parapets, you can wander in and out of 14 buildings that make up the fort. The barracks, officers' quarters, post hospital, and other buildings are filled with interpretive displays and feature period decor. Costumed guides lead reenactments, including musket firing and cannon

salutes. A short audiovisual presentation, *The Heritage of Mackinac,* explains the fort's basic history.

Admission to the fort also includes admission to the Benjamin Blacksmith House and the Biddle House. If you're planning to visit the sister parks on the mainland—Colonial Michilimackinac, Old Mackinac Point Lighthouse, or Historic Mill Creek Discovery Park—the Mainland Combo ticket ($26 adults, $15.50 ages 5-12) is the best deal. For information, stop by the park visitors center across from Marquette Park on Huron Street.

East Bluff

Some of the island's more impressive cottages line up along East Bluff. Wander east from the governor's mansion to see some of these Victorian marvels. Happily, most survived the Depression era—when they could be purchased for pennies on the dollar. Today, these well-tended homes are often valued at more than $1 million.

Work your way down one of the sets of public steps to the lakefront, where Main Street becomes Huron Street. Continue your walk east, passing smaller but no less appealing cottages and homes. Many are skirted with geraniums and lilacs, the island's signature

reenactors at Fort Mackinac

flowers, and boast a stunning view of the Straits.

Mackinac Island State Park

Too often overshadowed by cultural attractions and touristy diversions, Mackinac Island's natural history has drawn scientific interest for nearly 200 years. In the early 19th century, botanists discovered several species new to science, including the dwarf lake iris, still found only in the Straits of Mackinac region.

The island's landscape comprises fields, meadows, marshes, coastline, swamps, bogs, and a boreal forest. Early scientists marveled at the island's unusual topography, especially the brecciate limestone that has been sculpted by millennia of wind and waves. The result is some dramatic rock formations, like the giant inland slab of limestone called **Sugar Loaf Rock,** the lakeside caves of **Devil's Kitchen,** and impressive **Arch Rock,** which rises nearly 150 feet above the eastern shore and spans some 50 feet.

In recognition of the park's distinctive "natural curiosities" and growing tourism, the federal government created Mackinac National Park in 1875—following Yellowstone as the nation's second national park. Twenty years later it was returned to Michigan and became Mackinac Island State Park, Michigan's first. Today the park is managed by an entity known as **Michigan State Historic Parks,** which includes Fort Mackinac, Old Mackinac Point Lighthouse, Colonial Michilimackinac, and the Historic Mill Creek Discovery Park. Admission fees vary considerably, so it's best to visit www.mackinacparks.com/explore-mackinac/admission for full information. Keep in mind that "package and family deals" are available if you're planning on visiting more than one park or if you're traveling as a family.

Walk, run, ride, or bike, but make sure you get out of the center to really see Mackinac Island. You'll be surprised how quickly you can leave the crowds behind as you set out on Lake Shore Drive, the paved eight-mile path (which has a state highway designation, M-185) that circles the island. The trail never wanders far from the pleasant shoreline and passes many of the island's natural features, which are well marked. Traveling clockwise, the first you'll reach is Devil's Kitchen; heading in the opposite direction, you'll arrive first at Arch Rock, the most dramatic of Mackinac limestone oddities.

About halfway around, on the island's

British Landing at Mackinac Island State Park

northwestern side, is **British Landing,** where British soldiers infiltrated the island during the War of 1812. They hiked across Mackinac's interior, surprising the American garrison at the fort—who were apparently looking the other way—and recaptured the island. There's a small **nature center** here, staffed in summer by a helpful naturalist. Hike the short **nature trail,** which has several interpretive signs as it weaves up a bluff.

British Landing is also a good spot from which to head inland and explore the island's interior. British Landing Road bisects the island and links up with Garrison Road near **Skull Cave,** leading to the fort. It's a hilly three-mile trip from shore to shore. British Landing Road is considered a major thoroughfare by Mackinac standards, meaning it accommodates horses, carriages, and bikes.

Lighthouses

The **Round Island Light,** also known as the Old Round Island Point Lighthouse, was built in 1895 to guide ships among the shoals and channels between Mackinac Island and uninhabited Round Island, where it was built. Though unstaffed, the Round Island light still guides ships through the Straits today. Your best bet to see it is the eastbound lighthouse cruise offered in Mackinaw City by **Shepler's Mackinac Island Ferry** (E. Central Ave., Mackinaw City, 800/828-6157, www.sheplersferry.com, $49.50 adults, $27.50 ages 5-12).

ENTERTAINMENT

For the best of the island's **live music,** you'll want to check out the Grand Hotel, which offers plenty of live entertainment nightly. Catch live music at the Jockey Club at the Grand Strand, listen to the Grand Hotel Orchestra in the Terrace Room, or hear live bands at the Gate House. You can also find live entertainment at the Cupola Bar and at Woods. You'll find acoustic music at Mission Point Resort's Round Island Bar and Grill downtown. Redesigned in 2012, it features a number of HDTVs, providing a sports-bar atmosphere.

It's easy to understand why designated **pub crawls** are so popular on the island—it's hard to get an impaired driving infraction when there are no cars. Local retailers join in the game, selling T-shirts commemorating the experience (you might not remember it otherwise). Try not to overdo it; finish your crawl over the course of a few nights.

FESTIVALS AND EVENTS
★ Lilac Festival

For 10 days in early June, Mackinac Island celebrates the **Lilac Festival** (800/454-4227, www.mackinacisland.org), during which visitors can enjoy live music; A Taste of Mackinac, which showcases the talents of local chefs; and the Feast of Epona, the Celtic goddess of horses. Events culminate with the Grand Parade, one of North America's only all-hitch horse parades. Other events include a dog and pony show, an art print competition, and a 10K run. Each year the parade has a unique theme. The crowd is smaller than for the Labor Day Bridge Walk but still busy. Celebrations on this order represent Mackinac at its best.

Other Festivals

Early in August, the **Mackinac Island Horse Show** (www.mackinachorses.org) celebrates the island's love of all things equestrian, with events like showmanship and grooming, English and Western equestrian, and barrel racing. During the **Mackinac Island Fudge Festival** in late August, the Fudgies get their due as the entire island turns out to celebrate the estimated 10,000 pounds of fudge made each season.

SUMMER SPORTS AND RECREATION
Trails

Mackinac Island State Park has more than 2,250 acres with over 70 miles of trails and footpaths suitable for exploration on a bicycle or on foot. Pick up a free Mackinac Island Map, available all over town, and venture off. The map marks the location of old cemeteries, rock formations, and other points of interest, but it's even more appealing just to explore the smaller trails on your own and discover the pristine and tranquil side of Mackinac Island. Everything is well marked, and getting lost is difficult since you're on a relatively small island.

For walking or biking tours, join **Doc Crain** as he shares local legends on the way through the island's boreal forest trails. Hiking tours meet at 2pm Monday-Saturday at the Father Marquette statue, while biking tours depart at 10am Monday-Saturday from the **Mackinac Wheel Bike Shop** (6929 Main St.). Doc's tours can be called "infotainment," as he fascinates his guests with a wide array of facts about the island's plants and flowers, the glaciers that shaped its cliffs, and its long military history. Doc won't charge you a fee for the tours, but be generous and leave him a decent tip; he will certainly have earned it.

Runners can participate in the **Lilac Festival 10K** in early June, the **Mackinac Island Eight Mile** in September, or late October's **Great Turtle Half Marathon.** Visit **Run Mackinac** (810/487-0954, www.runmackinac.com) for more information.

There are plenty of shops that offer hourly **bicycle rentals** for single-speed bikes, mountain bikes, bikes for children, tagalongs, buggies, or tandems for the romantic. Most rentals run about $8 per hour or $45 per day, but rates vary depending on the equipment. **Ryba's Bicycle Rentals** (906/847-3208, www.rybabikes.com) on Main Street is a great resource and also offers baby carts, strollers, tagalongs, and electric wheelchairs for disabled people. Another reputable source is the **Mackinac Island Bike Shop** (7425 Main St., just east of Shepler's dock, 906/847-6337, www.bikemackinac.com), where no deposit is required and the price you pay is prorated to the quarter hour.

If you plan to do a lot of cycling, you may want to bring your own bike, since you can transport it on the ferry for about $10 round-trip. A hybrid or mountain bike is best for negotiating the island's myriad trails.

In order to accommodate visitors with disabilities, Mackinac Island has relaxed its ban on motorized transportation, albeit slightly. For those in need, motorized scooters or wheelchairs can now be rented from vendors on Market Street, right near the ferry embarkation point. This makes it possible for people with physical challenges to enjoy Mackinac Island, though be aware that most electric scooters are not powerful enough to climb the steeper inclines, such as the ramp up to Fort Mackinac.

On the Water

Open water sailing excursions are available on **Shepler's Ferry ships** (E. Central Ave., Mackinaw City, 800/828-6157, www.sheplersferry.com). Shepler's offers a variety of historic lighthouse and night sky cruises and can host charter trips for weddings or other special occasions. The **Star Line** (801 S. Huron St., Mackinaw City, 800/638-9892, www.mackinacferry.com) offers a similar schedule of cruises. Both lines depart from St. Ignace and Mackinaw City.

Mackinac Island's beautiful coastline is perfect for relaxation and picnicking, and often tempting for those looking to take a dip, especially children. The east side of the island is best for the little ones, but be warned: the rocky shores require swimming shoes or sandals, and there are no lifeguards, so swim at your own risk. The waters of the Straits can also be rather chilly, even late in the season.

Of course, you can always bring a rod and reel and fish off the rocks on Mackinac Island's shore, but the lure of the Great Lakes makes deepwater **fishing** one of the island's most popular summer activities. There are no fishing charter services based on the island, but, as with **parasailing,** a few private boats dock here.

Carriage Rides and Horseback Riding

With more than 600 horses calling the island their summertime home, you won't be able to turn a corner without bumping noses with these beautiful animals. But to be honest, who would want it otherwise? It isn't every day you get the chance to ride a carriage down Main Street or take a buggy on an island circuit. Just be certain to exercise appropriate courtesy. Do not pet or touch a horse until first asking permission from its rider, and do not step immediately behind a horse, as they can kick if they feel threatened.

Take a carriage tour with the island's largest livery, **Mackinac Island Carriage Tours** (7396 Market St., 906/847-3307, www.mict. com), operating since 1869, or **Arrowhead Carriages** (7671 3rd St., 906/847-6112, www. arrowheadcarriages.com), both offering personalized tours of the island in relatively small carriages. The guides are knowledgeable, and hourly rates run $110-189, depending on the total number of guests, but if the tour includes two or more families, they can split the fee among them, allowing for a cost-efficient hour. Both companies begin their tours on Market Street near the Father Marquette statue.

You'll be able to take the reins during a drive-it-yourself buggy tour from **Jack's Livery Stable** (Grand Ave. and Mahoney Ave., 906/847-3391, www.jacksliverystable. com, May-Oct., $70 per hour for 2 passengers, $88 for 4, $108 for 6). After gauging your skill with horses, one of the livery's professionals will give you driving instructions before setting you loose on the town with a free map. At their sister company, **Cindy's Riding Stable** (906/847-3572, www.cindysridingstable.com, May-Oct., $45 per hour), you can take one of the 30-plus saddle horses out on your own; located on Market Street across from the Biddle House, Cindy's Riding Stable rents horses only—no carriages.

Golf

In addition to a pleasant afternoon on the links, golfing Mackinac brings with it a unique thrill: golf carts are among the very few powered vehicles allowed on the island. So while other visitors are struggling to rein in an unruly horse or hoofing it across the island, you'll be driving something that's actually motorized.

Mackinac is the proud home of the oldest continuously played golf course in Michigan, **Wawashkamo** (906/847-3871, www.wawashkamo.com, $75 for 18 holes with cart, $53 without, 9 holes $50 with cart, $35 without). Vacationers have been golfing the course's nine holes since 1898, and the second set of tee placements makes it possible to play a full 18 holes on rough natural terrain, which includes traditionally Scottish thistle and heather. Wawashkamo means "walk a crooked trail," and it is built on a former battlefield from the War of 1812, adding to its historic appeal. Lower rates are available for twilight golf (4pm-7pm) and during the spring and fall months.

The Grand Hotel's 18 holes, known as **The Jewel** (906/847-3331, www.grandhotel.com, guests $120 for 18 holes, $55 for 9 holes, non-guests $135 for 18 holes, $70 for 9 holes, carts $50 pp for 18 holes, $25 pp for 9 holes), consists of two nine-hole courses—the original Grand Nine, across the street from the hotel, and the Woods Nine, in the island's interior. The Grand was built in 1901 and was redesigned in 1987 by noted golf course architect Jerry Matthews, who also designed the Woods course, added in 1994. Horse-drawn transportation is provided between the two courses.

Mission Point Resort hosts **The Greens at Mackinac** (906/847-3312, www.missionpoint.com, 18 holes $15 adults, $7 under age 13), the executive putting greens where even the most experienced putters can hone their skills or try out the merchandise from the pro shop selection of putters.

Other Activities

Three sets of **tennis courts** are available on Mackinac Island—there are public courts behind Fort Mackinac, and courts are available to guests at the Grand Hotel and Mission Point Resort. The Grand offers its guests organized matches, equipment rental, and private or semiprivate lessons. Contact tennis pro Nate Helmkamp (260/570-5871) for reservations.

WINTER SPORTS AND RECREATION
Ski and Snowshoe Trails

The island is a bit trickier to get to once the Straits freeze over, but for those willing to make the extra effort, a winter paradise awaits. The 70-plus miles of trails that bring out the hikers, bikers, and runners in summertime are transformed to cross-country ski and snowshoe trails for winter. Mackinac Island Ski Club volunteers team up with the state park to maintain a series of groomed winter trails. Perhaps best of all, the island is considerably less crowded, and a calming solace grips the island.

The Balsam Shop (Main St.; Surrey Hill, 906/847-3591, www.balsamshop.com) is open winter weekends and holidays for cross-country ski and snowshoe rentals. Since most of the island shuts down well before the snows come, winter lodging is limited. Check out **Bogan Lane Inn** (1420 Bogan Lane, 906/847-3439, www.boganlaneinn.com, $100-140), **Pontiac Lodge** (across Main St. from Shepler's dock, 906/847-3364, www.pontiaclodge.com, $100-425), or **Harbor Place Studio Suites** (7439 Main St., 800/626-6304, http://harborplace-studio-suites.michiganbesthotels.com, $275-325).

Horse-drawn taxis (bundle up!) are available from **Mackinac Island Carriage Tours** (906/847-3323, www.mict.com), with advance reservations. Charter flights to **Mackinac Island Airport** (MCD) are the only way on and off the island once the ferries stop running.

FOOD

One of the finest dining options on the island is the **Fort Mackinac Tea Room** (906/847-3331, www.grandhotel.com, 11am-3pm daily mid-May-mid-Oct.), located in the lower level of the Officer's Stone Quarters within the fort. Surrounded by thick masonry walls, the tearoom serves up both a great atmosphere and great food prepared by Grand Hotel chefs. Entrées run up to $30; good soups, salads, and sandwiches can be had for around $10. Ask for a spot on the terrace—the high setting offers a dramatic panorama.

Everyone should hit the ★ **Pink Pony Bar & Grill** (7221 Main St., 906/847-3341, www.pinkponymackinac.com, 8am-2am daily) at least sometime during a Mackinac visit. Located in the Chippewa Hotel, overlooking the marina, this is *the* party place following the famed Port Huron to Mackinac yacht race. The food's great too, with burgers, whitefish sandwiches, and such on the lunch menu and steaks, seafood, and ribs for dinner. Appetizers are especially popular in the dining room, where you'll find pan-fried calamari ($15) and honey apple brie flatbread ($14)—choices atypical of Mackinac Island. Dinner entrées average around $25. Outdoor patio dining is available in season.

The **Round Island Bar and Grill** (6633 Main St., 906/847-3312, www.missionpoint.com, 7am-midnight daily, only light snacks after 9pm, entrées $12-18) at Mission Point Resort has sandwiches and salads in a casual setting overlooking the Straits and neighboring Round Island. Wednesday is Crab Legs Night ($29). Sample some of Michigan's best regional beers and wines.

The island's best fine dining is at the high-end hotels and resorts. Try the **1852 Grill Room** (6966 Main St., 906/847-3347, www.theislandhouse.com, 6pm-10pm daily) at the Island House Hotel, where offerings include wild mushroom risotto ($23) and a 22-ounce T-bone steak ($52). Entrées at the Hotel Iroquois's **Carriage House Dining Room** (7485 Main St., 906/847-3321, www.iroquoishotel.com, lunch 11:30am-2:30pm daily Memorial Day-mid-Sept., dinner 5pm-9pm daily Memorial Day-mid-Oct.) emphasize seafood choices ($28-65) such as sautéed perch and broiled Maine lobster. Lunch selections include a wide variety of salads and sandwiches ($14-25).

For the treat of a lifetime, choose the **Main Dining Room** (286 Grand Ave.,

Mackinac Island Fudge

Mackinac's most famous sweet wasn't invented on the island. No one is really sure exactly how it happened, but it's commonly accepted that the sugary goodness was the result of a screwed-up, or "fudged," batch of caramels.

Fudge was first made on the island in the late 1800s by Newton Jerome "Rome" Murdick, who began selling the candy to vacationers who came to the island to stay at the recently opened Grand Hotel. Now in the fifth generation of the family, **Murdick's Fudge** (906/847-3530, www.murdicksfudgemackinacisland.com, 9am-10pm daily) is still selling their delicious treat on the island, in Mackinaw City, and at a few other locations. Rome Murdick began making his fudge on a marble slab; because of its tendency to remain cold, the marble helps to cool the fudge quickly so it can be shaped into bars. This gave summer tourists an incredible product and a show to boot.

Of course, Murdick's isn't the only place that sells fudge; it isn't even the only place that sells great fudge. There are currently 15 fudge shops on Mackinac Island, and each is worth a visit (though if you visit all of them, you'll end up with the stomachache of a lifetime).

Before long, Mackinac earned a reputation. It wouldn't be fair to say that people come just for the fudge, but while they're here, they buy it by the pound. Visitors' relentless appetite for fudge has earned them the nickname "Fudgies."

906/847-3331, www.grandhotel.com, 6:30pm-8:45pm daily, 5-course prix-fixe $80 pp) at the Grand Hotel. An exquisite five-course meal features choices from three rotating menus; you will not be disappointed. After 6:30pm, evening attire is required in all public areas of the Grand Hotel. For women, this means a dress, skirt, and blouse or a pantsuit; for men, a jacket, necktie, and dress slacks are required.

The Grand Hotel's **Woods Restaurant** (286 Grand Ave., 906/847-3331, www.grand-hotel.com, 11am-10pm daily) offers a more casual dining atmosphere than the hotel's Main Dining Room. Dinner selections include baked herb-crusted whitefish filet ($28) and prime New York strip ($49).

Fudge

Sooner or later you'll succumb to Mackinac Island's famous fudge. A visitor treat since Victorian times, the confection can be found in shops lining Main Street. Two of the oldest, **Murdick's Fudge** (906/847-3530, www.murdicksfudgemackinacisland.com, 9am-10pm daily) and **Ryba's** (906/847-3347, www.ryba.com, 9am-10pm daily) have multiple island locations, while Murdick's also has a shop in Mackinaw City. Ryba's also has two Chicago locations and another in the Detroit suburb of Fraser. You can buy a sizeable slab to take or mail home, or just a small sliver to nibble. Both stores also accept phone orders and will ship virtually anywhere. A little goes a long way—it's very rich stuff—and you might regret it later if you overdo it.

ACCOMMODATIONS

Along with the **Grand Hotel,** there are many other places to stay on Mackinac Island that still manage to offer the true Mackinac Victorian experience. Rates can be high, and prices can vary considerably even within one property, with water views commanding a considerable premium. But don't dismiss staying on Mackinac Island; you can find reasonable rates at smaller B&Bs and apartments, the latter of which often have good deals for week-long stays. The options below tip both ends of the scale. For information on more island accommodations, including rates and photos, visit www.mackinacisland.org. Unfortunately, there is no camping on Mackinac Island.

Hotels and Motels

The **Chippewa Hotel** (7221 Main St., 800/241-3341, www.chippewahotel.com, May-Oct., $109-579) is a venerable old Mackinac hotel that had a $3 million renovation several years back. The result is a classy and comfortable place to stay, with a location at the heart of the island on Main Street, overlooking the marina. The 24-person lakeside hot tub alone may be worth the stay. If you enjoy being pampered, check out the relaxing Lilac Tree Spa.

Two separate buildings—Cudahy Manor ($154-350) and the Summer House ($240-562)—make up the **Inn at Stonecliffe** (8593 Cudah Circle, 906/847-3355, www.theinnatstonecliffe.com, May-Oct.). More than 100 years old, the inn has been completely remodeled and restored. The Cudahy Manor is more B&B than hotel, a turn-of-the-century Tudor manor with 16 rooms, the more expensive of which have views of the Straits and the bridge. The Summer House has 33 studio suites.

One of the island's most striking buildings, the **Hotel Iroquois** (7485 Main St., 906/847-3321, www.iroquoishotel.com, rooms $130-185, suites $580-1,250), was built in 1900 as a home for the island blacksmith. It has since been converted into a 46-room hotel with a fine-dining restaurant (entrées $28-60) and a private sunbathing deck. Hotel Iroquois is a *Condé Nast Traveler* Gold List hotel and earned a perfect score for its stunning location. Still, with suite rates on par with the Grand Hotel's luxury rooms, you'll be better off sticking with Hotel Iroquois's competitively priced regular rooms.

Bed-and-Breakfasts

Cloghaun (7504 Market St., 906/847-3885, www.cloghaun.com, May-Oct., $97-204 high season, $84-199 off-season, including breakfast) was built in 1884 by Thomas and Bridgette Donnelly, who left Ireland during the potato famine and followed a relative to Mackinac Island. Today, this grand Victorian (pronounced CLA-han) with large grounds is still owned and operated by their descendants. It's located on Market Street, next to some of the island's historic attractions and just one block from Main Street. Eight rooms have private baths; two others share a bath.

Below East Bluff near Ste. Anne's Church, **Haan's 1830 Inn** (6806 Huron St., 906/847-6244, www.mackinac.com/haans, mid-May-mid-Oct., $90-215) is a Greek Revival built by Colonel Preston, one of the last officers to preside over Fort Mackinac, generally recognized as the island's first mayor. Just try to drag yourself out of the wicker chairs on the big front porch. Four of the seven rooms have private baths.

Only a few minutes' walk from the ferry docks, **Bay View Bed & Breakfast** (6947 Main St., 906/847-3295, www.mackinacbayview.com, May-Oct., $95-455) has rooms ranging from standards to suites facing the water. If you spend a little extra cash for a room with a view, you'll find yourself overlooking the yacht harbor. Breakfast is served on the veranda; make sure you try the custom Bay View Blend Coffee.

Other Lodging

★ **Mission Point Resort** (6633 Main St., 906/847-3312, www.missionpoint.com, $105-620) may have the island's very best location, spread across 18 acres at the island's southeastern tip. Though not of the Victorian era—it was built in the 1950s by the Moral Rearmament movement, a post-World War II patriotic group—the sprawling bright-white resort is attractive and well kept, offering beautiful lawns lined with Adirondack chairs. Amenities include an outdoor pool, tennis and volleyball courts, and loads of kids' activities.

In addition to the professional putting green, bicycle rentals, lawn bowling, croquet, tennis, and professional spa, Mission Point Resort offers hayrides around the island. The Tower Museum, eight stories up, provides a breathtaking panorama of the island and the Straits. Interpretive displays on each floor present fascinating looks at topics such as maritime shipping history, Native American heritage, and the construction of the Mackinac Bridge.

There are four restaurants, and the Lakeside Marketplace can provide you with a picnic lunch on your way out to explore the island; the Epicurean is the place for elegant dining and an impressive selection of wines. Rates are highest during the height of summer. With all it has to offer, Mission Point is a quintessential self-contained summer resort.

INFORMATION

For help with accommodations and other information ahead of time, contact the **Mackinac Island Chamber of Commerce & Tourism Bureau** (877/847-0086, www.mackinacisland.org). You can also get a visitors guide with maps of the state park at the **Mackinac Island State Park Visitors Center,** located on Main Street across from the island's Marquette Park and open from early May to mid-October.

GETTING THERE AND AROUND

Virtually all motorized vehicles are banned on Mackinac Island. The only exceptions are golf carts, scooters for the disabled, and a few public-service vehicles.

Boat

Two ferry lines offer service to Mackinac Island: **Shepler's Mackinac Island Ferry** (231/436-5023, www.sheplersferry.com, round-trip $25 adults, $13 ages 5-12) and the **Star Line** (800/638-9892, www.mackinawferry.com, $26 adults, $14 ages 5-12, discounts on the website). Both have departures from Mackinaw City and St. Ignace. Ferries run, in general, from Mackinaw City between May and October, and from St. Ignace from April through November. Free parking is available for day-trippers; overnight travelers have to pay to park (usually $20 per night).

If you're sailing your own boat, you can contact the **Mackinac Island State Harbor** (906/847-3561, www.michigan.gov/dnr) for reservations up to six months in advance of your stay. The marina's 76 slips are available

late May to mid-September. You can contact the marina on radio channel 9. It's located at 45°50.40 N, 84°36.42 W.

Air

Mackinac Island Airport (MCD) is the only way to get to the island in the winter, and it's always an option in the summer too. Year-round flights are available from St. Ignace ($32 adults, $16 under age 12) and Pellston ($100 adults, $50 under age 12) through **Great Lakes Air** (906/643-7165, www.greatlakesair.net), by reservation only, with a two-fare minimum. Horse-drawn taxi service is available from the airport to your hotel; contact **Mackinac Island Carriage Tours** (906/847-3323, www.mict.com).

Getting Around

While on the island, horses are certainly the most unique means of getting around. Taxis can be hired at **Mackinac Island Carriage Tours** (7278 Main St., 906/847-3323, www.mict.com).

If you enjoy walking and hiking, you can get around Mackinac Island on foot; the island is about eight miles in circumference. Mackinac is a wonderful place for casual strolls and all-day hikes.

The island is also a great place to cycle. **Mackinac Island Bike Shop** (Main St. next to Shepler's dock, 906/847-6337, www.mackinacislandbikes.com) at the Lake View Hotel has a wide array of choices, including mountain bikes for kids and adults, plus tagalongs and Burley trailers for babies. They also offer equipment for disabled people to use, including electric wheelchairs and motorized scooters. At **Ryba's Bicycle Rentals** (7463 Main St., 906/847-3208, www.rybabikes.com), you'll find a similar selection. There are a number of other bicycle rental shops on the island, or you can bring your own across on the ferry for about $10.

St. Ignace

St. Ignace is directly at the north end of the Mackinac Bridge, and is noteworthy for both its history and its less expensive off-island lodging. It has made a reputation of its own: with an annual auto show and plenty of tourism draws, this city, the first off the bridge, offers an introduction to the Upper Peninsula, where one instantly notices the more rustic feeling the U.P. is so known for. As such, St. Ignace doesn't have the glamour of Mackinac Island's resorts, and also lacks the touristy feel of Mackinaw City. Outdoors enthusiasts of all stripes will appreciate its access to the eastern branch of the Hiawatha National Forest.

SIGHTS
★ Mackinac Bridge

You can't miss it: it's that massive bridge, total length 26,372 feet. At mid-span, the roadway is 200 feet above the water. It has 42,000 miles of wire in the main cables, and its size and grandeur stand as a testimony to 20th-century engineering and the determination of the ironworkers who built it.

Known as "Mighty Mac" or simply "The Bridge," it stands out as Michigan's pride and joy. Stretching across nearly five miles of open water, Mighty Mac has the third-longest total suspension of any bridge in the world, and ranks as number one in the western hemisphere. There are other ways of measuring suspension, such as the length of the main span between towers. Some of these methods put the Bridge farther down on the list, but try telling that to a Michigander—of either peninsula.

There are several quality photo spots on either end of the bridge; just find St. Ignace's southern shore and you can't miss it. Try Straits State Park or Mackinac Bridge View Park just west of the toll plaza. Driving the bridge is different from looking at it, and if you can manage the approximately 10-minute-long and oddly exciting drive, you should do it. If you can't bring yourself to stay behind the wheel—and many can't—bridge personnel will drive your car across at no additional charge. Pedestrians, bicyclists, and snowmobilers are prohibited on the Bridge, but transportation is offered for them: $3.50 pp, $5 for

Mackinac Bridge

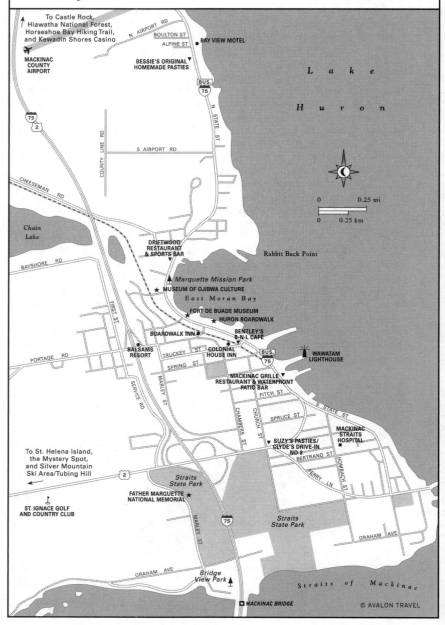

St. Ignace

To Castle Rock, Hiawatha National Forest, Horseshoe Bay Hiking Trail, and Kewadin Shores Casino

MACKINAC COUNTY AIRPORT

N AIRPORT RD

BOULTON ST

ALPINE ST

BAY VIEW MOTEL

BESSIE'S ORIGINAL HOMEMADE PASTIES

BUS. 75

N STATE ST

S AIRPORT RD

L a k e

H u r o n

COUNTY LINE RD

75
2

CHEESEMAN RD

Chain Lake

BAYSHORE RD

0   0.25 mi
0   0.25 km

DRIFTWOOD RESTAURANT & SPORTS BAR

Rabbit Back Point

Marquette Mission Park

MUSEUM OF OJIBWA CULTURE

East Moran Bay

FORT DE BUADE MUSEUM

HURON BOARDWALK

BOARDWALK INN

BENTLEY'S B-N-L CAFÉ

FIRST ST

BALSAMS RESORT

TRUCKEY ST

COLONIAL HOUSE INN

BUS. 75

WAWATAM LIGHTHOUSE

PORTAGE RD

SPRING ST

MACKINAC GRILLE RESTAURANT & WATERFRONT PATIO BAR

FITCH ST

S STATE ST

SERVICE RD

MARLEY ST

CHAMBERS ST

CHURCH ST

SPRUCE ST

MACKINAC STRAITS HOSPITAL

SUZY'S PASTIES/ CLYDE'S DRIVE-IN NO 3

BERTRAND ST

HOMBACH ST

To St. Helena Island, the Mystery Spot, and Silver Mountain Ski Area/Tubing Hill

2

Straits State Park

FATHER MARQUETTE NATIONAL MEMORIAL

FERRY LN

ST. IGNACE GOLF AND COUNTRY CLUB

MARLEY ST

75

Straits State Park

GRAHAM AVE

GRAHAM AVE

Bridge View Park

S t r a i t s   o f   M a c k i n a c

MACKINAC BRIDGE

© AVALON TRAVEL

Building the Bridge

It was an impossible dream since 1884, when a story in the *Grand Traverse Herald* reported that ferry service had failed as a means of traversing the Straits. The only way, it said, was a tunnel or a bridge.

Since its creation, Michigan had been cut in two by the Straits of Mackinac—the northern third isolated and rugged, the other two-thirds below. As early as 1897 and as late as the 1970s there was serious talk of the Upper Peninsula seceding from Michigan and forming its own state, the Superior State. It seems that the physical separation led to an ideological divide; even today, many Yoopers are Yoopers first and Michiganders second. For many travelers, the Straits were a time consuming obstacle, with ferry lines stretching for miles.

After years of planning and lobbying to get financial backing, bridge construction officially began in 1954. It was the largest bridge construction fleet ever assembled up to that time, and when the project was finally finished in 1957, designer David B. Steinman wrote that "the people of Michigan built the world's greatest bridge. They built it in the face of discouragement, of faintheartedness on the part of many of their leaders, of warnings that the rocks in the Straits were too soft, the ice too thick, the winds too strong, the rates of interest on the bonds too high, and the whole concept too big." It wasn't too big, but it wasn't easy either. It took three years of construction and $99 million dollars, and it regrettably cost five men their lives: Frank Pepper, James R. LeSarge, Albert Abbot, Jack C. Baker, and Robert Koppen. It's a steep cost for one of the world's finest engineering marvels.

"Mighty Mac" is five miles long, with a center span between the main towers of 3,800 feet. The main towers stand 552 feet above the water; the roadway is 200 feet up. It weighs 1,024,500 tons, has 4,851,700 steel rivets and 1,016,600 steel bolts, and can withstand winds up to an amazing 600 miles per hour. The suspended bridge is capable of moving as much as 35 feet east to west in high winds, but the bridge authority shuts the roadway down long before the swaying reaches that point.

The cost of operating and maintaining the bridge is paid by the toll you pay when crossing, and the maintenance it takes to keep a more than 60-year-old bridge safe for traffic is a staggering and unending job. But it's worth it—as frightening as it can be to drive across the bridge (it bows visibly in the wind, and you're 200 feet up), it's safe.

Michiganians are proud of their bridge, and they should be. It's gorgeous and convenient; without it, travelers from the south would be waiting in an hours-long line for the ferries; as it is, access to the entire Upper Peninsula is as easy as keeping your eyes on the road and your hands on the wheel.

a bike, and $15 for a snowmobile and driver. Snowmobile transport is only available 8am-8pm daily.

Father Marquette National Memorial

High above the open Straits of Mackinac, the largely open-air **Father Marquette National Memorial** commemorates French explorer and Jesuit missionary Jacques Marquette. In the 1660s and 1670s Marquette paddled through the Great Lakes, establishing dozens of cities along the way, including Sault Ste. Marie and St. Ignace. Marquette then linked up with Louis Jolliet and paddled another several thousand miles to become the first European explorer of the Mississippi River.

Walking trails feature interpretive signs that discuss Marquette's Great Lakes travels and the impact the area's geography had on settlement. Scant emphasis is given to the effect Marquette's missionary work had on Native Americans, thousands of whom Marquette converted to Christianity. A small museum on the site burned down several years ago, but it's still worth a visit for the National Memorial, the outdoor trail, and the panoramic view of the Mackinac Bridge.

The Memorial is on the grounds of **Straits State Park** (west of I-75 and south of U.S. 2, 906/643-8620, daily Memorial Day-mid-Sept.). A State of Michigan park sticker is required for entry.

Downtown St. Ignace

In contrast to the Father Marquette memorial, the **Marquette Mission Park and Museum of Ojibwa Culture** (500 N. State St., 906/643-9161, http://museumofojibwaculture.net, 9am-5pm daily Memorial Day-June, 9am-8pm daily late June-Labor Day, 9am-5pm daily Labor Day-early Oct., donation) tells the story of the Ojibwa and the effect the European explorers had on their culture. The museum is also the presumed site of Jacques Marquette's grave and the site of his Jesuit mission.

Displays housed in a former Roman Catholic church include artifacts, some dating to 6000 BCE, from archaeological digs on the grounds explanations of how the Ojibwa adapted and survived in the area's often harsh climate, and a discussion of how they allied with the French fur traders despite how it greatly diminished their traditional way of life. Don't miss the museum's adjacent gift shop, featuring authentic locally made crafts

such as ash baskets, quill jewelry, and more. It also offers an excellent selection of books on both Native American and French history in the area of the Straits.

The **Fort de Buade Museum** (334 N. State St., 906/643-6622, http://michilimackinachistoricalsociety.com, 10am-6pm Thurs.-Sat. summer, donation) interprets Native American, French, English, and American history. The museum has one of the city's largest collections, at more than 6,700 square feet, including historical Native American and military weapons. Unfortunately, it's also one of St. Ignace's least visited museums.

The **Huron Boardwalk** follows the shoreline for a mile, with interpretive signs explaining the role of the bay in the area's settlement. Outdoor displays explore the Straits of Mackinac history and include a rudder from a wooden steamer sunk in 1894 and the windlass from an 1891 shipwreck.

Castle Rock

Three miles north of St. Ignace is one of those tourist spots that is hopelessly, almost embarrassingly irresistible. **Castle Rock** (Castle Rock Rd., 906/643-8268, www.castlerockmi.com, daily early May-mid-Oct., $1) is a vertical tower that rises nearly 200 feet

Marquette Mission Park and Museum of Ojibwa Culture

and provides unparalleled views of Mackinac Island, the Straits, and Lake Huron. The oversize Paul Bunyan and Babe, his blue ox, is an exciting photo opportunity for children or adults with a certain sense of humor. Most visitors just head up the 170-step climb without looking twice. Nearby is a very touristy gift shop.

The Mystery Spot

The Mystery Spot (150 Martin Lake Rd., 906/643-8322, http://mysteryspotstignace.com, 9am-8pm daily May 10-June 15, 8am-9pm daily June 16-Labor Day, 9am-6pm daily Labor Day-Oct. 19, $9 adults, $7 ages 5-11) would hardly bear mentioning if it wasn't for the billboards you've seen around town and were no doubt wondering about. In the early 1950s, some surveyors apparently stumbled across an area where their equipment stopped working correctly. The laws of physics don't seem to apply here: tall people seem smaller, chairs balance with two legs in the air, and you'll be able to walk up a wall without falling. The experience can be fun. Whatever truth there is in the story of the Mystery Spot is magnified by the strange angles the buildings are built at, creating optical illusions that will no doubt make for some interesting photos.

An attraction just added is the zip line ($20). Riders are propelled by gravity for 1,000 feet along a cable about 20 feet in the air. Don't do it on a full stomach. Discounts are offered to those wanting to take in both attractions.

The Deer Ranch

It's not uncommon to see wild whitetail deer in the Upper Peninsula, but wouldn't it be great to get close enough to actually pet one? At the **Deer Ranch** (1540 W. U.S. 2, four miles west of I-75, www.deerranch.com, 9am-5pm daily mid-May-mid-June and Sept. 6-Oct. 16, 9am-8pm daily mid-June-Labor Day, $5 over age 5) you can do this and more. You'll find six large enclosures with a variety of deer habitats—from an open field to dense woods. Visitors can walk the perimeters and see 30 adult deer and about 15 fawns. Many of the deer are quite friendly, and often stick their noses through the fence looking for a bit of affection. Coin-operated food dispensers allow visitors to hand-feed the deer.

Lighthouses

There are no historic lighthouses in St. Ignace, but there is one close by on **St. Helena Island** (http://lighthousefriends.com), a few miles west of the city in the Straits of Mackinac.

Wawatam Lighthouse

Built in 1873, the 71-foot tower and attached keeper's quarters fell into disrepair after the lighthouse was automated in the 1920s. It has seen some restoration in the recent past, and it's open to the public by appointment (313/436-9150). The island is accessible by boat, but from land, you can get a decent view from a U.S. 2 turnout in Gros Cap, six miles west of St. Ignace. Near the St. Ignace marina is **Wawatam Lighthouse,** which is a recent construction.

LIGHTHOUSE CRUISES

The **Star Line** (587 N. State St., 906/643-7635 or 800/638-9892, www.mackinacferry.com, $28 adults, $12 ages 5-12) offers an exciting sunset cruise (8:30pm Mon. July-Aug.) departing from St. Ignace. The cruise passes under the Mackinac Bridge and around Round Island Lighthouse, Mackinac Island, Old Mackinaw Point Lighthouse, and Colonial Michilimackinac, and provides a running narration. **Shepler's Ferry** (556 E. Central Ave., Mackinaw City, 800/828-6157) also offers an evening lighthouse cruise ($49.50 adults, $27.50 ages 5-12) from its Mackinaw City dock only.

ENTERTAINMENT
Kewadin Shores Casino

The Upper Peninsula isn't much for metropolitan entertainment—nightclubs and lounges are almost nonexistent—but it does manage to get gaming right, although the local casinos tend to lack the Las Vegas-style flash and glitter. **Kewadin Shores Casino** (3105 Mackinac Trail, 906/643-7071, www.kewadin.com, year-round), more commonly called The Shores, has 25,000 square feet of space for games such as blackjack, poker, and roulette and more than 900 slot machines. From 4pm to 8pm Friday, each Kewadin location hosts its Friday Social, which includes bar specials, random draws for Kewadin Credits, match play, and double and triple points. The Northern Pines lounge features live entertainment Friday and Saturday night.

Eighty-one rooms are available at the casino's **hotel** ($80-95), on the shores of Lake Huron. Visitors can also enjoy the pool, fitness center, and game room. Dining options include **Horseshoe Bay Restaurant** (7am-9pm Sun.-Thurs., 7am-11pm Fri.-Sat.), which offers classic American fare and features a special each evening, including Italian selections on Tuesday and apple pork chops on Thursday. A summer dinner buffet is offered Sunday-Thursday ($11), and on Saturday the restaurant sets out a seafood buffet ($11). Daily lunch specials range $7-9. Breakfast is offered daily. Another dining option is the **Whitetail Bar and Grill** (11am-10pm daily, entrées $11-22).

FESTIVALS AND EVENTS
Powwows

A great way to learn about the Upper Peninsula's original inhabitants is to attend a powwow. Powwows celebrate Native American heritage through colorful dancing, feasting, ancient stories, and ceremonies. Many are open to the public and can be wonderful learning experiences. Know that powwows and many other Native American cultural events have a spiritual element to them; halter tops, bare chests, pets, drinking, smoking, and certain other behaviors are considered inappropriate. Take note of how others are dressed, or ask questions of the community's representatives. For a calendar of powwows, visit **Crazy Crow** (www.crazycrow.com/site/pow-wows-in-michigan). A powwow is held in Sault Ste. Marie each June by the **Sault Tribe of Chippewa Indians** (www.saulttribe.com).

Annual Mackinac Bridge Walk

On Labor Day, the Mackinac Bridge Authority dispenses with its no-pedestrian policy for the **Annual Mackinac Bridge Walk.** The walk begins in St. Ignace and ends in Mackinaw City, with the Governor of Michigan traditionally leading the crowd. To accommodate walkers, the bridge's two northbound lanes are closed to traffic. Walking begins at 7am, and no walkers are allowed to start after 11am, so make sure you get there on time—or earlier, if possible. It takes about two hours to make the five-mile walk. Note that there are no restrooms on the bridge. Transportation is provided from Mackinaw City back to St. Ignace ($5 pp, infants free).

Auto Shows

Perhaps St. Ignace's biggest claim to fame is its several summer and fall auto shows, which include the **Annual Antiques on the Bay** event, held the third week of June; the **St. Ignace Car Show Weekend,** the last weekend of June; and in September, the **On the Waterfront Car-Small Truck Show-Pedal Cars & Swap Meet,** the **Richard Crane Memorial Truck Show,** and the **Owosso Tractor Parts and Equipment Antique Tractor Parade and Show.** For details, visit http://stignace.com.

SUMMER SPORTS AND RECREATION

Hiawatha National Forest

Named after "The Song of Hiawatha," a poem by Henry Wadsworth Longfellow that tells the story of the 16th-century Iroquois chief, the **Hiawatha National Forest** is a swath of protected land stretching all the way from St. Ignace north to the Lake Superior shore. Many of the forest's 860,000 acres are found in the central U.P., but the separate eastern district is where you'll find most of St. Ignace's summer recreation opportunities.

Trails

Thirty-five miles of the **North Country National Scenic Trail** lie in the eastern district of the Hiawatha National Forest. Recently completed, it stretches from New York State to North Dakota. Off-limits to horses and motorized vehicles, the trail is perfect for hikers and leads through stands of cedar, aspen, pine, and northern hardwood. The flat to rolling trail is fully marked, but not all sections have been brought up to trail standards. The

website www.nps.gov/noco has a full map of the trail.

The **Horseshoe Bay Hiking Trail** is a two-mile (round-trip) trail that leads from Foley Creek Campground to a secluded, sandy Lake Huron beach and back. Only three miles from St. Ignace, the trail leads through northern white cedar lowlands, where you're likely to spot ducks and great blue herons in the numerous ponds. More information on the trail, including a complete map, is available from the **Michigan Department of Natural Resources** (www.michigan.gov/dnr).

The Hiawatha National Forest has more than 2,000 miles of forest road available for motor vehicle use, plenty of which is within easy reach of St. Ignace. Detailed maps of **ATV/ORV** trails are available from the Hiawatha National Forest's **St. Ignace Ranger District office** (1900 W. U.S. 2, 906/643-7900, www.fs.usda.gov/hiawatha, 8am-4:30pm Mon.-Fri.), along with trail maps, and information on other recreation opportunities. Rules are strictly enforced, so make sure you're thoroughly familiar with them before setting out.

Fishing

If you're into deepwater fishing, it's hard to beat the Great Lakes, where you'll find salmon, perch, walleye, whitefish, herring, pike, and more. Contact **E.U.P. Fishing Charters** (724 Cheeseman Rd., 877/475-3474, catchfish@lighthouse.net) or **Dream Seaker Charters & Tours** (888/634-3419, www.dreamseaker.com) for charters into the Straits.

Inland fishing is abundant in the area. Inland lakes, rivers, and streams provide famously good fishing from April right up to December's freeze. You'll need a valid Michigan fishing license. Visitors from outside Michigan need a temporary nonresident license. Both are available online at www.mdnr-elicense.com and through most fishing charter services.

Other Water Sports

Like the rest of the U.P., St. Ignace can be a

summertime paradise. Visitors have come to love the sandy **beaches,** and the relatively warm waters of the Straits can offer plenty of relaxation. You'll find ideal swimming spots at **Straits State Park** (720 Church St., 906/643-8620, www.michigan.gov/dnr) or at any number of smaller beaches along the Lake Huron and Lake Michigan shores.

If you thought the Straits were beautiful at eye level, imagine seeing them from a harness attached to a parachute and a 600-foot cable. Parasailing excursions are available from **Mackinaw Parasailing** (866/436-7144, www.mackinawparasailing.com, $75 single, $139 double, $189 triple), which docks at the Star Line Railroad Dock in St. Ignace. Mackinaw Parasailing has been giving visitors a new perspective for years from a custom boat that allows for easy flight-deck take-offs and landings. You can also catch a ride from Mackinac Island and Mackinaw City. Parasailing is an exhilarating activity, but clearly not for the faint of heart.

Golf

For some stunning scenery, the **St. Ignace Golf and Country Club** (223 U.S. 2, 906/643-8071, www.stignacegolf.com, $14 for 9 holes, $23 for 18 holes) offers a beautifully tended course with stunning views of the Mackinac Bridge, Lake Huron, and the Straits of Mackinac. Rental clubs are available for $10, and powered carts can be had for just $10. The golf course is located off U.S. 2, a short distance west of I-75, next to the Big Boy restaurant.

WINTER SPORTS AND RECREATION
Ski and Snowshoe Trails

The miles of hiking trails in St. Ignace don't disappear in winter, they just get covered in snow, perfect for **cross-country skiing** and **snowshoeing.** The North Country National Scenic Trail's 35 miles in St. Ignace are popular with skiers. There's a warming cabin at the trailhead to Sand Dunes Ski Trail, which has seven groomed trails suitable for every skill

level. Trails range 1.5 to 7.6 miles. While on Loop A, look for claw marks left by black bears climbing the trees in the fall (bears hibernate in the winter). For more information, contact Hiawatha National Forest's **St. Ignace Ranger District office** (1900 W. U.S. 2, 906/643-7900, 8am-4:30pm Mon.-Fri.).

Downhill Skiing

Believe it or not, you can actually find downhill skiing west of town, at **Silver Mountain Ski Area/Tubing Hill** (Cheeseman Rd. and U.S. 2 W., 906/643-6083, http://www.silvermt.com, gondola 8:15am-5pm, chairlift 9am-3:30pm, tubing sessions 9am-11am, 11am-1pm, 1pm-3pm Sat. only). While skiing is included and there are a few runs for beginner and intermediate skiers and snowboarders, Silver Mountain is very much an "all around," meaning it's a family-oriented winter resort that offers snow tubing with a rope tow, paddle towing, and groomed runs. Silver Mountain is an entertaining diversion, but serious skiers should head west to the Iron Mountain area for some of the U.P.'s best downhill skiing. Hours may vary, so check the website before visiting.

Snowmobiling

There are about 3,000 miles of snowmobile trails that spread across Michigan's Upper Peninsula, and a few of the trailheads are right in St. Ignace. Bundle up and hit the trails to pristine winter wilderness or popular destinations like Tahquamenon Falls. The local snowmobile club maintains many of the trails, and snowmobiles can be rented from the **Quality Inn** (561 Boulevard Dr., 800/906-4656). If you're bringing your own, be aware that snowmobile crossings are not allowed on the Mackinac Bridge; transportation is provided by the **Mackinac Bridge Authority** (906/643-7600) for $15 per sled.

Remember that snowmobiling in the Upper Peninsula can be very dangerous, especially for newcomers. Every year there are snowmobile-related deaths as reckless enthusiasts drive after a few drinks or plunge through the ice. Stay on marked trails and off rivers and lakes. Abstain from alcohol for at least one hour before driving or riding a snowmobile. Also, keep a close eye out for pedestrians, especially young children, who can be difficult to see. Before setting out, talk to locals who know what's going on, and check trail conditions with the **Straits Area Snowmobile Club** (www.straitsareasnowmobileclub.com).

FOOD

It's not impossible to visit the U.P. without sinking your teeth into the crust of at least one pasty (pronounced PASS-tee), but to get a complete U.P. experience, you should at least try one. Stop by **Bessie's Original Homemade Pasties** (1106 N. State St., 906/643-8487, http://bessiesoriginalhome-madepasties.com, 9am-9am Wed.-Mon. Apr.-Nov., $7-12) for the traditional Yooper nosh, a potpie creation of beef or chicken, potatoes, onions, rutabagas, and other vegetables. Bessie's also serves vegetarian pasties, deli subs, old-fashioned ice cream, and smoked fish. Everything on the menu is prepared fresh. **Suzy's Pasties** (W720 U.S. 2, 906/643-7007, 10am-6pm daily Apr.-Oct., $6.50-11) also serves a great version of this delicacy, and makes its own fudge as well.

Clyde's Drive-In No. 3 (U.S. 2, just west of the bridge, 906/643-8303, 9am-10am daily Apr.-Nov., $7-12) is another perennial St. Ignace favorite. Known throughout the U.P. as home of the best burgers on either side of the bridge, Clyde's Drive-In is not only an authentic curbside restaurant, it's also the best place for a meal on the cheaper side. You can choose to eat in if you prefer, but it gets pretty cramped. Clyde's menu includes fried shrimp, chicken, and perch, light breakfasts, old-fashioned malts and shakes, and the famous three-quarter-pound C Burger.

You'll find more old-fashioned dining at **Bentley's B-n-L Cafe** (62 N. State St., 906/643-7910, hours vary, $2-10), a fourth-generation diner that has a vintage soda fountain look.

Some of the town's best pizza, as well as

steak, seafood, and sandwiches, can be found at **Driftwood Restaurant & Sports Bar** (590 N. State St., 906/643-9133, www.the-driftwoodonline.com, 8am-12:30am daily, bar until 2am daily), a family restaurant and sports bar. Opening early for breakfast, the restaurant also offers great lunch choices ($8); dinner entrées can climb as high as $27, a little steep for family dining, but more moderately priced plates can be had for around $12.

For the best of St. Ignace's fine dining scene—which manages to stay stubbornly unpretentious—grab a table the **Mackinac Grille Restaurant & Waterfront Patio Bar** (251 S. State St., 906/643-7482, www.mackinacgrill.com, 11am-10pm Mon.-Sat., 9am-10pm Sun. summer, 11am-9pm Mon.-Sat., 9am-2pm Sun. off-season, lunch $7-10, dinner $12-18), which specializes in locally caught whitefish. Located on the marina, the restaurant offers a pleasant view of the Straits, Mackinac Island, and the Star Line ferry dock.

ACCOMMODATIONS

St. Ignace is jam packed with lodging options, which draw travelers who want to visit Mackinac Island without paying the high island prices. Unfortunately, many of St. Ignace's accommodations are rather run-of-the-mill and utilitarian. Don't expect to find the glitz of high-end lodging or expensive resorts like the island's Grand Hotel—but that doesn't mean you have to settle for a substandard room.

Hotels and Motels

Billed as St. Ignace's oldest lodging establishment, the **Boardwalk Inn** (316 N. State St., 800/254-5408, www.boardwalkinn.com, $89-180) was built in 1928, as the desk registers going back to 1929 will attest. Located across the street from the Huron Boardwalk, the classic boutique hotel is in the middle of downtown St. Ignace, an easy walk to most attractions, including ferries to Mackinac Island. The hotel fills up quickly, especially during the Labor Day Bridge Walk and St. Ignace's annual car show, so reserve well in advance. The Boardwalk serves a deluxe continental breakfast for guests each morning.

Considering the stunning views of Lake Huron and waterfront access to a private beach and boardwalk, the **Bay View Motel** (1133 N. State St., 906/643-9444, mid-May-Oct., $49-70) is surprisingly cheap and pet-friendly. Don't expect much from the Spartan rooms, of course, but what this motel lacks in decor it makes up for in its thrifty appeal and scenic location. Expect rates to jump during holidays and festivals.

Bed-and-Breakfasts

Although it also has seven motel rooms, the ★ **Colonial House Inn** (90 N. State St., 906/643-6900, www.colonial-house-inn.com, $79-135, motel $69-89) is first and foremost a bed-and-breakfast, and St. Ignace's only one at that. The Victorian-style home overlooks the Straits of Mackinac and features a wrap-around veranda and second-floor balcony. Each of the B&B's seven rooms is distinctively and individually decorated and has a double or a queen bed and a private bath. Occupancy is limited to two people per room, so families will need to stay in the adjacent motel. Pets are not allowed.

Camping

Of St. Ignace's many campgrounds, the most popular is **Straits State Park** (720 Church St., 906/643-8620, www.michigan.gov/dnr, $19-28). With 275 campsites, many with electricity and all with access to modern restrooms, the park's popularity is driven by a number of can't-say-no perks, including Lake Huron waterfront access, stunning views of the bridge, and the Father Marquette memorial and interpretive trail. Close to town, the campground is close to the center of activity, with easy access to Mackinac Island ferries and other attractions. It's almost worth putting up with the summertime crowds. Of the four modern campgrounds, aim for East Loop or West Loop, which have nicely wooded sites right on the Straits.

Smaller crowds can be found at **Brevoort**

Lake Campground (www.fs.usda.gov, from $18) in the Hiawatha National Forest, 20 miles west of St. Ignace. The 4,233-acre lake has about 70 large forested campsites with tables and fire rings. Campers have access to the lake for boating, fishing, and swimming, and three hiking trails explore the surrounding forest. You'll find boat and canoe rentals, as well as groceries and other necessities, at a small store adjacent to the campground. You might also want to try one of the 54 sites at **Foley Creek Campground** (www.fs.usda.gov, from $18). Although still in Hiawatha National Forest, Foley Creek is only six miles outside town. Smaller and more secluded than Straits State Park, this campground is close enough to the St. Ignace scene to use as a home base. Private campsites are set among large shade trees; Lake Huron beach access is a one-mile hike up Horseshoe Bay Trail. Contact Hiawatha National Forest's **St. Ignace Ranger District office** (1900 W. U.S. 2, 906/643-7900, 8am-4:30pm Mon.-Fri.) for information about both campgrounds.

Other Lodging

The cabins at **Balsams Resort** (1458 W. U.S. 2, 906/643-9121 June-Labor Day, 313/791-8026 Labor Day-June, www.balsamsresort.com, daily $100-140, weekly $800) are cozy, fully furnished homes away from home. Balsams Resort can put you up in a one- or two-bedroom log cabin where you can prepare your own meals in the kitchen, relax in front of the fireplace, or wander over the streams and through the 40-acre woods. You won't be able to see Lake Michigan from every cabin, but the motel ($60-75), which isn't quite as quaint, affords a decent view, and guests have access to a private beach.

Several area **cabins and cottages** are available for rent on a nightly or weekly basis, which is an attractive option for families or vacationers looking for a comfortable extended stay. With a wide range of rooms, locations, and availability, prices can be as low as $100 per night and can easily surpass $1,000 for weeklong rentals. Pets are welcome, but often with significant restrictions. Full details are on the website. For information and availability, contact the **St. Ignace Visitors Bureau** (6 Spring St., Suite 100, 800/338-6660, www.stignace.com).

INFORMATION

For visitor information, contact the **St. Ignace Visitors Bureau** (6 Spring St., Suite 100, 800/338-6660) or the **St. Ignace Chamber of Commerce** (560 N. State St., 800/970-8717). Both can be found online at www.stignace.com. More particulars on the trails, camping, and recreation available in Hiawatha National Forest are available from the **St. Ignace Ranger District office** (1900 W. U.S. 2, 906/643-7900, 8am-4:30pm Mon.-Fri.).

GETTING THERE AND AROUND

Car

Traveling from the south, follow I-75 north across the bridge to St. Ignace. From the north, I-75 drops into St. Ignace from Sault Ste. Marie, while travelers coming east from Wisconsin can take U.S. 2 into the city. If you're crossing the bridge from Mackinaw City, the 2015 passenger vehicle toll is $4, with an additional $2 for each axle if you're pulling a trailer. Trucks are $5 per axle. No toll increases are currently planned, but this is subject to change. Visit www.mackinacbridge.org for the latest.

Air

The two closest airports with scheduled passenger flights are **Pellston Regional Airport** (PLN, www.pellstonairport.com), south of Mackinaw City in the Lower Peninsula, and **Chippewa County International Airport** (CIU, www.airciu.com), in Sault Ste. Marie; both have rental-car providers.

It's possible to fly into St. Ignace's **Mackinac County Airport** (www.mackinaccounty.net) directly if you charter a flight through **Great Lakes Air** (906/643-7165, www.greatlakesair.net) from a number of nearby locations, including Detroit, Chicago Midway, and Chicago O'Hare, but it can be very costly.

Boat

Boaters can make reservations at one of the 120 slips at **St. Ignace Marina** (906/643-8131, www.michigan.gov/dnr). The harbormaster is on duty from mid-May through late September; you can reach the marina on radio channel 9. The location is 45°51.58 N, 84°43.06 W.

FERRY TO MACKINAC ISLAND

Since you're in St. Ignace, you'll likely want to visit Mackinac Island. You can catch a ride on a ferry at **Shepler's Mackinac Island Ferry** (231/436-5023, www.sheplersferry.com, round-trip $25 adults, $13 ages 5-12) or the **Star Line** (800/638-9892, www.mackinawferry.com, $26 adults, $14 ages 5-12).

Bus and Train

Greyhound (800/231-2222, www.greyhound.com) has a bus terminal just across from the ferry docks, providing service to St. Ignace from points across the country. **Amtrak** (800/872-7245, www.amtrak.com) has partnered with Greyhound to provide transportation to St. Ignace from several major cities in southwest Michigan. **Indian Trails** (800/292-3831, www.indiantrails.com) offers bus service to St. Ignace from Chicago and a number of Michigan cities.

Mackinaw City

Mackinaw City, located at the very tip of the Lower Peninsula, serves as a gateway for travelers bound for Mackinac Island and has several historic attractions of its own. Despite the high density of strip malls and souvenir shops, downtown Mackinaw City also offers some "serious" shops, including bookstores, antiques shops, and clothing stores that don't specialize in T-shirts. Mackinaw City shares a special trait with its island cousin—beautiful Great Lakes views. You'll also find excellent food and lodging here.

SIGHTS

Mackinac Historic State Parks

With a history as long and rich as Mackinac's, it isn't surprising to find a collection of historic sites that, together with Mackinac Island's Fort Mackinac and historic downtown, present nearly 300 years of Michigan history. If you're planning on visiting Colonial Michilimackinac, Old Mackinac Point Lighthouse, or the Historic Mill Creek Discovery Park, the "Mainland Combo" ticket ($26 adults, $15.50 ages 5-12) is the best deal, providing admission to all these sites. Families might want to take advantage of the Mackinac Family Heritage Membership ($85) for season-long unlimited entry to all of the sites for up to two adults and all dependent children or grandchildren ages 17 or younger.

HISTORIC MILL CREEK DISCOVERY PARK

Historic Mill Creek Discovery Park (9001 S. U.S. 23, 231/436-4100, www.mackinacparks.com, 9am-4pm daily early May-mid-Oct., 9am-5pm early June-late Aug., $9 adults, $6 ages 5-12) is an exceptionally pretty glen and rushing stream that creates a pleasant oasis for visitors, but it was once an innovative industrial site. When the British made plans to move from Fort Michilimackinac to Mackinac Island, Scotsman Robert Campbell recognized the obvious need for lumber. He purchased 640 acres of land surrounding the only waterway in the area with enough flow to power a sawmill. He built the mill in 1790 and later added a blacksmith shop and a gristmill.

The site was no longer profitable when the

downtown Mackinaw City

The Joy of Charter Fishing

Traveling with an expert guide is always memorable. Embarking on a charter fishing expedition is a special treat, and Northern Michigan offers them in spades along the Lake Superior and Lake Michigan shorelines. The proprietors—a.k.a. the ships' captains—take pride in offering hospitality and expert guidance to both amateur and experienced anglers. Highly knowledgeable of the local waters, your skipper can offer the latest information on how the fish are biting and the precise locations offering the best chances for a big catch.

Many charter operators also use their vessels to offer other adventures, including sunset cruises or lighthouse tours. While it's enjoyable to see the Great Lakes, being out on the water is something to savor.

To assure safety, the charter boat industry is highly regulated, and ship captains are required to be licensed by the U.S. Coast Guard. Ships carrying seven or more passengers must be inspected by the Coast Guard, while vessels ferrying six or fewer must be inspected by the State of Michigan. Remember that fishing anywhere in Michigan waters requires a valid state fishing license. For more information, visit the site for the Michigan Charter Boat Association (www.michigancharterboast.com).

Here are a few of the best in the UP:

- **E.U.P. Fishing Charters** (724 Cheeseman Rd., 251/504-1046, http://eupfishingcharters.net) offers half day trips from St. Ignace and Mackinaw City.

- **Kimar's Charters** (E3216 State Rd. M28, Shelter Bay, 906/892-8277, https://kimarscharters.com) offers serious sport trips of various lengths on Lake Superior between Au Train and Munising.

- **Lucky Line Fishing** (9052 26.6 Rd., Rapid River, Michigan 49878, 906/399-0760, https://lucklinefishingcharters.com) is situated in Gladstone on the Lake Michigan shore and offers charters geared to catching either Salmon or Walleye. There are also trips offered to Wisconsin shores.

fort ceased operation, so it was abandoned in the mid-1800s. Archaeologists and historians have worked together since the 1970s to recreate the water-powered sawmill on its original site. Today, visitors can see the splashing waterwheel in action and visit the Orientation Center, which has an audiovisual presentation and displays on other artifacts uncovered during the dig. Make sure to walk the park's 3.5 miles of trails, which wind through three kinds of forest or along the creek and mill pond, rising up to scenic overlooks with views of the Straits and Mackinac Island.

An extra $9 will gain you access to the park's new Treetop Discovery Tour, where you can stroll through the treetops on a canopy bridge, fly over a pond on a 425-foot zip line, or scale a climbing wall. Children have access to the Water Power Station and the Forest Friends Children's Play Area. Mill Creek is located just southeast of Mackinaw City.

OLD MACKINAC POINT LIGHTHOUSE

Old Mackinac Point Lighthouse (550 N. Huron Ave., 231/436-4100, www.mackinacparks.com, 9am-5:30pm daily, last admission 5pm, $8 adults, $5 ages 5-12) is Mackinaw City's third historic state park. Located on a point just east of the Mackinac Bridge, this 1892 cream-brick light guided ships through the busy Straits of Mackinac for nearly 70 years. When the Mackinac Bridge was completed in 1957, it became obsolete, since vessels could navigate by the bridge's necklace lights instead of this diminutive 50-foot tower. Today, this charming lighthouse, topped with a cherry-red roof, houses a maritime museum complete with hands-on exhibits, a tour to the top of the tower led by a costumed interpreter, and historic images. The lighthouse grounds serve as their own delightful little park, with impressive views of the Mackinac Bridge, a beach, and picnic tables scattered across the tidy lawn.

★ COLONIAL MICHILIMACKINAC STATE PARK

Believed to be the nation's longest-running archaeological dig, the site of **Colonial Michilimackinac State Park** (102 Straits Ave., 231/436-4100, www.mackinacparks.com, 9am-5pm daily early May-early June, 9am-7pm early June-late Aug., 9am-5pm daily late Aug.-early Oct., $13 adults, $7 ages 5-12) has provided archaeologists with treasures since 1959. The 18th-century military outpost and fur-trading village is the finest of the Mackinac Historic State Parks. The site was long a well-traveled Native American hunting and trading ground; the French built a post here in 1715. The French exploited the Native Americans, bribing them with gifts and alcohol as an incentive to assist them in the fur trade. Though this unfortunate relationship led many Native Americans to abandon their traditional ways of life, the two groups rarely fought. Instead, the French feuded with the British, who sought to expand their landholding in the region. For the next 65 years, the fort along the Straits alternately fell under French and British control.

The fort's most violent episode occurred while it was under British rule. In 1763, Pontiac, the Ottawa war chief, ordered an attack on British posts all over Michigan, an attempt to drive the growing British population out of Ottawa land. While Pontiac laid siege to Detroit, local Ojibwa stormed the fort, killing all but 13 soldiers. In the end, though, it was the feisty French colonists who sent the British fleeing from Fort Michilimackinac. They dismantled what they could and burned the rest to the ground in 1780, opting for a new, more defendable post on nearby Mackinac Island. In fact, much of the masonry from the original fort was used to build its successor on the island.

Today, Colonial Michilimackinac State Park portrays the lives of both the Native Americans and the European settlers, with costumed interpreters reenacting daily life at a Native American encampment and a stockade fort, a modern duplicate of the original. Displays include many of the artifacts excavated by archaeologists. Interpreters demonstrate various crafts and skills, from cooking and weaving to cleaning weapons. They're quite knowledgeable and able to answer most visitors' questions. Don't miss the underground archaeological tunnel exhibit,

A costumed interpreter demonstrates how to fire a musket at Colonial Michilimackinac State Park.

Mackinac or Mackinaw?

First-time visitors to the Straits will often notice the variant spelling of its name and become curious as to the reason. Simply put, the inconsistency can be traced to the area's multilayered history.

The original name given to the area by the Native Americans was Michilimackinac. Although scholarly opinion is mixed, the consensus is the term meant "great turtle," the giver of life, since the shape of Mackinac Island resembles a turtle. When the French constructed Fort Michilimackinac in 1715, they took the name and attempted to spell it in their language (a process known as transliteration), and ended the word (which is universally pronounced "-awe") in "-ac," in keeping with typical French spelling for this particular sound. Shortly after the name was shorted to Mackinac, while the fort was moved to Mackinac Island for strategic reasons. Eventually the new name became associated with the Straits themselves, which probably explains why the French spelling was chosen for the bridge.

When the British established the city on the tip of the Lower Peninsula in 1857, they took the name and spelled it with standard English pronunciation, "-aw" for "-awe." So while the city's name is distinguished by its spelling, the pronunciation is the same.

Today, the different ways of spelling the name of this beautiful place remains a small vestige of Michigan history.

"Treasures from the Sand." Other exhibits include "France at Mackinac 1670-1760," "Redcoats on the Frontier," and "Firearms on the Frontier," which describes the remaining underground ruins of the original fort.

Mackinac Bridge Museum

It's nothing fancy, but the small **Mackinac Bridge Museum** (231 E. Central Ave., above Mama Mia's Pizza, 231/436-5937, http://www.mightymac.org/bridgemuseum.htm, 8am-midnight daily May-Oct., free) is a treasure trove of fascinating information and artifacts on the construction of the $100-million Mackinac Bridge. A very well done video documents the bridge's design and construction.

Icebreaker *Mackinaw* Maritime Museum

When the U.S. Coast Guard Icebreaker *Mackinaw* was retired in 2006, ending 62 winters of clearing shipping lanes through the Great Lakes shipping channel, it was transferred to the Mackinaw Maritime Museum and docked in Mackinaw City. When it was built in the early 1940s to facilitate the transportation of war materials, the ship was the most cutting-edge icebreaker in the world. Located at the old railroad dock, the

Icebreaker *Mackinaw* Maritime Museum (131 S. Huron Ave., 231/436-9825, www.themackinaw.org, 9am-5pm daily mid-May-mid-June, 9am-7pm daily mid-June-early Sept., 9am-5pm daily Sept., $11 adults, $6 ages 6-17, free under age 6) is now open for tours.

Downtown Mackinaw City

Mackinaw City's downtown is partly a tourist trap but has some traditional businesses, including some worthwhile dining establishments. You will no doubt want to visit one or two of the city's innumerable **fudge shops** as well as **Mackinaw Crossings** (248 S. Huron Ave., 231/436-5030, www.mackinawcrossings.com), an outdoor mall with some good restaurants and shops; one that's especially noteworthy is **Enchanted Knights** (231/436-4059, www.shop.enchantedknights.com), the perfect place to get outfitted for a Renaissance fair, but which also appeals to more modern people. You'll find clothing, gifts, jewelry, and, yes, swords, all of which may make you feel like you've just been deputized by the Sheriff of Nottingham.

Another noteworthy destination and a great source for truly usual gifts is **Twisted Crystal** (301 E. Central Ave., 231/436-7020, www.twistedcrystal.com), with creative wire-wrapped jewelry utilizing rocks native to Michigan, including Petoskey stones, Leland bluestones, and greenstones, the official gemstone of Michigan.

The **Mackinaw Trolley Company** (410 S. Huron Ave., 231/436-7812, www.mackinawtrolley.com, May-Oct.) offers tours of Mackinaw City as well as a historical tour that crosses the bridge to St. Ignace. Can also be chartered for private tours or weddings. Prices vary widely depending on the tour and time selected.

Lighthouses

Mackinaw City is a place where lighthouse lovers will feel at home. The **Old Mackinac Point Lighthouse** stands guard in the shadow of the Mackinac Bridge. Visitors can tour the lighthouse and climb to the top, all while listening to a uniformed interpreter share secrets of the building's past. **McGulpin Point Lighthouse,** a few miles west, recently transitioned from life as a private home. There are plenty of other historic light stations nearby—enough to make the fascinating **lighthouse cruises** offered by **Shepler's Ferry** one of the city's more popular attractions.

★ MCGULPIN POINT LIGHTHOUSE

In 2009 Emmett County purchased **McGulpin Point Lighthouse** (500 Headlands Rd., 231/436-5860, www.mcgulpinpoint.org, 9am-8pm daily June-Sept., limited hours May and Oct., donation), decommissioned in 1906, and is gradually restoring it to its early-20th-century appearance. The residence is now a museum, displaying household items common during the late-19th century. Built in 1868, this is one of the oldest lighthouses in the area, and it is well preserved today due at least in part to its all-brick construction. The structure is nestled in a heavily wooded area just outside Mackinaw City. The lantern room and light at the top of the tower have been replaced, and visitors today can ascend the stairs to get a panoramic view of the Straits. Admission is free, but donations for the ongoing restoration of this gem are appreciated. Bringing the structure back to life has been a labor of love for the Emmet County Historical Commission, an accomplishment for which they are rightly proud.

LIGHTHOUSE CRUISES

The lighthouse cruises offered by **Shepler's Mackinac Island Ferry** (556 E. Central Ave., 231/436-5023, www.sheplersferry.com, June

McGulpin Point Lighthouse

9-Sept. 17, $49.50 adults, $27.50 ages 5-12) are very popular, and for good reason. Choose between cruising east into Lake Huron or west into Lake Michigan; either way, you'll pass below the Mackinac Bridge for a glimpse of its underside and get close enough to at least four historic lights to snap some photos. The trips last about three hours and are narrated by members of the Great Lakes Lighthouse Keepers Association. Historic lights include Mackinac Island's Round Island Light Station and Round Island Passage Light; St. Helena Island Light, west of St. Ignace; and the White Shoal and Waugoshance lighthouses. For the diehard lighthouse enthusiast, extended east and west cruises are offered. The eastern cruise ($68 adults, $39 ages 5-12) includes the difficult-to-access Spectacle Reef Lighthouse, while the western cruise ($61 adults, $35 ages 5-12) adds the Skillagalee Lighthouse to its itinerary. Cruises are subject to cancellation due to weather conditions, so be sure to call ahead.

The **Star Line** (801 S. Huron Ave., 231/436-5045 or 800/638-9892, www.mackinacferry.com, $28 adults, $12 ages 5-12) offers an exciting sunset cruise departing at 8:30pm Thursday July-August from Mackinaw City, and 8:30pm Monday July-August from their St. Ignace dock. The cruise passes Round Island Lighthouse, Mackinac Island, Old Mackinaw Point Lighthouse, and Colonial Michilimackinac, and provides a running narration.

FESTIVALS AND EVENTS

Hundreds of actors participate in Memorial Day weekend's **Colonial Michilimackinac Pageant,** which recreates historical events from the 1700s, including the famous 1763 attack. Perhaps taking a cue from St. Ignace's auto shows, Corvette enthusiasts gather at the **Corvette Crossroads Auto Show** in late August.

Mackinaw City's biggest event is Labor Day's **Annual Mackinac Bridge Walk,** which begins in St. Ignace and ends here. A few days later, in early September, thousands of people turn out for **Hopps of Fun,** the city's annual beer and wine festival, featuring more than 50 microbrews and 60 Michigan wines. Winter events include an annual **Winterfest** in early January. Information on all these events can be found at www.visitmackinawcitymichigan.com.

SUMMER SPORTS AND RECREATION
On the Water

One of the more popular fishing spots is the **Mackinaw City Fishing Pier,** built specifically for fishing, and where you may have some luck with perch, bass, salmon, or trout. You'll find the pier on the east side of town, near Railroad and Huron Avenues. **Cheboygan State Park** (4490 Beach Rd., 231/627-2811, www.michigan.gov/dnr), some 20 miles east of the city, is a favorite among anglers.

St. Ignace's **E.U.P. Fishing Charters** (724 Cheeseman Rd., 251/504-1046, http://eupfishingcharters.net) docks in Mackinaw City for offshore fishing trips with views of Mackinac Island and the bridge. For **parasailing** excursions into the Straits, contact **Mackinaw Parasailing** (209 S. Huron Ave., 866/436-7144, www.mackinawparasailing.com, $75 single, $139, double, $189 triple).

Beaches

There are miles of shoreline in and around the city, much of it with beaches. About four miles west of Mackinaw City on Wilderness Park Road, Lake Michigan curves into **Cecil Bay,** with sandy shores and shallow water. Public restrooms are available.

Golf

South of the city, the 18 holes and driving range of the **Mackinaw Club** (11891 N. Mackinaw Hwy., Carp Lake, 231/537-4955, http://mackinawclub.com, daily May 10-Oct., $17-30 for 9 holes, $25-45 for 18 holes) were built on the site of an emergency World War II landing strip for B-25 bombers.

Skydiving

Despite its name, **Mackinaw City Skydiving** (1040 Arbor St., Harbor Springs, 231/242-8822, www.skydiveharborsprings.com, spring-fall, tandem jump $299 adults) is actually in nearby Harbor Springs, a short drive west of the bridge, and has the best view of the bridge. You'll be able to see both peninsulas during one of the most exhilarating experiences in the region. Discounts are offered for groups and for online and cash payments. There is an extra charge for jumpers who weigh over 200 pounds.

FOOD

The **Historic Depot Restaurant** (248 S. Huron Ave., 231/436-7060, www.mackinawcrossings.com, 11am-10pm daily, entrées $8-20) in Mackinaw Crossings is a casual restaurant with nightly entertainment, a full bar, and usually a pretty long wait for a table. As its name implies, the restaurant channels the bygone days of train travel.

The two-story ★ **Dixie Saloon** (401 E. Central Ave., 231/436-5449, www.dixiesaloon.com, 11am-11pm daily, bar until 2am, entrées $10-25) was a Mackinaw City mainstay in the 1890s. The newly-renovated cedar building is wide open on the inside and features good all-American steak, ribs, and burgers. Stop by the Dixie Saloon on weekends for year-round live entertainment; the restaurant also features a full bar and weekly karaoke. Attached to the Dixie is **O'Reilly's Irish Pub** (www.oreillysmackinawpub.com), a casual yet elegant bar and grill. Despite the Irish decor, however, the menu is pretty much standard American bar fare.

An excellent choice for quality family dining is **Darrow's Family Restaurant** (301 Louvigney St., 231/436-5514, www.darrowsrestaurant.com, 7:30am-8:30pm Sun.-Thurs., 7:30am-9pm Fri.-Sat., entrées $8-18). A family-run establishment, Darrow's has evolved from a simple hot dog stand in the 1950s to a drive-in to today's incarnation as a sit-down restaurant. The eclectic menu includes soups, salads, sandwiches, and entrées, including Mackinaw-style smothered chicken breast, pot roast, and plenty of fish offerings from the Great Lakes, including several irresistible versions of fresh whitefish.

Fudge

Fudge shops are fairly ubiquitous in Mackinaw City. Noteworthy examples include **Joann's Fudge** (2 Main St.; 303 E. Central Ave., 231/436-5611, www.

In Mackinaw City, you're never far from a fudge shop.

joannsfudge.com, 8:30am-8pm Sun.-Thurs., 8:30am-9pm Fri.-Sat. early May-late Oct.), **Marshall's Fudge Shop** (308 E. Central Ave., 800/343-8343, www.marshallsfudge. com, 8:30am-8pm Sun.-Thurs., 8:30am-9pm Fri.-Sat. June-Sept., 9am-5pm daily Oct.-May), and **Kilwin's** (226 E. Central Ave., 231/436-5889; 176 S. Huron Ave., Mackinaw Crossings, 231/436-4067, www.kilwins.com, 10am-10pm June-Aug., reduced hours rest of the year), a national chain with a great number of Michigan locations.

ACCOMMODATIONS

With the Straits as a major tourism draw, Mackinaw City alone has more than 3,000 guest rooms. There's nothing quite as extravagant as the island's Grand Hotel or Mission Point Resort, but the city has plenty of lodging at affordable rates.

Hotels and Motels

Families will probably find the prospect of staying at the **Fairview Beachfront Inn and Waterpark** (907 S. Huron Ave., 231/436-8831, www.mackinaw-city.com, from $119, suites from $199 high season) irresistible. The 5,000-square-foot water park has plenty of room for the kids to splash and play with water cannons, waterfalls, buckets, and other toys that douse them with more than 1,700 gallons of water each minute. There's also plenty of private Lake Huron beach. The four floors of guest rooms and two- or three-bedroom suites can accommodate families of almost any size. That said, if you don't have kids, you may want to find rooms elsewhere.

Parkside Inn Bridgeview (771 N. Huron Ave., 800/827-8301, www.parkside-inn.com, from $99 d) is a very nice hotel located just shy of the bridge, which means that you should be able to get what everyone wants when they stay here—a room with a view—but you'll pay for it. If you're lucky, you can snag a discount rate and squeeze in for less than $100. The Parkside also offers a complimentary hot breakfast each morning and an indoor heated swimming pool.

If you're a bit less choosy, there are plenty of no-frills motels offering basic rooms that are very budget-friendly—you can pay as little as $50, but expect rates as high as $125 during the busy summer months. Try **Sunrise Beach Motel** (11416 W. U.S. 23, 231/436-5461, www.mackinawcitymotels. com), **Bell's Melody Motel** (11460 W. U.S. 23, 231/436-5463, www.mackinawcitymotels. com), or **Northwinds Motel** (11472 W. U.S. 23, 231/436-7434, www.mackinawcitymotels. com). Like a lot of Mackinaw City lodging, these are fairly bare-bones but relatively inexpensive.

Bed-and-Breakfasts

Located in one of Mackinaw City's oldest homes, the **Deer Head Inn** (109 Henry St., 231/436-3337, www.deerhead.com, $80-170) was built in 1913. The five rooms each try to capture the rustic Northern Michigan spirit, with names like Hemingway, Wilderness, and Hiawatha, and decorations that include bearskins, caribou and fox pelts, and mission-style furniture. Don't worry—the B&B doesn't compromise elegance to achieve its woodsy charm. Deer Head Inn is open year-round, and room rates vary seasonally.

The ★ **Brigadoon Bed & Breakfast** (207 Langlade St., 231/436-8882, www. mackinawbrigadoon.com, May-early Nov., $95-170) is located across the street from Huron Avenue, the Lake Huron shore, and the ferry docks. Its ten rooms mix modern appointments with a taste of the Old World. If you stay in the elegant butter-yellow building you'll find king or queen four-poster beds, heated marble floors in the private baths, and signature breakfasts on the veranda.

Camping

Mackinaw Mill Creek Camping (9730 U.S. 23, 231/436-5584, www.campmackinaw. com, May-Oct., $12-50) has more than 600 sites, including full hookups for RVs, tenting sites, cabins, and a mile of shoreline. The amenity-rich campground (free Wi-Fi!) is great for families. Rates vary depending on the site's view and the level of electrical service, while cabin rates vary wildly according to seasonal and holiday demand.

The nearest state campground is 12 miles west at wonderful **Wilderness State Park** (898 Wilderness Park Dr., 231/436-5381, www.michigan.gov/dnr, Apr.-Dec., campsites around $27), located at the end of a point. It offers 250 modern campsites, rustic cabins, and bunkhouses. The park has two campgrounds, one on the lakeshore and another tucked away in a grove of mature pines.

Twenty miles east of Mackinaw City, **Cheboygan State Park** (4490 Beach Rd., 231/627-2811, www.michigan.gov/dnr, campsites around $25) has modern sites near Lake Huron's Duncan Bay, although none are directly on the water. Reservations are available from late March through early December.

Other Lodging

Private cottages are the draw at **The Beach House** (11490 W. U.S. 23, 800/262-5353, www.mackinawcitybeachhouse.com, mid-May-mid-Oct., $80-120). The rooms are clean and well kept, but relatively Spartan. You'll want to stay here for the 250 feet of beach, the view of the bridge only a mile away, and the cottage-like feel. The rooms sleep one to five people and are pet-friendly. Kitchenettes are available. As a special touch of hospitality, owners Russ and Maxine Beyne serve muffins to guests every morning. The cottages book out quickly, so reserve far in advance.

INFORMATION

The **Mackinaw Area Visitors Bureau** (10800 W. U.S. 23, 231/436-5664, www.mackinawcity.com) can provide visitor information, adventure guides, and brochures. The **Mackinaw City Chamber of Commerce** (216 E. Central Ave., 231/436-5574, www.mackinaw-city.com) offers plenty of visitor information, a comprehensive calendar of events, and community information.

GETTING THERE AND AROUND
Car

Mackinaw City is accessed by I-75 north from Lansing or south from Sault Ste. Marie. If you're driving east from Wisconsin, take U.S. 2 to St. Ignace and join I-75 south across the bridge. If you're crossing the bridge from St. Ignace, the 2015 passenger vehicle toll is $4, with an additional $2 for each axle if you're pulling a trailer. Trucks are $5 per axle. No toll increases are planned, but this is subject to change; see www.mackinacbridge.org for the latest information.

Air

Delta Airlines currently has several scheduled flights daily to **Pellston Regional Airport** (PLN, www.pellstonairport.com), about 15 miles south of Mackinaw City. Shuttle transportation is available from **Wolverine Stages** (800/825-1450, www.wolverinestages.com, reservations preferred) and Mackinaw Shuttle (231/539-7005, www.mackinawshuttle.com). Make sure you call ahead for reservations and current rates. **Top of the Hill Taxi** (800/825-1450) provides taxi service, or you can rent a car through **Avis** (231/539-8302, www.avis.com) or **Hertz** (231/539-8404, www.hertz.com).

Boat

The **Mackinaw City Municipal Marina** (231/436-5269, www.michigan.gov/dnr) has a total of 104 slips and can be reached on radio channels 9 and 16. The harbormaster is on duty May 1-October 10, 7am-9pm. The marina is located at 45°46.55 N, 84°43.12 W.

FERRY TO MACKINAC ISLAND

To book a spot on one of the two **ferries** with service from Mackinaw City to Mackinac Island, contact **Shepler's Mackinac Island Ferry** (231/436-5023, www.sheplersferry. com) or the **Star Line** (800/638-9892, www. mackinawferry.com).

Bus and Train

There is no Greyhound service, public transportation, or car-rental outlets in the city, so having your own vehicle is a must. **Amtrak** (800/872-7245, www.amtrak.com) has partnered with Greyhound to provide bus service from some cities in southeast Michigan.

Escanaba and the Lake Michigan Shore

The main road west from St. Ignace that hugs the Lake Michigan shoreline, U.S. 2 has a succession of places to pull over, breathe in the fresh air, and admire the lake. Stop at one or two to stretch your legs on the way from St. Ignace to

Manistique, about 90 miles and two hours' drive. The beaches here are sandier than Lake Superior's, and the water is warm enough in late summer for swimming. Take a small detour to the north to discover the Seney National Wildlife Refuge, in summer an ideal place for hunting, fishing, berry picking, and photographing wildlife. In the winter, cross-country skiing and snowshoeing are hugely popular.

Like most U.P. towns, Manistique isn't quite the booming city it once was. Since its heyday as a lumber port in the early 1900s, Manistique has shrunk to about 3,000 people. Its size has made it quaint—the Manistique River flows through the center of town into Lake Michigan, and the scenic boardwalk makes for a pleasant stroll. Just past Manistique, the Garden Peninsula drops south into Lake Michigan, framing the northern reaches of Green Bay.

You'll pass through Garden, the largest community on the Peninsula, on your way to Fayette, the Upper Peninsula's most famous ghost town and a fascinating reminder of the area's industrial past. If you're curious, spend a morning or afternoon exploring the once bustling production town where pig iron was smelted during the Civil War.

The Green Bay shoreline, west of the Garden Peninsula, is known for its moderate climate, producing relatively mild (by Upper Peninsula standards) winters. The year-round temperate conditions make this corner of Lake Michigan shoreline a favorite destination for outdoors enthusiasts. Escanaba and Menominee (the U.P.'s third and fourth largest cities, respectively) make this region better than most for dining and lodging choices.

PLANNING YOUR TIME

There's plenty of scenic driving along the lakeshore and a few worthwhile stops along the way. You'll find more activity in Escanaba,

Previous: Snail Shell Harbor; Sand Point Lighthouse. **Above:** Fayette Historic State Park.

Look for ★ to find recommended sights, activities, dining, and lodging.

Highlights

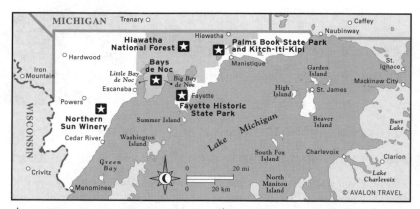

★ **Palms Book State Park and Kitch-Iti-Kipi:** Look down to the bottom of this crystal clear lake and you'll see bubbles emerging from the earth (page 70).

★ **Fayette Historic State Park:** This historic town site is one of the U.P.'s most famous ghost towns (page 79).

★ **Bays de Noc:** These bays have more than 200 miles of shoreline, 120,000 acres of water, and irresistible walleye fishing (page 81).

★ **Northern Sun Winery:** Sample some uniquely Northern Michigan varietals in an idyllic vineyard setting (page 87).

★ **Hiawatha National Forest:** Experience true wilderness by hiking, paddling, or camping in the eastern part of this national forest, which spreads north from U.S. 2 to Lake Superior (page 88).

Menominee, and Manistique than in the peninsula's smaller towns, but the biggest summertime draw is the fishing. Winter visitors will find miles of snowmobile trails packed into this small region. Pitching a tent at one of the forest campgrounds will encourage you to spend a whole week, but a visit to one of the larger towns should take only a day or two.

HISTORY

The cities along the Lake Michigan shoreline share a common history with many other Upper Peninsula towns: Native American communities gave way to the mining and logging industries, which in turn collapsed as the natural resources became depleted and demand began to wane. Manistique was a thriving port city central to the timber industry, while Escanaba flourished as an route for iron ore shipping. The Fayette historic town site—a preserved ghost town—is an example of what could have happened to these once-bustling communities. But Escanaba, Manistique, and Menominee endure as vibrant communities with economies supported mostly by the U.P.'s appeal as a tourism destination.

St. Ignace to Manistique

SIGHTS
Driving U.S. 2

U.S. 2 is one of the main east-west thoroughfares in the Upper Peninsula. There's not much entertainment or lodging along the shore, but the road to Manistique is lined with scenic turnouts, beaches, and other detours. You'll want to stop at one or two for a stunning view of Lake Michigan, but there's no need to stop at them all—even the most beautiful views tend to get repetitive.

Heading west along U.S. 2, you'll pass through Brevort, Epoufette, and Naubinway. You won't need to look far to find a short hiking trail or two, a sandy beach, or a restaurant to experience off-the-beaten-path dining and a bit of local culture. A trip north on M-33 will bring you to the town of Curtis, nestled between **Big Manistique Lake** and **South Manistique Lake** and home to plenty of outdoor activities. Take a small southern detour along County Road 432 for a glimpse of Seul Choix Point Light, a spot that affords a better view than a typical lighthouse. On a clear day you can catch a glimpse of Beaver, Garden, and High Islands, not to mention a few passing freighters. The road reconnects to U.S. 2 after passing between **McDonald** and **Gulliver Lakes.**

Siphon Bridge and Water Tower

Although it isn't nearly as big or impressive as Mighty Mac, Manistique's **Siphon Bridge,** which crosses the Manistique River, may very well be the Upper Peninsula's second most interesting bridge. An innovative engineering feat, the 1919 structure is partially supported by the water underneath it; as the roadway is four feet below water level. Its construction was prompted by a paper mill upstream that needed to dam the river for its water needs, thus raising the river.

Stop at the historic **Water Tower** (River St.) for a taste of regional history. Built in 1922, the 200-foot brick tower is located on the site of the Schoolcraft County Historical Park, which also includes a small **historical museum** (906/341-5010, http://schs.cityof-manistique.org, free). Unfortunately, the local historical society is unable to open the museum on a regular schedule; visit the website for updates.

Thompson State Fish Hatchery

In Thompson, just a few miles west of Manistique, you'll find the working **Thompson State Fish Hatchery** (944 S.

Escanaba and the Lake Michigan Shore

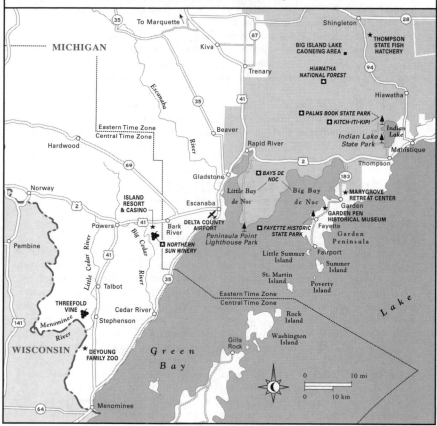

M-149, 906/341-5587, 7:30am-3:30pm daily, free), which produces several different fish species for the Great Lakes and inland lakes, including steelhead and brown trout, chinook salmon, and walleye. It isn't the prettiest stop on a tour of the U.P., but an interpretive center provides plenty of information about the importance of hatcheries and fisheries, small tributaries to the Great Lakes, and how watersheds work. The hatchery offers self-guided tours with informative signs that explain what you're seeing, and you can watch staff working with the fish in the ponds. The indoor portion of the hatchery is closed to the public.

★ Palms Book State Park and Kitch-Iti-Kipi

Located on Indian Lake's western shore, north and west of town, **Palms Book State Park** (M-149, 906/341-2355, www.michigan.gov/dnr) guards one of the U.P.'s most remarkable natural attractions. Kitch-Iti-Kipi, or "Big Spring," looks like a deep, dark pool tucked away in a grove of cedars—until you get close. Then you discover it's an enormous spring, where gin-clear water (with a noticeable aqua tint) bubbles out of the earth at a staggering 10,000 to 16,000 gallons per minute.

The park maintains a convenient raft

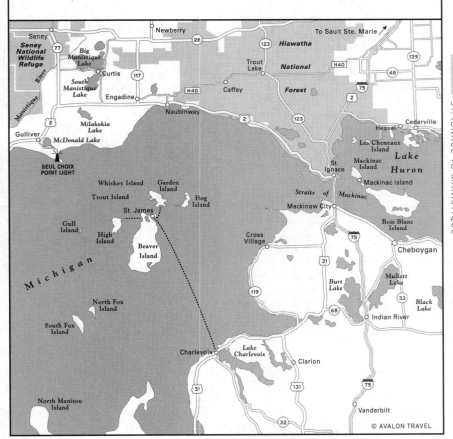

© AVALON TRAVEL

that allows you to propel yourself across the 200-foot-long spring with the help of a hand-powered cable tethered to either shore. It's an amazing view. Take your time to peer 45 feet down (it doesn't seem that deep) into the clear, slightly emerald waters and erupting sand bottom. You'll see brown, lake, and brook trout glide among the skeletons of downed trees. The spring is a popular attraction, so come during the early morning or evening, when the surrounding trees cast their reflections on the still water. You'll have to hike 100 yards or so up the park's gated entrance road, but Kitch-Iti-Kipi is such a magical place, you won't

mind. Winter is a great time to visit too, as the spring never freezes over.

Lighthouses

Ten miles south of Blaney Park at Gulliver, 14 miles east of Manistique, a road leads down a point to the 1895 **Seul Choix Point Light** (Seul Choix Rd., 906/283-3183, www.greatlakelighthouse.com, 10am-6pm daily Memorial Day-mid-Oct., $4 adults, $2 children, $10 families), a worthwhile detour. Pronounced "sul-SHWA"—French for "only choice"—it sits at the end of a finger of land that offers boaters the only choice for hiding from storms along this stretch of Lake Michigan. The township of Gulliver has done a splendid job restoring the light and creating a maritime museum in the fog signal building, complete with a third-order Fresnel lens. It includes an admirable scale model of the lighthouse, made by hand with thousands of miniature bricks. Climb the tower for great views of much of northern Lake Michigan. You'll have a good chance of seeing ship traffic, since Port Inland, just to the east, is an important commercial port. From U.S. 2 at Gulliver, go southeast on County Road 431 (a gravel road) and travel another four miles to the light.

The **Manistique East Breakwater Lighthouse** (906/341-5010) is located on the east side of Manistique, at the end of the east breakwater arm. The concrete breakwaters were built in the early 1900s as a means of creating safe harbor for large ships. You'll be able to see the red lighthouse, which dates from 1916, from throughout Lakeview Park; access to the pier and lighthouse can be found on the west side of the park. Visitors are not allowed inside, but you can get close enough for a good view. If weather permits, you can walk out to the lighthouse along the pier, but exercise caution.

SHOPPING
Bookstore

Despite the growing popularity of e-readers and the Internet, many people still like to sit down with a good book—especially if planning to spend time on an Upper Peninsula beach. If that describes you, take a detour off U.S. 2 to **The First Edition, Too Bookstore** (W4487 Worth Rd., Brevort, 906/292-5513, www.firsteditiontoo.com). Located adjacent to her home in an old five-room cabin, which feels more like an old library than a bookstore, owner Mary Carney takes pride in offering quality new and used titles, mostly on the history of Michigan and the Great Lakes region but also including modern fiction, crafts, and gardening. The artfully humorous sign out front reads "Open by chance or appointment."

pontoon boat at Kitch-Iti-Kipi

If you don't see Mary in the shop, just walk next door and knock.

Antiques

A little-known secret about the Manistique area is the cluster of antiques shops that can be found in Manistique and the surrounding towns of Gulliver, Thompson, and Garden Corners—all conveniently located along U.S. 2. If you have a passion for antiques, be sure to stop by any of these frequently overlooked gems. A few examples are **Heirlooms Past and Present** (5590 U.S. 2, Manistique, 906/341-7357) and **Christopher's Antiques & Collectibles** (211 Oak St., Manistique, 906/341-2570).

ENTERTAINMENT
Kewadin Manistique Casino

At **Kewadin Manistique** (U.S. 2 E., Manistique, 800/539-2346, www.kewadinmanistique.com), one of Kewadin's five Upper Peninsula casinos, gamers can try the slots or hit the tables for blackjack, Let it Ride stud poker, and three-card poker. At the end of each work week, the **Team Spirits Bar** hosts its popular Fantastic Friday Social, which feature drawings for casino credits and a monthly cash grand prize. Live local entertainment is offered the last Saturday of each month. Other nights, catch the game on the bar's big screens. If the bar menu isn't enough, visit Mariner's Cove, Kewadin Manistique's 60-seat restaurant, for breakfast, lunch, or dinner at surprisingly good prices. The casino is located on the north side of U.S. 2 in Manistique—you can't miss it.

Mackinaw Trail Winery
The small, simply decorated **Manistique on the Harbor Tasting Room** (103 W. Lakeshore Dr., 906/341-2303, www.mackinawtrailwinery.com) is a testimony to Michigan's growing wine industry. Hours of operation vary considerably, with spring hours 10am-6pm Mon.-Thurs. After Memorial Day and running until the end of tourist season, expect to see the tasting room open seven days a week, often well into the evening. With more than 14,000 acres of vineyards, Michigan is one of the most prolific grape-growing states, producing more than 375,000 cases of red, white, and fruit wines each year. Mackinaw Trail Winery uses grapes harvested from across the state to make their award-winning wines. The tasting room in Manistique is one of three such facilities operated by the winery, in addition to the production facility in Petoskey. The company is so named because its tasting rooms are located along various Northern Michigan locations, with Mackinaw City as its central point.

FESTIVALS AND EVENTS
Annual Manistique Folkfest
A special event on the Manistique calendar is the **Annual Manistique Folkfest** (www.cityofmanistique.org), held each year on the second Saturday in July. Arts and crafts vendors display their unique creations along Main Street, while an array of international foods is offered. For adults, there's the Paul Bunyan Beer Garden, while the kids can hang out at a children's play area.

SUMMER SPORTS AND RECREATION
Seney National Wildlife Refuge
Several miles north of U.S. 2 on M-77, the **Seney National Wildlife Refuge** (1674 Refuge Entrance Rd., Seney, 906/586-9851, www.fws.gov) has more than 95,000 acres in the area known as the Great Manistique Swamp. Established for resident wildlife, the area provides protection for endangered and threatened species and a habitat for migratory birds. The refuge is one of the U.P.'s most pristine wildlife viewing areas. Enjoy hiking, cycling, paddling, and fishing in the summer and cross-country skiing and snowshoeing in the winter. For those with physical limitations, the Marshland Wildlife Drive is open from May 15 until October 20. This seven-mile one-way road allows visitors to view portions of the refuge's wetlands, meadows, and forests. Stop at the **visitors center** (9am-5pm daily May 15-Oct. 20, including federal holidays) for an orientation slide show and information about the self-guided audio tour. The refuge is open year-round, and seasonal nature programs and special events are offered year-round when staff are available.

Indian Lake State Park
The Upper Peninsula's fourth-largest lake, Indian Lake is well known among anglers and RV campers, but be warned: Jet Skiers have discovered it too. The anglers come for the perch, walleye, and muskie that thrive in the lake's warm shallow waters. The RV campers come for the convenient location—just north of U.S. 2 and the Garden Peninsula, which includes plenty of campsites and sandy beaches.

The best-known campsites are at **Indian Lake State Park** (8970 W. County Rd. 442, 906/341-2355, www.michigan.gov/dnr), which has two units, one on the south shore and another three miles away on the west shore, both modern campgrounds with boat launches.

Following the U.P. Wine Trail

Long overshadowed by the winemakers of California, Michigan's vineyards and tasting rooms have in recent years found their way onto the connoisseur's map. Most, however, are located along the western coast of the Lower Peninsula, with the highest concentration in the Grand Traverse Bay area. An even more recent development has been the emergence of wineries on the northern side of the Mackinac Bridge.

The region of the Upper Peninsula stretching from Menominee up toward Escanaba has been identified by vintners as the "banana belt," an area that enjoys relatively mild winters as it is sheltered from the most severe cold coming off Lake Superior by the mountainous region to the northwest. In addition, the comparatively warm waters of nearby Green Bay further moderate winter temperatures.

Recent research done at the University of Minnesota has produced hardier grapes capable of flourishing at more northerly latitudes. These include Marquette, St. Pepin, Brianna, and Frontenac. The result is a variety of cabernets, chardonnays, and pinot grigios capable of pleasing even the most discriminating pallet.

Make a day of it and visit four of the best wineries north of the bridge. It takes about three hours to drive to each of these wineries, not including the stops. Be sure to go with a designated driver. Cheers!

- **Threefold Vine Winery** (S232 Menominee St., Stephenson, 906/753-6000, www.exploringthenorth.com/threefold/vine.html): Located in a historic bank building in Stephenson, Threefold is currently selling wines from grapes grown on a vineyard on the Garden Peninsula. A new farm in Menominee County is currently in development to produce a greater variety of grapes. For now, the current stock is on sale at their tasting room and at many retailers throughout the Upper Peninsula.

- **Northern Sun Winery** (983 10th Rd., Bark River, 906/399-9212, www.northernsunwinery.com): Known as an estate winery, Northern Sun, with over five picturesque acres, is an attraction itself as a setting for weddings and concerts. Carefully chosen grapes yield outstanding varieties of reds and whites. Try Marquette, a deep-red table wine that's a great complement to red meat and poultry.

The lake is the focus here, so hiking is limited. The western unit campsites, while not on the water, tend to be less busy. If you're looking for a waterfront site in the southern unit, plan to arrive midweek or during off-season, and keep your fingers crossed. This state park offers hunting and fishing, boating, beaches, and picnics, so it's in high demand. To reach the park, take U.S. 2 to Thompson, then go north on M-149 and east on County Road 442. To reach the west unit, stay on M-149.

Hiking and Biking

Directly south of U.S. 2 and about halfway between Naubinway and Manistique, a lovely trail hugs the Lake Michigan shoreline. Take Gould City Road south from Gould City until you hit **Gould City Township Park,** in the middle of the pathway. Head east along a moderately difficult off-trail route that extends about 3.5 miles before doubling back to your car; you can keep going west for another 2.5 miles or so. The trail is a little difficult to find, and the footing can be difficult at times, but the solitude and the views of the lake make it worthwhile.

With only two miles of hiking trails, Indian Lake State Park won't top any lists of hiking destinations. However, the **Indian Lake Pathway** has 8.5 miles of trails that are perfect for hikers and bikers. The three loops provide flat to rolling terrain and lengths from 1 to 4.5 miles. Don't confuse Indian Lake Pathway with the state park of the same name.

Northern Sun Winery

- **Leigh's Garden Winery** (904 Ludington St., Escanaba, 906/553-7799, www.leighsgarden. com): Offering an extensive list of white, red, rosé, and seasonal varieties, Leigh's can ship your selections anywhere in Michigan.

- **Mackinaw Trail Winery** (103 W. Lakeshore Dr., Manistique, 906/341-2303, www.mackinawtrailwinery.com): The vineyard is in the northern Lower Peninsula, but Mackinaw Trail operates a cozy little tasting room off U.S. 2 near where the Manistique River empties into Lake Michigan. Here you'll find some unusual varieties, including Cranberry, White Ibis, and Traminette, a dry wine that's very compatible with fish.

The pathway is located west of the park; the easiest way to reach the trailhead is to take M-149 about 12 miles north of Thompson.

There's also a much easier three-mile trail at **Camp Seven Lake Recreation Area,** 24 miles north of Manistique in the Hiawatha National Forest, which can be completed in about two hours. There are picnic grounds and a swimming area here. The **Rainey Wildlife Area,** on the north side of Indian Lake, has a hiking trail and boardwalks that lead to a wildlife observation platform, where there is a decent chance of seeing bald eagles in spring and early summer. Head north from Manistique on M-94 for about five miles, then take a left on Dawson Road. After 1.5 miles, take the access road north to the parking lot. It's definitely worth the detour.

Canoeing and Kayaking

You'll find some of the area's best canoeing in and around Curtis. You can paddle Big Manistique Lake, South Manistique Lake, and the smaller North Manistique Lake, but one of the area's most popular trips will take you down the **Manistique River,** which begins at the west end of Big Manistique Lake and empties into Lake Michigan some 70 miles downstream, wending its way through the **Seney National Wildlife Refuge.** The river constantly twists and turns and promises to be anything but boring. There are a few access points just west of Big Manistique Lake and then a long 27-mile stretch between easy take-outs at Mead Creek and Merwin Creek campgrounds. From the other direction, put in to the **Indian River** a good distance north,

a campsite at Indian Lake State Park

near Steuben, or farther west, where the river passes beneath Forest Road 13. From here, take the river about 30 miles east and south to Indian Lake.

Fishing

The abundance of rivers, streams, and large lakes in the area gives this stretch of the Upper Peninsula a bevy of fishing options. Camping or building fires is prohibited in the **Seney National Wildlife Refuge** (1674 Refuge Entrance Rd., Seney, 906/586-9851, www.fws.gov), but you can cast a line at Walsh Creek and the Ditch, Creighton, Driggs, and Manistique Rivers as well as at a number of fishing pools. The more than 20,000 acres of the **Manistique Lakes** is generally less than 30 feet deep. Fishing here includes muskie, northern pike, walleye, large and smallmouth bass, perch, bluegill, and more. Be warned—these waters are accessible to Jet Skis and water skiers. Try **Camp Seven Lake** (906/341-5666) in Hiawatha National Forest for smaller waters. For more information on popular fishing spots, contact the **Manistique Tourism Council** (800/342-4282, www.visitmanistique.com), the **U.S. Forest Service** (2727 N. Lincoln Rd., Escanaba, 906/786-4062, www.fs.fed.us), or the **Michigan Department of Natural Resources** (906/452-6227, www.michigan.gov/dnr).

Open-water fishing trips can be chartered through **Delta Dawn Charters** (906/428-9093, www.dawndeltachartersup.com), which docks at Manistique for salmon fishing. Morning, afternoon, and evening charters are available. Half-day charters are $325 for up to four people, $50 each for each additional person, up to six total. Full-day charters cost $425 for up to four people, $50 for each additional person, up to six total.

Golf

If you've come to the U.P. to golf, you can find 18 holes at **Indian Lake Golf and Country Club** (1305 N. Birch St., Manistique, 906/341-5600, www.indianlakegolfclub.com, unlimited play $45, including golf cart), on the northeast shore of Indian Lake. The course has a pro shop, cart and club rentals, a full bar and restaurant, and bent grass greens and fairways. There were only nine holes here for more than 70 years, but the club added an additional nine in 2000, and did a thorough renovations of the entire course in 2017. Travel north on M-94 from downtown Manistique for 2.5 miles, turn left at the school, and travel 1 mile to the golf course.

Great Lake Awards

- **Prettiest beach:** Twelve Mile Beach, Pictured Rocks National Lakeshore
- **Best area for swimming:** Mackinaw City
- **Best place to catch a sunset:** Little Girl's Point
- **Best fishing spot:** Stannard Rock in Lake Superior
- **Best place to sail:** Straits of Mackinac

Stony Point Golf Course (8102 W. U.S. 2, Manistique, 906/341-3419, http://stonypointgolf.com, mid-Apr.-mid-Nov., $20-28) is a nine-hole course located just two miles west of Manistique. The par-35 family-owned course has bent grass greens and fairways and is nestled in the Upper Peninsula's renowned scenery.

Off-Road Vehicles

Unlike Michigan's Lower Peninsula, the Upper Peninsula allows off-road vehicles to operate on any state forest road, as long as it isn't specifically posted as prohibited. Although much of the U.P. is accessible via these roads, a designated trail system is also set aside specifically for ORV use. Plenty of multiuse trails thread through the U.P. along and north of U.S. 2. Try the 36-mile **Sandtown Trail,** just east of the Manistique Lakes. Take M-117 north to Sandtown Road and turn right on Hayes Road to the parking area. The **Brevort-Trout Lake Trail** starts north of Brevort Lake, a short distance from St. Ignace; from here, connect to the Newberry-Rexton Trail and a system of trails that makes its way west. Additionally, all Schoolcraft County roads are open to ORVs, provided you keep to the shoulder at a speed below 25 mph. Detailed off-road vehicle maps are available from Michigan Department of Natural Resources (DNR) Service Centers; the closest ones are in Newberry and Marquette.

You can also contact the **Manistique Area Tourism Council** (800/342-4282, www.visitmanistique.com).

WINTER SPORTS AND RECREATION

Ski and Snowshoe Trails

The **Indian Lake Pathway** provides some of the area's finest groomed ski trails, with 8.5 miles of flat to rolling terrain. There are more than nine miles of trails at the **Seney National Wildlife Refuge,** where cross-country skiers might see winter wildlife, such as wolves or coyotes. The wooded surroundings and views of the frozen Manistique River alone make the trek worthwhile.

Snowmobiling

The area near U.S. 2 and north of Lake Michigan can be traversed by snowmobile on **Trail 2,** which starts in St. Ignace and makes its way west to Escanaba and beyond. A number of smaller trails, too numerous to list, branch off and provide access to much of the U.P., including state and national forests and the Manistique Lakes. Nearing Manistique, Trail 2 skirts the Seney National Wildlife Refuge before dropping south into town. Take Trail 41 or Trail 7 northwest into the Hiawatha National Forest.

Ice Fishing

Fishing on a frozen lake is becoming a popular winter pastime, and if you'd like to try it, the Manistique Lakes near Curtis are a great choice. The ice tends to form in early December, providing some of the U.P.'s best seasonal fishing for northern pike, walleye, and perch.

FOOD

If you didn't stop at Clyde's Drive-In No. 3 outside St. Ignace, make a point of going to ★ **Clyde's Drive-In No. 2** (201 Chippewa Ave., 906/341-6021, 9am-7pm Mon.-Thurs., 9am-8pm Fri.-Sat., 11am-7pm Sun. Memorial Day-Labor Day, $9-12) in Manistique. You'll find the same old-school service, malts, and

Big C burgers as at Clyde's other well-known U.P. drive-ins. You'll swear they're among the most delicious burgers you've ever tasted.

ACCOMMODATIONS

Several **chain motels** are represented along U.S. 2, especially near Manistique, but there are also many independent motels. Let's hope places like **Star Motel** (1142 E. Lakeshore Dr., 906/341-5363, $50-66) continue to prosper. Located about two miles east of Manistique on U.S. 2, this tidy, vintage 1950s motel has large rooms, meticulous owners, and a nice setting on the lake. It allows well-behaved dogs.

For Indian Lake lodging, try **Mountain Ash Resort** (3 N. County Rd. 441, Manistique, 906/341-5658, www.mtashresort. com, July-Aug. $300-575 weekly, off-season $45-105 daily). Proprietors Rick and Becky Bayer have 12 log cabins and a more expensive three-bedroom lodge. All are open year-round and are easily accessible to all sorts of recreation—fishing and hiking in the summertime, snowmobiling and cross-country skiing in the winter. The cabins are stocked with dishes, cooking utensils, appliances, and bed linens. Just bring your own towels and food. Pets are allowed with a deposit. Take County Road 149 north of U.S. 2 at Thompson, turn right on County Road 442 and left on County Road 441; the lodge is located on the east side of Indian Lake.

Camping

Sherman's Resort & Campground (W18155 Nezor Point Rd., Curtis, 906/586-6761, www.shermansresort.com) offers both cabin rentals and campsites right on beautiful South Manistique Lake. With 800 feet of pristine beach and numerous modern campsites ($28), complete with a bathhouse and fire pits, it's truly an idyllic lodging choice. The resort also offers a variety of comfortable two- and three-bedroom cabins. Rates vary depending on the season and length of stay.

The **Log Cabin Resort and Campground** (W18042 County Rd. H-42,

Curtis, 906/586-9732 or 888/879-6448, www. uplogcabin.com, campsites $2-39, cabins $69-129) has 600 feet of Big Manistique Lake frontage on more than 23 acres. You'll find boat slips, a games room, a sandy beach, and 50 campsites, 34 of which are full-service RV sites.

About 20 miles north of Manistique, just off M-94, the **Indian River Campground** (Hiawatha National Forest, 906/341-5666, single site $18, double $36) sits on a bluff overlooking the Indian River. The 10 private wooded sites provide plenty of seclusion and a feeling of solitude despite the camp's close proximity to the highway. This is an excellent stop for paddlers making their way down the Indian River Canoe Trail, offering clean drinking water, picnic tables, and grills.

The larger **Camp Seven Lake Campground** (906/341-5666, $18-44 depending on amenities), in the Hiawatha National Forest, has 41 campsites, each with a table and a fire ring. Camp Seven Lake is perfect for boating, fishing, swimming, and hiking along a three-mile trail. Take County Road 442 eight miles east of Forest Road 13, about 24 miles northwest of Manistique.

INFORMATION AND SERVICES

The **Manistique Area Tourist Council** (800/342-4282, www.visitmanistique. com) is the source for visitor information in Manistique. You can also contact the **Schoolcraft County Chamber of Commerce** (1000 W. Lakeshore Dr., Manistique, 906/341-5010 or 888/819-7420, www.schoolcraftcountychamber.org) and the **Michigan DNR** (906/228-6561, www.michigan.gov/dnr).

Schoolcraft Memorial Hospital (500 Main St., Manistique, 906/341-3200, www. scmh.org) is 0.25 miles east of M-94. For banking and an ATM, stop at **Wells Fargo** (226 S. Cedar St., 906/341-1900, www.wellsfargo.com) or one of Manistique's many other banks.

GETTING THERE AND AROUND

Car

U.S. 2 winds from St. Ignace, just north of the Bridge, for about 90 miles before it runs into Manistique. It continues to Escanaba and on toward Wisconsin, but the long, easy stretch between St. Ignace and Manistique parallels the lakeshore for much of the drive. You'll want to detour on highways north and south of U.S. 2 along the way. Coming from Wisconsin, take U.S. 41 north from Green Bay, cross into Michigan at the twin cities of Marinette, Wisconsin, and Menominee, Michigan, then take M-35 north to U.S. 2 and Manistique. From Munising on the Lake Superior shore, drive south on M-94.

Boat

There's a small marina in Manistique, where the river flows into Lake Michigan, that offers a small selection of seasonal and transient slips. The **Manistique Marina** (906/341-6841, www.michigan.gov/dnr) has a harbormaster on duty mid-June-September 1 and can be reached on channel 9 or 68. Marina coordinates are 45°57.08 N, 86°14.08 W.

Bus

Regular bus service is provided to Manistique as well as several small towns along U.S. 2 by **Indian Trails** (800/292-3831, www.indiantrails.com), originating from St. Ignace, Escanaba, and Milwaukee.

Garden Peninsula

The Garden Peninsula, just a short 20-mile drive past Manistique, is a quiet, peaceful point of land, filled with little-used asphalt roads perfect for cycling and a handful of sleepy farms and orchards. Garden, the largest city on the Peninsula, is a pleasant stop on the way to Fayette, the Upper Peninsula's most famous ghost town. A bit of history, a moderate climate, and scenic beauty make the peninsula one of the U.P.'s more tranquil destinations.

SIGHTS

Garden Peninsula Historical Museum

If you're curious about the town of Garden and its history, stop at the **Garden Peninsula Historical Museum** (State St./ M-183, 906/644-2398, 11am-3pm Wed.-Sat. Memorial Day-Labor Day, donation). There isn't much here aside from genealogy and community history, such as the logging and fishing industries, but the quaint museum, located in a former one-room schoolhouse, will likely appeal to local history buffs. It also includes a genealogy library. If you're looking for a faster

tour of the Garden Peninsula, keep heading south to Fayette Historic State Park.

★ Fayette Historic State Park

By far the Garden Peninsula's most notable attraction is **Fayette Historic State Park** (4785 II Rd., 906/644-2603, www.michigan.gov/dnr). If you make time for just one stop in this part of the U.P., make it this outstanding state park. Once the site of a large smelting operation, Fayette's limestone furnaces converted raw iron ore from U.P. mines into pig iron that was loaded onto barges bound for Escanaba. In the 1880s, this gritty industrial town claimed a population of 500, and its loud, hot blast furnaces worked seven days a week. By 1891, the nearby forests that provided the furnaces with fuel were all but depleted, and more efficient steelmaking methods came into use. The furnaces shut down, leading to the town's demise.

Nearly a century later, Fayette was reborn as a wonderfully restored historic site and state park. Today, Fayette is one of the nation's most scenic ghost towns, its dozen limestone buildings tucked alongside the sheer white

U.P. Trivia

- The toll for an automobile crossing the Mackinac Bridge today is $4. When the bridge opened in 1957, it was $3.75—equivalent to $32.19 today.

- In 1923, Harvey Firestone, Thomas Edison, and Henry Ford embarked on a camping trip to the Upper Peninsula. Their favorable impression of the area motivated them to make considerable investments here, including the Thunder Bay Inn.

- Isle Royale National Park, an archipelago in Lake Superior, is Michigan's only national park, and the least visited property in the National Park system. In a typical year, it receives only 16,000 visitors.

- The word "Yooper" as a vernacular for a resident of the Upper Peninsula only dates to the 1970s.

- The northwestern portion of the Upper Peninsula, including the Keweenaw, is the only place in the United States where Finnish Americans are a majority.

- Ironwood, the westernmost city in the U.P., is 600 miles from Detroit—approximately the same distance from Detroit to New York City.

bluffs and deep clear waters of Snail Shell Harbor. Start at the visitors center, which gives a good historical overview and features a helpful scale model of the village. You can wander in and out of the hotel, opera house, homes, and other buildings, some intact, some more decayed. Horse-drawn carriage rides around the grounds and boat tours are available from Memorial Day to Labor Day. The town cane be explored at any time, and a very early morning or off-season visit can add to the ghostly appeal of the place, a big plus when one considers the obvious irony of a crowded ghost town.

While the historic town site is certainly the biggest draw, don't overlook the rest of the 750-acre park. It includes a semi-modern campground (with electricity but no modern restrooms or showers) and several miles of hiking trails, including one that swings

Fayette Historic State Park

north along the bluffs above Snail Shell Harbor.

Marygrove Retreat Center

Although it's clearly a Roman Catholic retreat center, as indicated by shrines and other religious icons, **Marygrove Retreat Center** (906/644-2771, www.marygrove.org, rates vary) welcomes non-Catholics as well for retreats that provide tranquility, renewal, and rest. The 1920s building, a former cancer hospital, is being continuously restored in shape, and the work has paid off. The 36 guest rooms are clean, well-kept, and inviting. Located on Garden Bay, the center has 40 acres of wooded property, gardens, a library, a conference center, and an intriguing labyrinth patterned out of stone. Specialized retreats are offered to guests with specific interests or needs. Take M-139 south of U.S. 2 for nine miles.

Fairport

If commercial fishing interests you, continue down County Road 513 to Fairport, near the tip of the peninsula, where a commercial fleet still operates. There's little else in this small town, but it's fun to watch the comings and goings of the fishing boats, especially in mid-afternoon, when they usually return with the day's catch.

Fayette Heritage Days

For more than 20 years, Fayette Historic State Park has come to life during the annual **Fayette Heritage Days** (www.michigan.gov/dnr) festival, celebrating the town's history. The second Saturday in August brings visitors to the state park for period music, food, and displays that channel the ghost town's once busy iron-smelting days.

SUMMER SPORTS AND RECREATION
★ Bays de Noc

With the exception, perhaps, of Green Bay, Lake Michigan's best-known inlets are the Bays de Noc. The Big and Little Bays are positioned at the northwest end of the lake and are known primarily for their world-class walleye fishing. Equally popular is the water itself—more than 120,000 acres between the two bays, making them one of the U.P.'s top summer destinations for fishing, boating, paddling, or swimming.

Hiking and Biking

There's more to **Fayette Historic State Park**

Big Bay de Noc

(4785 II Rd., 906/644-2603, www.michigan. gov/dnr) than the historic town site. A five-mile footpath affords views of the ghost town from the area's limestone bluffs, and some 17 miles of trails wind through the forests surrounding the town. **Portage Bay State Forest Campground** (906/452-6227, www. michigan.gov/dnr) has just over two miles of nice trails on the Ninga Aki Pathway. Take County Road 483 south of Garden for 10 miles.

Canoeing and Kayaking

If you're into kayaking—and sea kayaking in particular—you won't want to miss the opportunity to put in to Lake Michigan at **Fayette Historic State Park**. From here, head north to Snake Island and Garden Bay or south to Sac Bay. The waters close to shore are suitable for all but the least experienced kayakers, offering views of towering limestone cliffs and sandy beaches. Experienced kayakers can head south from the southern point to nose around the offshore islands, but there's plenty of open water involved, so caution is advised.

Fishing

Although you'll be able to find some fishing at **Fayette Historic State Park** and the campground at **Portage Bay State Forest** (906/452-6227, www.michigan.gov/dnr), you might want a more adventurous option. **Fishing Bay de Noc** (www.baydenoc.com) provides information on several charter services that can provide full-day or half-day trips on either bay.

Boating

With 90,000 acres of water, the larger of Delta County's two bays, **Big Bay de Noc,** fills the gap between the Garden Peninsula and Stonington Peninsula to the west, providing some of the area's best boating. There are boat landings at Fayette Historic State Park and Garden Bay, as well as at Little Fishdam River to the north and Nahma, a few miles south of U.S. 2 on County Road 497. Fayette Historic State Park's Snail Shell Harbor has 300 feet of

dock available for overnight or day use, and the waters here are deep enough for larger craft. Boaters in search of larger marinas will need to dock at Gladstone or Escanaba on Little Bay de Noc or Manistique to the east, on the opposite side of the Garden Peninsula.

Beaches

Located on Lake Michigan's Big Bay de Noc, **Sac Bay Beach** (906/786-4902 or 906/786-1020, www.deltacountymi.org) is a 65-acre county park and beach. The beach is no-frills, offering a sandy lakeshore, a small play area, and a few picnic tables. It makes a nice rest stop while traveling the Garden Peninsula. **Fayette Historic State Park** also has a small swimming beach just south of the town.

Golf

There is one adequate but basic golf course on the Garden Peninsula. More serious golfers may want to head west for the Bays de Noc golf trail near Escanaba, but on the Garden Peninsula, with its unbeatable scenery, you'll find a good venue at the **Nahma Golf Course** (8588 LL Rd., 906/644-2648, http://nahma-golfcourse.com, $12 for 9 holes, $18 for 18 holes), with nine holes on fairly flat terrain. Cart rentals available at additional cost. Take County Road 494 south of U.S. 2.

WINTER SPORTS AND RECREATION
Ski and Snowshoe Trails

The same Garden Peninsula trails that make for popular summertime hiking become pathways through the Upper Peninsula's winter wonderland. The five miles of trail that overlook the **Fayette Historic State Park** (4785 II Rd., 906/644-2603, www.michigan.gov/dnr) are regularly groomed for skiing each winter. Although the path is suitable for beginners, more advanced skiers will enjoy the views of Big Bay de Noc and the town, even if they do miss the challenge of a more difficult trail. Strap on some snowshoes for a trek through the town site itself—although it can be brutally cold, you'll bypass the summer tourist crowds.

Snowmobiling

Connect to the U.P. snowmobile trail system via **Trail 415** (the only designated snowmobile trail in the Garden Peninsula), which starts in the city of Garden and makes its way north to Trail 2. From there, the U.P. is yours.

FOOD

As its name implies, **Sherry's Port Bar** (4424 M-123, 906/644-2545, 9am-9pm Sun.-Thurs., 9am-10pm Fri.-Sat.), south of Garden, is primarily a drinking establishment, but it has managed to become a catch-all family restaurant with reasonably priced food and a hearty breakfast. Burgers and steaks are $7 and $23, respectively. Its proximity to Fayette Historic State Park makes it a popular stop.

ACCOMMODATIONS

On the north end of Big Bay de Noc and the Garden Peninsula, where U.S. 2 and M-183 meet, **Moose Manor Resort & Motel** (16086 U.S. 2, Cooks, 906/644-2318, www.moosemanormi.com, mid-Apr.-Nov., $85-135) has 12 modestly priced rooms, two with kitchenettes. The resort offers lake access, beach views, and best of all, a diner-style restaurant next door. Pets are not allowed.

Camping

Camping is readily available at dozens of rustic campgrounds within Hiawatha National Forest, and a particularly nice one is the very secluded—and difficult to reach—**Portage Bay State Forest Campground** (906/644-2603, from $13) on the Garden Peninsula's eastern shore.

It's southeast of Garden, at the end of Portage Bay Road. For modern campsites, the best bets are often state parks (reservations 800/447-2757, www.michigan.gov/dnr) like **Indian Lake State Park** or **Fayette Historic State Park.**

INFORMATION

For visitor information and assistance for the Garden Peninsula, contact the **Bays de Noc Convention & Visitors Bureau** (230 Ludington St., 906/789-7862 or 800/533-4386, www.travelbaysdenoc.com) and the **Delta County Chamber of Commerce** (230 Ludington St., 906/786-8830 or 888/335-8264, www.deltami.org).

Bank choices are limited in Garden, but you can do some banking at **First Bank Upper Michigan** (6322 State St., Garden, 906/644-3535, www.first-bank.com, 8:30am-4pm Mon.-Fri.). An ATM is offered.

Your best option for medical attention will be to head to Manistique to the **Schoolcraft Memorial Hospital** (7870 U.S. 2, Manistique, 906/341-3200, www.scmh.org).

GETTING THERE AND AROUND

Having your own vehicle is really your only viable option for getting to and getting around the Garden Peninsula. There's no public transportation and no airport south of U.S. 2, and although there are boat landings and docks at Fayette Historic State Park, Garden Bay, and Portage Bay, there are no large marinas such as those in Escanaba, St. Ignace, or Manistique.

Escanaba and Vicinity

A large city by U.P. standards, Escanaba and neighboring Gladstone (just a few miles north) are home to some 20,000 people, serving as the industrial and commercial center for the south-central Upper Peninsula. The natural deepwater port gave Escanaba its start during the Civil War, when a hastily built rail line linked the iron mines in Negaunee with the port, bringing needed raw materials to support the Union war effort. Today iron ore is still shipped out of Escanaba's modern port facilities in the form of iron-clay taconite pellets, bound for steelmakers in the Lower Peninsula, Indiana, and Ohio.

Best of all, if you started your day near the Garden Peninsula, Escanaba is less than 50 miles away, a drive of 1 hour and 20 minutes.

Unlike M-35 north of Gladstone, the stretch of road between Gladstone and Menominee runs close to the coast, and it has been designated the **U.P. Hidden Coast Recreation Heritage Route.** Follow it south from Gladstone to Escanaba.

SIGHTS
Downtown Escanaba

Downtown Escanaba focuses on Ludington Street, an east-west route that runs from

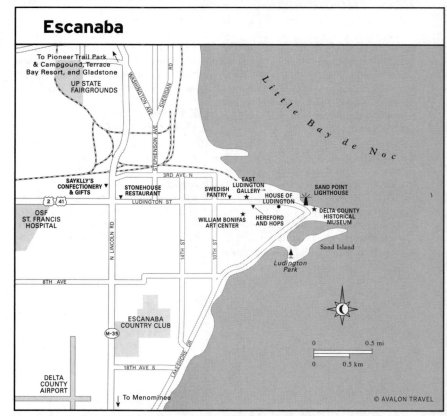

M-35 to the waterfront. Here's where you'll find most of the town's restaurants and shops and a growing local arts presence. If you're a science junkie, check out the sidewalk kiosks scattered around downtown, each of which focuses on a particular planet of the solar system.

The town's most iconic landmark is the **House of Ludington** (223 Ludington St.), a grand old Queen Anne resort hotel built in 1865. After enjoying a second heyday in the 1940s and 1950s, the old hotel has stuttered and stumbled with some shoddy interior remodeling and mismanagement. The most recent owners have reopened the hotel's restaurant, which offers some of the U.P.'s best dining. Today, the building's imposing facade continues to anchor the downtown.

At the foot of Ludington Street, lovely **Ludington Park** offers paved pathways along the water and to a small island (in-line skates permitted), interpretive signs explaining local history, a band shell that hosts concerts on Wednesday and Sunday evenings in summer, a playground, a beach, tennis courts, and a boat launch.

Escanaba's art scene can perhaps best be witnessed during a visit to the **William Bonifas Art Center** (700 1st Ave. S.,

906/786-3833, www.bonifasarts.org, 10am-5:30pm Tues.-Wed. and Fri., 10am-8pm Thurs., 10am-3pm Sat.), a community arts facility housed in a 1938 building that was originally a gymnasium and auditorium. Today, the center hosts changing free gallery exhibits, theatrical productions, and classes. The **East Ludington Gallery** (1007 Ludington St., 906/786-0300, www.eastludingtongallery. com, 10am-5pm Mon.-Sat.) displays and sells works by more than 35 regional artists.

Delta County Historical Society

Just to the south, the **Delta County Historical Museum** (16 Water Plant Rd., 906/786-3428, www.deltahistorical.org, 11am-4pm daily Memorial Day-Labor Day, $3 adults, $1 children, $5 family) has interesting and informative displays on local logging, Native American cultures, military history, and maritime history. The four-room museum has been collecting historical artifacts for more than 50 years, and the result is an important documentation of regional heritage.

Waterfalls

They're pleasant enough, and certainly pretty, but with a drop of about five feet spread out

Ludington Street in downtown Escanaba

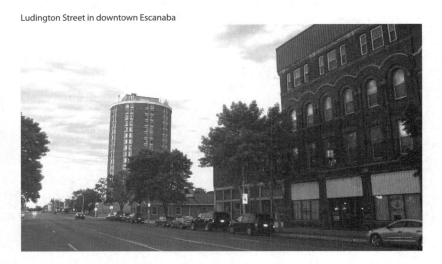

over several tiers, the **Rapid River Falls** aren't quite as impressive as some of its larger counterparts. Still, they're peaceful, relaxing, and visually interesting. A park on the river has picnic tables and grills as well as a playground. Take U.S. 41 seven miles north of Rapid River and follow the signs to the left.

Lighthouses

One of Ludington Park's most popular attractions is the **Sand Point Lighthouse** (end of Ludington St., 906/786-6790, 9am-5pm daily Memorial Day-Aug., 1pm-4pm daily Sept., donation), an 1868 brick light that was restored and reopened in 1990 by the Delta County Historical Society. It was a big job: In the 1940s, the Coast Guard remodeled the obsolete light for staff housing, removing the lantern room and the top 10 feet of the tower. You can climb the tower and take a look at the restored keeper's house. The light's first custodian, by the way, was Mary Terry, one of the nation's earliest female light keepers. The Delta County Historical Museum is located nearby.

At the tip of the Stonington Peninsula, across Little Bay de Noc from Escanaba, **Peninsula Point Lighthouse Park** (9am-5pm Mon.-Fri. Memorial Day-Labor Day, 1pm-4pm Tues.-Wed. Sept., free) is the perfect place to sprawl out on a sunny day: an open meadow, a grassy picnic area, a great shoreline for beachcombing, and—the main attraction—an 1865 lighthouse. Climb the spiral stairway for one of the most expansive views around: a 270-degree survey of Green Bay, and in clear weather even Wisconsin's Door County. The lighthouse was abandoned in the 1930s and replaced by a more effective shoal light several miles offshore. Local volunteers restored and reopened the old light, but it was subsequently ravaged by fire in 1959. The keeper's home was destroyed, but the tower survived the blaze. The lighthouse is operated by the Hiawatha National Forest.

Peninsula Point Lighthouse

ENTERTAINMENT
Island Resort and Casino

Harris, a small town some 13 miles west of Escanaba, has one of the U.P.'s finest gaming resorts. **Island Resort and Casino** (W399 U.S. 2/41, 906/466-2941 or 800/682-6040, www.chipincasino.com) is a 24-7 casino with more than 1,400 slot machines and plenty of table games—craps, blackjack, roulette, poker, Texas hold 'em, and more. When you get hungry, stop at the Firekeeper's Restaurant for cheap breakfast and lunch or daily all-you-can-eat dinner specials. Other on-site dining can be found at the Beachcomber Restaurant and Bar, Coral Reef Grille, and Bingo Snack Bar. The Island Showroom seats more than 1,300 for headliner shows; for lesser-known acts, visit Club Four One for weekly live bands and comedy nights every Sunday. A golf course, a 113-room hotel with an indoor pool, a salon, and an RV park cement Island Resort's reputation as one of the Midwest's premier resort destinations.

FESTIVALS AND EVENTS

Upper Peninsula State Fair

On M-35 between Escanaba and Gladstone, you'll pass the U.P. State Fair Grounds. For decades Michigan had the rare distinction of hosting two state fairs, the event in Detroit as well as its Upper Peninsula counterpart. However, the tumultuous economy of the last several years caused the State of Michigan to end many traditions, and the fairs unfortunately were among them. Since 2010 the U.P. edition has been operated by the Upper Peninsula State Fair Authority, a quasi-public body governed by a board consisting of representatives from all 15 Upper Peninsula counties. Recently a private nonprofit has revived Detroit's edition of the fair in suburban Novi. The **Upper Peninsula State Fair** (www.upstatefair.net) continues to be held during the third week of August. For additional information, contact the **Delta County Chamber of Commerce** (230 Ludington St., 906/786-2192 or 888/335-8264, www.deltami.org).

the tasting room at Northern Sun Winery

★ Northern Sun Winery

In Bark River, just a short drive west of Escanaba, you'll find another addition to the growing list of Upper Peninsula wineries. Visiting the **Northern Sun Winery** (983 10th Rd., 906/399-9212, www.northernsunwinery.com, 1pm-6pm Thurs.-Sun. May-Sept.) will make you feel like you've been transported to the French countryside. Vintner David Anthony and his wife, Susie, have perfected the art of growing high-quality grapes in a region often thought to be inhospitable. Northern Suns produces a variety of wines ranging from the St. Pepin, a dry white wine, to the Léon Millot, a fruity sweet wine that even has a chocolate subnote. From Escanaba, take U.S. 2 west for 10 miles before turning onto D Road. Continue for two miles until you come to 10th Road, and make a right. Go one more mile and you'll see the winery on your left.

Balloons on the Bay and Pioneer Days

The combination is interesting, to say the least—hot air balloons and pioneer heritage. Every year in late June, the U.P. State Fair Grounds become the staging ground for hot air balloons that fill the air above Lake Michigan. Jump in the basket for a tethered balloon ride or experience a bit of the old days while watching lumberjack exhibitions, old-fashioned craft demonstrations, and a barbecue cook-off. For more information, get a hold of the **Delta County Chamber of Commerce** (230 Ludington St., 906/786-2192 or 888/335-8264, www.deltami.org).

Monarch Migration

There really isn't anything official about the annual monarch butterfly migration, aside from volunteers, organized by the U.S. Forest Service, who count the populations and help tag the insects for tracking.

Escanaba in da Moonlight

Travelers who haven't been to the Upper Peninsula and don't quite know what to expect might want to track down a copy of the film *Escanaba in da Moonlight*, an off-color love song to the beautiful, quirky, often misunderstood Yooper culture.

The movie, starring, written, directed, and produced by Michigan native Jeff Daniels, tells the story of the "buckless Yooper," Reuben Soady, a 42-year-old man in the humiliating position of never having shot a buck, considered an essential rite of passage in Soady's home of Escanaba. Most of the film takes place at the Soady deer camp, and at the core of it, it's about hunting and family and expectations—and the spirit of the Upper Peninsula itself. It's really quite good.

That said, the story is also rather odd; things go a bit off when talk turns to UFOs. But the rest of the film is an accurate depiction of the area's culture: the local vernacular ("Yoo betcha!"), the conviction that euchre is the only card game worth playing, the flannel shirts, the hunting camp. This is the Upper Peninsula viewed from a somewhat stereotypical perspective, told by someone who understands and appreciates the land and its people.

Clearly, the movie is not for everyone (the film's website attributes the PG-13 rating to "uncultured humor") and has not been well received by critics, but it may still be worth a place in your rental queue.

But when it comes to monarch viewing, you can join the throng of enthusiasts who make the trek to the **Stonington Peninsula** each August. The peninsula, which extends south into Lake Michigan between the Bays de Noc, is an annual gathering point in the butterflies' great migration south to Mexico; they stop in and around Peninsula Point Lighthouse Park before the long flight across Green Bay and the open waters of the lake. The brilliant orange and black monarchs are best seen in August, although the migration continues into September, often overlapping with the autumn colors Michigan is known for, and combining to form a spectacular display of color.

SUMMER SPORTS AND RECREATION
★ Hiawatha National Forest

The 860,000-acre **Hiawatha National Forest** spans much of the central U.P., with its western unit stretching from the Lake Michigan shoreline of the Stonington Peninsula to the Lake Superior shore near Munising. For information on hiking trails, campgrounds, canoe routes, and other attractions, stop at the **Visitor Information Station** (U.S. 2, just east of Rapid River,

906/474-6442). You can talk with rangers and pick up a wide selection of maps and handouts. The station also includes interpretive displays and a small bookshop.

Hiking and Biking

Hiawatha National Forest's 40-mile **Bay de Noc/Grand Island Trail** follows an old Ojibwa portage route, used to carry canoes and supplies between Lakes Michigan and Superior. Today it ends just short of both lakes, beginning just northeast of Rapid River and ending 10 miles shy of Lake Superior at Ackerman Lake. The trail parallels the Whitefish River, about 0.5 to 2 miles away, tracing its eastern bluff and offering high, sweeping views of the forested river valley. Along the way, it hopscotches over several streams and passes a number of inland lakes. The high density of hardwoods makes the route especially beautiful during the fall color season.

Horses and mountain bikes are allowed on the Bay de Noc/Grand Island Trail, but not motorized vehicles. Primitive camping is permitted throughout the national forest, and no permit is required. To find the trailhead, follow U.S. 2 east from Rapid River two miles, then turn left on County Road 509 and drive another 1.5 miles. You'll see a parking area on the west side of the road.

A few miles east of the Hiawatha National Forest Visitor Information Station, turn north off U.S. 2 onto County Road H-13 to reach the great hiking and mountain biking trails of **Pine Marten Run.** The trail network lies between the Indian River to the north, County Road 440 to the south, Forest Road 2258 to the west, and County Road 437 to the east. This newly signed area includes 26 miles of rolling single-track and overgrown double-track. Various loops wind through groves of huge hemlocks and white pines, a dozen lakes, and the stunning Indian River. From County Road H-13, turn right on County Road 440, and watch for the Forest Service sign directing you to Iron Jaw Lake. Alternatively, head north from County Road 440 on Forest Road 2258, where you'll find another trailhead just before the road crosses the Indian River. Maps and more information are available from the Hiawatha National Forest Visitor Information Station (U.S. 2, just east of Rapid River, 906/474-6442).

Just three miles north of Gladstone, the Escanaba River State Forest maintains the **Days River Pathway,** a fine nine-mile hiking trail that loops through forest and along the scenic Days River, which cuts a deep gorge near the trailhead. This is a good stream for brook trout, so be sure to bring a fly rod. A camera and a set of binoculars are useful too since the area is thick with warblers and other songbirds. To reach the trailhead, follow U.S. 2 east of Gladstone three miles, then turn left onto Days River Road. For more information, contact the **Escanaba Forest Area Office** (906/293-3293, www.michigan.gov/dnr).

On the opposite side of Little Bay de Noc, the Stonington Peninsula is largely bypassed by travelers, as it lacks accessible sandy beaches or significant commercial attractions. It's a soft and peaceful place, with smooth slabs of bedrock shoreline and sunny meadows that have reclaimed abandoned farmland. The Hiawatha National Forest manages a nice stretch of shoreline along the peninsula's west side, including a few campgrounds and hiking trails. Look for the Forest Service signs south of Garth Point. The peninsula preserves several stands of old-growth hemlock, hardwood, and pine. One of the most notable examples is now protected as the **Squaw Creek Old Growth Area,** a part of the Hiawatha National Forest. Though these woods are not virgin timber, 19th-century loggers practiced selective cutting, quite unusual in those days,

entrance to Hiawatha National Forest

ESCANABA AND THE LAKE MICHIGAN SHORE

ESCANABA AND VICINITY

and left behind several large trees that have grown to be enormous. Trails are few—you'll find just a couple of abandoned logging roads open only to foot traffic. Walking is easy, however, since the high shade canopy created by the trees crowds out the underbrush usually found in the woods. Be sure to take a compass, or use the compass app on your smart phone.

The southern part of the 65-acre tract is particularly scenic, with the clear tea-colored waters of Squaw Creek sloshing between the massive trunks. You'll find the largest hemlocks south of the creek and huge hardwoods just to the north. Squaw Creek is not marked by a sign and shows up on only a few maps. To find it, drive south nine miles on County Road 513; just before and after the road crosses the creek, you'll see turnouts on the east side of the road and old roads leading inland.

Canoeing and Kayaking

Just north of Pine Marten Run and the Indian River, the **Big Island Lake Canoeing Area** offers paddlers a quiet chain of nine lakes. Since there are few launches for powerboats, the lakes usually remain quite peaceful even in the height of summer. Again, be sure to obtain information and maps from the Visitor Information Station (U.S. 2, just east of Rapid River, 906/474-6442); they will be a great asset during your adventure.

You'll find good paddling on the **Escanaba River.** Put in northwest of Gladstone and take the river all the way to Green Bay. There are more than 40 miles of good paddling between Gwinn and Gladstone, with periodic access points; most of the river is suitable for those with moderate experience, though some sections are more challenging.

You can paddle a few miles along the **Ford River,** southwest of Gladstone. Beginners can take the river between County Road 414 and U.S. 2, but there's some white water as you get closer to Green Bay. There's an access point at U.S. 2 if you're nervous about continuing. Experienced open-water kayakers can paddle Little Bay de Noc and Green Bay. Rent a canoe, kayak, or a number of other types of boat from

Richards Boatworks and Splash Rentals (4528 E. M-35, Escanaba, 906/789-1009, 9am-6pm Mon.-Fri., 10am-2pm Sat.).

Fishing

Although it's the smaller of the two bays, **Little Bay de Noc,** with more than 30,000 acres of water, is still a sight to behold. The bay is known for its fishing, particularly for walleye during the fall. **Delta Dawn Charters** (1328 Lake Shore Dr., Gladstone, 906/396-4001, www.deltadawncharters.com) is a great way to fish Little Bay de Noc and its environs. Captain Bill Myers is a seasoned pro who will lead you to the best spots for trout, salmon, and walleye. Rapid River's **Bay de Noc Charters** (7989 U.S. 2, 906/553-4850, www.baydenoccharters.net), on the northern tip of the bay, can take you on a fishing trip in Little Bay de Noc, and charters into Big Bay de Noc are available as well. Gladstone is home to a bevy of fishing charters—contact the **Bays de Noc Convention & Visitors Bureau** (230 Ludington St., Escanaba, 800/533-4386, www.travelbaysdenoc.com).

If you'd rather set off on your own, contact **Uncle Ducky Boat Rentals** (434 E. Prospect St., Marquette, 877/228-5447, www.paddlingmichigan.com). Local tackle shops and outfitters include **Bayview Bait and Tackle Shop** (7110 U.S. 2, 906/786-1488, www.baydenoc.com, 7am-7pm daily), between Gladstone and Escanaba, and **Walleye's Choice** (10132 M-35, 906/428-1488, www.walleyeschoice.com, hours vary). Walleye's Choice also offers fishing charters. Cast a line into the **Whitefish River,** which flows into Little Bay de Noc at Rapid River, for trout and smallmouth bass.

Beaches

In Gladstone, visit **Van Cleve Park** (906/428-2916) on Lake Shore Drive. There's a sandy beach for swimming in the waters of Little Bay de Noc, and a number of other facilities make this one of the area's best beaches for family fun—a fitness course, sand volleyball courts, horseshoes, basketball courts, a softball diamond, a gazebo, a playground, and more. You'll find the beautiful Gladstone Harbor here as well.

Golf

Golfing in the Upper Peninsula is like most U.P. activities—casual and unpretentious, without the pomp found at more expensive destinations. One of the U.P.'s finest golf trails consists of four top-notch courses in Delta County, each within 20 minutes of the others. The **Escanaba Country Club** (1800 11th Ave. S., 906/786-4430, www.escanabacc.com, 9 holes $15 walking, $25 with cart, 18 holes $25 walking, $40 with cart) is the oldest country club in Delta County, founded in 1915. The 18-hole par-71 course has a PGA professional on staff and one of the hardest finishing holes around.

Nearby **Gladstone Golf Club** (6514 Days River Rd., 906/428-9646, www.gladstone-golf.com, 9 holes $15 walking, $25 with cart, 18 holes $55 walking, $40 with cart) is surrounded by thousands of acres of forests. The Days River runs through 5 of the 18 holes. Take U.S. 2 about three miles north of Gladstone, turn left on County Road 446, and proceed for two miles.

Rated one of the best courses in the area, the 18-hole **Terrace Bluff Golf Club** (7146 P Rd., Gladstone, 906/428-2343, 9 holes $16, 18 holes $25) features views of the bay and is suitable for golfers of every skill level. The amenities of Terrace Bay Resort and Convention Center are close at hand. Finally, seven miles west of Escanaba on U.S. 2, the **Highland Golf Club** (906/466-7457, www.highlandgolfclub.net, 9 holes $15, 18 holes $25) was Delta County's first 18-hole course.

Off-Road Vehicles

The Forest Islands Trail begins about 10 miles south of Escanaba, west of M-35. Take 4.25 Road to H Road and turn right, then turn left on F Road to the parking area. The 33-mile trail ends in Cedar River and is broken into the Limpert Road Loop, the Seven Mile Marsh Loop, and the Westman Road Loop near Cedar River at the south end of the trail.

WINTER SPORTS AND RECREATION
Downhill Skiing

The Escanaba area is only a short distance east of Iron Mountain and the Upper Peninsula's best-known skiing runs, but beginning and intermediate skiers can try **Gladstone Sports Park** (900 N. Bluff Dr., 906/428-9130, http://gladstonemi.org, hours vary, $12 skiing, $10 tubing), just east of the city. It's a relatively low-key resort, but its combination of easy hills and tubing runs makes it ideal for families who want to avoid the crowds and prices of the bigger resorts to the west. There are a few rope tows and a T-bar, three tube runs with the only return lifts in the U.P., and a snowboard terrain park that includes a half pipe for riders. Food and drink are sold in the Ski Chalet.

Ski and Snowshoe Trails

The nine miles of **Days Rivers Pathway** (906/293-3293, www.michigan.gov/dnr), three miles south of Rapid River, are among the most popular groomed ski trails in the area. Choose among loops of one to eight miles, suitable for beginners as well as experts. Six miles north of Rapid River, the **Rapid River Ski Trails** (906/786-4062, www.fs.fed.us) provide an especially beautiful excursion through varied terrain. Pay attention to the signs, and stay off the 10-mile loop unless you're an expert cross-country skier—the other loops are suitable if you're less experienced. Snowshoers can make tracks alongside both trails, and both trails have donation boxes to help support trail maintenance and upkeep.

Dogsledding

In the winter, the Bay de Noc-Grand Island Trail area is the stomping grounds for the sled dogs of **Triple Creek Sled Dog Kennels** (906/439-5242 or 877/275-7533). Owner Bob Johnson, one of the U.P.'s most experienced mushers, offers a variety of dogsled trips ranging from two-hours to as long as five days. Package tours include an overnight stay at **Johnson's Buck Sporting Lodge,** his solar-powered wilderness lodge north of Rapid River.

Snowmobiling

Gain access to the Michigan's seemingly endless 6,100 miles of interconnected snowmobile trails via the **Nahma Grade Snowmobile Trail;** the trailhead is a few miles east of Rapid River. After following a natural gas pipeline for 11 miles, the trail heads north. From Escanaba, **Trail 2** takes you west toward Iron Mountain.

FOOD

You'll find your best dining options in downtown Escanaba. The hottest spot in town is ★ **Hereford and Hops** (614 Ludington St., 906/786-1945, www.herefordandhops.com, 11am-9pm Mon.-Sat., noon-8pm Sun., longer hours in summer, entrées $9-26), a cook-your-own-steak place and microbrewery in the 1914 Delta Hotel. You'll find excellent seafood choices to, such as grilled salmon and tilapia bruschetta.

You can get traditional American meals at the ★ **Swedish Pantry** (819 Ludington St., 906/786-9606, www.swedishpantry.com, 8am-6pm daily, entrées $10-22), but you'll also find that, true to its name, the cute little restaurant serves up traditional food the way a Swedish grandmother used to make it. No one will stop you from ordering the meatloaf or roast beef, but you really should try the Swedish meatballs, potato sausage, and rutabaga. Grab a massive fresh-baked cookie from the bakery, and browse the traditional Scandinavian merchandise at the gift shop.

The **Stonehouse Restaurant** (2223 Ludington St., 906/786-5003, www.stonehouseescanaba.com, lunch 11am-2pm Mon.-Fri., dinner 5pm-9:30pm Mon.-Thurs., 5pm-10pm Fri.-Sat.) doesn't look like much on the outside, but it has some fine food and a casual atmosphere. Lunch runs around $10 for sandwiches, salads, and entrées (look for the daily

plate special), but plan on spending $18-33 for a dinner entrée—steak, lobster, scallops, duck, and more. The Carport Lounge serves mixed drinks and a passable list of wines by the glass.

Of course, you can always make reservations at an Escanaba landmark. The historic ★ **House of Ludington** (223 Ludington St., 906/786-6300, www.houseofludington. net, 5pm-9pm Thurs.-Sat., dinner $12-24) has two dining rooms: the King George Dining Room is an elegant choice, where you'll dine with antique silver, while the Emerald Dining Room is slightly more casual. The restored hotel serves gourmet meals, but during dinner hours only. The varied menu offers something for everyone, including a roast chicken breast in pesto sauce and portobello mushroom pie. Special mention, however, must be given to the outstanding cashew strawberry salad.

Sayklly's Confectionery & Gifts (1304 Ludington St., 906/786-2928) is one of those unexpected special places you find that make a vacation more memorable. A community institution since 1906, Sayklly's has been producing and selling delicious treats including assorted chocolates, peanut brittle, and saltwater taffy to generations of visitors and locals alike. They even ship anywhere in the world. Their U.P. notoriety earned them national attention when the company was featured on the Food Network's *Unwrapped* in 2011. The store also features unique gift items from manufacturers such as Lladro, Waterford, Swarovski, and Dept. 56.

ACCOMMODATIONS

The typical sprawl of chain motels runs along M-35 between Escanaba and Gladstone, but some nice family owned operations are still holding their own along the waterfront, with rates in the $50-100 range. The ★ **Terrace Bay Resort** (7146 P Rd., 906/786-7554, www. terracebay.com, $85-165), on Little Bay de Noc between Escanaba and Gladstone, has immaculate and up-to-date rooms featuring great views of the bay. The 200-acre golf resort complex includes an 18-hole course, indoor and outdoor pools, tennis courts, a games room, and more. To find Terrace Bay, watch for signs on U.S. 41 south of Gladstone. About six miles south of Escanaba on M-35, **Fishery Pointe Beach Cottages** (E5043 M-35, 616/361-1386, www.fisherypointe.com, Memorial Day-Labor Day, 616/430-1343 $570-700 weekly) and **Sandy Shores Cottages** (4717 M-35, 906/786-3625, www.sandyshorescottages. com, May-Oct., $65, cabins $575-725 weekly) offer housekeeping cottages on a nice stretch of sandy beach.

Downtown Escanaba's **House of Ludington** (223 Ludington St., 906/786-6300, www.houseofludington.net, $65-105) hasn't exactly been restored to its former glory, but the current owners, Ed and Suzell Eisenberger, have certainly made a good faith effort. The hotel's 17 rooms are decorated with different themes, each with an eye to highlighting the hotel's storied past. The House of Ludington was constructed in 1865, renamed in 1871, and torn down and rebuilt in 1883. It's passed through numerous hands in the decades since. It was closed for a few years during the 1990s. A new bar occupies the spot that was once a courtyard, and the building also includes two dining rooms and modern amenities in each guest room.

A few miles south of Escanaba, travelers can find some of the remote peace and tranquility the U.P. is known by visiting **St. Michael's in Cedar Dells** (2726 M-35, Bark River, 906/280-2165, www.escanabacottages. com, $115-145), a resort tucked away in a cedar grove overlooking Lake Michigan. The rustic but clean one- to three-bedroom cottages are perfect for families. Pets are welcome too.

Camping

Haymeadow Creek Campground (Rapid River Ranger District, 499 E. Lake Shore Dr., Manistique, 906/474-6442, www.fs.fed.us) is about 10 miles north of U.S. 2 on County Road 509 in Hiawatha National Forest. Each of the 15 campsites has a fire ring and a picnic table, and drinking water is available on-site. You'll

be able to connect to the Bay de Noc-Grand Island Trail from here.

Closer to town, you'll find both tent and RV camping at the **Pioneer Trail Park and Campground** (906/786-1020, www.delta-countymi.org, $19-23 tents, $29-35 RVs), a county park a few miles north of Escanaba. Of the 75 sites, only 17 are for tenting, but these include fire pits and picnic tables. The rest of the campsites have electric hookups for RVs, and most of them have water. Pioneer Trail is ideal for families: Amenities include a playground and a playing field, a picnic area, showers, and optional cable TV. The campground is on U.S. 2/M-35 between Gladstone and Manistique. There are 25 additional campsites at the **O. B. Fuller Park and Campground** (906/786-4902, www. deltacountymi.org, $29-38), another county park on Lake Michigan, 15 miles south of Escanaba. The campground features more than 80 wooded acres, Lake Michigan shoreline, fishing on the Bark River, and electricity and water at each campsite. Follow M-35 south from Escanaba to the Bark River crossing.

INFORMATION AND SERVICES

Visitor information for Escanaba and the surrounding area can be obtained from the **Bays de Noc Convention & Visitors Bureau** (230 Ludington St., 906/789-7862 or 800/533-4386, www.travelbaysdenoc.com) and the **Delta County Chamber of Commerce** (230 Ludington St., 906/786-8830 or 888/335-8264, www.deltami.org). For recreation information, contact the **Michigan DNR** (6833 U.S. 2, Gladstone, 906/786-2351, www.michigan.gov/dnr) or the U.S. Forest Service's office for the **Hiawatha National Forest** (2727 N. Lincoln Rd., Escanaba, 906/786-4062, www. fs.fed.us).

Seek medical attention at **OSF St. Francis Hospital** (3401 Ludington St., Escanaba, 906/786-3311, www.osfstfrancis.org). There are plenty of banks and ATMs in downtown Escanaba and in Gladstone, including **Wells Fargo** (1205 Ludington St., 906/789-5236, www.wellsfargo.com), as well as a number of smaller local and regional banks.

GETTING THERE AND AROUND
Car
If you're coming from the Mackinac Bridge or south on I-75 from Sault Ste. Marie and Ontario, you really couldn't have an easier time driving to Escanaba—take U.S. 2 east from St. Ignace until you hit the city. Since Escanaba is far closer to Wisconsin than to the Lower Peninsula, many drivers will want to drive along Green Bay (the bay) from Green Bay (the city) on U.S. 41 to M-35, which runs to Escanaba from the south.

Boat
There are two quality marinas in the vicinity of Escanaba, one in Escanaba itself and the other in Gladstone, a few miles north. The **Escanaba Municipal Marina** (906/786-9614, www.michigan.gov/dnr) has 37 transient and 128 seasonal slips. The marina is open May 9 to October 7, and the harbormaster can be reached 7am-4pm daily on channel 9. The marina offers showers, gas and diesel fuel, day-use dockage, pump out, launch, bicycle rentals, a dog run, and snacks, plus cable TV hookups and free Internet access. Its location is 45°44.34 N, 87°02.05 W.

The **Gladstone Marina** (906/428-2916, www.michigan.gov/dnr) is located at 45°50.15 N, 87°01.00 W, and the harbormaster is on duty from May 15 to September 1. Gladstone Marina monitors radio channels 9 and 68.

Air
Delta Airlines has flights to **Delta County Airport** (ESC, 3300 Airport Rd., 906/786-4902, www.deltacountymi.org), a small airport just southwest of Escanaba, from Detroit. You can rent a car from **Alamo Car Rental** (3300 Airport Rd., 906/786-0603, www.nationalcar.com); you really will need a car while you're here.

Bus
Regular bus service runs to Escanaba from Green Bay, Ironwood, Marquette, St. Ignace, Green Bay, Chicago, and Detroit by **Indian Trails** (800/292-3831, www.indiantrails.com).

Menominee and Vicinity

Spiking like a canine tooth between Wisconsin and the waters of Green Bay (and only about 55 miles from Escanaba), the triangle of land comprising Menominee County and southern Delta County has been dubbed the peninsula's "banana belt." It's a fitting name, as it does have the U.P.'s most temperate climate, thanks to the relatively warm waters of Green Bay, and the lightest snowfall in the Upper Peninsula—just 50 inches a year on average, a quarter of what typically falls on the rest of the peninsula.

Locals take advantage of this quirk of nature not by growing bananas but by raising dairy cattle and crops like corn and soybeans. Farms dot the countryside, many on land long ago clear-cut by loggers. The logging industry still echoes through the region, however, in the historic waterfront district of Menominee and the mammoth NewPage paper plant near Escanaba—a key factor in the area's stable economy. Many visitors have a tough time getting past the big lake always looming on the eastern horizon—the lapping waters of Green Bay are infinitely enticing and easily accessible.

Remember that Menominee is located in the central time zone, an hour earlier than Escanaba and the majority of the Upper Peninsula.

SIGHTS
The Menominee River spills into Green Bay between the twin cities of Marinette,

Menominee and Vicinity

To Escanaba

41

M-35

Henes Park

0   400 yds
0   400 m

BAY DE NOC RD

13TH ST

RIVER DR

38TH AVE

Watertower Park

577

MARINETTE TWIN COUNTY AIRPORT

30TH AVE

22ND ST

18TH ST

13TH ST

SUNSET RD

SCHLOEGEL'S BAY VIEW RESTAURANT

ECONO LODGE

23RD AVE

Green Bay

581

18TH AVE

14TH AVE

RIVERSIDE GOLF CLUB

MICHIGAN

Menominee

MENOMINEE COUNTY HERITAGE MUSEUM

Menominee Marina

Blueberry Island

Menominee River

10TH AVE

Boom Island

10TH ST

NORTH SHORE GOLF CLUB

SPIES PUBLIC LIBRARY

SERVING SPOON CAFE

TRENDS AND TRADITIONS

Great Lakes Marina Park

RIVERSIDE AVE

VAN CLEVE AVE

LAUERMAN HOUSE

41

6TH AVE

BERG'S LANDING

WISCONSIN

W-64

BEST WESTERN RIVERFRONT INN

Tourist Park

MINNESOTA AVE

MARINETTE AVE

STATE ST

M&M VICTORIAN INN

Marinette

41

MERCHANT ST

MICKEY-LU'S BAR-B-Q

City Park

PIERCE AVE

CHURCH ST

SHORE DR

MAIN ST

CARNEY BLVD

OGDEN ST

HOSMER ST

© AVALON TRAVEL

Wisconsin, and Menominee, Michigan, once the region's richest lumber port. Menominee's bustling business district is centered on 1st Street, along the waterfront. Fortunately, most of the 19th-century brick and sandstone buildings have survived, and their restoration is an ongoing task. You can explore the **historic district** guided by a walking tour brochure available at **Spies Public Library** (940 1st St.). Its 1905 beaux arts facade is one of the tour's most beautiful buildings. A growing number of shops and restaurants along 1st Street are adding new life to this pleasant area.

Menominee County Heritage Museum

The Menominee County Historical Society maintains the **Menominee County Heritage Museum** (904 11th Ave., 906/863-9000, 10am-4pm Mon.-Sat. Memorial Day-Labor Day, donation) in a former Catholic church. Like many of the Upper Peninsula's regional history museums, the very local focus may be of limited interest to visitors, but it does outline the county's history since its beginnings and has displays about logging, Native American artifacts, and other aspects of Menominee's heritage, making it worth the stop for local history buffs.

Bayside Parks

The waterfront district is home to bayside parks, easily accessible on foot. **Great Lakes Marina Park** stretches along the water between 6th and 10th Avenues, flanked by a new marina and a band shell that hosts summer concerts on Tuesday and Thursday evenings. For a longer walk or bike ride, head south along the water to the **Tourist Park** swimming beach. Continue farther south to the **North Pier Light,** which marks the entrance to Menominee Harbor with a beacon at the end of a rocky breakwater. Although the light is attractive, it's not open to the public.

De Young Family Zoo

Just north of Menominee is the **De Young Family Zoo** (N5406 County Rd. 577, Mellen, 906/788-4093, www.thedeyoungfamilyzoo. com, 10am-5pm daily summer, call for hours off-season, $12 adults, $10 seniors, $8 ages 5-16, free under age 5), a pleasant diversion at the end of a long day's drive. You'll find some of the animals you'd expect in big-city zoos, including big cats, bears, primates, wolves, and foxes. Special programs including animal shows and feeding demonstrations.

SHOPPING

Ready for a bit of retail therapy? Head over to 1st Street in downtown Menominee for a visit to **Trends & Traditions** (615 1st St., 906/864-1568, www.trendstraditionsmi. com, 9:30am-6pm Mon.-Thurs., 9am-5pm Fri.-Sat., 10am-4pm Sun.), a charming gift store and boutique with a wide assortment of women's clothing and accessories, including purses, scarves, and jewelry, plus numerous giftware choices—wine and bar accessories, candles, kitchen items, and home decor. From 2011 through 2017, readers of the Marinette *EagleHerald* have voted the store the area's best gift shop.

ENTERTAINMENT
Threefold Vine Winery

In downtown Stephenson is the tasting room of the **Threefold Vine Winery** (S232 Menominee St., 906/753-6000, www.threefoldvine.com, 11am-5pm daily May-Dec., 11am-5pm Thurs.-Sat. Jan.-Apr.) in a former bank building. Here you can take your time sampling any of 19 varieties of wines crafted by grapes grown in the Upper Peninsula, ranging from dry to sweet and to "dessert style." This is the perfect place to choose a bottle to complement a picnic on the beach.

FESTIVALS AND EVENTS
Art for All

If you happen to be in town on the last Sunday of June, be sure to visit **Art for All** (www.artforallinc.com) in Great Lakes Marina Park along 1st Street. The event is both a juried art fair and an exhibition featuring works in various media: paintings, drawings, photographs, pottery, glasswork, and sculpture. All the work is for sale, so if you see a piece you like, remember that a fine painting or photograph will make a much nicer remembrance of your trip than a T-shirt. The event runs from 10am to 4pm.

Menominee Waterfront Festival

Pay a visit to Menominee's Historic Waterfront district for the **Waterfront Festival** (www.menomineewaterfrontfestival.com), held every year on the first weekend in August. This popular four-day celebration offers plenty of fun activities and events, including live music at the band shell, a parade, boat races, and food vendors. Be sure not to miss the amateur lumberjack competition or the stunning fireworks display.

SUMMER SPORTS AND RECREATION
Hiking and Biking

Menominee's most popular park is a bit farther away, at the north end of town off M-35. **John Henes Park** (906/863-2656) occupies a 50-acre point that juts out into Green Bay. Designed by noted landscape architect Ossian Cole Simonds, this unusual park combines tracts of virgin hemlock and pine with traditional park amenities, walking trails, swimming beaches, and playgrounds.

At the Cedar River, 25 miles north of Menominee on M-35, the **Escanaba River State Forest** (906/786-2351) offers a network of hiking and mountain biking trails, with four loops ranging two to seven miles over hilly terrain sculpted by ice age glaciers. The Cedar River Trail and Timber Trail in nearby **J. W. Wells State Park** (906/863-9747) both follow the Green Bay shoreline.

Canoeing and Kayaking

The 100-mile stretch of the Menominee River from above Iron Mountain all the way through Menominee separates the Upper Peninsula from Wisconsin. The strong current offers paddlers an intense high-current ride. You'll have to portage around several dams and reservoirs, but the wildlife viewing and rugged scenery make the effort worthwhile. The upper reaches of the river are not for beginners, however—the Class IV and V white water is some of the U.P.'s fastest. If you're an inexperienced or timid paddler, put in at an access point closer to Menominee, where the flow is gentler and the slower rapids are more navigable.

Beaches

In the 55 miles between Menominee and Escanaba, several parks and beaches lure you off the highway. About 13 miles north of Menominee, **Bailey Park** is a favorite swimming beach for locals, with fine sand and low dunes on a point that stretches away from the highway. Just to the north, **Kleinke Park** is more exposed to M-35 but offers campsites overlooking the bay as well as a sandy beach. There are small swimming beaches at **Tourist Park,** near the Menominee Harbor and the North Pier Light, and at **Henes Park,** on M-35 just north of town.

Fishing

There's some fishing available at **Cedar River,** north of Menominee, as well as at the Menominee River and several smaller local lakes and rivers—try **Hayward Lake** or **Walton River.** In town, anglers can cast a line off the Menominee Municipal Pier— the same pier that leads to the North Pier Light—but some of the best fishing is in Green Bay and Lake Michigan. Currently there are no fishing charter services operating from the Menominee area, although in nearby Peshtigo, Wisconsin you'll find **Walleye Madness Guide Service** (County Road B, Peshtigo, WI, 906/290-2939 or 715/582-9090, www.walleyemadnessfishing.com). Captain Steve Paulsen will take patrons just about anywhere in Green Bay they wish, on either the Michigan or Wisconsin sides.

Boating

Green Bay, Little and Big Bays de Noc, and northern Lake Michigan are among the Midwest's most beautiful, temperate, and sailable waters. Along with sites in Escanaba and Gladstone to the north, boaters can put in at the **Menominee Marina** (906/863-8498, www.michigan.gov/dnr).

Golf

In Stephenson, several miles north of Menominee on U.S. 41, golfers can enjoy a relaxing game at the rural **Indian Hills Golf Course** (N8881 Walnut Rd., Stephenson, 906/753-4781, www.indianhillsgolf.net, nine holes $10, unlimited play $15, pull cart $2; riding cart). Perhaps due to its remote location, surrounded by fields of grain and corn, this nine-hole course holds a certain quaint attraction. Closer to Menominee, golfers can visit the **North Shore Golf Club** (2315 M-35, 906/863-3026, greens fees $35, including cart) a few miles north of town on M-35. The club's 18 holes are well maintained, and—one of the most compelling reasons to swing a club here—a few holes provide views of Green Bay. You'll find many of the amenities you'd expect at a higher-level course: a

PGA professional, a restaurant, a banquet hall, a pro shop, and a driving range.

WINTER SPORTS AND RECREATION

Ski and Snowshoe Trails

One of the best places for ungroomed ski trails is **J. W. Wells State Park** (906/863-9747), on M-35 about 25 miles north of Menominee. The park, open year-round, has almost 700 acres of land for public use crossed by eight miles of ski and snowshoe trails, some of which lead skiers along the Green Bay shoreline. You'll find the groomed trails of **Cedar River Pathway** (906/786-2354, www.michigan.gov/dnr) several miles north of J. W. Wells State Park, where M-35 and County Road 551 meet. The pathway has several loops, ranging two to nine miles, that are perfect for beginning skiers.

Snowmobiling

The expansive Michigan DNR trail system doesn't extend south into Menominee County. The best bet for snowmobiling is to head north on U.S. 41 to Powers, where the trailhead for **Trail 331** connects to **Trail 2** a few miles north. Take Trail 2 west toward Iron Mountain or east to Escanaba.

the Menominee Marina

Many of Menominee County's unpaved roads and the shoulders of paved roads are accessible by snowmobile; double-check local ordinances for exceptions. Always use extreme caution when riding on public roads. More information about statewide snowmobile regulations is available from the website of the **Michigan DNR** (www.michigan.gov/dnr). Remember, safety first.

FOOD

Dining in Menominee is mostly classic American fare, with an emphasis on fish from the local waters. **Berg's Landing** (450 1st St., 906/863-8034, www.menomineelanding.com, lunch and dinner daily, entrées $19-27) offers terrific views of Green Bay and good reliable steaks, seafood, chicken, and vegetarian dishes. Reservations are recommended after 2pm. Locals will likely point you to **Schloegel's Bay View Restaurant** (2720 10th St., 906/863-7888, http://tastefullydifferent.com, 6:30am-8pm Mon.-Sat., 7:30am-8pm Sun.), right on U.S. 41, for pies (baked daily), generous sandwiches, and international items like Swedish pancakes and Cornish pasties—all at very reasonable prices. Salads and sandwiches run $6.50-8 and dinner entrées range $9-15. You can enjoy a great view of Green Bay as well.

In addition to the traditional café offerings—coffee, espresso, soups—the **Serving Spoon Cafe** (821 1st St., 906/863-7770, 6:30am-2:30pm daily, under $10) has earned a reputation for its Mediterranean-style pitas, light salads, vegetarian sandwiches, and gluten-free options. Across the river on the Wisconsin side, **Mickey-Lu's Bar-B-Q** (1710 Marinette Ave., Marinette, WI, 715/735-7721, www.jldr.com, 9am-10pm Mon.-Thurs., 9am-11:30pm Fri.-Sat., 11am-10pm Sun.) looks like a hole in the wall, but it's the place to go for *very* cheap food—authentic old-fashioned butter burgers, malts, and ice cream sundaes.

ACCOMMODATIONS

Lodging choices are limited to a few chain motels in Menominee and neighboring Marinette, Wisconsin. Two of the best values are **AmericInn Lodge Suites** (2330 10th St., Menominee, 906/863-8699, $115-139), **Econo Lodge** (2516 10th St., Menominee, 906/863-4431, $92-117), which has rooms overlooking the bay, and in Wisconsin, **Best Western Riverfront Inn** (1821 Riverside Ave., Marinette, WI, 715/732-1000, $119-145), just west of U.S. 41 at the river.

Cross the river into Wisconsin for comfortable lodging at one of the area's nicest historic inns, the ★ **M&M Victorian Inn** (1393 Main St., Marinette, 715/732-9531, www.lauermanhouse.com, $100-160). The M&M is named after the twin cities, not the candy, and is a stunning restored 1893 Queen Anne-style home with elegant original woodwork, stained glass, and five guest rooms. Travelers can also stay at its sister facility, the **Lauerman House Inn** (1975 Riverside Ave., 715/732-7800, www.lauermanhouse.com, $100-160).

Camping

J. W. Wells State Park (906/863-9747 or 800/447-2757, www.michigan.gov/dnr), about 25 miles north of Menominee on M-35, is the most extensive park along the highway. Flanking both sides of M-35, the 800-acre park is known for its three-mile stretch of rocky beach and large modern campground. The campground doesn't offer much privacy, but all 178 sites are near the beach and 30 back up right to the water. All sites often fill on summer weekends. If you've planned well ahead, you might be able to claim one of the park's five rustic cabins ($60), stone and log buildings built as a Civilian Conservation Corps (CCC) project in the 1930s and tucked in secluded woods near the water. They sleep 8 to 16 people and feature barrel stoves for both warmth and cooking.

The **Cedar River North State Forest Campground** (906/786-2354, $15, no reservations) in Escanaba River State Forest is a quiet, rustic campground right on the banks of the river, just a few miles upstream from the mouth. The 18 sites are for tent and small trailer use, and 4 of them are walk-in tent-only

The Spirit of the CCC

The Civilian Conservation Corps (CCC) program began in 1933 after President Franklin Roosevelt proposed to Congress a program to provide meaningful work to unemployed young men whose families were drawing relief as a result of the Great Depression. The program represented a creative approach to severe unemployment and a deterrent to potential delinquency.

Often nicknamed Roosevelt's "tree army," the participants performed all sorts of outdoor forestry tasks. Working at a vast network of rural camps, the young men planted trees, built roads, fought fires, and stocked rivers and lakes with fish. In addition, the CCCers dug canals and constructed cabins and wildlife shelters throughout the nation's national parks, monuments, and forests.

Participants were initially required to be age 17 to 25 and unmarried. The camps operated along a paramilitary model. Commanders had disciplinary authority over the corpsmen, who were required to address their superiors as "Sir." Participants were organized into companies comprising the corpsmen stationed at a particular camp. Each man was initially paid $30 per week, of which $25 was sent to his parents.

The sheer volume of work performed by the CCC is astounding. Over nine years, the corps planted approximately 3 billion trees and built over 800 parks nationwide. Many of the building projects undertaken by the CCC are still in use today.

The nature of their work varied depending on the region. In the Upper Peninsula, the Seney National Wildlife Refuge was built by CCC corpsmen from nearby Camp Germfask. In 1936 on Isle Royale, men from the 2699th Corp built the Rock Harbor Camp and the nearby Daily Farm Landing, which is still in use today.

At its peak in 1935, the program enrolled over 500,000 participants in some 2,900 camps nationally. During the life of the program, 1933 to 1942, a total of 2.5 million men participated, including over 100,000 in Michigan. The program was so successful that in recent decades the concept has been replicated by many states as an answer to chronic unemployment. Noteworthy enrollees in the original CCC included actors Walter Matthau, Robert Mitchum, and Raymond Burr, in addition to Admiral Hyman Rickover and test pilot Chuck Yeager.

The Michigan DNR operates several volunteer programs for citizens interested in keeping the spirt of the CCC alive. **Adopt-A-Park** enlists volunteer groups to participate in spring cleanups, park maintenance, and various special projects. Visit http://www.michigan.gov/dnr for details.

---

sites. You'll find potable water from a rustic hand pump. From M-35 at the village of Cedar River, follow County Road 551 west for eight miles.

Fox Park (906/753-4582), seven miles north of Cedar River, has a 25-site primitive campground that rarely fills along with a nice sandy beach. The more popular **Fuller Park** (906/786-1020), nine miles north, has 25 modern sites, a sandy beach, a bathhouse, a boat launch, and access to the Bark River.

River Park Campground (502 5th Ave., 906/863-5101, www.cityofmenominee.org, $20-30) offers several amenities but has one significant drawback—it's located behind a Kmart. Otherwise, the modern campground's 58 sites are clean, with paved parking pads

and a playground. You'll also be within walking distance of a coin laundry. This is the exception rather than the norm; in Michigan's Upper Peninsula, most people come to find a campsite within walking distance of absolutely nothing at all.

INFORMATION AND SERVICES

Perhaps the most important piece of information (or at least the one plenty of travelers forget) is that Menominee County is in the central time zone, the same as Wisconsin. Most of the Upper Peninsula and the entire Lower Peninsula are in the eastern time zone. When traveling between Menominee and Escanaba, set your watch forward an hour when heading north to Escanaba, and back an hour when driving south. Most cell phones and GPS-enabled devices will reset automatically.

For visitor information, contact the **Marinette-Menominee Area Chamber of Commerce** (601 Marinette Ave., Marinette, 906/863-2679, www.marinettechamber.com).

Menominee banks include two **Wells Fargo** locations (M&M Plaza, 906/863-5523; 962 1st St., 906/863-5515, www.wellsfargo. com) with ATMs; **Stephenson National Bank and Trust** (1111 10th St., 906/863-2526, www.snbt.com); and **First National Bank and Trust** (3805 10th St., 906/863-7861, www.fnbimk.com).

The closest hospital is Marinette's **Bay Area Medical Center** (3100 Shore Dr., 715/735-4200 or 888/788-2070, www.bamc. org) in Wisconsin. Take U.S. 41 south to Main Street and turn left, then go right on Shore Drive for 1.5 miles.

GETTING THERE AND AROUND
Car

Menominee is located on the border of Michigan and Wisconsin, across the river from Marinette. Take U.S. 41 from the north or south into town, or drive along the Green Bay coast south from Escanaba on M-35.

Boat

The **Menominee Marina** (906/863-8498, www.michigan.gov/dnr) has 20 transient slips and a whopping 243 seasonal slips. Open mid-May through mid-October, the marina has restrooms and showers, gasoline, laundry, and a picnic area with tables and grills. Contact the harbormaster on channel 22 or 16. Menominee Marina is located at 45°06.21 N, 87°35.58 W.

Air

The airport that's most accessible to Menominee is the small **Delta County Airport** (ESC, 3300 Airport Rd., 906/786-4902, www.deltacountymi.org) near Escanaba, served by Delta Airlines from Detroit. You can rent a car from **Alamo Car Rental** (3300 Airport Rd., 906/786-0603, www.nationalcar.com).

Bus

Bus service to Menominee is provided from Green Bay, Ironwood, Marquette, St. Ignace, Green Bay, Chicago, and Detroit by **Indian Trails** (800/292-3831, www.indiantrails.com).

The Superior Upland

The western interior is largely defined by its austere, beautiful land.
Known as the Superior Upland, this por-
tion of the peninsula is filled with rocky crags, rugged landscape, and old-growth forest. In short, it's the wildest region

of an already remote destination. Here the eastern U.P.'s flat and tame landscape gives way to the Porcupine Mountains, roaring streams, and pristine forests.

Gogebic County and the region surrounding Ironwood are known as the Big Snow Country, with the U.P.'s top destinations for downhill skiing. Though Michigan's "mountains" don't reach 2,000 feet, the resorts at Bessemer and Wakefield make for some of the best skiing between the Mississippi and the Alleghenies. Summertime visitors can enjoy the region's numerous waterfalls and hiking trails.

The Porcupine Mountains, or the Porkies, as they're affectionately known, are among the oldest highland ranges in the United States. Bring your hiking boots. Much of the Porkies—particularly the 85 miles of trails in Porcupine Mountains Wilderness State Park—are only accessible on foot. If you're looking for old-growth hemlock, rustic

cabins, remote backpacking—plus fishing, canoeing, or camping—this is surely the place for you.

PLANNING YOUR TIME

The western U.P. is made for rugged isolation during the summers. In winter, it's where you'll find the best of Michigan's downhill skiing. Plan on two or three days to explore—and longer for ski trips or backcountry hiking. No matter the season, you'll want to set some time aside for the Porkies. Speaking of time, be mindful of the time change in the four Michigan counties (Gogebic, Iron, Dickinson, and Menominee) that border Wisconsin and are in the central time zone, one hour earlier than the rest of Michigan's eastern time zone.

HISTORY

This corner of the Upper Peninsula traces its heritage to iron. You can see it reflected in the town names: Iron Mountain, Iron River,

---

Previous: paddling on Lake of the Clouds; downtown Crystal Falls. **Above:** Ontonagon Lighthouse.

Look for ★ to find recommended
sights, activities, dining, and lodging.

Highlights

© AVALON TRAVEL

★ **IXL Museum:** This museum recreates the office environment of the Wisconsin Land & Lumber Co., a giant of the timber industry during the late 19th and early 20th centuries. It's probably the most realistic historic site you'll ever visit (page 108).

★ **Piers Gorge:** Here you'll find the ultimate wilderness river: rugged, tranquil, and picturesque, with rolling rapids to boot (page 109).

★ **Iron County Heritage Trail:** With the Iron County Historical Museum as its centerpiece, this fun string of attractions is a great destination for anyone interested in the area's iron mining past (page 114).

★ **Sylvania Wilderness and Recreation Area:** Over these 20,000 acres of land, you'll find 36 crystalline glacial lakes and endless opportunities for recreation (page 116).

★ **Bond Falls:** Don't miss one of the Upper Peninsula's most beautiful waterfalls (page 120).

★ **Little Girl's Point:** At this dramatic spot high on a bluff over Lake Superior, you'll find a spectacular view of both the lake and the mountains (page 124).

★ **Copper Peak:** Even if you're not here to ski off the highest artificial jump in the world, this is a great spot to enjoy spellbinding views (page 124).

★ **Downhill Skiing:** The immense snowfalls of the western Upper Peninsula make the Superior Upland the finest destination for downhill skiers between the Rockies and the Appalachians (page 127).

★ **Porcupine Mountains Wilderness State Park:** Virgin forest, Lake Superior shoreline, and miles of trails make the Porkies a rugged, secluded paradise that's perfect for getting away from the crowd (page 130).

The Superior Upland

N

0   15 mi

0   15 km

Apostle Islands National Lakeshore

122

182

Superior Falls

Hurley

51

Ironwood

J

W

Bessemer

Wakefield

28

H

M

M

51

B

M

B

45

70

W I S C O N S I N

73

189

70

C

U

N

8

N

141

Kingsford

Iron Mountain

Norway

8

141

2

Hermansville

Escanaba River State Forest
© AVALON TRAVEL

Sturgeon River

IXL MUSEUM

M I C H I G A N

State Forest

Pier Gorge

Montreal River

Black River

505

BIG POWDERHORN MTN

DOWNHILL SKIING

INDIANHEAD

BLACKJACK

64

2

Isle River

Presque Isle River

Lake Gogebic State Park

64

Lake Gogebic

Bergland

64

SYLVANIA WILDERNESS AND RECREATION AREA

Clark Lake

Crooked Lake

Watersmeet

45

Lake Ottawa Recreation Area

Lake Ottawa

73

Iron River

Caspian

189

Bewabic State Park

2

IRON COUNTY HERITAGE TRAIL

Amasa

Crystal Falls

69

95

Menominee River

Michigamme Reservoir

141

Bond Falls Flowage

BOND FALLS

Paulding

PAULDING MYSTERY LIGHT

Agate Falls

Kenton

National

28

Sidnaw

TRIANGLE RANCH

Eastern Time Zone
Central Time Zone

141

Ottawa

Sturgeon River Gorge Wilderness Area

141

Three Lakes

Michigamme River

Republic

Lake Michigamme

95

28

Escanaba River

Ishpeming

Negaunee

41

Champion

41

WISCONSIN
MICHIGAN

Little Girls Point

Copper Peak

COPPER PEAK

Sandstone Falls

Chippewa Falls

Algonquin Falls

513

519

Summit Peak

Porcupine Mts

Mirror Lake

LAKE OF THE CLOUDS OVERLOOK

107

PORCUPINE MOUNTAINS WILDERNESS STATE PARK

Silver City

64

SOUTH BOUNDARY ROAD

Ontonagon

45

Rockland

Ontonagon River

26

To Keweenaw Peninsula

Sturgeon River

41

L'Anse

Loon Lake

Craig Lake

Crooked Lake

White Deer Lake

Yellow Dog River

Huron Mts

Big Bayou

Lake Independence

Marquette

Lake Superior

Keweenaw Bay

Lake Superior

Ski Brule

SKI BRULE

Sturgeon River

Ironwood, National Mine, Mineral Hills. You see it in the faces of the residents, descendants of immigrant mine workers from Scandinavia, Italy, and Cornwall.

Federal surveyors first discovered iron ore in 1844 near present-day Iron River. As workers systematically surveyed this unfamiliar land recently acquired by Michigan, their compasses swung wildly near Negaunee, where iron ore was so plentiful it was visible on the surface, intertwined in the roots of a fallen tree. That tree is the official symbol of the city of Negaunee. The symbol became both literal and metaphorical, as the fortunes of the community became intertwined with the rise and fall of the iron industry.

Apart from a handful of small mining operations, the potential wealth of the Upper Peninsula's iron deposits remained largely untapped for decades until the nation's ever-expanding web of railroad lines reached the area. In the 1870s, the arrival of the railroad prompted the development of the first major mines. World War II and its insatiable demand for iron forced area mines to maintain peak production, driving some to depletion. By the 1960s and 1970s, the western U.P. iron industry had grown quiet, after producing nearly two billion tons of ore. All underground iron mines in the U.P. were closed by 1978, casualties of foreign steelmaking and newer manufacturing methods that relied more on plastics.

Iron Mountain and Vicinity

Iron Mountain lacks the glamour of a typical tourist destination. You need to look a little harder here: The surrounding forest is beautiful, and the area's long heritage of logging and mining yield a trove of compelling historical sites.

Iron Mountain was first settled in about 1880 when vast deposits of iron were discovered underfoot. The Chapin Mine, located near present-day U.S. 2 and Kent Avenue on the north end of downtown, boosted the town's population to almost 8,000 by 1890. Italians were among the numerous groups of European immigrants working at the Chapin Mine. Italian neighborhoods still thrive today around the mine on Iron Mountain's north side, evidenced by the tempting array of Italian restaurants and corner markets.

The city's long-abandoned mines still serve an important role, however—as a magnet for brown bats. An estimated two million bats winter in the Millie Mine shaft, protected from predators while able to enter and exit freely due to the bat-friendly grates installed at the mine entrance. As the weather turns cool in the fall, the bats congregate all around Iron Mountain, creating an amazing sight, before returning to the mine.

While iron mining formed the backbone of the local economy, Henry Ford added some measure of diversification in the 1920s when he bought up huge tracts of nearby forest and built his first company sawmill on land southwest of town, which he dubbed Kingsford, in honor of Iron Mountain's Ford dealer, Edward Kingsford. Soon Ford's Kingsford empire included the main plant for making floorboards for the Model T, residences for workers, a refinery, and even a chemical plant to make newfangled charcoal briquettes. The businesses were eventually closed or sold, including the briquette plant, which relocated to Oakland, California, and has since been acquired by the Clorox Corporation, but which still manufactures the ever-popular Kingsford charcoal briquettes.

During World War II the facilities were devoted to the production of military hardware. The sawmill began building Waco CG-4A gliders for the Army Air Force, an indispensable tool during the Allied invasion of France.

Henry Ford's influence can also be found

Iron Mountain

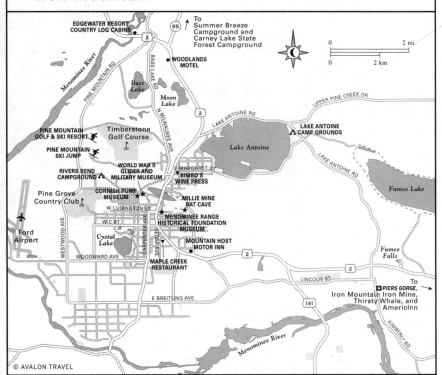

Map labels:
EDGEWATER RESORT COUNTRY LOG CABINS
95
To Summer Breeze Campground and Carney Lake State Forest Campground
2
Menominee River
PINE MOUNTAIN RD
BASS LAKE RD
WOODLANDS MOTEL
Bass Lake
Moon Lake
N MILWAUKEE AVE
2
LAKE ANTOINE RD
UPPER PINE CREEK DR
0 — 2 mi
0 — 2 km
PINE MOUNTAIN GOLF & SKI RESORT
Timberstone Golf Course
LAKE ANTOINE CAMP GROUNDS
Lake Antoine
LAKE ANTOINE RD
Fumee Lake
PINE MOUNTAIN SKI JUMP
RIVERS BEND CAMPGROUND
WORLD WAR II GLIDER AND MILITARY MUSEUM
E MARGARET ST
BIMBO'S WINE PRESS
Pine Grove Country Club
CORNISH PUMP MUSEUM
MILLIE MINE BAT CAVE
W LUDINGTON ST
MENOMINEE RANGE HISTORICAL FOUNDATION MUSEUM
WESTWOOD AVE
W C ST
CEDAR AVE
Ford Airport
Crystal Lake
MOUNTAIN HOST MOTOR INN
2
Fumee Falls
WOODWARD AVE
MAPLE CREEK RESTAURANT
LINCOLN ST
2
E BREITUNG AVE
141
To PIERS GORGE, Iron Mountain Iron Mine, Thirsty Whale, and AmericInn
KIMBERLY RD
Menominee River
© AVALON TRAVEL

in some surprising places. The local airport and main city park bear his name, and the nickname of the athletic teams at Kingsford High School is the "Flivvers," an early nickname for the Ford Model T. But perhaps the most telling example is a name Kingsford shares with Detroit: Both cities' main streets are named Woodward Avenue, while other major arteries sport names of Detroit counterparts: Cass, Hamilton, and Milwaukee.

SIGHTS
Iron Mountain Iron Mine

If you're going to spend any amount of time in Iron Mountain and the rest of the Superior Uplands, it's helpful to get a firsthand look at the mining industry that made the area

what it is today. You can't miss the **Iron Mountain Iron Mine** (906/563-8077, www. ironmountainironmine.com, 9am-5pm daily Memorial Day-mid-Oct., $15 adults, $10 ages 6-12, free under age 6) in Vulcan, nine miles east of Iron Mountain. Big John, a towering two-dimensional miner with a pickax in his hands, welcomes westbound motorists on U.S. 2. The 40-minute tour takes visitors 400 feet below the surface on a 0.5-mile journey. Outfitted in rain slickers and hard hats, visitors board an underground train to learn about the history and process of mining, including equipment demonstrations. You'll get set up for the tour in the gift shop, where you can also browse rock and mineral samples.

★ IXL Museum

A lot of museums bill themselves as a "step back in time," but you truly feel it at the **IXL Museum** (5551 River St. N., Hermansville, 906/498-2498, www.hermansville.com, 12:30pm-4pm Thurs.-Sun. Memorial Day-Labor Day, donation) in downtown Hermansville, 28 miles east of Iron Mountain. For more than a century, this wood-frame building served as the northern office of the Wisconsin Land & Lumber Company, which in the 1860s began building doors and window sashes in central Wisconsin. After the Great Chicago Fire of 1871, founder C. J. L. Meyer moved north to tap into the vast pine reserves of the Upper Peninsula. He built the Hermansville office and adjacent sawmill in 1881. IXL stands for "I excel," and was used as a logo on all the company's products.

Today, the preserved IXL building exists in a time warp and is one of the most fascinating museums in the Upper Peninsula; the Dictaphones, mimeograph machine, and payroll records are all still here, as if you'd stepped into the office on a weekend when everyone was off-duty. The second floor, which was originally apartments for Meyer and his family, now displays more historic documents and an assortment of machinery from the logging days. When Meyer expanded the business into Michigan, he came up with an ingenious invention: tongue-and-groove flooring, precision-milled in one operation. The Hermansville operation quickly became the largest flooring plant in the country, crafting the floors for notable clients that included the main Mormon temple in Salt Lake City and Yellowstone National Park's main lodge. At its peak, it held 30 million board feet of lumber in its yards and operated three railroads to handle the ever-increasing shipments.

Cornish Pump and Mining Museum

Iron Mountain's Chapin Mine once led Menominee Range mining production, but it was also one of the wettest mines ever

Big John welcomes visitors to the Iron Mountain Iron Mine.

worked. In 1893, an immense steam-operated pump, a 54-foot-high, 725-ton behemoth and the largest in the world at the time, was put into service. Electric pumps replaced it just 20 years later. The pump is on display at the Menominee Range Historical Foundation's **Cornish Pump and Mining Museum** (300 Kent St., Iron Mountain, 906/774-1086, www.menomineemuseum.com, 9am-5pm Mon.-Sat., noon-4pm Sun. Memorial Day-Labor Day, $5 adults, $4.50 seniors, $3 ages 10-18, free under age 10), one block east of U.S. 2 in downtown Iron Mountain. Along with the impressive pump, this comprehensive museum includes a good-size collection of mining equipment, photos, and period clothing as well as a small theater.

World War II Glider and Military Museum

Adjacent to the pump museum is the **World War II Glider and Military Museum** (302 Kent St., Iron Mountain, 906/774-1086, www.menomineemuseum.com, 9am-5pm

Mon.-Sat., noon-4pm Sun. Memorial Day-Labor Day, $8 adults, $7 seniors, $4 ages 10-18, free under age 10), which shares the fascinating story of the Waco World War II glider. The museum also contains some small military planes and displays of uniforms and equipment.

Combination tickets for the two adjacent museums is $11 adults, $10 seniors, $4 ages 10-18. Tickets for the two museums plus the Menominee Range Historical Museum are $15 adults, $12 seniors, $6 ages 10-18.

Menominee Range Historical Museum

The Menominee Range Historical Foundation's other museum, the **Menominee Range Historical Museum** (300 E. Ludington St., 906/774-4276, www.menomineemuseum.com, 11am-3pm Tues.-Fri. June-Labor Day, call for hours Labor Day-mid-Oct., $5 adults, $4 seniors, $3 ages 10-18, free under age 10), provides an overview of the area's history from the 1800s on. More than 100 exhibits are housed in the town's former Carnegie Library, most of them focusing on the everyday life of those who lived in the Menominee Iron Range. You can visit a Victorian parlor, a livery stable, an interactive general store, and much, much more. There's also a historical archive available for research.

Badwater Ski-Ters Water Ski Show

Although it's located in Wisconsin, a trip to **Badwater Ski-Ters Water Ski Show** (www.exploringthenorth.com) at Vagabond Park is definitely worthwhile. Located on the Menominee River, just five miles west of Iron Mountain, this world-class and nationally renowned water-ski team performs jumps, trick and barefoot skiing, and the pyramid. In 2015 the team took first place in the national jump team championship competition. Best of all, the shows are free. Catch the Ski-Ters at 6pm Wednesday and Sunday and on a few Saturday nights mid-June through late-August. Take

U.S. 2/141 west from Iron Mountain and look for the signs.

Millie Mine Bat Cave

While bats are often perceived as a bit creepy, there's something impressive about the million-plus bats that spend winters in the abandoned mine shaft of **Millie Mine Bat Cave.** Bats have free access to the mine through a grate, which was constructed to prevent people from falling several hundred feet to the floor of the mine shaft. The mine's constant 40°F temperature makes it ideal for the bats, which can be viewed entering or leaving the mine each spring (late Apr.-early May) and autumn (Aug.-Sept.). The best viewing time is at dusk. Take Park Street north from U.S. 2 east until you get to the marked viewing area. All seven viewing sites are listed at www.michigan.gov/dnr, the website of Michigan's Department of Natural Resources (DNR).

★ Piers Gorge

Where the U.P. isn't bordered by lakes, it's bounded by rivers: The grand Menominee rambles from near Iron Mountain all the way to Lake Michigan's Green Bay, forming nearly half the Wisconsin-Michigan boundary. Just south of Norway, it narrows through **Piers Gorge,** a pretty run of frothing white water and waterfalls. In the mid-1800s, loggers relied on the Menominee to float logs to the river's mouth; they cursed this stretch of river for the logjams it caused, and they built a series of wooden piers in an attempt to slow the current and channel the flow—hence the name. To view the gorge, follow U.S. 8 south from Norway and turn right on Piers Gorge Road just before you cross the river into Wisconsin. Follow the road about 0.5 miles until it ends at a trail. Along the one-mile trail, you'll be treated to several views of the gorge that become progressively more dramatic, some as high as 70 feet. There are several side trails of varying degrees of safety, some of which wind down to the river, but views of each of the falls can be enjoyed from the main trail. This is not a good choice for small children or those with physical limitations, since there are several narrow passes and steep drop-offs.

FESTIVALS AND EVENTS

Pine Mountain Music Festival

The **Pine Mountain Music Festival** (906/482-1542, www.pmmf.org), an annual summer event since 1991, has a lineup of opera, symphony, and chamber music performances that take place across the region at venues in Marquette, Houghton, Munising, and Iron Mountain. In 2017 folk singer-songwriter and native son Joshua Davis, a finalist on the NBC's *The Voice,* featured prominently in the schedule. The festival also features a special concert series called UPStarts!, a platform for emerging musicians from the Upper Peninsula.

SUMMER SPORTS AND RECREATION

Hiking and Biking

The trails that encircle the large lake at **Fumee Lake Natural Area** (www.fumeelakes.org) give hikers the chance to see plenty of natural beauty, still untouched by motorized vehicles and development. There are five miles of shoreline and more than 500 acres of water in Fumee Lake and Little Fumee Lake. Choose among loops of one, two, or seven miles. Each offers different views of the lakes and wildlife. Bring your camera and a pair of binoculars. Fumee Lake Natural Area is located east of Iron Mountain, near Norway. Take Upper Pine Creek Road north of U.S. 2.

Canoeing and Kayaking

Only experienced white-water kayakers who can handle Class III and IV rapids should consider running the **Menominee River.** The narrow canyon walls of Piers Gorge produce some of the Midwest's most thrilling and difficult white water. For an easy paddle on the nearby Brule or Pine Rivers, contact **Northwoods Wilderness Outfitters** (N4088 Pine Mountain Rd., Iron Mountain, 906/774-9009, www.northwoodsoutfitters. com). This excellent shop will set you up for an afternoon or an extended trip, with canoe and kayak rentals as well as drop-off and pickup service.

Fishing

Even though Lakes Michigan and Superior don't border the Iron Mountain region, the abundance of inland lakes offer plenty of great fishing. Try **Bass Lake** near the Wisconsin

rapids on Piers Gorge

border, north of Iron Mountain and two miles west of U.S. 2, or larger **Lake Antoine,** four miles north of Iron Mountain (take U.S. 2 to Lake Antoine Rd.). **Carney Lake** is a little farther away, 16 miles northeast of Iron Mountain on M-95 and Merriman Truck Trail, but it has over 100 acres and includes a boat launch and rustic campgrounds to make it worth the drive. For more sites and advice on fishing the area's rivers, contact the **Dickinson Area Partnership** (800/236-2447, www.ironmountain.org).

Off-Road Vehicles

After the mining and logging industries petered out, they left behind a vast network of unpaved roads, making the backcountry around Iron Mountain perfect for off-roading. There are also nearly 30 miles of ORV routes on the **Norway Trail.** Take County Road 573 east of Norway to Norway Truck Trail, then go north to the parking area, or take Foster City Road several miles north of U.S. 2 in Waucedah.

Golf

The **Pine Grove Country Club** (1520 W. Hughitt St., Iron Mountain, 906/774-3493, http://pinegrovecc.org, $54 for 18 holes Mon.-Fri., $64 Sat.-Sun., cart $18) has been around for more than 100 years, but the semiprivate course's elegant new clubhouse is only about a decade old. There is limited play time for nonmembers: any time Monday, before noon Thursday and Friday, and after 11am Saturday and Sunday.

You'll have a better choice of tee times at **Oak Crest Golf Course** (N1475 U.S. 8, 906/563-5891, www.oakcrestgolf.com, $25-27 for 9 holes, $42-45 for 18 holes) in Norway. The 18 holes are surrounded by oak trees, which gives the course both a naturally stately feel as well as its name. You can also play at **TimberStone Golf Club** (N3332 Pine Mountain Rd., 906/776-0111, www. pinemountainresort.com, $79-99 for 18 holes), part of Pine Mountain Resort. The course's 18 holes are set on 240 wooded acres, certified a

five-star course by *Golf Digest* magazine; of 6,000 courses nationwide, only 24 are in this category. Playing can be pricey, but look for package deals that combine lodging and golf.

Waterfalls

You'll find a couple of waterfalls in the area, although they aren't the Upper Peninsula's most dramatic. The pretty but small **Fumee Falls** has minimal water flow but is very easy to get to. A trail and viewing platform just off U.S. 2, just east of Iron Mountain, allow you to see the 20-foot cascade fairly easily. The **Sturgeon Falls Dam,** not to be confused with Sturgeon Falls, isn't quite as accessible, but it's worth a visit. The falls are 3.5 miles south of Loretto on the Menominee River.

WINTER SPORTS AND RECREATION
Ski and Snowshoe Trails

Perhaps the most appealing feature about **Fumee Lake Natural Area** is its year-round accessibility. The summer hiking trails transition nicely into cross-country ski and snowshoe pathways during the long and intense Upper Peninsula winters. There are loops of varying distance and difficulty, all wonderfully isolated from the nearby towns. An excellent example is the **Upper Pine Creek Road,** north of U.S. 2, a few miles west of Norway and east of Iron Mountain. Also, the **Merriman East Pathway,** some 13 miles northeast of Iron Mountain on M-95 at Merriman Road, has nearly 10 miles of trails that make for pleasant cross-country skiing.

Downhill Skiing

Although Michigan's biggest and best ski resorts are farther west in the Ironwood area, the Iron Mountain region holds its own with two downhill ski resorts—plus a little something extra. **Pine Mountain Resort** (N3332 Pine Mountain Rd., 906/774-2747, www. pinemountainresort.com, $35-45 adults, $31-37 ages 13-17, $15-25 under age 13), in Iron Mountain, has multilevel skiing and lighted nighttime runs, two terrain parks, and a half pipe. But that pales in comparison to the **Pine Mountain Ski Jump** (N3330 Pine Mountain Rd., 800/236-2447, www.kiwanisskiclub.com), a towering 175-foot-tall scaffold with a run of 380 feet. There's an international competition here that draws 20,000 people each year to the world's largest artificial ski jump; the current Pine Mountain record is a 468-foot jump by Austria's Stefan Kaiser.

Snowmobiling

More than 120 miles of snowmobile trails cross Dickinson County, connecting to trails throughout the U.P. and northern Wisconsin. Iron Mountain and Norway are connected by a trail that skirts Fumee Lake (you can take it east toward Escanaba), while Trail 5 will take you north toward Marquette and Lake Superior.

FOOD

Italian is the way to go if you're eating out in Iron Mountain. Homemade ravioli, slow-roasted pork, Italian sausage, Roma red sauce—you'll find it all in the town's unassuming Italian eateries. **Bimbo's Wine Press** (314 E. Main St., Iron Mountain, 906/774-8420, 9am-10pm Wed.-Sat., around $8) serves hearty Italian sandwiches like porketta and Italian hot beef for incredibly reasonable prices. Except for the thin-crust pizzas, **Famers** (N3332 Pine Mountain Rd., Iron Mountain, 906/774-2747, www.pinemountainresort.com, 7am-9pm Sun.-Thurs., 7am-10pm Fri.-Sat., dinner entrées $13-24) is the place to go when you're looking for something a bit less Italian. Part of Pine Mountain Resort, Famers is a sports bar complete with good appetizers, five TVs, cocktails, and big steaks, and is the perfect place to catch the big game.

For good hearty fare (try the half-pound burger), head to the ★ **Thirsty Whale Bar and Grill** (825 Murray Rd./U.S. 2, Norway, 906/563-5466, lunch and dinner Mon.-Sat., $8-20), west of town. Friday nights feature a tempting fish fry. A good choice for families is the **Maple Creek Restaurant** (1052 S. Stephenson Ave., Iron Mountain, 906/774-1777, www.maplecreekim.com, 6am-9pm Mon.-Sat., 6am-8pm Sun., breakfast $7-10, lunch and dinner entrées $12-17), where you'll find satisfying family-style fare at moderate prices.

ACCOMMODATIONS

Look for standard chain motels in downtown Iron Mountain. The ★ **Pine Mountain Resort** (N3332 Pine Mountain Rd., Iron Mountain, 877/553-7463, www.pinemountainresort.com, lodge rooms $70-90, condos $200-260) anchors a full-service ski and golf resort on the northwest side of town, complete with a dining room, indoor and outdoor pools, a sauna, tennis courts, and hiking and mountain biking trails.

Just off U.S. 2, the ★ **Edgewater Resort** (N4128 U.S. 2, Iron Mountain, 800/236-6244, www.edgewaterresort.com, $505-790 weekly) makes the most of its fine setting overlooking the Menominee River, with 10 log cabins scattered across its grounds, along with a picnic area, a playground, a volleyball court, and canoes and fishing boats for rent. One-, two-, and three-bedroom cabins with kitchens rent by the week but can sometimes be rented by the day; pets are permitted. The resort also offers wireless Internet, laundry facilities, a playground for children, and a boat for fishing. Either a Michigan or Wisconsin license is valid for fishing on the Menominee.

The **Mountain Host Motor Inn** (1451 S. Stephenson Ave., Iron Mountain, 906/776-0700, $52-80) is a reasonably priced motor lodge that offers some unusual amenities. Each room is equipped with a fax modem in addition to wireless Internet, plus hair dryers and in-room cable TV with movies. The motel offers an exercise room with a sauna and tanning bed, a copy service for the business traveler, and daily continental breakfast.

The **Woodlands Motel** (N3957 U.S. 2, Iron Mountain, near M-25, 906/774-6106, reservations 800/394-5505, $68-95) is a classic mom-and-pop operation. Each of the 19 clean and comfortable rooms has a kitchenette, queen beds, and wireless Internet access. There's a playground for kids, and as an extra bonus for winter vacationers, it's close to the area's snowmobile trails.

In Norway, you'll love the comfort and serenity of the ★ **AmericInn** (W6002 U.S. 2, Norway, 906/563-7500 or 800/634-3444, www.americinnofnorway.com, $80-120) at the end of a long day's drive. The rustic feel of the lobby and the soothing water of the hot tub will easy your tension and recharge your batteries for the next day. AmericInn offers complimentary continental breakfast, a cocktail lounge, and a pool with a dry sauna. All rooms are nonsmoking.

Camping

Carney Lake State Forest Campground (906/875-3324, www.michigan.gov/dnr, $13) has 16 rustic sites suitable for tents and trailers. There are no showers or laundry, but you will find vaulted toilets and clean water from the campground's hand pump. The sites are first-come, first-served and fill quickly in summer high season. The fishing is excellent. Take M-95 north of Iron Mountain and head east on Merriman Truck Trail.

Summer Breeze Campground (W8576 Twin Falls Rd., 906/774-7701, www.summerbreezecampground.com, May-Oct. 15, tents $20, hookups $28-32, weekly and seasonal rates available) represents "upscale" camping—amenity-rich, busy, and plenty of room for even the largest RVs. Beyond the hot showers and a camp store are a heated swimming pool, DVD rentals, Wi-Fi, and a book exchange. There are fire rings and tables at every site. The 70 campsites are grassy and shaded, 28 with full hookups and 42 with water and electricity. There is also a cabin with electricity but no running water that rents for $45 per night. Take M-95 North to Twin Falls Road and turn left.

You can also find campsites at **Lake Antoine Park** (N3393 Lake Antoine Rd., 906/774-8875, $29) and **Rivers Bend Campground** (N3905 Pine Mountain Rd., 906/779-1171, $29). Both are modern

campgrounds offering sites with or without electricity. Also available are flush toilets, showers, and potable water. Both operate from Memorial Day through Labor Day. For reservations, call the County Parks Office (906/774-8875).

INFORMATION AND SERVICES

For information on Iron Mountain and the surrounding area, contact the **Tourism Association of the Dickinson County Area** (600 S. Stephenson Ave., 800/236-2447, www.ironmountain.org). Also remember that Iron Mountain is in the central time zone, an hour earlier than most of the Upper Peninsula.

If medical attention is necessary, the **Dickinson County Hospital** (1721 S. Stephenson Ave., Iron Mountain, 906/774-1313, www.dchs.org) is located on U.S. 2/141 heading southeast from town. In addition to a few local banks, **Wells Fargo** (www.wellsfargo.com) has locations both in Iron Mountain (1805 S. Stephenson Ave., 906/774-0930) and north in Crystal Falls (1352 U.S. 2, 906/875-6651).

GETTING THERE AND AROUND
Car

Iron Mountain is located on Michigan's border with Wisconsin, at the intersection of two major highways. Driving into town from the east, take U.S. 2, which is U.S. 2 and U.S. 141 when you come from the west. North from Wisconsin or south from other parts of the U.P., U.S. 141 leads into town. Take U.S. 2/141 north to Crystal Falls, U.S. 2 east to Norway, and U.S. 2 west to Iron River.

Air

There are a few nearby options for flying to Iron Mountain. **Ford Airport** (IMT, 500 Riverhills Rd., Kingsford, 906/774-4870, www.fordairport.org) in Kingsford has flights on Delta Airlines from Minneapolis and Detroit. Car rentals are offered by Avis (www.avis.com). If you arrive by air, a car will be an absolute necessity during your stay.

Delta County Airport (ESC, 3300 Airport Rd., Escanaba, 906/786-4902, www.deltacountymi.org), a small airport just southwest of Escanaba, has flights from Detroit on Delta. You can rent a car from **Alamo** (3300 Airport Rd., 906/786-0603, www.alamo.com).

Sawyer International Airport (MQT, 125 G Ave., Gwinn, 906/346-3308, www.sawyerairport.com), has daily American Eagle flights from Chicago, and Delta has daily flights from Detroit and Minneapolis. You'll find major car rental agencies, including **Alamo** (906/462-5266), **Avis** (906/346-6398), **Budget** (906/372-9240), **Dollar** (906/346-4355), **Hertz** (906/346-4355), **National** (906/346-6378), and **Thrifty** (906/346-4355). Sawyer is just south of Marquette and about two hours' drive from Iron Mountain, but with more regular flights, it can be the easier option.

Bus

Iron Mountain is served by the **Indian Trails** (800/292-3831, www.indiantrails.com) bus line.

Taxi

For taxi service, call **Tri-City Cab** (906/774-7878).

Iron River and the Ottawa National Forest

Iron County's population centers around **Iron River,** an iron mining center, and **Crystal Falls,** the picturesque county seat 15 miles east. Both retain their small-town charm. Like Iron Mountain, Iron River is just a simple town to pass through while on your way to some great skiing or backwoods campsites. Still, it makes for a quaint visit and a convenient stop.

The real draw to the region is the **Ottawa National Forest.** Sprawling on nearly 100,000 acres, the Ottawa National Forest blankets much of the western peninsula from the Wisconsin border to U.S. 141, which runs north from Iron River. The Ottawa National Forest doesn't have contiguous boundaries but rather is a patchwork of protected lands overlaying towns, private property, and various state parks and forests.

Named for the indigenous Ottawa people who lived and traded in this region (although they actually populated the eastern half of the U.P. in greater numbers), the Ottawa National Forest encompasses more than 400 lakes, seven major river systems, some of the U.P.'s most spectacular waterfalls, 27 campgrounds, and three wilderness areas: Sylvania, the Sturgeon River gorge, and the McCormick Tract.

SIGHTS
★ Iron County Heritage Trail

There are 12 stops along the Iron County Heritage Trail (www.ironheritage.org), a path of historic places scattered throughout the county. You won't find a lot of dramatic lighting and fancy display cases at the **Iron County Historical Museum** (100 Brady Ave., Caspian, 906/265-2617, www.ironcountyhistoricalmuseum.org, 10am-4pm Mon.-Sat. Memorial Day-Labor Day, noon-4pm Mon.-Sat. Sept., by appointment Oct.-Memorial Day, $10 adults, $5 ages 5-18, free under age 5), two miles south of U.S. 2 off M-189 in Caspian. What you will find is an interesting, appealing, and eclectic blend of local history and culture at this rambling, funky, and homegrown museum. Located on the site of the once productive Caspian iron mine—the mine's rusting head frame still looms over the complex—it survives largely on the admission fees, donations, and plenty of volunteer labor. In the main building, displays cover Native American history, logging, mining, sporting equipment, and kitchenware from the early 1900s. The perennial favorite display is the mechanized iron mine and railroad model: for a nickel, a miniature ore skip hauls rocks to the surface and loads them on the railroad.

Other displays not to miss: the Mining Memorial, with a database of area mines and miners along with a video of life in the mines; a 3-D acrylic mine diagram that will enable to appreciate the depths of the mine, precisely where the ore has been extracted, and where it remains. You'll also see a 50-foot-long diorama of a logging camp, complete with hundreds of folk-art figures by local artist William Monogal; newspaper clippings on Iron River's 1920 "rum rebellion," when federal agents from Chicago stormed the home of the priest and discovered eight barrels of rum, only to be condemned by the county prosecutor. Topping it off is an exhibit depicting the history of the local labor movement, which helped boost miners' earnings from $365 per year in 1931 to $1,886 per year a decade later.

Outside, several relocated buildings occupy the grounds. One is a streetcar barn that includes the actual car that once traveled between the mines in Caspian and Iron River.

Head to Crystal Falls for a look at the small-town life of miners at the turn of the 20th century. Tour the **Harbour House Museum** (906/875-4341, www.crystalfallsmuseum-harbourhouse.org, guided tours 10am-2pm Thurs.-Sat. or by appointment June-Aug., $2 adults, $5 families), a restored Queen Anne colonial revival home that houses a two-story museum, complete with authentic furnishings and decorations and several exhibits displaying regional artifacts. The first floor contains a music room, library, and dining room, all preserved to look as they did in the early 1900s. Five exhibit rooms on the second floor celebrate the area's mining heritage.

Visit **Mile Post Zero and Treaty Tree** as well; as you might expect, this spot is simply a mile marker and a tree, but its historical significance is certainly noteworthy. The site marks the precise location of the survey point that set the boundary between Michigan and Wisconsin in 1840. To get here, follow M-73 west of Iron River until you come to Ottawa Lake Road and turn right. Continue to West Brule Lake Road, and proceed west until you arrive at the Stateline Picnic Grounds. Follow the trail signs until you come to the marker, which is about a 0.5-mile hike.

Other sites on the Iron County Heritage Trail include a museum, the county courthouse, and a pioneer church. Contact **Friends of the Heritage Trail** (906/875-6642, www.ironheritage.org) for maps and additional information.

Triangle Ranch

Much of the U.P. is dotted with ghost towns, but **Triangle Ranch** may be its only ghost farm. In the 1920s, a developer had grand plans for some of Iron County's clear-cut logging land. He purchased nearly 10,000 acres and built pens, corrals, barns, and a rancher's home with the intention of raising beef cattle. The idea went bust after just one year—it proved too costly to care for the animals over the long U.P. winter. Most of the land was sold back to a pulp-and-paper company and has since been reforested, but the skeletons of the beef operation remain. Triangle Ranch remains on the Michigan state map; from Crystal Falls, take U.S. 141 north about 15 miles to the marked Triangle Ranch Road, which is a few miles north of Amasa. Follow the road east about one mile to the remains of the ranch.

Paulding Mystery Light

If inexplicable or supernatural happenings fascinate you, or if you don't believe in them but are simply curious, a fun evening pastime is visiting the **Paulding Mystery Light,** alternatively known as the Lights of the Paulding or the Dog Meadow Light, in Watersmeet. The small mysterious light reportedly appears in the distance almost every night. According to the sign at the site, "Legend explains its presence as a railroad brakeman's ghost, destined to remain forever at the site of his untimely death. He continually waves his signal lantern as a warning to all who come to visit." To get here, take U.S. 2 east of Iron River, then follow U.S. 45 about five miles north of Watersmeet to Robbins Pond Road—brown signs will help you find the way from there. Over the years several attempts have been made to explain this bizarre phenomenon, though none have proved conclusive.

★ Sylvania Wilderness and Recreation Area

Sylvania protects its assets well—36 crystalline glacial lakes hidden among thick stands of massive old-growth trees. Sylvania can be a truly magical place for anglers who dream of landing that once-in-a-lifetime smallmouth bass, paddlers who yearn to glide across deep quiet waters and along untrammeled shoreline, and hikers who want to travel under a towering canopy of trees and hear nothing more than the haunting whistle of a loon. This is nature's solitude at its very finest.

One of three wilderness areas within Ottawa National Forest, the **Sylvania Wilderness** (www.fs.fed.gov), near Watersmeet, stretches across 18,000 acres roughly bordered by U.S. 2 to the north, U.S. 45 to the east, and the Wisconsin border to the south. The adjacent **Sylvania Recreation Area** acts as a buffer, extending by an additional 3,000 acres this area of lakes and woodlands. There are a few modern services, including a drive-in campground, a nice beach, flush toilets, and running water.

Once viewed as just another tract of good timber, Sylvania's fate turned in the late 1890s, when A. D. Johnston, a lumberman from Wisconsin, purchased 80 acres near the south end of Clark Lake decided it was too lovely to cut, and instead kept it as his personal fishing retreat. Johnston invited his wealthy friends, some of whom were executives at

U.S. Steel, who were also captivated by the land. Together, they purchased several thousand additional acres and formed the private Sylvania Club.

Like other upscale U.P. "great camps," the Sylvania Club soon had grand log lodges along its shores, guards to keep trespassing anglers away from its bountiful lakes, and caretakers to squelch forest fires as they cropped up. Ownership shifted over the decades, and eventually it fell into the hands of Lawrence Fisher, one of the seven brothers of the famous Fisher Body Works, which eventually became part of General Motors. When he died, his heirs sold the property to the federal government for $5.7 million. It was operated as a recreation area from the late 1960s until 1987, when the bulk of it was converted to wilderness status.

We can partly thank old money for the condition of the land today. With most people previously barred from fishing here, Sylvania's lakes are now a paradise for anglers, especially those looking for smallmouth bass. Its waters remain pristine due to the lack of development and powerboat access, as well as the area's topography. Sylvania lies on the watershed divide between Lake Superior and the Mississippi, so it isn't exposed to runoff from nearby lands. And whatever your thoughts on fire management, Sylvania's decades of fire protection mean that visitors today can marvel at a virgin forest of white pines, hemlocks, maples, and basswood trees more than 200 years old.

Begin a trip to Sylvania with a call or visit to the **Ottawa National Forest Visitors Center** (906/358-4724), at the intersection of U.S. 2 and U.S. 45. The staff can help you with maps, regulations, campsite reservations, and other information. Sylvania's rules can be quite idiosyncratic, especially the fishing regulations. Take time to ask questions and read through the materials rangers provide. To reach Sylvania, follow U.S. 2 west about four miles from the visitors center and turn south on Thousand Island Lake Road. Travel about four miles, and follow the signs to reach the entrance building. All visitors are required to register on arrival.

The entrance is in the recreation area, near the drive-in campground on Clark Lake. If you intend to travel into the wilderness area, plan on treating your own water; you'll find water pumps only in the recreation area. Cooking stoves are encouraged as well to lessen the number of feet tramping through the forest in search of deadwood. During summer months, make sure you also have ample insect repellent or, better yet, a head net to combat mosquitoes and blackflies.

ENTERTAINMENT
Lac Vieux Desert Resort Casino

If you're looking for local U.P. gaming, you can find it at **Lac Vieux Desert Resort Casino** (N5384 U.S. 45, Watersmeet, 906/358-4226 or 800/583-3599, www.lvdcasino.com) in Watersmeet. It's a bit of a drive west on U.S. 2 and then north on U.S. 45, but it's worth the trip from Iron River. The 24-7 gaming room has more than 700 video and reel slots, roulette, blackjack, craps, bingo, a poker room, and plenty more gaming fun. Stop by the Thunderbird Sports Lounge for food, drinks, and free live entertainment every Friday and Saturday night until 1am. There's a snack bar for light fare and a restaurant with several buffets in addition to a full menu.

FESTIVALS AND EVENTS
Annual End of Summer Blues Fest

During the fourth weekend of August, head over to the tiny community of Alpha for its **Annual End of Summer Blues Fest** (888/879-4766, $15) presented by the Iron County Chamber of Commerce. The event features a Veterans Freedom Memorial Ride for both motorcycles and cars, followed by an afternoon blues concert. Alpha is located along County Road 424 just two miles off U.S. 2 and just southwest of Crystal Falls. If you're heading out from Crystal Falls, Take U.S. 2/141 south about three miles until you get to the County Road 424 turnoff. Make a right onto 424 and continue for about two miles.

Rodeo

One of the biggest events to hit Iron County is the annual **U.P. Championship Rodeo** (888/879-4766, www.upprorodeo.com), which has been hosting professional rodeo events since 1968. The rodeo is usually held during the third weekend of July. Popular events like steer wrestling, bull riding, and bareback riding, among others, continue to draw crowds for a good serving of Western-style fun.

SUMMER SPORTS AND RECREATION
Biking and Hiking

In the far south of the Ottawa National Forest, a few miles south of Iron River, the **Lake Ottawa Recreation Area** (Lake Ottawa Rd., 906/265-9259, www.fs.fed.us) has about nine miles of trails. One of the more popular is the primitive but nice Ge-Che Trail, which follows a 2.5-mile loop from the boat landing area. Try the two-mile Brennan Lake Loop too. The Lake Ottawa Recreation Area is listed as part of the Iron County Heritage Route. Hikers in search of a short, easy trail will find it at **Bewabic State Park** (1933 U.S. 2 W., Crystal Falls, 906/875-3324, www.michigan.gov/dnr), located just off U.S. 2 between Iron River and Crystal Mountain, closer to Crystal Mountain. The two-mile nature trail leads visitors from the campground to the day use area and back—expect to spend about an hour on the trail.

Sylvania Wilderness Area and Recreation Area maintains 15 miles of trails, including a seven-mile trail, marked with blue blazes, around Clark Lake. It provides access to campsites and trails to other lakes. Most of Sylvania's trails are old roads from its fishing camp days. While not always well marked, the trails are quite easy to follow. These same roads become a great **cross-country ski** network in the winter months.

Ottawa National Forest staff groom 15 miles of trails within Sylvania.

The marked and mapped **Pines and Mines** trail system gives a glimpse of the enticing opportunities for mountain biking in the western Upper Peninsula. A joint effort of local tourism and economic development groups, the Ottawa National Forest, and a local trail-access organization, Pines and Mines comprises some 200 miles of trails in three networks. Routes range from tame gravel roads to single-track trails deep in the woods. Many of the trails reveal stunning waterfalls, remote lakes, and historical landmarks.

Near Marenisco in Gogebic County, the **Pomeroy-Henry Lake Network** offers 100 miles of gentle biking on wide gravel roads around a national forest area peppered with small lakes. It's a good choice for families. The **Ehlco Network,** just south of Porcupine Mountains Wilderness State Park, includes more single-track deep in the forest on grass or dirt paths. This area can be wet, due to some lowlands and the work of local beavers, so avoid it after a rain. Perhaps the best of the three networks is the one located outside the national forest: the **Iron County (Wisconsin) System.** Trails radiating out of Hurley, Wisconsin, lead past waterfalls, large flowages, and old mining relics like the Plummer head frame near Pence, Wisconsin. Good interpretive signs help make sense of historic sites. Routes in this system range from gravel to single-track roads, though the map makes it difficult to distinguish between them. Single-track trails 6 and 13 are the best.

While the Pines and Mines trails are great, the map provided is mediocre. It's best to bring your own topographic map, and before you set out, get some local advice from Ottawa National Forest rangers or local bike shops such as **Hobby Wheel** (1435 E. Cloverland Dr., 906/932-3332) in Ironwood. Pick up a map at the Wisconsin or Michigan state information centers; both are on U.S. 2 near the border. You can also find maps at local bike shops or at the **Ottawa National Forest**

Headquarters (E6248 U.S. 2, Ironwood, 906/932-1330, www.fs.fed.us, 8am-4pm Mon.-Fri.) in Ironwood.

Canoeing and Kayaking

Seven major river systems flow within the Ottawa National Forest; a staggering total of 1,000 miles of navigable waters. Congress has designated more than 300 of those miles as "wild and scenic" or "recreational" rivers, protecting their pristine condition. In general, rivers like the Ontonagon and Presque Isle offer quiet water in their southern reaches, winding through relatively flat woodlands. North of M-28, they begin a more rugged descent through hills and bluffs, requiring more advanced skills and boats appropriate for white water. For strong paddlers with good white-water skills, these rivers offer some of the finest paddling in the Midwest.

Remember, however, that this can all change depending on rainfall and the time of year. Rivers that normally flow gently often become torrents in the spring. Always check with U.S. Forest Service officials before setting out. Also, the Forest Service distributes an extensive *River Digest,* a free publication that outlines navigable rivers, launch areas, liveries, in addition to high and low flow times. Pick one up at a district ranger office.

The three branches of the mighty Ontonagon spread across the western U.P. like a spiderweb; at times it seems every road you travel crosses one branch or another. While many parts of the river system are worth exploring, one spot gets particular attention: the upper reaches of the middle branch of the Ontonagon, where **Bond Falls** cascades down a series of black boulders.

Paddling is the best way to explore the **Sylvania Wilderness.** Most of the lakes are linked by water or by relatively easy portages, though there are a couple "grunt portages" of two miles or more. Many campsites are accessible only by water. Motors and other mechanized equipment are forbidden, including sailboats. The one exception is Crooked Lake, which allows electric motors of 4 hp or less.

From the entrance road, you can park your vehicle and put in at Clark Lake or Crooked Lake. According to rangers, Clark (the largest), Crooked, and Loon Lakes are the three busiest. Some of the smaller lakes see less traffic and are just a short portage away; these include Mountain and High, which are both accessible from Crooked Lake. One ranger recommends bringing snorkel gear. The crystal-clear waters provide great visibility for viewing several species of large fish. Canoes and kayaks can be rented from **Sylvania Outfitters** (23423 U.S. 2, 906/358-4766, www.sylvaniaoutfitters.com) in Watersmeet. You can outfit your entire trip here, with boats, food, fishing gear, and maps. You can even arrange to have your equipment delivered and picked up at the water's edge.

A small but pleasant chain of lakes is the highlight of **Bewabic State Park** (1933 U.S. 2, 906/875-3324, www.michigan.gov/dnr), five miles west of Crystal Falls. Boaters can put in at the first of the Fortune Lakes and make their way to Fourth Lake, which is an easy day's paddling. Though First Lake can be somewhat frenetic on summer weekends, the waters get quieter and downright pristine as you proceed down the chain. Paddlers can escape fishing boats by darting under the low U.S. 2 bridge to Mud Lake. The park itself has a modern 144-site campground with good privacy, a small stretch of sandy beach, tennis courts, and other amenities. Camping reservations are generally not necessary, but can be made via the state park reservation system (800/447-2757, www.michigan.gov/dnr).

Fishing

Bewabic State Park (1933 U.S. 2, 906/875-3324, www.michigan.gov/dnr) has some fine fishing for perch and bass on First Lake, the park's largest (192 acres) and deepest (72 feet). There are more than 300 lakes here, and miles of rivers and streams for fishing. Iron County is home to five of the Upper Peninsula's 13 blue-ribbon trout streams, the highest certification the state DNR confers. Try the 12-mile stretch of **Iron River** extending upstream

from the city, wade into **Brule River** between M-73 and M-189 south of town, or head to **Cooks Run,** south of U.S. 2. For more information on fishing in Iron County, contact the **Chamber of Commerce** (50 E. Genesee St., Iron River, 906/265-3822 or 800/879-4766, www.iron.org).

Golf

Iron County is also home to some of the most interesting golfing in the entire U.P. You won't want to miss the 18 holes at the **George Young Recreational Complex** (159 Young's Lane, 906/265-3401, www.georgeyoung.com, $55 per day in peak season). Not only is it the area's only 18-hole venue, but as a professional course measuring 7,030 yards, it's also the U.P.'s longest. You can play the standard course at just shy of 5,400 yards if you prefer. The elegant complex is run by a nonprofit corporation dedicated to recreation and preservation. Its lands include miles of trails for biking, hiking, and cross-country skiing. The **Crystal View Golf Course** (602 Wagner St., 906/875-3029, www.crystalfalls.org, $15) in Crystal Falls is a nine-hole course owned by the city, located on the banks of Paint River. Another nine-hole course, **Iron River Country Club** (110 Hiawatha Rd., 906/265-3161, $16), located nearby in Iron River, allows nonmembers to play before noon and after 6pm daily.

Off-Road Vehicles

Off-road enthusiasts can find a designated ORV route stretching 67 miles from Iron River northwest to Marenisco. There are miles of additional trails that network throughout Ottawa National Forest, some of which used to be the roadbeds of railroad tracks. Be careful to stay on designated and marked roads and trails. Contact the **U.S. Forest Service** (E6248 U.S. 2, Ironwood, 906/932-1330, www.fs.fed.us, 8am-4pm Mon.-Fri.) for maps and more information.

Waterfalls

Just off the Black River Road National Scenic

Byway, the Black River rolls and tumbles over seven magnificent waterfalls north of Bessemer before rushing into Lake Superior. The site is believed to be the largest concentration of waterfalls in the state. The first two, **Chippewa Falls** and **Algonquin Falls,** 9.5 and 9 miles north of Bessemer, are a little tough to find without a topographic map, since they don't lie near well-marked trails. The next five are a different story. Ottawa National Forest has marked and mapped a good trail network, beginning from a parking lot off County Road 513, about 13 miles north of Bessemer. From this lot you can hike, from south to north, to **Great Conglomerate, Potawatomi, Gorge, Sandstone,** and **Rainbow Falls.** Only strong hikers and serious waterfall enthusiasts should try to cover them all in one 10-mile outing—it's huge number of steps and several waterfalls.

Like babies and sunsets, each waterfall is beautiful in a different way, and it's impossible to name the best one. Potawatomi is the closest, just a few minutes' walk from the lot, and accessible by wheelchair. It is a lovely delicate fretwork of foam cascading over remnants of an ancient lava flow. The last falls, Rainbow, is the largest of the group, cascading 40 feet. The resulting spray sometimes creates a rainbow effect, hence the name. The best view of Rainbow Falls is from the east side of the river, which you can access from a suspended footbridge near the river's mouth at **Black River Harbor.**

★ BOND FALLS

Some consider **Bond Falls** one of the most spectacular falls in the Upper Peninsula—a mighty big claim—while others feel the setting is far too developed with walkways and viewing platforms, distorting its natural beauty. Decide for yourself; head for Paulding on U.S. 45 in Ontonagon County. Bond Falls is three miles east on Bond Falls Road and is well marked by signs. Though virtually surrounded by national forest land, the falls themselves sit on power company property, just below a dam that forms the adjacent **Bond Falls Flowage,** a popular area for fishing, swimming, and camping. To view the falls, follow the trail down the west side of the river. Ignore the spillway, cement retaining wall, and other power company additions. Once you begin descending the stairs, the falls come into view on the right, close enough to touch. Continue down the path to a footbridge that spans the base of the falls for an up-close view. Water gushes down a

Bond Falls

50-foot face of chiseled rocks, so dramatic it almost looks artificial. A few miles north of Bond Falls **Agate Falls** is another striking waterfall, this one offering a bridge for easy viewing. Take U.S. 45 north from Watersmeet, then M-28 east from Bruce Crossing.

WINTER SPORTS AND RECREATION
Downhill Skiing

Without the benefit of the Big Snow Country marketing muscle that serves the ski resorts of Gogebic County, **Ski Brule** (397 Brule Mountain Rd., Iron River, 906/265-9346 or 800/362-7853, www.skibrule.com, prices vary) is left to its own devices to sell this appealing ski area six miles south of Iron River. Its gimmick is that it's "first to open, last to close," which translates to about six months of skiing. Brule is reliably open for downhill skiing by mid-November and continues through April. The terrain is nice, with 500 vertical feet, eight chairs and T-bars, and a decent half pipe for snowboarders.

Ski and Snowshoe Trails

Ski Brule (397 Brule Mountain Rd., Iron River, 906/265-9346 or 800/362-7853, www.skibrule. com) is an ideal place for cross-country skiing. Skiers can check out 14.2 miles of groomed and tracked trails, some of which wind along the Brule River. Because they aren't covered by the resort's snowmaking, the cross-country trails don't always open as soon as the downhill area. There are some 8.5 miles of groomed trails at **The Listening Inn** (339 Clark Rd., Crystal Falls, 906/822-7738, www.thelisteninginn. com, trail use $7), a splendid log lodge and B&B located nine miles north of Crystal Falls. Two beginner loops, separate snowshoe trails, and ski rentals make the inn an ideal ski destination. As with hiking, one of the finest trails for cross-country skiing in the **Lake Ottawa Recreation Area** (Lake Ottawa Rd., Iron River, 906/265-9259, www.fs.fed.us) is the groomed and marked Ge-Che Trail.

Ottawa National Forest grooms 15 miles of trails within the **Sylvania Wilderness Area and Recreation Area,** which provide a great cross-country ski network in winter months.

Snowmobiling

As with ORV trails, a network of snowmobile trails leaves Iron River and winds through the Ottawa National Forest. **Trail 2** heads west into the forest, eventually reaching Ironwood, while plenty of routes branch off to the north and south into Wisconsin. Trails 2 and 16 head east for Escanaba.

FOOD

At ★ **Alice's Restaurant** (402 W. Adams St., 906/265-4764, 4:30pm-9pm Tues.-Sun., entrées $17-28) you'll find authentic Italian specialties brought over from the old country and passed down through generations, such as homemade ravioli and other pasta dishes, gnocchi, and soups.

For picnics, pick up supplies at **Angeli's Foods** (833 Riverside Plaza, U.S. 2 E., 906/265-5107, http://angelifoods.com, 7am-10pm daily). An ordinary-looking modern supermarket from the outside, inside it surprises with a superb bakery, produce department, and deli.

ACCOMMODATIONS

The **Lakeshore Motel** (1257 Lalley Rd., Iron River, 906/265-3611, www.lakeshoremotelicelake.com) sits on the edge of spring-fed Ice Lake in Iron River, just east of downtown on U.S. 2, with tidy motel rooms (from $51), some with kitchenette units (from $82), and cabins (from $62). It's a great find complete with a sandy beach and a boat launch. Iron River also has an ★ **AmericInn** (40 E. Adams St., Iron River, 906/265-9100, www.americinn. com, $114-160) on U.S. 2 just east of downtown, with a nice indoor pool, a whirlpool, and a sauna; suites are available.

You'll find great lodging at ★ **Chicaugon Lake Inn** (1700 County Rd. 424, 906/265-9244, www.chicaugonlakeinn.com, $79-121), predictably located near Chicaugon Lake in Iron River. The year-round hotel has sparsely decorated but well-kept rooms, whirlpool suites, and free wireless Internet access. Check out their special rates for the fall color season. **Lac O' Seasons Resort** (176 Stanley Lake Dr., 906/265-4881 or 800/797-5226, www.lacoseasons.com, $170-345) rents 14 cabins and cottages on the shores of Stanley Lake. In Crystal Falls, **Michi-Aho Resort** (2181 M-69, 906/875-3514 or 800/875-3514, www.michi-aho.com, $69-79) has rooms and cottages on the banks of the Michigamme River.

Camping

The ★ **Ottawa National Forest** maintains 27 auto-accessible campgrounds, all with tent pads, fire grates, and some form of toilet facilities. Many are located along rivers and lakes. Most tend to be quite rustic and secluded, with the exception of Black River Harbor, Sylvania, and Bobcat Lake. A few, like Black River Harbor, require a fee and allow reservations through a central reservation system (800/280-2267 or 800/283-2267). Rates for these campgrounds are $16 per day, with a 14-day maximum stay. For more information on a specific campground, contact a district ranger station or the **Ottawa National Forest Headquarters** (E6248 U.S. 2, Ironwood, 906/932-1330 or 800/562-1201, 8am-4pm Mon.-Fri.).

INFORMATION AND SERVICES

For more information on the Iron River area and Iron County, contact the **Iron County Chamber of Commerce** (50 East Genesee St., Iron River, 906/265-3822, www.iron.org). All of Iron County is in the central time zone.

Aspirus Iron River Hospital (1400 W. Ice Lake Rd., Iron River, 906/265-6121, www.aspirus.org) can see to your medical needs. For financial needs, including ATMs and branch locations, try **Wells Fargo** (234 W. Genesee St., 906/265-5144, www.wellsfargo.com) or **Miners State Bank** (312 W. Genesee St., 906/265-5131, www.msbir.com).

To make sense of what the Ottawa National Forest has to offer, start with a map. You can pick up a small free brochure or large topographic map ($4) at the **Ottawa National Forest**

Headquarters (E6248 U.S. 2, Ironwood, 906/932-1330, 8am-4pm Mon.-Fri.) in Ironwood or at the **Watersmeet Ranger District Office** (U.S. 2 and U.S. 45, Watersmeet, 906/358-4551). Other district offices, in Bessemer, Bergland, and Ontonagon should have maps and brochures, although budget cuts have forced them to curtail other visitor services.

GETTING THERE AND AROUND
Car

Like many of the larger cities in the U.P.'s western reaches, Iron River is located close to the state's border with Wisconsin. If you're coming from Wisconsin, take W-139 across the border; it becomes M-189 in Michigan. U.S. 2 runs from Ironwood east to Iron Mountain. If you're traveling to or from the Keweenaw Peninsula, take U.S. 141.

Air

Generally, the farther west you go in the Upper Peninsula, the farther you get from conveniently located airports. One of the downsides to all this rugged isolation is that no matter where you fly in, you'll also have to drive a good distance from the airport. Thankfully, both **Delta County Airport** (ESC, 3300 Airport Rd., Escanaba, 906/786-4902, www.deltacountymi.org), near Escanaba, and **Sawyer International Airport** (MQT, 125 G Ave., Gwinn, 906/346-3308, www.sawyerairport.com), near Marquette, offer plenty of options for car rentals. Wisconsin's **Rhinelander-Oneida County Airport** (RHI, 3375 Airport Rd., Rhinelander, WI, 715/365-3416, www.fly-rhi.org) is a bit closer and has daily flights to and from Minneapolis-St. Paul on Delta Airlines and vehicle rentals through Alamo, Avis, Budget, and National.

Bus

Getting to Iron River is easy on **Indian Trails** (800/292-3831, www.indiantrails.com) buses, which run regular trips from Escanaba to Ironwood.

Ironwood

With mammoth Lake Superior providing the requisite moisture, the northwestern corner of the U.P. isn't exaggerating when it markets itself as Big Snow Country. Cool air moving across the warmer waters of Lake Superior creates lake effect snow when it hits land, generating an astounding average of 200 inches per season. This combines nicely with the area's rugged hills, home to many of the Midwest's largest downhill ski resorts. As a result, the western U.P., especially around Ironwood, is one of Michigan's most heavily marketed tourism areas, luring sizable crowds of skiers up U.S. 51 every weekend from Wisconsin, Chicago, and Detroit.

Ironwood hugs the Montreal River, which forms the border between Michigan and Wisconsin. On the other side lies its sister city of Hurley, Wisconsin. Together they were once the center of activity for the iron miners of the Gogebic Range. Ironwood had the stores and services; Hurley provided the bars and brothels. During the heyday of iron mining—from the early 1900s to about 1930—the population topped 15,000. But as the industry grew less profitable, the money made from iron left the region, but without leaving opulent mansions or other monuments of wealth, as was the case in copper country.

Consequently, Ironwood today is a hardscrabble town that barely hints at its prosperous past. Still, locals are friendly, and they would probably agree that the natural beauty of the land surrounding Ironwood is what attracts visitors much more than the city itself.

SIGHTS
Downtown Ironwood

There are a few interesting diversions in Ironwood's downtown, one of which is the **Ironwood Memorial Building** (213 S Marquette St.), a beautiful structure that serves as a memorial for area residents killed in combat. World War I scenes are portrayed in stained glass, a statue of a soldier stands guard in the lobby, and displays outline the history of the region. Stop by the **Old Depot Park Museum** (150 N. Lowell St., 906/932-0287, noon-4pm Mon.-Sat. Memorial Day-Labor Day, free), once the train station and

downtown Ironwood

now an interesting museum devoted to the area's history. Another noteworthy site is the **Miners Memorial Mural** (E. McLeod Ave., just east of S. Suffolk St.). Painted on the side of a building, it shows the faces and names of several dozen miners who died on the job. You can also visit the **Historic Ironwood Theater** (906/932-0618, www.ironwood-theatre.net, office open noon-4:30pm Wed.-Fri.) to learn more about the town's heritage. Docent-led tours (Wed.-Fri. summer, donation) are usually offered in the late morning or early afternoon.

Hiawatha

After encountering Big John, the absurdly tall miner at the Iron Mountain Iron Mine, you'd be correct for thinking the Upper Peninsula has a thing for oversize historical figures. Case in point: **Hiawatha** (Suffolk St.), the 50-foot fiberglass rendering of a Native American that serves as a very touristy roadside attraction.

Hiawatha sculpture in downtown Ironwood

★ Little Girl's Point

Just minutes from the strip-mall world of U.S. 2, a genuine U.P. experience awaits. Follow County Road 505 north from Ironwood to reach **Little Girl's Point,** an area favorite. Perched high on a bluff over Lake Superior, this tranquil county park features a sandy beach, a boat launch, picnic tables, grills, and fantastic views. Take time to absorb the stunning Porcupine Mountains to the east and the Apostle Islands to the west.

Black River Road National Scenic Byway

Gogebic County tourism folks heavily promote this 15-mile stretch of County Road 513 from Bessemer north to Lake Superior, and for good reason. The two-lane road itself is pleasant enough, a wooded drive that twists in tandem with the Black River, hidden away in the forest just off the road's eastern shoulder. But even better, it links together several noteworthy attractions.

The end of County Road 513, Black River Harbor, is a popular Ottawa National Forest campground on Lake Superior, with a large day-use area, sand beach, and boat launch. You can also pick up the North Country Scenic Trail here. For campground reservations, call the U.S. Forest Service central reservation system (800/280-2267 or 800/283-2267).

★ Copper Peak

You'll see the peak long before you reach it. About nine miles north of Bessemer, the rocky outcrop of Copper Peak rises 364 feet above the surrounding countryside, crowned by the 421-foot **Copper Peak Ski Flying Hill** (906/932-3500, www.copperpeak.org). Ski flying is similar to ski jumping but uses different equipment to achieve even longer distances. The current record is 512 feet. Copper Peak, built in 1970, is the only ski flying hill in the western hemisphere and the highest artificial jump in the world.

From Memorial Day to Labor Day, and on weekends through mid-October, a chairlift, elevator, and steps run to the top for a heart-thumping skier's-eye view of the chute. This is not a trip for the faint of heart. But if you can get over a little knee knocking, you'll be wowed by the panorama of the surrounding countryside, with views stretching across the undulating green of the national forest, the serpentine Black River, and the aqua blue horizon of Lake Superior. The Copper Peak complex also offers 12 miles of mountain biking trails.

FESTIVALS AND EVENTS
Festival Ironwood

A midsummer tradition, **Festival Ironwood** (906/932-1122, www.ironwoodchamber.org) celebrates this resilient town's culture and character. Held at Depot Park, near the museum, the event features food, music, games, plus other fun diversions. This event is a great way to meet and chat with local people, who are known for their friendliness.

SUMMER SPORTS AND RECREATION
Hiking and Biking

The lengthy **North Country National Scenic Trail** has been mentioned before, but the footpath really is the area's best hiking.

When it's completed, the North Country Trail's 4,600 miles will make it the longest off-road hiking trail in the United States, more than double the length of the renowned Appalachian Trail. The section that passes through Ontonagon and Gogebic Counties cuts through the Ottawa National Forest and Porcupine Mountains Wilderness State Park and into Wisconsin near Ironwood. Although it's one of the nation's longest trails it's also one of the least traveled, providing plenty of solitude for long stretches along the path.

In a land filled with stunning views, you'll find one of the best on the **Gogebic Ridge Hiking Trail,** a spur from the North Country Trail about 40 miles northeast of Ironwood. The trail is eight miles long and reaches its pinnacle at an overlook on one of the longest, tallest cliff faces in the state, complete with views of Lake Gogebic and the forested countryside. The south end of the trail skirts Weary Lake. Contact the **U.S. Forest Service** (906/884-2411) for additional information about both the North Country and Gogebic Ridge trails.

When the snow isn't on the ground, the extreme western U.P. is prime mountain biking territory. More than 100 miles of the **Pines and Mines Mountain Bike Trail**

Little Girl's Point, a tranquil spot to view Lake Superior

cut through Gogebic County alone, while nine miles of trails form the **Wolverine Mountain Bike Trail.** One of the fat-tire highlights is **Copper Peak,** where cyclists can enjoy a ride up the hill that would be a ski lift in the wintertime, then tear through the woods on the way back down.

Canoeing and Kayaking

Some of the best paddling the U.P. can offer is in Ottawa National Forest's 2,000 miles of streams and rivers. Paddlers in the Ironwood region will likely want to make the short trip east to the forest.

Fishing

Lake Superior, the largest, deepest, and coldest of the Great Lakes, offers spectacular opportunities for deepwater fishing. An excellent partner is **Nomad Lake Superior Fishing Charters** (211 W. Lime St., 906/932-1576, www.nomadcharters.com) for full-day ($500-600) and half-day ($400-450) charters. Your best bet for stream, river, and inland lake fishing is to head east to Ottawa National Forest's 2,000 miles of waterways and 500 lakes.

Golf

One of the western U.P.'s finest golf courses can be found in Ironwood itself. The **Gogebic Country Club** (200 Country Club Rd., 906/932-2515, www.gogebiccountryclub.com, $23 for 18 holes, $15 for 9 holes) has been a favorite Michigan golf spot since the early 1920s, when the attractive stone clubhouse was constructed. Its 18 holes measure around 6,000 yards. Take U.S. 2 a few miles west of Ironwood and turn south on Country Club Road. In Bessemer, you'll find the beautiful nine-hole **Boulder Creek Golf Course** (N11868 Heron Lane, Bessemer, 906/932-9066, $25 for 18 holes, with cart $35). Hours and greens fees fluctuate seasonally at both courses.

Off-Road Vehicles

The closest major off-road vehicle trail in Ottawa National Forest is the 67-mile route that runs from Marenisco, 25 miles east of Ironwood on U.S. 2, to Iron River. There are, of course, smaller trails closer to Ironwood, but remember that ORVs are prohibited in the national forest except on designated, marked trails. Maps are available from the **U.S. Forest Service** (E6248 U.S. 2, Ironwood, 906/932-1330, www.fs.fed.us, 8am-4pm Mon.-Fri.), and also the **Michigan DNR** (427 U.S. 41 N., Baraga, 906/353-6651, 8am-5pm Mon.-Fri.).

Waterfalls

From Little Girl's Point, north of Ironwood on County Road 505, continue west on County Road 505 to reach **Superior Falls.** The rushing Montreal River puts on its final spectacular show here, plummeting more than 40 feet, then squeezing through a narrow gorge before spilling into Lake Superior a short distance away. You can also reach the falls by taking U.S. 2 about 11 miles west from Ironwood and turning north on W-122, which becomes County Road 505 when you cross back into Michigan. In about 4.8 miles, watch for a small brown sign that directs you west into a small parking area near a Northern States Power substation. From there, it's a short walk to the falls. You can also continue down the path past the falls to the shores of Lake Superior, an excellent place to watch the sunset. Be advised that the power company sometimes limits access to the falls, and the gate is occasionally locked.

As you can no doubt guess from its name, **Interstate Falls** is located on the border of Michigan's Upper Peninsula and Wisconsin. Like Superior Falls, Interstate Falls is part of the Montreal River, but this waterfall is shorter, at 20 feet, and wider, with a fairly impressive flow when the water level is high. You'll want to cross into Wisconsin to see it. Take U.S. 2 west into Wisconsin to an unpaved road about 0.25 miles past the border and follow the signs for **Peterson Falls,** which is a short walk upstream.

Heading north from Bessemer on the Black River Road National Scenic Byway will take you to a beautiful and popular lineup of five waterfalls on the Black River, which run roughly parallel to the byway. In the last few miles before Lake Superior, you'll be able to see the **Great Conglomerate, Potawatomi, Gorge, Sandstone,** and **Rainbow Falls.**

WINTER SPORTS AND RECREATION
★ Downhill Skiing

With the exception of the ski area in the Porcupine Mountains Wilderness State Park, the area's downhill ski resorts line up conveniently along a short stretch of U.S. 2 just east of Ironwood. Each venue welcomes both downhill skiers and snowboarders. Lift ticket prices vary with the season; package rates that include lodging usually offer the best deals. For those who want to explore all the area's terrain, ask about the interchangeable lift ticket, which is available at each participating resort. It's good on weekdays only at the area's four major resorts: Powderhorn, Blackjack, Indianhead, and Whitecap Mountain, located just over the border in Wisconsin.

Heading east from Ironwood, the first resort you'll reach is **Big Powderhorn Mountain** (N11375 Powderhorn Rd., Bessemer, 906/932-4838 or 800/501-7669, www.bigpowderhorn.net, daily in season, day pass $65 adults, $54 ages 10-17 and over age 64, $44 ages 7-9) in Bessemer. Powderhorn radiates an early 1970s feel, and the giant fiberglass skier at the entrance—complete with red and blue vintage '70s skiwear—says it all. The resort's 25 downhill runs are on two faces, with 700 vertical feet and nine double chairlifts. Perhaps more than the others, Big Powderhorn Mountain caters to families, with affordable lift tickets, mostly tame runs, and plenty of ski-in, ski-out lodging bordering its slopes. In the main lodge at the base you'll find a cafeteria, ski rental and repair, a ski school, and a bar.

In 2014, Indianhead Mountain Resort and Blackjack Ski Resort merged under the management of a new company, **Big Snow Resort** (800/346-3426, www.bigsnow.com, $49 Mon.-Fri., $65 Sat.-Sun. and holidays adults, $40 Mon.-Fri., $52 Sat.-Sun. and holidays ages 10-17 and over age 64). Both resorts

Choosing a Ski Resort

When thinking of downhill skiing, destinations such as the Rocky Mountains or the Alps usually are the first to come to mind—certainly before the Great Lakes region. And while it's probably misleading to say Ironwood has the same caliber of skiing found in the West, it is fair to say that the abundance of ski runs and resorts, plus the immense snowfalls of the western Upper Peninsula, combine to make it perhaps the finest destination for downhill skiers between the Rockies and the Appalachians.

There are numerous ski resorts within a short drive of Ironwood. Whether you like carving a half pipe or leaving the first tracks on a backcountry slope, you'll find enough variety and deep snow to keep you satisfied, often for a fraction of what you'd pay at one of the large Colorado resorts. A handy list to help you choose:

- Best for families and newbies: **Big Powderhorn Mountain**
- Best for ungroomed trails and snowboarders: **Blackjack Ski Resort**
- Cheapest choice: **Ski Brule**
- Most challenging slopes: **Indianhead Mountain Resort**
- Best terrain and views: **Porcupine Mountains Ski Area**
- Highest jumps: **Pine Mountain Ski Jump** and **Copper Peak Ski Flying Hill**

continue to operate under their legacy names, but Big Snow lift tickets are valid at both resorts. **Indianhead Mountain Resort** (500 Indianhead Rd., Wakefield, 9am-4pm Sun.-Fri., 9am-8pm Sat. and holidays) is the area's largest resort, with 638 vertical feet, five chairlifts, two T-bars, and 22 runs. Indianhead offers some of the region's most challenging, although overly groomed, skiing and pleasant runs that wind for more than a mile through the woods. Indianhead's lodging and sales, rentals, and repair services are located at the top of the resort and offer more choices than area competitors. The day lodge even offers great views of the Ottawa National Forest spilling out across the valley and far beyond the slopes.

Blackjack Ski Resort (N11251 Black Jack Rd., Bessemer, 9am-4pm daily) makes the most of its terrain. Cameron Run and Spillway are often left ungroomed and offer good bump skiing, and Blackjack is arguably the best resort for snowboarders, with the area's best half pipe, served by its own rope tow, and a great terrain park on Broad Ax. Look to Blackjack for a variety of snowboard events, including camps and competitions. Blackjack offers 16 runs, four double chairlifts, and 465 vertical feet. A day lodge at the base offers food service along with ski rental and repair. A limited number of condo accommodations line the slopes. The Loggers Lounge upstairs hosts the area's liveliest after-ski scene.

Ski and Snowshoe Trails
Active Backwoods Retreat (E5299 W. Pioneer Rd., Ironwood, 906/932-3502, www.michiweb.com/abrski, $10-12), or ABR for short, grooms 25 miles of trails for skiing and striding on hundreds of acres of private land three miles south of Ironwood. The trails are open daily as well as some nights for lighted skiing or moonlight skiing. A warming hut, lessons, and rentals are available.

Between Ironwood and Bessemer, take Section 12 Road north from U.S. 2 to reach **Wolverine Nordic Trails** (www.

wolverinenordic.com, donation). Situated on private land and maintained by volunteers, the 9.3 miles of groomed trails wind through the hilly country south of the Big Powderhorn ski area. In fact, you can ride one of Powderhorn's chairlifts ($3) to access the network. Otherwise, begin at the lot with the warming hut on Sunset Road off Section 12 Road.

If solitude is more important to you than set trails, don't overlook the vast terrain available in the 982,895-acre Ottawa National Forest. The **U.S. Forest Service** (E6248 U.S. 2, Ironwood, 906/932-1330, www.fs.fed.gov, 8am-4pm Mon.-Fri.) office has national forest maps and can suggest trails to try.

Snowmobiling
Of the western U.P.'s hundreds of miles of snowmobile trails, plenty are accessible from Ironwood. **Trail 2** heads east from Ironwood across the rest of the U.P. Take **Trail 11** north to Porcupine Mountains State Park and Lake Superior. Heading the opposite direction, Trail 11 runs northwest to Lake Superior where Michigan and Wisconsin meet. Plenty of these trails drop south into Wisconsin and connect with that state's network of snowmobile trails.

FOOD
It looks like a classic corner tavern, but **Don & GG's** (1300 E. Cloverland Dr., 906/932-2312, 11am-9pm Mon.-Thurs., 11am-10pm Fri.-Sat., under $10), on U.S. 2 in Ironwood, might surprise you with its vegetarian dishes and smoked trout salad. Don't worry—you can still get burgers and chicken dinners. The **Hoop 'N' Holler Tavern** (115 Hoop 'N' Holler Rd., Merriweather, 906/575-5555, 11am-10pm Mon.-Thurs., 11am-11pm Fri., 11am-midnight Sat., noon-11pm Sun., under $10) is a tavern in the classic mold, complete with plenty of good cheer and some very good tavern food, including burgers, sandwiches, and pizza. Located on Lake Gogebic's northwest side, Hoop 'N' Holler has a beach available in the summertime. Merriweather and

the tavern are in the eastern time zone, one hour later than Ironwood.

The ★ **Kimball Inn** (6622 U.S. 2, Hurley, WI, 715/561-4095, www.kimballinn.com, 4pm-9pm Tues.-Thurs., 4pm-9:30pm Fri.-Sat., 4pm-9pm Sun., $8-17) is actually in Wisconsin, but it's worth the extra four-mile drive west on U.S. 2 from the border to sample its smoked barbecue, charbroiled steaks, grinders (Italian sandwiches), and more.

ACCOMMODATIONS

You'll find a large selection of independent motels along U.S. 2, many of which offer great deals and clean and comfortable if simple rooms. A couple of good choices are the **Classic Motor Inn** (1200 Cloverland Dr., 906/932-2000) and the **Crestview Motel** (906/932-4845, http://crestviewmotel.net) at the west end of U.S. 2. Both run $50-75, although rates may be higher during peak ski season.

The larger area ski resorts have slope-side or near-slope accommodations that range from dormitories to simple motel rooms to deluxe condominiums. Prices range widely for almost every budget, and good value can be had outside ski season. Try **Indianhead Reservations** (800/346-3426) or **Big Powderhorn Mountain and Lodging** (800/222-3131) for plenty of choices. Ask about package deals with lift tickets if you're traveling in winter.

For something more intimate, you can't beat the **Bear Track Inn** (N15325 Black River Rd., Ironwood, 906/932-2144, http://beartrackcabins.tripod.com, from $85). National forest land practically surrounds the inn's three log cabins, which have a great location one mile from Lake Superior's Black River Harbor and near scores of hiking, biking, and skiing trails. Each cabin has a full kitchen and use of the Finnish sauna. From the outside, the **Regal Country Inn** (1602 E. U.S. 2, Wakefield, 906/229-5122, www.regalcountryinn.com, $95-125, higher in winter season) looks nothing like an old Victorian home, but if you're in one of its historic or

Victorian rooms you'll swear you've booked a B&B. Antique beds and decorations, pictures of local historic figures, quilted bedspreads, and a gourmet breakfast (for an additional charge; continental breakfast is included) all add to this inn's charm. Free wireless Internet is an added plus.

Finally, chain motels cluster near the U.S. 2/U.S. 51 interchange, including the **Days Inn** (13355 U.S. 51, Hurley, WI, 715/561-3500, $75-129), with an indoor pool. Some rooms include microwaves and refrigerators.

Camping

True to Michigan state park form, **Lake Gogebic State Park** (800/447-2757, www.michigan.gov/dnr) offers a fine modern campground, with large but rather open sites on the western shore of Lake Gogebic. A boat launch, a small sandy beach, and a nice picnic area are nearby. Lake Gogebic is known for great walleye and perch fishing, so pack a rod even if you don't come with a boat. Reservations are accepted but generally not needed.

INFORMATION AND SERVICES

For visitor information, assistance, and planning, contact the **Ironwood Area Chamber of Commerce** (150 N. Lowell St., 906/932-1122, www.ironwoodchamber.org) or the **Western Upper Peninsula Convention and Visitor Bureau** (906/932-4850 or 800/522-5657, www.westernup.info).

Ironwood's hospital is the **Aspirus Ironwood Hospital** (10561 N. Grand View Lane, 906/932-2525, www.aspirusgrandview.org), just north of U.S. 2 between Bessemer and Ironwood. There's no shortage of banks in Ironwood and Bessemer. You'll find both local and regional banks as well as two Wells Fargo locations.

GETTING THERE AND AROUND
Car

Ironwood is tucked just about as far into the U.P.'s western corner as you can get—in fact,

Ironwood is as far from Detroit as Detroit is from New York City. U.S. 2 runs through Ironwood from the east or the west. From the south, drive up W-77 or U.S. 51. M-28 connects the north and east in the Upper Peninsula.

Air

Sawyer International Airport (MQT, 125 G Ave., Gwinn, 906/346-3308, www.sawyerairport.com), near Marquette, is the largest facility in the Upper Peninsula and has daily flights on **American Airlines** nonstop service from Chicago O'Hare Airport and on **Delta Airlines** to Minneapolis-St. Paul and Detroit.

Closer to the Ironwood area are **Houghton County Memorial Airport** (CMX, 23810 Airpark Blvd., Calumet, 906/482-3970, www.houghtoncounty.org), which has scheduled flights from Chicago on **United Airlines,** as well as vehicle rentals by **Alamo** and **National**. In Wisconsin, **The Rhinelander-Oneida County Airport** (RHI, 3375 Airport Rd., Rhinelander, WI, 715/365-3416, www.fly-rhi.org) has daily flights from Minneapolis-St. Paul on **Delta Airlines** and vehicle rentals by **Alamo, Avis, Budget,** and **National.**

Bus

Getting to Ironwood by bus is pretty easy, even if you're coming from Chicago, Detroit, or farther afield. A combination of Greyhound and **Indian Trails** (800/292-3831, www.indiantrails.com) routes can get you there without too much trouble. Ironwood is on Indian Trails' St. Ignace-Escanaba-Ironwood line.

Porcupine Mountains and Ontonagon

If the Superior Upland is known for its ruggedness, the jagged, heavily wooded terrain of the Porcupine Mountains region can be virtually impregnable. Here you'll find the closest thing Michigan has to offer in the way of highlands, with steep trails descending into rocky valleys amid thick hardwood and evergreen forests. There are cities here, but they almost seem to be an afterthought. Many of the businesses exist to serve the hardy hikers, anglers, and campers who make treks here each summer. If you're looking to have your outdoors skills tested, you've come to the right place.

SIGHTS
★ Porcupine Mountains Wilderness State Park

Anchored along the Lake Superior shore in the northwest corner of the U.P., **Porcupine Mountains Wilderness State Park** (906/885-5275, www.michigan.gov/dnr) covers 60,000 acres, making it the largest in Michigan's excellent state park system. The Porcupine Mountains were a national park site in the 1940s, but came under state control in 1945 when loggers threatened the virgin timber resources before the state acted.

According to legend, someone once decided that this rumpled landscape of low mountains and tall pines resembled the silhouette of a porcupine. The name stuck, along with an endearing nickname: "The Porkies." The area is a focal point for casual hikers and hardcore backpackers, with 90-plus miles of well-marked and well-maintained trails—more than you'll find in many national parks, and certainly more than you'll find in most of the Great Lakes region.

In this case, bigger means better. The park preserves vast stands of virgin hemlock, pine, and the largest tract of virgin hardwoods between the Rockies and the Adirondacks. There are also secluded lakes, wild rivers, and some of the Midwest's highest peaks. Summit Peak tops out at 1,958 feet. Unlike most state parks, Porcupine Mountains Wilderness is large enough to provide a true sense of

Porcupine Mountains

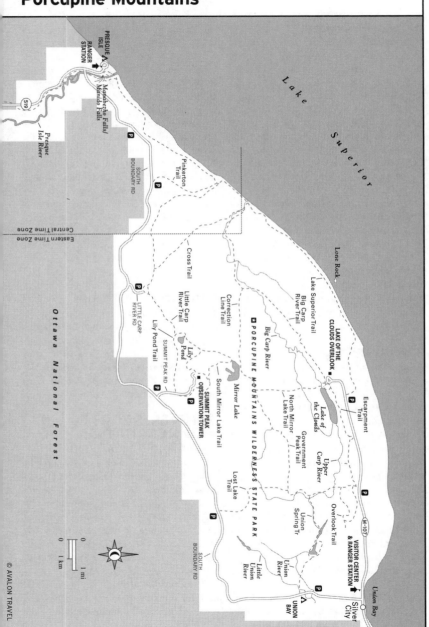

© AVALON TRAVEL

wilderness and serenity, a treasured escape from the civilized world.

Ontonagon County Historical Museum

The Ontonagon Boulder was pried from its namesake riverbank a few miles upstream from the Lake Superior shoreline community of Ontonagon. Today, the two-ton mass of native copper resides at the Smithsonian, and Ontonagon's mining heritage thrives only in museums, especially since the mine and smelter in nearby White Pine closed in 1995. White Pine now is little more than a forlorn ghost town of 1950s tract housing. You can see Ontonagon's happier days presented at the very worthwhile **Ontonagon County Historical Museum** (422 River St., 906/884-6165, www.ontonagonmuseum.org, 10am-5pm Mon.-Sat., 10am-2pm Sun. May-Sept., 10am-5pm Tues.-Sat. Oct.-Dec., 11am-4pm Thurs.-Sat. Jan.-Apr., $5), a lavender building on U.S. 41/M-38, downtown's main street. The historical society also offers periodic tours of the nearby Ontonagon Lighthouse, which is time well spent.

Adventure Copper Mine

In Greenland, 12 miles southeast of Ontonagon, the **Adventure Copper Mine** (200 Adventure Ave., Greenland, 906/883-3371, www.adventureminetours.com, 9am-6pm Mon.-Sat., 11am-6pm Sun. late May-mid-Oct., tours $14-120), operated for 70 years without turning a profit. Today, it's more successful as a tourism destination, offering a number of surface and underground tours that last from 45 minutes to five hours. One of the tours recreates the experience of old-time miners by having visitors rappel down a mineshaft in total darkness, explore small areas, and get a little dirty. There are some tamer underground tours too. To get here, take Adventure Road off M-38 in Greenland.

Old Victoria

Originally established by copper miners in the 1840s, the tiny town of **Rockland** was nearly destroyed by fire in 1890. It was rebuilt in the popular Victorian style of the day. Several Victorian facades still decorate this small community in the Ontonagon River valley, which is 14 miles south of Ontonagon on U.S. 45. From downtown Rockland, follow Victoria Dam Road southwest two miles to **Old Victoria** (906/886-2617, donation), a cluster of miners' log homes huddled around a once-lucrative copper mine shaft. Locals have worked strenuously to save this historic site, which is still a work in progress. Its new designation as a Keweenaw National Historic Park cooperating site may attract new attention and needed funds. The homes are open most summer afternoons when guides are available. Visitors are welcome to wander the grounds at any time; donations are needed and appreciated. Continue past Old Victoria to the **Victoria Dam,** a hydroelectric facility and a surprisingly pretty spot popular with local anglers.

Ontonagon Lighthouse

The county historical society's current project is the restoration of the 1866 **Ontonagon Lighthouse,** which replaced the original built in 1853. Contact the **Ontonagon County Historical Society** (906/884-6165, www.ontonagonmuseum.org) for information on public tours and the restoration effort.

SUMMER SPORTS AND RECREATION
Hiking and Biking Trails

Many visitors to the Porkies head immediately toward the justly famous **Lake of the Clouds Overlook.** From the parking lot at the end of M-107, it's just a few steps to the overlook, where the placid lake slices a long sliver of blue through a thick blanket of jade forest hundreds of feet below. The exquisite view is arguably the most dramatic in Michigan; it really has to be seen to be appreciated.

The overlook also serves as the trailhead for some the park's most rugged and scenic routes. To full appreciate the Lake of the Clouds view, hike the aptly named

Saving the Porkies

Long before Europeans arrived and began harvesting the area's abundant resources, the Ojibwa people had already named the peaks and crags along the Lake Superior shore the Porcupine Mountains. In the 1700s the area was a principle trapping area in the fur trade. In the mid-1800s, copper was first discovered, and by the latter half of the 19th century and into the early 20th century, there were no fewer than 45 copper mines operating inside what is now Porcupine Mountains Wilderness State Park. Loggers also soon discovered the area and began to pursue their trade.

In the era before modern conservation methods, logging had a drastic, often damaging impact on the landscape, and the threat to the Porcupine Mountains became real. As tree cutting began to encroach on the virgin forests in the early 1920s, discussion of preservation began. The dream became a reality 20 years later, when the State of Michigan established the park and the Porcupine Mountains ("The Porkies") were saved. Despite some minor conflicts with copper mining companies, the park has remained virtually untouched.

Today, the Porkies are home to one of the Great Lakes region's largest remaining old growth forests, hardwoods, and eastern hemlock trees. It's a remarkably beautiful park, offering almost boundless recreational opportunities.

Escarpment Trail, which winds east and skims over Cloud Peak and Cuyahoga Peak. Bordered by a sheer cliff, the four-mile trail is considered by many to be the most beautiful in the park. Allow ample time to stop and enjoy the shimmering lake and valley floor spreading out around you.

At its eastern trailhead, the Escarpment Trail links up with the 7.5-mile **Government Peak Trail.** This secluded route drops south over the Upper Carp River and past Trap Falls, then swings west and scales Government Peak. As quickly as it rises, the trail drops down to quiet Mirror Lake, a perfect spot to soak weary feet after a full day of hiking.

From Mirror Lake, the dull and heavily wooded **Correction Line Trail** heads west, where it meets the **Big Carp River Trail,** another good choice. Running nine miles from Lake Superior to the Lake of the Clouds

Ontonagon Lighthouse

Overlook, this fine route leads hikers along a shaded river valley of hemlocks and ferns, past the park's highest waterfall, the 25-foot Shining Cloud Falls, and along a dry ridge top with more dramatic peeks at the unspoiled Lake of the Clouds.

Several miles south, visitors get another soaring view from the **Summit Peak Observation Tower.** At 1,958 feet, Summit Peak is even taller with a 40-foot observation tower at its crest. It's an inspiring panorama, a vast landscape unscarred by humans. In fact, the only sign of civilization is a spindly ski jump 18 miles away, rising above the tree line like a circus clown on stilts. On a clear day, scour the horizon for a glimpse of Lake Superior's Apostle Islands, nearly 40 miles west.

One of the park's most spectacular trails is probably its most accessible: the **East and West River Trail** parallels the wild and turbulent Presque Isle River. From the Presque Isle Campground at the park's west end, you can follow the river one mile upstream and down the opposite bank as it corkscrews through narrow rock walls and tumbles into Lake Superior. Keep a tight hold on children and pets along this trail, and don't think about wading—the current is swift and dangerous.

To dangle your toes or let your dog take a swim, there's a wonderfully deep, clear, and placid backwater pool just east of the main channel right near Lake Superior.

Long before the Porcupine Mountains were preserved for their virgin forest and natural beauty, miners harvested the rich minerals buried in the bedrock. At the east end of the park, the **Union Mine Trail** provides a glimpse into life in the 1840s, when the Porkies were part of the area's copper rush. Marked with white mine shovels to indicate points of interest, this self-guided interpretive trail forms a one-mile loop along the spring-fed Union River and the site of an old copper mine, now largely reclaimed by nature. In the shadow of lofty hemlocks, you'll see how miners tunneled shafts into the riverbank and learn about their lives in the wilderness—still untamed today.

Fishing

Fishing is one of the many recreational benefits in this vast expanse of wilderness. The park's most striking location, Lake of the Clouds, is accessible to anglers, along with a number of other lakes and streams. Try Mirror Lake and the Carp River, Presque Isle River, and Union River. Contact the **DNR**

Lake of the Clouds in the Porcupine Mountains

suspension bridge over the Presque Isle River

to Houghton, a distance of more than 41 miles. Throughout the state, the DNR has purchased many of these old grades and removed the rails, maintaining them as multiuse trails. In the U.P., that usually means snowmobiles and ATVs. Near the intersection of M-26 and M-38 at Lake Mine, the trail spans the Firesteel River on three bridges, which range from 65 to 85 feet high. Stop at the **Michigan DNR Office** (427 U.S. 41 N., Baraga, 906/353-6651, 8am-5pm Mon.-Fri.) in Baraga for a map of the rail trail that shows access points. Where the trail crosses roads, look for a yellow-and-black snowmobile crossing sign on the highway or a DNR ATV wooden trail sign on the trail.

Waterfalls

The Porcupine Mountains' more than 60 waterfalls can seem a bit overwhelming, but despite the many choices, some stand out. Make the brief trek to **Presque Isle Falls** in the western portion of the park. You can also take South Boundary Road southwest from the visitors center to a boardwalk that follows the river to a number of falls, including **Manabezho Falls** and the smaller, less impressive **Manido Falls.**

WINTER SPORTS AND RECREATION
Downhill Skiing

Downhill skiers are often surprised to find a state-run downhill ski area within Porcupine Mountains State Wilderness Park, and even more astonished to find it offers 42 beginner to advanced runs with 787 vertical feet. The runs at **Porcupine Mountains Ski Area** (906/885-5275, www.porkiesfun.com, 9:30am-5:30pm Mon.-Fri., 10am-5pm Sat.-Sun., $20-35) just west of the park headquarters on M-107, span a north-facing flank served by two chairlifts, one T-bar, and a tow rope. The ski area recently added more than 100 acres of backcountry terrain when it opened Everest, a 0.5-mile-wide section of virgin forest with more than 17 runs and snowcat service. A day lodge at the base offers food

Park Headquarters (906/885-5275) for regulations and information.

Beaches

Porcupine Mountain State Park is known for its beaches along more than 50 miles of Lake Superior shoreline. The most popular is **Union Bay,** which is easily accessible by car at the east end of the park. It's a lovely place, but the water can be bone-chillingly cold.

Golf

Golfers can play the nine holes at **Ontonagon Golf Course** (19906 Firesteel Rd., Ontonagon, 906/884-4130, $30 for 9 holes). The clubhouse is fairly Spartan, but the par-35 course makes for a nice round, and the pro shop can provide you with everything you need for an afternoon on the links.

Off-Road Vehicles

The old Copper Range Railroad grade bisects Ontonagon County and the southern Keweenaw Peninsula from Mass City north service, rentals, and a small ski shop. The lifts may be old and a bit creaky, but the terrain is wonderful, the snow is reliable (the annual average tops 175 inches), and the views of Lake Superior from the top are phenomenal. But for all its charms, this is not a good choice on a day when a strong north wind is blowing.

Ski and Snowshoe Trails

The **Porcupine Mountains Ski Area** (906/885-5275, www.porkiesfun.com, 9:30am-5:30pm Mon.-Fri., 10am-5pm Sat.-Sun.) chalet and base area also serve cross-country skiers, who can access a terrific network of trails. The park grooms and tracks 14.2 miles of the park's hiking trails, which wind through the eastern end of the park. Some skirt the Lake Superior shoreline, where snow and ice sculptures form. Others scale the hilly terrain in the interior of the park and can be reached via one of the ski lifts. For day visitors, there is no admission cost. Lift tickets ($39 adults, $30 under age 18) can also be bought in a package that includes ski rentals. Check the website for complete pricing information.

Snowmobiling

In addition to the marked trails in Ottawa National Forest, you can take unplowed M-107 to Lake of the Clouds for a great groomed snowmobile trail in the Porkies that ends at a spectacularly beautiful location.

FOOD

Paul's Restaurant (120 Lincoln Ave., Silver City, 906/885-5311, noon-9pm daily, dinner entrées $12-28), in Silver City's AmericInn Porcupine Mountain Lodge, gets high marks for fish and other supper club fare. In Ontonagon, **Syl's Cafe** (713 River St., Ontonagon, 906/884-2522, 7am-9pm daily, entrées $7-12) is a classic small-town café, with some of the best pasties around. Fifteen minutes south of Ontonagon on U.S. 45, **Henry's Never Inn** (74 National Ave., 906/886-9910, 10am-2am Mon.-Sat., 9:30am-2am Sun., $10) in Rockland draws crowds in from far and wide for its enormous buffets with various fish dishes on Friday night and Italian delicacies on Saturday. Soups and sandwiches are great too, but it's really the spirited locals who add flavor to this old mining haunt. Henry's has a very colorful history, having served as a "blind pig" (speakeasy) during Prohibition.

If you're camping in the Porkies, your closest full-service grocery is in Ontonagon, 17 miles east of the park. For last-minute supplies, try the **Silver City General Store** (107th Engineers Memorial Hwy., 906/885-5885). It has basic camping and fishing supplies as well as picnic staples like cheese and bread.

ACCOMMODATIONS

You'll find a string of motels along M-64 between Silver City (two miles east of park headquarters) and Ontonagon. Many are plain, somewhat Spartan independent establishments, but they'll work just fine after a long day outdoors. **Mountain View Lodges** (34042 107th Engineers Memorial Hwy., Silver City, 906/885-5256, www.mountainviewlodges.com, minimum 2 nights for $450) feature two-bedroom cottages on Lake Superior with amenities like fireplaces and fully equipped kitchens that include dishwashers. The **AmericInn Porcupine Mountain Lodge** (120 Lincoln Ave., Silver City, 906/885-5311, www.americinn.com, $125-175) offers the full array of motel services, including an indoor pool, a sauna, meeting rooms, a dining room, and a bar. For other options, contact the **Ontonagon Chamber of Commerce** (424 River St., 906/884-4735, http://ontonagonmi.org).

Camping

Campers have their choice of two modern campgrounds, both with a number of sites overlooking Lake Superior: **Union Bay** (full hookups) at the east end of the park or **Presque Isle** (no hookups) near the mouth of the Presque Isle River on the park's western edge. Both offer flush toilets and showers. In addition, three rustic campgrounds (called "outposts") with 3 to 11 sites each are located off the South Boundary Road, accessible by car, but with no facilities. They tend to offer more privacy than the modern campgrounds. Reservations (800/447-2757, www.michigan. gov/dnr) are recommended for all campsites in summer.

As another option, the park offers 16 hike-in **rustic cabins** (reservations 906/885-5275, www.midnrreservations.com, $65). These are great retreats after a day on the trail. They come with two to eight bunks, mattresses, a woodstove, basic utensils, and protection from the elements, but no electricity or running water. Bring your own stove for cooking. Cabins situated on inland lakes even come with a rowboat, so you can finish the day with a lazy drift across the water. Reserve a cabin as much as a year in advance.

Two more options for backpackers: There are three hike-in **Adirondack shelters** with sleeping platforms, available only on a first-come, first-served basis, as well as backcountry camping. Trailside camping is permitted throughout the backcountry, as long as you stay 0.25 miles or more from cabins, shelters, scenic areas, and roads. All backpackers must register at the visitors center before setting out.

INFORMATION AND SERVICES

Visitor information can be had from the **Porcupine Mountains Convention and Visitor Bureau** (906/884-2047, www.porcupinemountains.com) or the **Western Upper Peninsula Convention and Visitor Bureau** (906/932-4850 or 800/522-5657, www.explorewesternup.com). For maps and information about the state park, visit the **Porcupine Mountains Wilderness State Park Headquarters** (412 S. Boundary Rd., Ontonagon, 906/885-5275, www.michigan.gov/dnr, 10am-6pm daily mid-May-mid-Oct.).

If you need a hospital, you'll find the **Aspirus Ontonagon Hospital** (601 S. 7th St., 906/884-4134, www.aspirus-ontonagon. org), in Ontonagon; take Greenland Road (M-38) to 7th Street and turn north. Banking services can be found at **Citizens State Bank of Ontonagon** (501 River St., 906/884-4165, www.csbont.com).

GETTING THERE AND AROUND
Car
M-38, M-64, and U.S. 45 all converge on Ontonagon, located on the shores of Lake Superior. From Ironwood, take U.S. 2 to M-28/64 before turning north on M-64. From Ontonagon, take M-64 to M-107 to get to Porcupine Mountains Wilderness State Park—the headquarters are on South Boundary Road, just south of 107th Engineers Memorial Highway.

Boat
Ontonagon has a small marina that has 29 seasonal slips and 7 transient slips. The **Ontonagon Village Marina** (906/884-4225, www.michigan.gov/dnr) operates May 1-October 5 and can be reached on radio channels 16 and 68. Coordinates are 46°52.57 N, 89°19.58 W.

Air
Ontonagon's county airport doesn't offer scheduled flights, but you'll be able to catch a plane into **Houghton County Memorial Airport** (CMX, 23810 Airpark Blvd., Calumet, 906/482-3970, www.houghtoncounty.org), which has scheduled flights from Chicago on United Airlines. Alamo and National offer vehicle rentals, and taxi and limo service is available through **Copper Country Limo and Taxi** (906/370-4761). Marquette's **Sawyer International Airport** (MQT, 125 G Ave., Gwinn, 906/346-3308, www.sawyerairport.com) is a more distant option, over two hours' drive from Ontonagon.

Keweenaw Peninsula and Isle Royale

If Lake Superior resembles the head of a wolf, then the Keweenaw Peninsula (KEE-wuh-naw) is seized firmly in its jaw. Parts of the land do look like they've been gnawed on: Vestiges of the 19th-century copper boom are still in evidence, earning

this narrow strip of land the nickname "Copper Country."

Today, the Keweenaw's wealth is measured not in copper but in its boundless natural beauty. The peninsula is a mother lode of wild rivers, hidden waterfalls, and lonely Lake Superior beaches. There's civilization here too, but the Keweenaw is thinly populated even by Upper Peninsula standards. Houghton is the largest city, with Hancock, just across the river, a close second. Together they have a combined population of around 11,000—although the student population of two universities increases that figure during the school year. The cities are separated by Portage Lake, part of the Keweenaw Waterway, which splits the peninsula in half. Occasionally, locals will refer to the portion from Hancock north to Copper Harbor as "Copper Island."

Copper Harbor, on the shores of Lake Superior at Michigan's extreme north, is the end of the road, literally and figuratively; it's the terminus of U.S. 41, which originates in Miami, but the surroundings also announce the area's extreme northern latitude—which look and feel different from almost any other place in Michigan. Copper Harbor enjoys a well burnished reputation as an outdoor destination for kayakers, bikers, and snowmobilers. Rugged travelers on the way to Isle Royale National Park can catch the ferry here.

Some 48 miles north, and also part of Michigan, Isle Royale National Park is a wild, craggy, roadless archipelago in Lake Superior of lakes and forests, moose and hiking trails. This wonderfully remote location makes possible the park's status as the least visited property in the National Park system.

The remote Keweenaw has never had the tourism appeal and associated amenities of a larger community like Marquette, but this is slowly beginning to change. With the Keweenaw National Historic Park as a draw, more museums and other attractions are

Previous: downtown Calumet; Copper Harbor Lighthouse. **Above:** an old-growth pine tree at Estivant Pines Nature Sanctuary.

Look for ★ to find recommended
sights, activities, dining, and lodging.

Highlights

★ **A. E. Seaman Mineral Museum:** Get a fascinating glimpse of "natural art"—a sampling of thousands of colorful minerals from Michigan and around the world (page 144).

★ **Quincy Mine:** This mine north of Hancock tops the list of Keweenaw Historic Sites. The full two-hour tour takes you deep into the mine (page 145).

★ **Downtown Calumet:** This diamond in the rough is a three-dimensional reminder of the once prosperous copper industry. Friendly townspeople make it all the more enjoyable (page 147).

★ **Downtown Laurium:** Take a self-guided walking tour of some of the grandest homes in Michigan (page 149).

★ **Fort Wilkins Historic State Park:** Learn about one of the few remaining wooden forts in the country. During the summer, costumed interpreters recreate military life (page 159).

★ **Brockway Mountain Drive:** Don't miss this scenic lookout on the way to Copper Harbor—or the view of the city on the way back down (page 160).

★ **Lighthouses:** Sand Hills, Eagle Harbor, Copper Harbor...some of the U.P.'s finest historic lighthouses are here in the Keweenaw. A few of them double as bed-and-breakfasts (page 160).

★ **Hiking Isle Royale:** It takes some work to get here, but once you do, you'll find 165 miles of trails and some of the country's last true wilderness (page 176).

Keweenaw Peninsula and Isle Royale

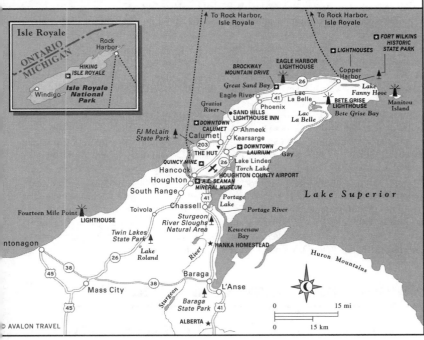

opening, and each year more people are discovering the peninsula's unspoiled beauty. The backcountry is filled with amazing hiking and mountain biking trails that lead to waterfalls and other gems.

Yet for those who crave adventure and solitude, the Keweenaw Peninsula and Isle Royale offer it up generously. As it was for those early copper miners, the Keweenaw today remains a remarkable land of discovery.

PLANNING YOUR TIME

It's only about a two-hour drive from the base of the Keweenaw Peninsula to Copper Harbor, but with scenery this stunning and outdoor activities this isolated, you're going to want to plan on spending considerably more time here. Houghton and Hancock make a great base for outdoor excursions—you can get pretty much anywhere in the peninsula in a

little more than an hour at most. Depending on how many hours you're looking to spend on the trail or in the kayak, visitors often find that a weekend is plenty of time for a good recreation and sightseeing vacation. If you're planning on a visit to Isle Royale, you'll want to add several days. The island wilderness is vast, with over 165 miles of trails, several inland lakes, and other natural curiosities.

HISTORY

Like a ragged dorsal fin on the back of the Upper Peninsula, the Keweenaw Peninsula was quickly shunned by early European immigrants to the Michigan Territories as hopelessly remote and rugged: nearly surrounded by Lake Superior, laden deep in snow for half the year and blanketed by impenetrable forests that grew from untillable rock and infertile sand. They dismissed it as nothing more than a wasteland, even more so than the rest of the Upper Peninsula.

But around 1840, state geologist Douglass Houghton confirmed the presence of copper—vast deposits of pure native copper, much of it near the surface, that no one had claimed. The still young United States quickly developed an insatiable appetite for the metal, first for use in new industrial machinery and later for Civil War hardware, electrical wiring, and other innovations. The value of Houghton's discovery seemed incalculable.

The copper rush commenced almost immediately, beginning with prospectors and followed by large mining enterprises that flocked to the remote Keweenaw. It was the nation's first mineral rush. Copper employed thousands of immigrant laborers, built cities, made millionaires, and financed extravagant luxuries like opera houses and mansions for the copper barons. Before it was over, King Copper generated more than $9.6 billion in wealth, exceeding the value of the California gold rush tenfold.

Today, the aftermath of the copper boom looms large, taking the form of abandoned mines, ghost towns buried in the forest, and the peculiar sight of lavish buildings in almost forgotten towns. Neglected for most of the 20th century, efforts by historic preservationists began in the 1970s. The result is the Keweenaw National Historic Park, established in 1992 and still very much a work in progress. Unfortunately, a great deal of this rich history has been demolished, thrown away, or crushed under the weight of winter snows. But a remarkable amount remains. While chain restaurants across the United States line their walls with fake tools and implements, here you'll find the real thing: scores of mining artifacts decorating restaurants, front porches, and other public venues.

Houghton, Hancock, and Vicinity

In 2014, *Outside,* a magazine dedicated to outdoor sporting life, listed Houghton (HOE-ton) among the nation's 16 best place to live. *Outside* may indeed have been on to something. Houghton and the adjacent city of Hancock offer great sporting diversions and boast a robust multicultural flair. Streets lined with beautifully preserved early-1900s buildings and the presence of a university add an atmosphere of culture and sophistication.

While the Keweenaw's cities provide a refreshing dose of urbanity, there are plenty of outlying towns and destinations that are also worthy of exploration. Houghton and Hancock's central location make it a great place for hub-and-spoke traveling—find your lodging, spend the evenings in the city, and make your way out on engaging day trips throughout the Keweenaw.

SOUTH OF HOUGHTON AND HANCOCK

The Keweenaw Peninsula begins at Ontonagon on its western shore and at L'Anse on the east, an imaginary line traced roughly by M-38. Between this highway and the Portage Waterway, the southern Keweenaw is quiet and sparsely populated. It's quite a change from the turn of the 20th century, when the Copper Range Company operated a network of successful mines across this whaleback of a peninsula. Like elsewhere in the Keweenaw, the tall skeletons of mining shaft houses, dying relics of the copper rush, frequently lurch skyward out of the pines.

At the foot of Keweenaw Bay, between Baraga (BARE-a-ga) and L'Anse (LAHNS), the enormous wooden statue *Shrine of the Snowshoe Priest* looms 35 feet above Red Rock Bluff. It commemorates the life of Bishop Frederic Baraga, a Roman Catholic missionary from Slovenia who gained recognition for his work with local Ojibwa people in the mid-1800s, traveling by snowshoe to reach distant communities. Unlike most missionaries in his day, Baraga is believed to have worked to support the Ojibwa's rights by helping them gain title to their land, a stance unpopular with the local European fur traders and government Indian agents. Baraga spoke the Ojibwa language fluently, and his guidebook of Ojibwa vocabulary and grammar is still consulted today.

A few miles south of L'Anse, on U.S. 41, a white clapboard lumber mill marks your arrival in **Alberta**. In 1935, Henry Ford built the mill, dammed nearby Plumbago Creek for the mill's water supply, and constructed housing for the mill's workers. It's a classic example of a company town, one that has changed little since operations shut down in the early 1950s. Today the facility is operated by Michigan Technological University as a forestry research center. The grounds, including a small museum, are open to the public (9am-5pm Mon.-Fri.). Admission is free, but donations are appreciated. The sawmill is currently being renovated and is open by appointment only (906/487-3603).

Ford built many other facilities across the western U.P., mostly sawmills to harvest the nearby timber for automotive applications. The outpost in Alberta, however, is much smaller, and was built mostly for PR purposes.

Hanka Homestead

The Hanka family from Finland established this farmstead, hidden away in the creases of the landscape above Keweenaw Bay between Baraga and Houghton, in 1896. The buildings include a log house, a barn, a milk house over a spring for natural refrigeration, and a sauna, in keeping with Finnish tradition. The self-sufficient Hankas raised dairy cows and chickens, grew vegetables and grains, and tanned hides to eke out a living and get through the harsh winters. What they didn't do much was modernize. Even though Jalmar Hanka, the last surviving family member, lived here until the mid-1960s,

the **Hanka Homestead** (906/334-2601 summer, 906/334-2575 fall-spring, www.hanka-homesteadmuseum.org, noon-4pm Tues. and Thurs.-Sun. Memorial Day-Labor Day, $4 adults, $2.50 ages 5-12) remains as it was in about 1920, complete with the Hankas' belongings filling the home and its nine outbuildings. Guides offer comprehensive tours, and the homestead is a cooperating site of the Keweenaw National Historic Park. It's best to call ahead before driving out here. To find the homestead, head north about 10 miles on U.S. 41 from Baraga, turn west on Arnheim Road, and follow the small wooden signs, which may refer to it as the "Finnish Homestead Museum."

HOUGHTON AND HANCOCK

Houghton (pop. 7,000) and Hancock (pop. 4,000) face each other across the Portage Waterway, with homes and churches tumbling down steep 500-foot bluffs reminiscent of San Francisco, especially on the Hancock side. The Portage Waterway effectively slices the Keweenaw in two, a 21-mile passage that saves boaters the 100-mile trip around the peninsula.

Native Americans used the route for centuries to cross the peninsula, traveling from Keweenaw Bay across Portage Lake and along the ancient Portage River, then crossing over land the rest of the way to the shores of Lake Superior. In the late 1800s a dredged canal eliminated the need for the west-end portage. Commercial traffic plied the waterway, largely to serve the smelters, stamping plants, and vibrant cities of the burgeoning copper trade.

A unique **lift bridge** spans the waterway that links Houghton and Hancock. Functioning in a way similar to a drawbridge, its huge center section rises like an elevator to let water traffic pass below. Today the Portage Waterway largely serves pleasure boaters and the 125-foot *Ranger III*, a ferry that transports hikers to Isle Royale National Park, which is operated by the National Park Service. Houghton and Hancock are

Houghton and Hancock

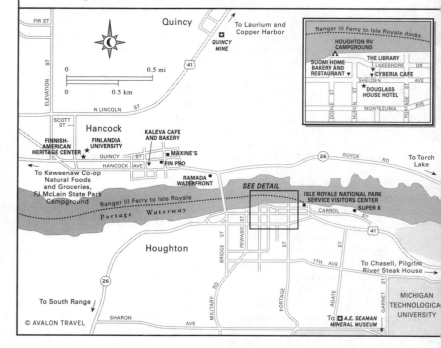

considered the gateways to the Keweenaw and to Isle Royale, but visitors just passing through will miss an appealing slice of the region. The twin cities offer the studious atmosphere of college towns combined with pride in their Finnish heritage.

Downtown Houghton

You can conduct your own historic walking tour of Houghton by strolling down Shelden Avenue, the city's main street. Tall facades of redbrick and red sandstone line the street, including the **Douglass House Hotel** (517 Shelden Ave.), built in 1860 as a luxury hotel and dining establishment for travelers through the Portage Waterway. An addition in 1899 made it the lavish building you see today. Inside, the Victorian interior of the **Douglass House Saloon** (906/482-2003) still reflects those genteel days, with original Tiffany chandeliers, leaded glass windows, and frilly curtains.

On the east end of town, the campus of **Michigan Technological University** stretches out along the Portage Waterway. Over 6,500 students attend Michigan Tech, the majority of whom study some type of engineering. Geology, mining, and industrial archaeology are some of the school's notable fields. Students in the mining field get real-world experience here, learning hands-on mining practices deep inside the nearby Quincy Mine.

★ A. E. SEAMAN MINERAL MUSEUM

Michigan Tech is home to the highly regarded **A. E. Seaman Mineral Museum** (1404 E. Sharon Ave., 906/487-2572, www.museum. mtu.edu, 9am-5pm Mon.-Sat., $6 adults, $5 seniors, $3 students, $2 ages 9-17, free under age 9), the official mineralogical museum of the state of Michigan. The Keweenaw is considered one of the most geologically rich and fascinating regions in the world, and the Seaman Museum holds the premier collection of area minerals and gemstones, including crystallized copper, silver, datolites, greenstones, and agates. Don't miss the informative exhibit on an iron mine and glowing fluorescent minerals. The museum also houses an impressive collection of minerals from around the world numbering more than 30,000 specimens. The museum recently relocated to a new and expanded freestanding facility. Parking is plentiful and free.

Downtown Hancock

Michigan Tech isn't the only local university: Across the waterway is **Finlandia University,** which began in 1896 as a Finnish academy to serve the area's ever-growing number of immigrant miners' families. Today, enrollment is approximately 550. The institution's **Finnish-American Heritage Center** (435 Quincy St., 906/487-7302, 8am-4:30pm Mon.-Fri.) maintains a gallery open to the public that highlights Finnish artists and the archives of the area's Finnish settlement.

Even those not enthusiastic about shopping might be drawn into some of Hancock's stores, with their emphasis on unusual Finnish products. Where else will you find sauna supplies but **Fin Pro** (208 Quincy St., 906/487-5628)? The shop owners, who retired here from Helsinki, also carry an excellent selection of Finnish textiles, glassware, books, and music. You'll also find a good array of Finnish glassware and gifts at **Maxine's** (129 Quincy St., 906/482-5101).

★ Quincy Mine

Just north of Hancock, the mammoth shaft house of the **Quincy Mine** (906/482-3101, www.quincymine.com, daily May-mid-Oct., hoist and mine tour $25 adults, $22 over age 54, $10 ages 6-12, free under age 6, surface tour and tram ride $15 adults, $14 over age 54, $8 ages 6-12) dominates the skyline. The Quincy ranked as one of the world's richest copper mines in the late 1800s, producing over a billion pounds of copper. Today, a few of its buildings still stand, and the land beneath it remains riddled with the shafts (vertical tunnels) and adits (horizontal tunnels) of the mammoth mine, which stretch more than 1.5 miles deep on 92 levels and 2 miles wide.

The Quincy Mine is a key site in the

the shaft house at Quincy Mine

Keweenaw National Historic Park, and it offers a fascinating tour that takes you through the historic buildings and deep into the mine itself. Many of the tour guides are mining students at nearby Michigan Tech, so they can handle just about any mining or engineering question. The tour begins with a look at the gargantuan steam hoist, the world's largest. A giant spool of sorts, it powered the steel pulleys that hauled the miners and mine cars loaded with copper in and out of the mine. The machine's mammoth size—more than double the size of the average hoist—was necessitated by the extreme depth of the mine.

The building itself is as interesting as the hoist. In an era when miners made $1 a day, a good wage for the time, the Quincy Mining Company built its hoist house of poured concrete, then decorated it with tasteful arched windows, lined the walls with Italian tile, and topped it off with green tiles imported from Spain. Because it was so overengineered, the immense room remains in excellent shape today. It also houses plenty of artifacts and photos, including bilingual safety instructions posted next to the machinery, due to the high number of immigrant Finnish miners.

From the hoist house, the tour continues with a rather dramatic ride in a glass enclosed tram down the side of a steep hill. Views of Houghton and Hancock are terrific as the tram descends to an entrance to the mine, an adit at Level 7. A tractor carries you about 2,000 feet into the mine, where guides demonstrate mining techniques and give you a feel for what it was like to work deep inside the earth; a drippy, damp environment with only hand tools and candles. Contact the **Quincy Mine Hoist Association** (49750 U.S. 41, 906/482-3101, www.quincymine.com) for tour times and other information.

Lighthouses

Two of the lighthouses in the Houghton and Hancock area are the **Portage Lake Upper and Lower Entry Lights,** the upper located at the end of the breakwater at McLain State Park. Built in 1950, the steel tower is one of the Keweenaw's newest lights, which takes nothing away from its beauty. Take M-203 about 10 miles north of Hancock to F. J. McLain State Park. The Portage Lake Lower Entry Light is on the east side of the Keweenaw Peninsula at the Portage River in the town of Lake Linden. This light was built 30 years earlier than its companion on the other side of the river. A long walk along the breakwater pier will allow you to get close.

Near the Lower Entry Light, the **Portage River Light,** also called the Jacobsville Light, has been converted into a pleasant, unique bed-and-breakfast in Lake Linden. The **Jacobsville Lighthouse Inn** (38741 Jacobs St., 906/523-4137, www.jacobsvillelighthouse. com) offers regular tours of the lighthouse and grounds. Call ahead for an appointment, or just stop by to see if they're available.

NORTH OF HOUGHTON AND HANCOCK

At the height of the Keweenaw's copper mining glory, the Calumet and Hecla Consolidated Copper Company, which operated largely in Calumet, proved the grandest operation of all. At the turn of the 20th century, C&H employed some 11,000 workers who extracted more than 1.5 billion tons of copper from a web of mines that tunneled under Calumet and adjacent Laurium. A surface plant in town, considered the most efficient in the nation, roared and whistled with the sound of 50 steam engines at work.

C&H ultimately generated more than $72 million in revenue. It built low-cost housing for its miners, consisting of some 1,000 dwellings lined up like chess pieces. Groups of homes formed towns and were named Swedetown or Limerick—American namesakes of their ancestral homes. Most significantly, C&H spawned the city of Calumet, known then as Red Jacket, a booming community of more than 60,000 residents. Striking red sandstone buildings with false fronts and cornices lined the 12-square-block business district. Downtown Calumet was filled with elegant shops, soaring churches, some 70 saloons, and even a lavish theater that attracted the nation's leading vaudeville stars. The city buzzed day and night, both above and below ground.

After the mining industry declined, Calumet's economy became stagnant and the city remained largely frozen in time. Today, downtown's sturdy sandstone buildings have survived the decades beautifully, and Calumet is a trove of early 1900s architecture—the pivotal reason for its national historic park status. "We are fortunate that this area has been little disturbed since those glory days," said a park supporter. "Few modern intrusions have marred the area's scale and the feeling of its mining heritage." Today, Calumet (pop. 800) anchors the new Keweenaw National Historic Park, one of the park's two key units and a designated historic district.

★ Downtown Calumet

Thanks to its new federal status and renewed civic pride, downtown Calumet's historic character is more evident than ever. Ugly mid-century facades have been removed from the elegant sandstone and brick buildings, and new investment is gradually coming in to restore and preserve them further. To appreciate this architectural legacy, stop by the **Keweenaw Convention and Visitors Bureau** (56638 Calumet Ave., 906/337-4579 or 800/338-7982, www.keweenaw.info) and pick up a walking tour guide. A few stops of particular note: The **Union Building** (5th St. and Red Jacket Rd.) was home of one of the area's first banks in 1888 and remains in excellent shape, with a decorative metal cornice. **Shute's Bar** (322 6th St.) doesn't look that special on the outside, but inside you can see the preserved ornate plaster ceilings and the magnificent back bar with a stained-glass canopy. Across the street, the **Red Jacket Fire Station** typifies the Romanesque style favored for public buildings and churches at the time. Examine the detail on the **Red Jacket Town Hall and Opera House,** now called the **Calumet Theatre** (340 6th St., 906/337-2610, www.calumettheatre.com).

Free self-guided tours are possible during box office hours (noon-5pm Mon.-Fri.) and guided tours are available by appointment. Perhaps more than any other, this building was truly the pride of the community. The theater portion, added in 1898 and the first municipally owned theater in the country, was a showy extravagance of plaster rococo in cream, crimson, green, and gilt. It even had electric lights, a rarity at the time. Referred to as "the greatest social event ever known in copperdom's metropolis" when it opened in 1900, the theater attracted A-list celebrities such as John Philip Sousa, Harry Houdini, Douglas Fairbanks Jr., and Sarah Bernhardt.

Keweenaw National Historic Park

The **Keweenaw National Historic Park** (200 5th St., 906/337-3168, www.nps.gov/kewe) is not so much a place on a map but a place in time. One of the National Park Service's newest units, it was established in 1992 "to commemorate the heritage of copper mining on the Keweenaw Peninsula; its mines, its machinery, and its people."

Rather than a park with simply defined boundaries, the Keweenaw National Historic Park consists of historic attractions throughout the peninsula. Two units anchor the park, the Quincy Unit at the Quincy Mine in Hancock, and the Calumet Unit in historic downtown Calumet, although some of this land remains privately owned. The National Park Service owns a limited amount of land outright to preserve key sites and conduct interpretive activities. In addition, the park has designated "cooperating sites" throughout the peninsula, including mine tours and museums that remain in private ownership but will benefit from increased visibility and federal funding.

The park will continue to be under development for many years while continuing to restore buildings, create interpretive displays, and develop educational programs. The **park headquarters** (25970 Red Jacket Rd., Calumet, 906/337-3168) currently

Copper Mining in Copper Country

Copper Country, the nickname associated with the Keweenaw Peninsula, is well earned. After the discovery of copper in the mid-1800s, mines near the tip of the Keweenaw were among the first to open. The copper business grew slowly for several years until just before the Civil War, and by 1860 Copper Country was producing some 12 million pounds of the metal per year. By 1890 the region was sending about 100 million pounds of copper annually on ships that traveled through the Great Lakes or on trains headed to Chicago and the rest of the nation. Over the course of 40 years, Michigan produced more copper than any other state, occasionally accounting for as much as 90 percent of the nation's total output.

As the boom took off, the Keweenaw region soon saw an influx of workers from all over North America, followed by immigrants from Cornwall. Cornish miners were later joined by large numbers of Norwegians, Finns, Danes, and Swedes, who came to the Upper Peninsula to work tirelessly in both the copper and iron mines to make an honest living. The newcomers brought with them their cultures, foods, and languages. Many of the old mining communities in Keweenaw and around the U.P. are still influenced by this heritage. Even today, Finns are among the most prominent ethnic groups in Michigan's Upper Peninsula.

Copper Country mining camps and small towns grew seemingly overnight to become large cities and industrial centers. In Hancock, the region's mining and immigrant heritage survives, exemplified by the Quincy Mine, a national historic site, and Finlandia University, founded in 1896. Other towns born of the copper boom include Calumet, Laurium, and Lake Linden.

As the copper deposits became depleted, the industry began its long decline, culminating with the last mines closing by the 1970s.

The economic impact on the area was severe and long-lasting. In most U.P. communities, the hole left by the demise of mining has yet to be filled with another industry. Today, logging (conducted in a responsible and sustainable manner) and tourism hold the best hope for the area's economic future. These industries permit utilization—but not exploitation—of the Upper Peninsula's prized natural resources.

operates with just a skeleton administrative staff. For visitor information, contact the **Keweenaw Convention and Visitors Bureau** (56638 Calumet Ave., Calumet, 906/337-4579 or 800/338-7982, www.keweenaw.info).

C&H Industrial Core

One of Calumet and Hecla's mines was located right in town, in an area bisected by Red Jacket Road, just west of U.S. 41. Beginning at the Coppertown USA museum, a self-guided industrial core walking tour takes you past a drill shop, a powder house, a machine shop, and several other mining buildings in various states of restoration. The National Park Service is adding interpretive signs to guide you along and share mining information, but you'll also want an information sheet that maps the route, available from the Keweenaw

Tourism Council, the park headquarters, or the Coppertown USA museum.

Coppertown USA

The mine's pattern shop, where wooden patterns were made as molds for machine parts, now serves as the home of **Coppertown USA** (25815 Red Jacket Rd., 906/337-4354, www.keweenawheritagesites.org, 11am-5pm Mon.-Sat. June-Aug., $4 adults, $3 with National Park Pass, $2 ages 6-15, free under age 6), a privately run museum and national park cooperative site that traces the region's copper industry. It includes numerous artifacts, a display of area minerals, a replica of a mining captain's office, a diorama of Native American mining, and more. Don't miss the pattern shop area, which still houses thousands of patterns, lined up on shelves as if they haven't been touched for 50 years (some have been relocated to the Smithsonian). Another interesting exhibit is a 1976 scale model that shows elaborate plans for Calumet, including a cultural center, a festival plaza, and a products exhibit center. The museum is located near the intersection of U.S. 41 and Red Jacket Road.

★ Downtown Laurium

Just across U.S. 41 from Calumet is Laurium. Largely a residential district for the area mines, the west end (closest to Calumet) has a few streets of plain company homes that remain, looking rough and dilapidated—like much of Laurium. But a few blocks farther east, around Pewabic and 3rd Streets, mining management built their homes, and today the area is a quiet and stately neighborhood well worth visiting. Pick up a *Laurium Walking Tour* guide from the **Keweenaw Convention and Visitors Bureau** (56638 Calumet Ave., 906/337-4579 or 800/338-7982, www.keweenaw.info) in Calumet. It will direct you to impressive homes like the one at 305 Tamarack Street, where a wise mining investor made enough to create this grand home with seven fireplaces, a third-floor ballroom, and a carriage house.

But the finest home belonged to Captain Thomas Hoatson, founder of the Calumet and Arizona Mining Company, who built his dream mansion at 320 Tamarack Street. Today it operates as the **Laurium Manor Inn** (906/337-2549, www.laurium.info, tours 11am-5pm daily, $7 adults, $4 children), which means the public can enjoy a glimpse of this remarkable place. Sprawling across 13,000 square feet, the 45-room mansion includes ceilings covered in silver leaf, elephant hide wall coverings, a triple staircase of hand-carved oak, and a turntable in the carriage house so carriages could be rotated to face forward. The inn is open year-round, with room rates of $89-175.

Football or cinema fans may want to view the decidedly less dramatic home at 432 Hecla Street. Laurium's most famous citizen was born here—**George Gipp,** the Notre Dame football star, immortalized in the movie *Knute Rockne, All American.* "The Gipper" was undoubtedly Ronald Reagan's most famous role until he became president. A George Gipp Memorial decorates the corner of Tamarack Street and M-26.

Ghost Towns

Ghost towns litter the Keweenaw, faded testament to the boom and bust days of copper. The ruins of old mines and stamping plants

downtown Laurium

(facilities that separated copper from rock) line M-26 between Hancock and Calumet. The gray piles of residue are mine tailings or stamping plant leftovers called "stamp sand." Several bona fide ghost towns hide in the woods too, especially between Calumet and Copper Harbor. At **Central** (watch for the small brown sign on U.S. 41, about 11 miles north of Mohawk), an exceptionally rich mine produced nearly $10 million worth of copper by 1898 while the surrounding town grew to 1,200. Today, nature has all but reclaimed Central, with just a few clapboard houses creaking in the breeze. Turn right near the top of the hill for a look at the mine ruins and rows of house foundations. Be sure to watch your step while walking.

Just south of Copper Harbor on U.S. 41, another sign announces your arrival in **Mandan,** directing you down a dirt road disappearing into birches. Follow it south for about 50 yards and a tidy row of homes suddenly erupts out of the woods. Welcome to Mandan, the last stop on a trolley line from Hancock.

ENTERTAINMENT
Ojibwa Casino and Resort
The **Ojibwa Casino** (16449 Michigan Ave., Baraga, 906/353-6333 or 800/323-8045, www.ojibwacasino.com) in Baraga is tucked away in the southeast corner of the Keweenaw Peninsula, where the long land formation meets the rest of the U.P. There's enough gaming here to satisfy all but the choosiest players, with more than 300 slot and video poker machines that take denominations as low as a penny and up to $5. If you prefer table games, the casino offers craps, roulette, blackjack, poker (including 3-5-7 and Texas hold 'em), and more. Get something to eat at the **PressBox Sports Bar** (11am-1:30am daily), which serves up exactly the type of food you'd expect at a sports bar. You'll find other sports bar trappings here too, like happy hour specials and big-screen TVs. You'll also see a few things you might not expect, such as an eight lane bowling alley and a dance

floor. The PressBox hosts DJs or live bands on weekends. The lodging here is good too. The Ojibwa Casino hotel has gone through a series of renovations to their 40 guest rooms, which include double rooms and whirlpool suites at remarkably modest rates ($75 d, $90 suites). To get there from Houghton and Hancock, take U.S. 41 south to M-38, turn right, and go a little more than a mile. From Ontonagon, take M-38 east.

Calumet Theatre
Built more than a century ago, the **Calumet Theatre** (340 6th St., Calumet, 906/337-2610, www.calumettheatre.com) was Keweenaw's destination for live opera since 1900. The theater enjoyed a good run, hosting greats such as John Philip Sousa, among others. But as the era of live theater declined, the theater's fortunes faded. Later, as copper mining waned and motion pictures grew in popularity, the Calumet was converted into a cinema. Summer stock took place a few times during the 1950s and the 1970s, but didn't enjoy a permanent resurgence until the Calumet Theatre Company was incorporated in 1983, which brought year-round entertainment back to this glamorous hall. And it is glamorous: The auditorium, with its bowl-shaped proscenium, stunning paintings, and elegant woodwork, was restored in the 1970s, followed by exterior work during the late 1980s. Today, the Calumet is a National Historic Landmark that regularly hosts theater and opera performances as well as symphony concerts, dance, and music. Some 30,000 people come through the doors each year. You can take a self-guided tour of the historic theater during box office hours (noon-5pm Mon.-Fri., donation), and guided tours are available by appointment. Take U.S. 41 into town and turn north on 6th Street to get to the theater.

FESTIVALS AND EVENTS
Leave it to those engineering students at Michigan Tech to design and build elaborate snow sculptures at the university's **Winter**

Carnival in January. Houghton also hosts the **Bridgefest and Seafood Fest** the second weekend in June, with food and music in Ray Kestner Park. Chassell's **Strawberry Fest** is the second week in July, just in time for the sweet and juicy harvest. Perhaps the most elaborate annual event is the **Heritage Days Celebration** (www.mainstreetcalumet. com) in Calumet. Running a full week during mid-August, the occasion celebrates the area's Finnish heritage and includes ethnic foods, a parade, and art and craft vendors.

SUMMER SPORTS AND RECREATION
Hiking and Biking

Mountain bikers new to the area can hardly believe the wealth of terrific trails in the Keweenaw, literally hundreds of miles of old mining and logging roads, overgrown double-track routes, and technical single-track. They loop through towering pines to backwoods waterfalls, to otherwise inaccessible Lake Superior shorelines, and even past ghost towns now buried deep in the woods. Note that many trails may dead-end suddenly.

Vast tracts of land in the Keweenaw are privately owned by large corporations; either mining firms or paper companies. In exchange for a break on state taxes, the companies allow public use of the land for recreation, including hiking, fishing, and mountain biking. Still, for liability reasons, some outfitters and bike shops are reluctant to hand out maps or endorse these lands for riding. If you ask, though, most bike shops tend to be quite helpful about suggesting trails, especially the **Keweenaw Adventure Company** (155 Gratiot St., 906/289-4303, www.keweenawadventure.com) in Copper Harbor. If you're going on your own, snowmobile maps make decent trail guides. Cross-reference them with a topographic map. Snowmobile trails often cross frozen lowlands that are impassable during summer months.

Always remember to use common sense. Don't venture out without a map and compass and the skill to use them. Stay away from active logging areas, which are usually marked by signs, and the audible presence of buzzing logging equipment. If you hear a logging truck coming, don't just move to the side, get completely off the trail. Logging trucks are wide and heavy, and they can blaze down roads at surprising speeds.

Many old railroad grades threading across the northern Keweenaw have been converted to public multiuse trails, intended for snowmobiles, ATVs, and perhaps to a lesser extent, mountain bikes. For cyclists not comfortable venturing deep into the woods, they're a nice way to get off the road. The **Jack Stevens Rail Trail** runs 14 miles from Hancock north to Calumet on the former Soo Line grade. Somewhat less appealing, because it parallels M-26 for a lengthy stretch, is the **Keweenaw Rail-Trail,** an 18-mile route from Hancock along Torch Lake, also ending in Calumet. Trail surfaces can be a rough collection of rock, gravel, wood, and sand or whatever happened to be there when they removed the rails, so they're not appropriate for narrow-tire bikes. For more information and a map listing access points, contact the Keweenaw Tourism Council at 800/338-7982.

If you're skilled with a map and compass, some fine single-track winds down along the **Gratiot River** about five miles north of Calumet. As a bonus, you can check out the little-visited Upper and Lower Gratiot Falls as the river rolls and tumbles its way to Lake Superior. For other ideas, check in at **Cross Country Sports** (507 Oak St., Calumet, 906/337-4520, www.crosscountrysports.com). Most of the staff are willing to divulge at least a couple of their favorite trails.

For something a little less adventurous, pedal the **Swedetown Trails** (www.swedetowntrails.org), a cross-country trail network on the southwest edge of Calumet. From 6th Street near St. Ann's Church, pick up Oceola Road and follow it south. The trail network has about 15 miles of trails over rolling hills and through woods and all are great for biking except the northernmost loop (the Red Trail), which is usually too wet. From this small network, you can veer off onto what seems like an endless network of side trails. In winter, these trails offer great cross-country skiing, including a charming chalet with a snack bar and a warming stove (noon-5pm Mon.-Tues., noon-8pm Wed.-Fri., 10am-8pm Sat., 10am-5pm Sun.). For information, contact the **Keweenaw Convention and Visitors Bureau** (906/337-4579 or 800/338-7982, www.keweenaw.info).

Canoeing and Kayaking

Rivers in the Keweenaw tend to be somewhat rocky, so white-water kayaking is limited, although river levels vary with each year's level of precipitation. Sea kayaking, on the other hand, is outstanding. It's the perfect way to access bluffs, caves, sea stacks, and rocky islands all along the Lake Superior shoreline. The Keweenaw Water Trail, still under development, guides small craft around the peninsula and through the Portage Waterway. Canoeing is popular on inland lakes, but open boats are not recommended on Lake Superior.

The **Keweenaw Water Trail** provides a mapped passageway of more than 100 miles through the Portage Waterway and along the Lake Superior shore, indicating accommodations, campgrounds, launches, and more. For more information and to purchase a water trail map, contact the **Keweenaw Convention and Visitors Bureau** (906/337-4579 or 800/338-7982, www.keweenaw.info). For white-water boaters, **Down Wind Sports** (308 Shelden Ave., 906/482-2500, www.downwindsports.com) in Houghton is your best source for local information on river conditions.

Fishing

One of the finest fishing rivers in the Houghton and Hancock area is the Salmon Trout River. Flowing for about 12 miles from tiny Perrault to Lake Superior, the river is an excellent spot to cast for steelhead and brook trout. Take M-26 a few miles south of Houghton to Old M-26/Erickson Drive in the village of Atlantic Mine. Turn right, then right

again on County Road A-65, which continues as Obenhoff Road to an access point a few miles west.

Another popular site is **McLain State Park** (18350 M-203, 906/482-0278), seven miles north of Hancock on M-203. You can also try both Portage Lake and Torch Lake for walleye, bass, and northern pike.

Golf

The only choice for 18 holes in the Keweenaw Peninsula is **Portage Lake Golf Course** (906/487-2641, www.mtu.edu, 7:30am-9pm daily May-mid-Oct., $40 for 18 holes, $24 for 9 holes), a fine course belonging to Michigan Technological University. Although it's located off the main drag as you enter town, the well-kept greens are peaceful and the holes have the tree-lined horizons you'd expect from a U.P. golf course. The clubhouse has a pro shop and a bar and grill, the cleverly named Par and Grill. Players can get a beer at the grill or from one of the beverage carts. There's also a putting green and a driving range that closes at dusk.

About 15 miles south of Houghton, in Toivola, the **Wyandotte Hills Golf Club and Resort** (5821 E. Poyhonen Rd., 906/288-3720, May-Oct., $23 for 18 holes, $18 for 9 holes) is a nine-hole course that does double duty as an overnight getaway, with four cabins that can be rented year-round. The wooded and watered course makes for good golfing, while the clubhouse serves an excellent lunch and dinner Monday to Friday and lunch only on Saturday. In Calumet, you'll find the **Calumet Golf Club** (1501 Golf Course Rd., 906/337-3911, http://calumetgolfclub.com, $30 for 18 holes, $20 for 9 holes), another nine-hole course with club rentals and a reasonably priced restaurant.

Bird Watching

Bird watchers will find a variety of northern species in the Keweenaw, including red- and white-winged crossbills, Canada geese, hawks, peregrine falcons, and bald eagles. An

the big snow gauge on U.S. 41

more suitable for ORV riders. Bear in mind that you'll likely be sharing the pathway with nonmotorized travelers.

Waterfalls

Far south of Houghton and just north of the imaginary line that forms the base of the Keweenaw Peninsula, the **Wyandotte Falls** drop 20 feet down multiple steps in a beautiful display. Take Wyandotte Hills Golf Course Road less than a mile west of M-26 to the parking area, then follow the trail to the falls. The **Hungarian Falls,** north of Hancock, are better still. Take M-26 north to Hubbell, and then turn left on 6th Street. Take the left fork two blocks up, and turn left onto the second trail road. Both forks lead to the falls. The right fork leads to the Upper Falls, while the left heads to the Lower Falls. At 25 feet, the Upper Falls drop farther, but the Lower Falls are more beautiful, at a still impressive 15 feet.

WINTER SPORTS AND RECREATION
Downhill Skiing

If you're into serious skiing, head north to Mount Bohemia near Copper Harbor, but for novices or skiers who appreciate tamer terrain, **Mont Ripley** (906/487-2340, www.aux. mtu.edu/ski, full day $47, half day $40), near Houghton and Hancock and owned and operated by Michigan Technological University, also offers some good downhill runs and is lit for night skiing.

Ski and Snowshoe Trails

A giant **snow gauge** on U.S. 41 south of Phoenix proudly marks the Keweenaw's record snowfall, a staggering 390.4 inches in the winter of 1977-1978. It wasn't an aberration; the surrounding waters of Lake Superior routinely produce colossal lake-effect snows, often exceeding 300 inches per year. That reliable level of snow, combined with the remarkable local terrain, makes the Keweenaw a haven for snowmobilers.

Thankfully, skiers and snowshoers will find there's more than enough wilderness to

estimated 20 species of warblers are frequently spotted throughout the peninsula.

Just north of the Hanka Homestead, the Sturgeon River bleeds across the lowlands before emptying into Portage Lake, forming sloughs that attract migrating waterfowl. For the best access, stop at the **Sturgeon River Sloughs Natural Area,** marked by an observation tower along U.S. 41 near Chassell. The 1.5-mile De Vriendt Nature Trail follows a series of dikes and boardwalks back into the slough, with interpretive signs describing herons, ospreys, eagles, kestrels, ducks, and dozens of other species that frequent the area.

Off-Road Vehicles

The Michigan DNR's ATV route, the Hancock-Calumet Trail, stretches all the way from Hancock to Calumet. Like other DNR trails, this one is kept lightly groomed. All state forest roads are open to ORV use, unless specifically marked otherwise. The rail trails and other old railroad grades that can cause headaches for mountain bikers are go around. Many towns have developed cross-country ski trail systems. For backcountry skiing and snowshoeing, pick up a snowmobile map and avoid the marked trails. Also note that some accommodations located on signed and groomed trails cater to snowmobilers, and the roar can get pretty deafening. Don't be afraid to ask about the presence of "sleds," as they're sometimes referred to, before booking lodging in winter months.

Snowshoers should stay off groomed ski trails, but Michigan Tech in Houghton has a series of marked snowshoeing trails. In Calumet, try the marked Swedetown trails.

Snowmobiling

There are more than 2,000 miles of snowmobile trails in the U.P., and at last count, the Keweenaw had more than 200 of them. They stretch from south of Houghton all the way to the tip. Most are clearly identified, well groomed, and between 10 and 16 feet wide. And they do connect to the other 1,800-plus miles of trails above the bridge. The **Keweenaw Trail** (Trail 3) is the main route into and out of Houghton and Hancock, and it connects to numerous other branches: The North and South Freda trails lead toward Lake Superior, while Stevens Trail connects to Calumet.

Keweenaw Trail joins the 55-mile **Bill Nichols Trail,** which ends farther south in Mass City, near Ontonagon. A popular multiuse trail during warmer weather, this converted rail line is one of the most popular scenic snowmobile routes in the Keweenaw. For a detailed map, including the locations of gas stations, contact the **Keweenaw Convention and Visitors Bureau** (56638 Calumet Ave., Calumet, 906/337-4579 or 800/338-7982, www.keweenaw.info).

FOOD

Combine a college town with a large multicultural population, and you come up with a good range of eating options in the Houghton and Hancock area.

★ **The Library** (62 North Isle Royale St., Houghton, 906/487-5882, www.library-brewpub.com, 11:30am-10pm Mon.-Thurs., 11:30am-11pm Fri.-Sat., 9am-10pm Sun., entrées $14-26) ranks as the most popular place in town, drawing both students and locals. Offerings include homemade beers, steaks, salads, pizza, pastas, and a bevy of sandwich choices. The ★ **Pilgrim River Steak House** (47409 U.S. 41, Houghton, 906/482-8595, www.pilgrimriversteakhouse.com, 11am-10pm Mon.-Thurs., 11am-11pm Fri.-Sat., noon-9:30pm Sun., entrées $17-36), on U.S. 41 on the southeast end of Houghton, is *the* place to go for beef of all sorts, especially prime rib.

Just north of Calumet in Kearsarge is an undiscovered gem. **The Hut** (58540 U.S. 41, Kearsarge, 906/337-1133, www.hutinn.com, 11am-10pm Mon.-Sat., 8am-10pm Sun., $12-25) restaurant resides in a 1950s-era building that resembles a Frank Lloyd Wright structure and offers great food and warm hospitality. Steaks, seafood, and a great array of pasties make this place well worth the stop.

Along with basic eggs-and-hash-browns fare, **Suomi Home Bakery and Restaurant** (54 N. Huron St., Houghton, 906/482-3220, 6am-3pm Mon.-Sat., 7am-2pm Sun., under $10) includes a few Finnish specialties on the menu. Try the *pannukakku,* billed as a Finnish pancake but more like deep-dish custard pie topped with raspberry sauce. Most breakfasts come with *nisu,* a Finnish yeast bread spiced with cardamom. The restaurant can be a bit hard to find. It's partially hidden under Houghton's covered walkway, a block down the hill from Shelden Street.

Cyberia Café (800 Sharon Ave., Houghton, 906/482-2233, 7am-11pm Mon.-Fri., 9am-11pm Sat.-Sun.) is an Internet café that offers terrific java and the best cinnamon rolls you've ever tasted.

Over on the Hancock side, find good food, relaxation, and a splendid view in the Ramada Hancock at the **Waterfront Restaurant** (99 Navy St., Hancock, 906/484-8494, www.ramadahancock.com, 11am-9pm Mon.-Thurs., 11am-10pm Fri.-Sat., 9am-9pm Sun., entrées

$16-25). For adults, there's a full bar. On Hancock's main street, the **Kaleva Cafe and Bakery** (234 Quincy St., Hancock, 906/482-1230, www.mykaleva.com, 7am-9pm Mon.-Sat., 8am-9pm Sun., under $10) draws the locals for its baked goods, including its self-proclaimed "famous" whipped-cream cakes. Kaleva makes a good pasty, which is a potpie creation of beef, potatoes, onions, and ruta-bagas—just the kind of hearty self-contained meal that miners could take with them deep underground. You'll also find pasties at coffee shops and grocery store deli counters throughout the Upper Peninsula.

Though you'll find plenty of traditional grocery stores along M-26 south of town and U.S. 41 north, a better choice just might be the **Keweenaw Co-op Natural Foods and Groceries** (1035 Ethel Ave., Hancock, 906/482-2030, www.keweenaw.coop, 8am-8pm daily). Friendly staff, excellent organic produce, and plenty of reasonably priced staples make this a great option for picnic supplies. As you head up the hill on U.S. 41, veer left onto Ethel when the highway swings hard right. Watch for the colorful wooden sign. The co-op is a couple of blocks ahead on the right.

You can find homemade coffee-shop fare and Finnish bakery items like saffron bread at ★ **Toni's Country Kitchen** (79 3rd St., Laurium, 906/337-0611, 7am-5:30pm Mon.-Fri., 7am-5pm Sat.).

Despite its name, the **Lindell Chocolate Shoppe** (300 Calumet St., Lake Linden, 906/296-8083, www.lindellchocolateshoppe.net, 6am-4pm Mon.-Thurs., 6am-8pm Sat., 6am-2pm Sun., under $10) is actually a full restaurant. Visitors come to marvel at the beauty of this untouched 1920s shop, gleaming with golden oak, stained glass, and marble. Locals, though, come for the food, especially the extensive breakfast offerings and Friday-night fish fry.

ACCOMMODATIONS

There are a few good options south of Houghton. **Carla's Lake Shore Motel** (14258 U.S. 41, Baraga, 906/353-6256, www.

carlasinn.com, from $79), on U.S. 41 north of Baraga, has both clean, inexpensive motel rooms and a few cabins, all with a stunning view of Keweenaw Bay; pets are welcome. An attractive option in Baraga is the **Baraga Lakeside Inn** (900 S. U.S. 41, 906/353-7123, www.baragalakesideinn.com, $98-145).

For such a small place, Houghton accommodations can be on the pricey side, perhaps due to the presence of the university. But bargains are available. Tucked below downtown Houghton along the Portage Waterway, **Super 8** (1200 E. Lakeshore Dr., Houghton, 906/482-2240, www.super8.com, $96-135) offers one of the best locations in town, right on the water and the bike path. Also included are an indoor pool and included continental breakfast.

East of town, on the Lake Superior shore in the town of Lake Linden, the comparatively expensive but charming **Jacobsville Lighthouse Inn** (38741 Jacobs St., Lake Linden, 906/523-4137, www.jacobsvillelighthouse.com, $185-300, $20 extra for single-night stays) offers five rooms in a well-kept keeper's home with an attached lighthouse tower. The 50-foot tower offers stunning panoramic views of Lake Superior and the surrounding land, plus more than 350 feet of lakeshore.

In Hancock you can find clean rooms, moderate amenities, and a terrific location at the **Ramada Waterfront** (99 Navy St., Hancock, 906/482-8400, www.ramadahancock.com, $90-140). Enjoy the complimentary breakfast and the indoor pool.

The ★ **AmericInn Motel and Suites** (5101 6th St., Calumet, 906/337-6463, www.americinn.com, $110-140), north of Hancock, is the only full-service motel in greater Calumet, with an indoor pool and other amenities. The lobby's comfortable lodge-like setting is a calming oasis at the end of a long travel day. For something more traditional, look into the opulent copper-baron mansion at the ★ **Laurium Manor Inn** (320 Tamarack St., Laurium, 906/337-2549, www.lauriummanorinn.com, $95-209) in

Laurium. Across the street, the owners have also restored the 1906 brick **Victorian Hall** (906/337-2549, $99-149). Most rooms have private baths.

Camping

For campsite reservations at any Michigan state park, contact **Michigan DNR Reservations** (800/447-2757, www.midnrreservations.com). To rent rustic cabins or walled tents, contact the parks directly.

At Toivola, head 6.2 miles west on Misery Bay Road, then north and west on Agate Beach Road for 4 miles to **Agate Beach Park** (906/482-8319), a rather unknown little spot on Lake Superior. There's electricity but no modern plumbing. You will find an idyllic and quiet sandy beach, Lake Superior sunsets, and a low $8 tenting fee ($11 for sites with electricity). **Baraga State Park** (1300 U.S. 41 S., Baraga, 906/353-6558, www.michigan.gov/dnr, $18-22) is almost entirely campground. Most come for its more than 100 modern sites, with electricity, showers, and a convenient location: just off U.S. 41, one mile south of the town of Baraga. Reservations are usually not necessary. Across the highway, a day-use area offers a sand beach and a bathhouse.

The Bill Nichols Rail-Trail passes through **Twin Lakes State Park** (6204 E. Poyhonen Rd., Toivola, 906/288-3321, www.michigan.gov/dnr, $21-24) in the southern Keweenaw. There is also a former single-family home that is now a park lodge ($135-170). Though situated along the highway, many of its modern sites sit on the shores of Lake Roland, which was once determined to be the warmest lake in the Upper Peninsula. Sunsets get top billing at **McLain State Park** (18350 M-203, 906/482-0278, www.michigan.gov/dnr, campsites $18-28, cabins $70), where the sky often glows peach and pink before the sun melts into Lake Superior. Like most Michigan state parks, the 98 campsites are more than adequate, and many come with waterfront views.

Continuing up M-203 seven miles north of Hancock, the **City of Houghton** maintains an RV-only campground (1100 W. Lakeshore Dr., Houghton, 906/482-8745, first 6 nights $40 per night, $36 thereafter). Each site is located near the water; no pets are allowed. Tent campers will be more attracted to the **Hancock Recreation Area** (2000 Jasberg St./M-203, Hancock, 906/482-7413, www.cityofhancock.com, May 15-Oct. 15, $14-22), which sits on the Portage Waterway. Following M-203 a mile from downtown, the primitive sites are situated in a quieter area apart from the 50 RV sites that are so modern they even include cable TV. Showers and laundry are on the premises.

INFORMATION AND SERVICES

The twin towns of Houghton and Hancock represent the area's largest population center, where you'll find most of the area's essential services, including tourism information and medical care. The area also serves as the unofficial gateway to the upper Keweenaw. The **Keweenaw Convention and Visitors Bureau** (56638 Calumet Ave., Calumet, 906/337-4579 or 800/338-7982, www.keweenaw.info) serves as an excellent one-stop source for attractions and lodging information. If you're interested in Copper Country's interesting history, you won't want to miss the fascinating **Keweenaw National Historic Park** (200 5th St., Calumet, 906/337-3168, www.nps.gov/kewe, 9am-5pm Mon.-Fri.).

If you need medical attention while in Houghton and Hancock, **Portage Health** (500 Campus Dr., Hancock, 906/483-1000 or 800/573-5001, www.portagehealth.org) is the place to go. The hospital is located just west of U.S. 41; take U.S. 41 north or south to Campus Drive, turn west, and follow for 0.5 miles until you reach the Portage Health sign. Farther north, just outside Calumet, is **Aspirus Keweenaw Hospital** (205 Osceola St., Laurium, 906/337-6500, www.aspirus.org). Take U.S. 41 into town to M-26/School Street and go east to 2nd Street. Turn right on 2nd Street and then left on Osceola to arrive at the hospital.

There are several banks on either side of

the river. You can find national banks such as **Wells Fargo** (600 Sheldon Ave., Houghton, 906/482-5500, www.wellsfargo.com), Midwestern banks such as **Citizens Bank** (400 Quincy St., Hancock, 906/482-6002, www.citizensbanking.com), and local banks such as **Superior National Bank and Trust** (235 Quincy St., Hancock, 906/482-0404; 56788 Mine St. Station, Calumet, 906/337-5983; 53115 M-26, Lake Linden, 906/296-6611, www.snb-t.com).

GETTING THERE AND AROUND
Car
By car, U.S. 41 west from Marquette and M-26 north from Mass City are the main routes to the peninsula, meeting and crossing in Houghton and Hancock and then merging again at Calumet. Many of the secondary roads in the Keweenaw are dirt or gravel. For old logging roads and other questionable routes, a 4WD vehicle is strongly recommended.

Air
Houghton County Memorial Airport (CMX, 23810 Airpark Blvd., Calumet, 906/482-3970, www.houghtoncounty.org) is located a short distance northwest of Hancock. United Airlines (800/864-8339) has the only scheduled flights, twice daily to and from Chicago. Ground transportation is available for both local and long-distance trips with **Neil's Taxi** (906/482-5515) or **Copper Country Limo** (906/370-4761). Houghton County Memorial Airport also offers car rentals through **Alamo** (906/482-6655) and **National** (906/482-6655).

It's not entirely accurate to say that the only scheduled air service at Houghton's airport is offered by United; **Royale Air Service**

(906/483-4991 or 877/359-4753) offers daily one-way ($210) or round-trip ($310) seaplane flights to Isle Royale National Park.

Boat
You have multiple options for boating into Houghton and Hancock, since there's a marina in each city. **The Houghton County Marina** (906/482-6010, www.michigan.gov/dnr, May-Sept.) is located in Hancock, with 44 seasonal 10 transient slips. The marina is amenity-rich and offers close-up views of the lift bridge. You can contact of the harbormaster on channels 16 and 68. Entry into the Portage Waterway is at 47°14.08 N, 88°34.19 W from the east, or at 46°57.40 N, 88°26.00 W from the west, with the marina itself located at 47°07.30 N, 88°34.19 W. Your other option, albeit a limited one, is to put in at Houghton City Marina, located just across the Portage Waterway with 300 feet of broadside dockage but no overnight use. Channel entrances are the same as above; the dock is located at 47°07.21 N, 88°34.20 W.

Bus
Bus service tends to be spotty in the U.P., especially in the Keweenaw. The city's **Houghton Motor Transit Line** (906/482-6092, www.cityofhoughton.com, $2 adults) runs a regularly scheduled Downtowner Route that loops around from the Michigan Tech campus and ends at the Copper Country Mall. It's convenient but doesn't go much farther than you could get walking or on a bicycle. It does offer on-demand service for locations inside ($5) and outside ($6) city limits, but its scope is limited to the immediate area. Likewise, **Hancock Public Transportation** (906/482-3450, www.cityofhancock.com, $4 adults) runs a door-to-door on-demand service within a limited area.

Copper Harbor and Vicinity

Wedged between Lake Superior to the north and long and lovely **Lake Fanny Hooe** to the south, Copper Harbor has always been an outpost in the wilderness—for the copper prospectors who came in the mid-1880s, for the military who built a fort to keep the miners and the Native Americans at peace, and today for those who come for its water and woods.

Copper Harbor literally marks the end of the road in the Keweenaw Peninsula: U.S. 41 ends here in a small unceremonious loop 1,990 miles from its other end in Miami. The tip of the peninsula undoubtedly draws people because it is the end of the road. When they get here, they discover one of the Upper Peninsula's most scenic natural areas and one of its most appealing little towns.

This serene tip of the Keweenaw is a favorite vacation spot for kayakers, canoers, and boaters. With its location in the far north of the U.P. and surrounded on three sides by Lake Superior, Copper Harbor feels like the end of the earth, or, at the very least, the end of Michigan.

SIGHTS
Copper Harbor

Tiny Copper Harbor, population 75, offers much more than you might expect from its size. In a town just a few blocks long, street addresses are only used by the postal service. If you enjoy shopping, check out the **Laughing Loon** (1st St., 906/289-4813) for nontouristy gifts that reflect the true nature of the north. Rock hounds will like the **Swede's Gift Shop** (Gratiot St./U.S. 41 and 4th St., 906/289-4596), both with a good selection of local minerals. **The Fisherman's Daughter** (5th St. at the waterfront, 906/289-4285, www.fishermansdaughter.org, summer) is another shop offering ceramic pottery, clothing, jewelry, and rare minerals.

The **Thunderbird Shop** at the **Minnetonka Resort** (562 Gratiot St., 906/289-4449, www.minnetonkaresort.com, hours vary) is a terrific source for books on mining, shipwrecks, and other historical subjects. The shop also has a lot of interesting artifacts for sale, such as lanterns and clay pipes

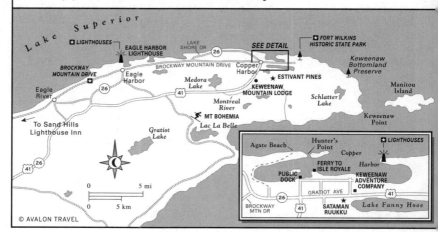

Copper Harbor and Vicinity

discarded long ago by miners. The motel's adjacent **Astor House Antique Doll and Indian Artifact Museum** (562 Gratiot St., 906/289-4449, 10am-5pm daily June-mid-Oct., $2, free under age 12) is well worth a visit too.

You won't find a full-service grocery store in Copper Harbor, so load up in Houghton or Calumet if you're planning a campout or cabin stay. However, the exceptionally friendly **Gas Lite General Store** (Gratiot St. near 1st St., 906/289-4652) has all the basics, and also happens to be the spot to catch up on local news. What you don't learn there, you'll hear about at the Pines across the street. For fresh or smoked fish, head to the ferry dock and **Jamsen's Fish Market** (4 Waterfront Landing, 906/289-4000, www.jamsen.biz, 7am-3pm daily summer high season), run by the last commercial fishing family still working the local waters.

Around Town

You can enjoy a couple of nice walks right around downtown. From the parking lot of the municipal marina west than the ferry dock, a 3.2-mile round-trip trail winds through the woods and over twisted roots to **Hunter's Point.** This small appendage of land forms the west end of the harbor. On the open Lake Superior side, **Agate Beach** is a good spot to look for the eponymous banded rocks. Downtown, a sign will point you south toward **Estivant Pines,** a 377-acre sanctuary of virgin white pines just a few miles south of town. As recently as the 1970s, local conservationists like the late Jim Rooks saved the magnificent trees from loggers. Some tower nearly 10 stories high and date back nearly 1,000 years. At first the pines will seem hidden by the maturing oaks and maples, but just look up.

★ Fort Wilkins Historic State Park

The history of Fort Wilkins, at **Fort Wilkins Historic State Park** (15223 U.S. 41, 906/289-4215, www.michigan.gov/dnr, 8am-4:30pm daily mid-May-mid-Oct.), sounds like one of those over-the-top military spending stories of the 1980s. With miners pouring north during the copper rush, the federal government feared fighting would surely erupt between the newcomers and the local Native Americans, so it ordered the construction of a garrisoned fort. In 1844 the government sent around 100 soldiers who built barracks, a mess hall, a hospital, and other buildings

Fort Wilkins Historic State Park

behind a tall stockade fence. But the anticipated fighting never occurred, and the winters proved long, cold, and desolate. Half the troops were pulled out in 1845 and sent south, where the country faced the threat of war with Mexico; by 1846 the rest were gone.

Today, Fort Wilkins stands as one of the few remaining wooden forts east of the Mississippi, with 16 whitewashed buildings meticulously restored and filled with exhibits of life on the northern frontier. From mid-June to late August, costumed interpreters recreate military life. Along with the fort, the state park includes rocky and scenic Lake Superior frontage, a few short hiking trails, the 1866 Copper Harbor Lighthouse (accessible only by boat), plus an excellent **campground** (reservations 800/447-2757, www.midnrreservations.com) on Lake Fanny Hooe.

★ Brockway Mountain Drive

Dubbed "the most beautiful road in Michigan," this 10-mile route traces the spine of a 735-foot-high ridge between Copper Harbor and Eagle Harbor and is the highest paved road between the Rockies and the Allegheny Mountains. A parking area midway allows you to stop and soak in the panorama of Lake Superior and the rolling forests of the Keweenaw. Watch for ravens, bald eagles, and peregrine falcons, which will sometimes soar below you. Traveling west to east, the end of the drive offers an opportunity to get a postcard-quality shot of Copper Harbor, tucked between Lake Superior and Lake Fanny Hooe.

Scenic Lakeshore Drive

This stretch of M-26 between Copper Harbor and Eagle River lives up to its name: Lake Superior looms alongside the road, studded with rocky islands and swelling dunes. Unfortunately, you miss about 10 miles of the route if you take Brockway Mountain Drive. A good strategy is to try both—Brockway is better when traveling east, while this drive is better heading west.

About five miles south of Copper Harbor,

Hebard Park is a good picnic, sunset, or agate-hunting spot. Where M-26 and Brockway Mountain Drive meet, watch for the small sign marking **Silver Falls.** It's a short downhill walk to this lovely little waterfall that splashes and pools in the forest.

West of Eagle Harbor, the road climbs above **Great Sand Bay** toward Eagle River. From this high vantage point, you can sometimes see huge 1,000-foot-long lake freighters out in the shipping lanes, which squeeze close to shore to round Keweenaw Point. Inland, beach peas, sand cherries, and wild roses cling to windswept, volatile mounds of sand. Like beach grasses, the plants' spreading root systems help trap the sand, stabilizing and building dunes.

The Keweenaw's tilted fault line is particularly pronounced in this part of the peninsula. To the south rises the exposed basalt face of the Cliff Range, while to the north, the fault line drops away so quickly that Great Sand Bay plummets to depths of more than 1,000 feet. In between, deep ridges allow microclimates to thrive. Along the south side of the road, watch for faintly marked **Michigan Nature Association Trails** that dip into dark, deep forests, where lichen drapes from the pines and deep cushions of moss cover the rocky path.

★ Lighthouses

Although it's located on the mainland, **Copper Harbor Lighthouse** is accessible only by boat, since the adjacent property owners refuse to grant an easement. Until recently, a DNR-sanctioned business would ferry visitors from the Copper Harbor Marina for tours, but since the company recently went out of business, there is currently no way to access this magnificent structure. Originally built in 1849, the stone lighthouse is the oldest operating light on Lake Superior. Today an automated tower built during the 1930s allows ships to navigate. It was on this point where Douglass Houghton first spotted a thick green stripe in the rock indicating the presence of copper, a discovery that unleashed the Keweenaw's copper boom.

There are a few other lighthouses around Copper Harbor: Gull Rock Lighthouse and Manitou Island Lighthouse, the oldest light on the Great Lakes. Like the Copper Harbor light, they're only accessible by private boat.

A few miles west of Eagle Harbor, the **Eagle River Lighthouse** is worth a brief look and makes for a nice picture, but today it's a private residence and not open to the public. The light went out of service in the early 1900s. On the other side of the peninsula, in Bete Grise, historic lighthouse aficionados will want to track down **Mendota Lighthouse** for a picture, but it's also a private residence not open to the public. The owner maintains an excellent website (www.mendotalighthouse.com) that offers an abundance of information on the history, evolution, and ongoing restoration of this historical gem.

If you're looking to get inside a lighthouse, and especially if you'd like to stay the night, try the **Sand Hills Lighthouse Inn** (5-Mile Point Rd., Ahmeek, 906/337-1744, www.sandhillslighthouseinn.com, $165-225), south of Eagle Harbor. The 1917 lighthouse, made for three keepers and their families, underwent a three-year restoration in the early 1990s. Today the building looks just as stunning inside as out.

Eagle Harbor

One of the Keweenaw's most charming little towns, Eagle Harbor, has a sleepy, comfortable feel to it, with a wonderfully protected natural harbor, a perfect crescent of beach, and even a historic lighthouse with an observation deck out on the rocky point. In short, it's a classic summer getaway.

The redbrick **Eagle Harbor Lighthouse,** built in 1861, is one of the area's prettiest. Its outbuildings contain a small museum (hours vary) filled with information on shipwrecks, mining, and commercial fishing. In 2013 a new museum was opened, covering the lifesaving efforts of the Coast Guard over the years.

The **one-room schoolhouse** (Center St., 2 blocks west of the harbor) was the birthplace of the Knights of Pythias, a secret fraternal society known for its elaborate rituals and fanciful costumes.

FESTIVALS AND EVENTS

Copper Harbor hosts the peninsula's best **Fourth of July** fireworks show, and Sam Raymond, owner of Copper Harbor's Keweenaw Adventure Company, puts on a growing **Fat Tire Festival** the day before

Eagle Harbor Lighthouse

Labor Day. For more information on area festivals and celebrations, contact the **Keweenaw Convention and Visitors Bureau** (56638 Calumet Ave., Calumet, 906/337-4579 or 800/338-7982, www.keweenaw.info).

SUMMER SPORTS AND RECREATION
Hiking and Biking

You'll need a map to reliably navigate this complex area. A snowmobile trail map (available through local shops and the Keweenaw Convention and Visitors Bureau) is adequate for major routes, the *DeLorme Atlas and Gazetteer* includes a few more, although a topographic map is best. However, no map yet shows even half the trails in the area. Sam Raymond, owner of the **Keweenaw Adventure Company** (145 Gratiot St., Copper Harbor, 906/289-4303, www.keweenawadventure.com, hours vary), has mapped and signed dozens of miles of mountain biking routes, although the signs keep disappearing. He's also clearing and maintaining the trails with only the help of a few friends. It's a huge undertaking for minimal return, so show Sam your appreciation by giving him your business. Keweenaw Adventure Company rents and services mountain bikes and sells those ever helpful maps.

Not surprisingly, Keweenaw Adventure Company is also your best source for trail suggestions in the area. The **Red Trail** is the region's classic route, a single-track trail with plenty of technical twists and turns. It runs roughly from the gravel **Burma Road Trail,** past the south end of the Keweenaw Mountain Lodge golf course and the north shore of Lake Manganese, where you can pick up **Paul's Plunge** back to Lake Fanny Hooe. Another good loop is the two-track **Surprise Valley Trail,** which hooks up with the **Kamikaze Trail** that traces the southern side of Lake Fanny Hooe.

In the same general area, the **Clark Mine Trail** dips south away from Copper Harbor at the south end of Lake Fanny Hooe. Just outside town, brown-and-white signs will direct you to **Manganese Falls,** a pleasant walk down into a ferny oasis; **Manganese Lake,** a popular fishing and swimming hole; and the **Clark Mine,** where the old brick furnace chimney still stands against a backdrop of mine tailings. Where the Clark Mine Trail swings east, make your way south to meet up with the Montreal River if you're interested in a little trout fishing.

In addition to the trails south of Copper Harbor, there are other destinations to consider. A wide dirt-and-gravel road continues from the end of U.S. 41; follow it for about a mile to the first main left branch, which winds north and east to the Lake Superior shore and **Horseshoe Harbor,** a fine place to spend an afternoon scrambling around the rock ledges and beaches. This picturesque sliver is owned by the Nature Conservancy, and mountain bikes are not allowed on the property. Backtracking to the main road, continue east about three miles to another left (northeast) turnoff, which skirts **Schlatter Lake** and continues on to **High Rock Bay** at the tip of the peninsula. Don't be surprised to see a camp or two set up here. A word of warning: The dirt road that leads from the end of U.S. 41 is very rough in places. Only vehicles capable of off-road travel should be used here.

Copper Harbor it at the top of the Keweenaw Peninsula, but it's not at the end. The tip of the peninsula curves to the east and slightly south and continues about 10 miles beyond town, leaving about 60 square miles east and south of Copper Harbor with no pavement, development, or attractions. In short, it's a nature lover's dream, where you can hike, mountain bike, fish, or just get out alone in the woods.

Probably more than 100 miles of trails crisscross the tip of the peninsula; there is no accurate count. They range from deer trails to tight single-track to wide gravel and dirt roads used by logging trucks and snowmobiles. Aside from a few tracts held by the state and the Nature Conservancy, the vast majority of the land is owned by International Paper, which uses it for logging. The paper company has put the land in what is called a Commercial Forest Reserve (CFR). These lands, common throughout the U.P., provide tax breaks to companies that agree to keep the land open to the public for recreation. That means you are free to hike, bike, and otherwise explore this area. Avoid any active logging areas and follow the same guidelines you would anywhere: respect "no trespassing" signs, take nothing but photographs, and leave nothing but footprints.

Canoeing and Kayaking

Paddling is at its finest in the Keweenaw, where there are plenty of islands, rock formations, and wilderness coastlines to explore. **Keweenaw Adventure Company** (145 Gratiot St., 906/289-4303, www.keweenawadventure.com, hours vary) rents kayaks, guides trips, and offers lessons. Beginners should try the 2.5-hour introductory paddle, which includes novice dry land instruction and a fine little trip around the harbor and along the Lake Superior shoreline. Keweenaw Adventure Company also offers some daylong trips around the peninsula to Horseshoe Harbor, Agate Harbor, and the mouth of the Montreal River, as scheduling permits. Check the website or give them a call for specifics.

If you have your own boat, don't overlook the peninsula's inland waters. Fanny Hooe, Medora, and other nearby lakes offer classic north woods peace and scenery, often with the company of bobbing loons or black bears on the shoreline.

Fishing

The **Gratiot River,** which crosses M-26/U.S. 41 north of Amheek and Mohawk and continues west to Lake Superior, is a good place to cast a line for brook and rainbow trout, as well as the occasional steelhead. There's an access point on M-26/U.S. 41. To find access where the Gratiot River crosses Cliff Drive, take the turnoff in the village of Amheek and follow Cliff Drive to the water. For another fishing spot, follow Five Mile Point Road from Amheek to Farmer's Road and turn left to the river and its Upper Falls.

You can cast a line at Gratiot River Country Park. To get here, take U.S. 41 to Allouez and turn at the gas station onto Bumbetown Road; continue onto Gratiot River Road for just over four miles.

Boat Trips and Tours

The Kilpela family, who run the Isle Royale ferry service, also offer **sunset cruises** (906/289-4437, visit www.isleroyale.com, Tues.-Thurs. and Sat. July 4-late Aug., $25 adults, $20 over age 59, $15 ages 5-14) on the *Isle Royale Queen IV.* From mid-May through the end of September, the *Queen* earns her keep by ferrying passengers from Copper Harbor to Isle Royale National Park, a 4.5-hour trip. Call for reservations and to check the schedule, which varies throughout the summer as the time of sunset changes.

Diving

The crisp water of Lake Superior offers outstanding visibility for divers. Although there's little in the way of plant and animal life—the cold water makes for a pretty sterile environment—there are interesting geologic formations and shipwrecks.

Ships have been running aground for well over 100 years around the Keweenaw Peninsula, a major navigational hazard. Within the 103-square-mile **Keweenaw Underwater Preserve,** divers can explore the *Tioga,* a freighter that ran aground near Eagle River in 1919, and the *City of St. Joseph,* which met its fate north of Eagle Harbor in 1942. Both ships are in less than 40 feet of water, with large sections of their hulls, deck machinery, and other artifacts clearly visible.

One of the Upper Peninsula's oldest shipwrecks, the *John Jacob Astor,* lies just offshore of Copper Harbor, near the Fort Wilkins State Park Lighthouse Overlook. An Underwater Trail marks the location of the rudder, anchor, and other remnants of the *Astor,* which sank in 1844. Local lore explains that before the Keweenaw Underwater

Golf in Northern Michigan

When thinking of Upper Peninsula recreation, hiking, fishing, and boating might first come to mind. But the great game of golf also ranks as a popular leisure pursuit—and the Upper Peninsula delivers in spades.

By far the biggest draw of U.P. courses is the relative lack of crowds—even during the peak of the summer. In addition, U.P. courses blend harmoniously with their wooded surroundings in a way that their counterparts in more populated areas don't. Many stay open until just before the snow flies, treating fall duffers to an exquisite palette of red, gold, and amber. And despite a lower number of patrons, most U.P. courses have all the amenities, including pro shops, restaurants, and shower facilities.

Try one of the following major U.P. golf destinations:

- **Wild Bluff** (page 252) near the Bay Mills Resort and Casino in Sault Ste. Marie offers both scenic fairways and a stunning view of Lake Superior.

- **The Rock** (page 261) on Drummond Island will make you feel like you're at a private club (which it once was). This is a rare find.

- The **Keweenaw Mountain Lodge** (page 164) near Copper Harbor is as close to wilderness as a golf course get. You'll likely see deer, fox and sand hill cranes crossing the fairway as you line up your shot.

Preserve was established in 1989, townspeople learned of a small group of salvage divers who were planning to retrieve one of the anchors. Without the legal protection of an underwater preserve, the divers took the matter into their own hands: They hauled up the anchor themselves and hid it in nearby Lake Fanny Hooe, where it remained until recently, when it was safely returned to its original wreck site. Today, disturbing or removing any artifact is a felony under Michigan law.

The U.S. Coast Guard has to be more than a little embarrassed about the preserve's most popular dive site, the cutter *Mesquite*. In 1989, the 180-foot *Mesquite* ran aground on a reef off Keweenaw Point while tending to a navigational buoy. Efforts to free the ship failed and winter winds battered it so badly that the Coast Guard decided to sink it as a dive site rather than pay the costs of retrieving and repairing the aging vessel. Today the *Mesquite* sits in 110 feet of water in Keystone Bay with virtually all its equipment on deck. Experienced divers can explore the *Mesquite's* interior. Currently there are no sources in the Keweenaw for diving equipment or instruction, so you'll need to be prepared before arriving in the area.

Golf

The nine holes of the **Keweenaw Mountain Lodge** (906/289-4403 or 888/685-6343, www. atthelodge.com, $18 for 9 holes, $25 for 18 holes, cart $20 for 9 holes, $25 for 18 holes) have a reputation for their beautiful scenery as well as for a good game of golf. One of the Keweenaw's best rounds, there's a pro shop and meals available at the lodge. If the weather's nice and the blackflies aren't circling, try dining on the porch. After a full day on the links, you'll appreciate the full bar, wine list, and great food.

Off-Road Vehicles

Since there aren't any DNR-designated trail systems this far north in the Keweenaw Peninsula, your best bet for off-roading is the state forest roads in Copper Country State Forest. All state forest roads are open to ORV use unless they're specifically marked otherwise.

Waterfalls

The Montreal River tumbles over some beautiful waterfalls before joining Lake Superior just to the southeast, but they're difficult to reach. The best way is to start at Bete Grise (bay-duh GREE). Just before you reach Bete Grise Bay, you'll see two dirt routes heading east into the woods. One is signed "This is not the road to Smith Fisheries." Take the unsigned road. It will lead you around Bear Bluff to an old commercial fishing enterprise, which is now private property. Continue on the smaller trail behind the fishery, a terrific path that traces the steep bluffs of the shore. It's about another 1.5 miles to the mouth of the Montreal River and its stellar waterfalls. West of Bete Grise, the pleasant **Haven Falls** are located at a roadside park. Take Lac La Belle Road south for 4.5 miles, then turn right at the fork and take it to the park.

In Copper Harbor, you won't want to miss the **Manganese Falls,** a thin but inspired flow that drops about 45 feet into a narrow gorge just outside town. To get there, turn south on Manganese Road for less than a mile; the falls are located a short walk from the roadside. Eagle Harbor has a few shorter falls, each about seven feet high. There are taller, more impressive falls in the Keeweenaw Peninsula, but these are pretty easy to get to. **Silver River Falls** is a short walk from M-26, a little more than four miles east of Eagle Harbor. The falls are wide and reasonably picturesque, with a picnic area and roadside park nearby. **Copper Falls** is located about three miles south of Eagle Harbor, on the cutoff road between U.S. 41 and town. As you pass Owl Creek on your way south, take the second trail road to the left and park. The falls are a very short walk straight off the end of the road.

Eagle River's falls are much more impressive than Eagle Harbor's and even more convenient to get to. Both **Eagle River Falls** and **Jacob's Falls** are more or less on the shoulder of M-26. There's a parking area and pedestrian bridge just off the highway as it enters Eagle River, providing great access to the 60-foot falls. You can see the smaller Jacob's Falls as you drive past on M-26, three miles northeast of Eagle River, but you'll want to stop to admire the 40-foot drop.

WINTER SPORTS AND RECREATION
Downhill Skiing

Downhill skiers can check out Michigan's most challenging terrain at **Mount Bohemia** (6532 Lac La Belle Rd., 906/360-7240 or 888/937-2411, www.mtbohemia.com, lift tickets $62), near Lac La Belle. Mount Bohemia offers one of the Midwest's highest vertical drops, at 900 feet, with some steep pitches, rocky outcrops, and gladded terrain that may make you think you're somewhere in the Rockies.

Ski and Snowshoe Trails

A few trails stand out from the northern Keeweenaw's many miles of cross-country skiing possibilities. First among these is the **Copper Harbor Pathway.** With a number of regularly groomed loops and trails that range from beginner to expert, the miles in and around Copper Harbor provide pleasant skiing and include marked snowshoe trails. The **Fort Wilkins State Park Loop** is in the region between Copper Harbor and the north shore of Lake Fanny Hooe, while the long **Kamikaze Trail** (not for beginners) hugs the lake's southern shore for more than two miles. Snowshoers will want to make their way into **Estivant Pines Nature Sanctuary,** 350 acres of virgin pine and towering hardwoods south of town that are purported to be the oldest living trees in the state. You'll be able to choose among three loops ranging 1 to 2.5 miles, and the ancient woods are worth going out of your way for. It's also going to be quiet, since no snowmobiles or motorized vehicles are allowed.

Snowmobiling

The Copper Harbor region, like the rest of Keeweenaw, has plenty of well-groomed snowmobile trails. The Keeweenaw Trail curves north to east as it ascends from Hancock, eventually connecting with the Lac La Belle Trail (steer clear of the Mount Bohemia skiers), Eagle's Loop, Mandan Trail, Harlow Trail, and other snowmobile routes with trail numbers in the 130s. Take the Brockway Mountain or Powder House Trails into Copper Harbor, and for an end-of-the-road journey to the point of the Keweenaw, take the High Rock Trail to Lake Superior, east of the city. A good trail map is available from the **Keweenaw Convention and Visitors Bureau** (56638 Calumet Ave., Calumet, 906/337-4579 or 800/338-7982, www.keweenaw.info).

FOOD

The ★ **Pines** (160 Gratiot St., 906/289-4222, www.pinesresort.net, 6:30am-3pm daily, $8-17), a small café, is an unbeatably warm, inviting place complete with knotty pine, a stone fireplace, and good basic Yooper fare, burgers, hearty sandwiches, and a delicious turkey dinner on Sunday. Get a booth by a window and take in a true "up north" experience. The adjacent **Zik's Bar** is the hangout for Copper Harbor locals. The ★ **Harbor Haus** (77 Brockway Ave., 906/289-4502, www.harborhaus.com, 4pm-8:30pm daily, dinner entrées $22-39) in Copper Harbor offers top-notch dining overlooking the harbor. Think entrées like sautéed lamb rib chops ($29) or pan-seared duck breast ($24). When the *Isle Royale Queen IV* passes by, the staff drop what they're doing to rush outside and perform the cancan. A good choice for whitefish, not to mention pan-fried walleye and beer-battered haddock, is the **Mariner North** (245 Gratiot St., 906/289-4637, http://manorth.com, 11am-10pm daily, entrées $14-21), featuring seafood, steaks, and even some vegetarian dishes. This Copper Harbor institution lost some of its spirit when the original log building burned to the ground several years ago, but it remains a popular gathering place.

Inside the Eagle River Inn, ★ **Fitzgerald's Restaurant** (5033 Front St., 906/337-0666, www.eagleriverinn.com,

4pm-8pm Mon.-Thurs., noon-9pm Fri.-Sun., dinner entrées $16-29) offers upscale dining overlooking Lake Superior. The menu features filet mignon, Memphis-style ribs, fresh fish and seafood, pecan walleye, and a comprehensive wine list.

ACCOMMODATIONS

Located high on a ridge above Copper Harbor, the log lodge and cabins of the **Keweenaw Mountain Lodge** (906/289-4403 or 888/685-6343, www.atthelodge.com, motel $135, cabin $150-220) were built as a WPA project in the 1930s. Reservations can be difficult to obtain, but try for a cabin rather than the uninspired motel rooms, which were added much later than the other buildings. Near the western tip of Lake Fanny Hooe, **Lake Fanny Hooe Resort and Campground** (505 2nd St., 906/289-4451, www.fannyhooe.com, from $105) offers a variety of accommodations, including a lakefront motel, cottages, and a chalet. Each motel room includes queen beds, cable TV, a kitchenette, a full bath, and individual room heat. Canoes and boats can be rented to enjoy the peaceful lake.

The no-frills rooms at the **King Copper Motel** (906/289-4214 or 800/833-2470, www.kingcoppermotel.com, $95-136) come with great views of the harbor and are just a few steps from the ferry dock—perfect for a warm shower and a real bed after a week on Isle Royale.

Between Copper Harbor and Eagle Harbor on M-26, **Eagle Lodge** (13051 Lakeshore Dr./M-26, Eagle Harbor, 906/289-4294 or 888/558-4441, www.eaglelodgecabins-lakeside.com, $100-155) offers simple housekeeping cabins perched on Lake Superior's shore. In Eagle River, the **Eagle River Inn** (5033 Front St., Eagle River, 906/337-0666, www.eagleriverinn.com, $120-150) offers motel-style accommodations in a similarly outstanding setting, right at the water's edge and flanked by a long sand beach. All rooms come with lake views. South of Eagle Harbor, check out the ★ **Sand Hills Lighthouse Inn** (5-Mile Point Rd., Ahmeek, 906/337-1744, $165-225).

It may not be cheap, but with a 90-foot tower to climb and rooms with balconies overlooking Lake Superior, you can justify the cost. Owner Bill Frabotta has restored the 1919 lighthouse, filled it with antiques, and decorated it in lavish Victorian style. There's a great breakfast too. Take M-26 west from Ahmeek to Five Mile Point Road.

Camping

Fort Wilkins State Park (15223 U.S. 41, 906/289-4215, www.michigan.gov/dnr) has 165 modern sites in two campgrounds, both on Lake Fanny Hooe. Many sites back up to the water and offer decent privacy. To reserve a spot (but not a specific site), contact the Michigan state parks central reservations system (800/447-2757, www.midnrreservations.com). **Lake Fanny Hooe Resort and Campground** (505 2nd St., 906/289-4451 or 800/426-4451, www.fannyhooe.com, $30-42) offers uninteresting sites in an open grassy area, but with a decent location near town and the south shore of Lake Fanny Hooe.

West of Ahmeek on Five Mile Point Road, **Sunset Bay Campground** (2701 Sunset Bay Beach Rd., 906/337-2494, www.sunset-bay.com, late May-mid-Oct., $25-30) indeed offers a fine view of the sunset from your tent flap. Several of its 12 primitive sites sit on Lake Superior. There are 18 RV sites available. Many locals simply head out into the woods on weekends and set up camp near a favorite stretch of beach or river. If you choose to do the same, respect the "no trespassing" signs and observe all backcountry camping practices (bury waste, hang packs, stay 50 feet from the water)—you'll be sharing the woods with plenty of black bears.

INFORMATION

For Copper Harbor visitor information, contact the **Copper Harbor Improvement Association** (906/289-4212, www.copper-harbor.org) or stop by the **Visitors Center** (Grant Township Bldg., U.S. 41 and 2nd St.). The booth is staffed during the summer months, but even if no one is working, you can get brochures from the lobby at any time. The **Keweenaw Convention and Visitors Bureau** (56638 Calumet Ave., Calumet, 906/337-4579 or 800/338-7982, www.keweenaw.info) is a great source for information and maps.

Medical emergencies will necessitate going south again, though not all the way to Hancock, to the **Aspirus Keweenaw Hospital** (205 Osceola St., Laurium, 906/337-6500, www.aspirus.org). Heading into Laurium from Copper Harbor or northern Keweenaw, take U.S. 41 to M-26/School Street and turn left. Take School Street to 2nd Street, turn right on 2nd, then left on Osceola to the hospital.

You'll have to head south of Copper Harbor to find a bank. Keweenaw's regional bank, **Superior National** (80 Mohawk St., Mohawk, 906/337-6807, www.snb-t.com) has a branch in Mohawk, six miles north of Calumet on U.S. 41. You can find an ATM at the Gas Lite General Store on the corner of U.S. 41 and 1st Street.

GETTING THERE AND AROUND
Car

The two main roads that lead north and east to Copper Harbor are the same highways from the base of the Keweenaw to Houghton and Hancock. U.S. 41 and M-26 merge at Calumet until Phoenix, where they split again. U.S. 41 doubles as the Copper Country Trail Scenic Byway, which starts in Hancock, and it really is a pleasant drive, striking more or less through the middle of the peninsula. The trail pairs Keweenaw's natural beauty, which is especially striking during the fall, with a smattering of history at old mines, museums, and other heritage sites. Drivers may want to consider M-26 for the journey between Phoenix and Copper Harbor. Not only does it pass through Eagle Harbor, a pleasant town in its own right, but it also hugs the Lake Superior shore the entire way. As pleasant as the Copper Country Trail is, you'll get a more scenic drive on the detour east. The best combination is to take Brockway Mountain Drive (U.S. 41) east to Copper Harbor and the Scenic Lakeshore Drive (M-26) when traveling west toward Eagle Harbor.

Air

If you're flying in, the closest airport is the **Houghton County Memorial Airport** (CMX, 23810 Airpark Blvd., Calumet, 906/482-3970, www.houghtoncounty.org), with daily flights from Chicago. For car rentals at the airport, contact either **Alamo** or **National** at 906/482-6655.

Boat

The northern part of the Keweenaw is small, but it has a lot of shoreline and a couple of harbors and marinas to boot. The **Copper Harbor State Dock** (906/289-4698, www.

michigan.gov/dnr) is small, with only 10 transient slips available, but there are basic amenities (gas, showers, restrooms), unlike Eagle Harbor. The harbormaster is on duty 9am-5pm daily and can be reached on radio channel 9. Copper Harbor's dock is located at 47°28.42 N, 87°51.50 W.

The **Eagle Harbor State Dock**, about 14 miles west of Copper Harbor, has transient docking, but no other amenities. There's an emergency phone number (906/289-4215), but no harbormaster on duty. You can find the dock at 47°27.52 N, 88°09.33 W.

Public Transportation

There is no public transportation in the Copper Harbor area, save for limited taxi and shuttle service in Houghton and Hancock and at the airport, but this is a very expensive option. There is no bus service to the area.

Isle Royale

Stranded in the vast waters of Lake Superior, Isle Royale is perhaps the model of an ideal national park: wild, rugged, and remote. A 45-mile-long archipelago, Isle Royale is the least visited property in the National Park Service system, attracting just 18,000 visitors a year—fewer than Yosemite receives in a single weekend. Here, wireless communications are the only contact with the outside world.

Civilization on Isle Royale (ROY-al, as if there were no "e") is concentrated in two small developments at opposite ends of the island. Windigo, on the southwest end, includes a National Park Service information center, a camp store, and a marina. Rock Harbor, near the east end, offers the same, plus a no-frills lodge and restaurant across from the ferry dock, and a handful of cabins overlooking Tobin Harbor. The rest of the island is backcountry, 210 pristine square miles of forested foot trails, rocky bluffs, quiet lakes, and wilderness campsites.

Those who make the trek either by boat

or by seaplane come primarily to hike Isle Royale's 165 miles of trails, fish its 46 inland lakes, and paddle its sawtooth shoreline. Wildlife viewing is popular too, especially for the moose that swam across from Ontario several decades ago, and the eastern timber wolves that later followed their prey across the rock solid winter ice. Wolves are notoriously elusive, but rest assured that your sightings of wildlife will far outnumber your human contacts while on Isle Royale.

GEOGRAPHY

Backpackers will take note of Isle Royale's distinctive topography as they traverse the long, narrow island, which runs southwest to northeast and is less than nine miles across at its widest point. A series of ridges and valleys fall away from the park's high interior backbone, the Greenstone Ridge, creating a washboard of forest and rock. Mount Desor marks the highest point on the island, rising from the Greenstone Ridge to 1,394 feet.

The same Precambrian lava flows that formed the Keweenaw Peninsula more than a billion years ago also formed Isle Royale. After each lava flow, wind and rain carried sand and other sediments into the area, producing slabs of softer rock sandwiched between the hard layers of basalt, creating the island's characteristic ridge and trough pattern. Hikers crossing the width of the island will feel this layout in their quads, as the trail continually rises and falls with each ridge. This feature becomes most apparent on the park's northeastern edge, where it meets Lake Superior. The ridges become long rocky fingers, and the valleys become narrow slivers of water wedged between the rocky points.

When the center of the Superior Basin began to subside, it thrust the layers of rock on Isle Royale upward at an angle, giving the island a northeast side of steep ridges and bluffs, and a southwest shore that slopes gradually to the water and includes lowlands and bogs. The northern Keweenaw Peninsula is a near mirror image of Isle Royale, with a gradual northern shore and more steeply angled southern side.

The geography of Isle Royale is intimately related to the water that surrounds it. Along with its namesake island, the largest in Lake Superior, Isle Royale National Park actually consists of an archipelago of some 400 islands, all of them remnants of the same landmass. More than 80 percent of the national park lies underwater, beneath shallow ponds, bogs, inland lakes, and the clear, cold water of Lake Superior. An interesting bit of trivia: Ryan Island, located on Isle Royale's Siskiwit Lake, is the largest island in the largest lake on the largest island in the largest lake in the world.

CLIMATE

Isle Royale is the perfect escape from a hot, sticky summer. With its water temperature rarely exceeding 45°F, Lake Superior does a fine job as North America's largest natural air conditioner. It also has a significant moderating effect on the island: summers are generally a little cooler than on the mainland,

with daytime temperatures from mid-May to mid-August ranging 65-75°F. Nights are north woods cool, often dipping into the 40s and even 30s. Clouds obscure the sun more than half the time in summer, and fog can strike anytime. More than one disappointed backpacker has returned from Isle Royale without any memories of the island's lovely vistas.

Lake Superior's moderating effect works in reverse during the cold months. Winters are slightly warmer than on the mainland, though that can be small consolation in this part of the world. Once Lake Superior turns from cobalt to dark gray in late autumn, and its infamous winter storms begin churning, the island becomes shrouded in fog, whipped by wind, and buried under several feet of snow.

Isolation isn't the only reason Isle Royale has few visitors. Come mid-October, the island closes down much like a summer resort, the only national park to do so. The ferries stop running, the concessionaires in Rock Harbor shut down, and the rangers head for Houghton or take seasonal work in warmer climes. Only the wildlife researchers continue their work, tracking free-roaming wolves and moose by air.

PLANTS AND ANIMALS

Isolated from the effects of civilization, Isle Royale acts as a living laboratory, a study of how plants and animals interrelate in the ebb and flow of nature's cycles. Owing to these unique natural qualities, the United Nations declared the park an International Biosphere Reserve in 1980.

Plants

Spruce, fir, and jack pine share the island with beech and maple forests, but numerous varieties of wildflowers take center stage in June and July. Forests can be dotted with yellow lady's slipper and American starflower; lowlands are brightened by wild irises, calla lilies, and yellow pond lilies. In July and August different species of berries make their appearance; look for blueberries, thimbleberries, and red

Isle Royale

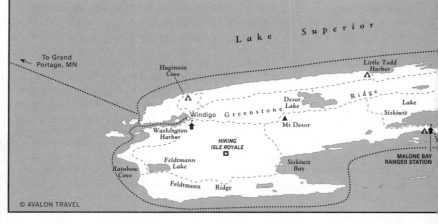

raspberries, especially in the sunnier, rockier high areas.

Moose and Wolves

Naturalists believe **moose** first arrived at Isle Royale in the early 1900s, when several swam the 15 miles from mainland Ontario. With ample vegetation for food and no natural predators, the moose multiplied rapidly, their numbers soaring to somewhere between 1,000 and 3,000 by the late 1920s. Soon after, their numbers outstripped their food sources. Starvation and a succession of harsh winters killed off hundreds of the huge mammals in the 1930s. A fire in 1936 prompted a regrowth of vegetation. With revived food sources, the moose population skyrocketed again, followed by another round of starvation.

The seesaw pattern might have continued for decades, but nature intervened in the form of the eastern **timber wolf** (also known as the gray wolf). During the exceptionally cold winter of 1948-1949, the lake iced over between Ontario and Isle Royale, and a small pack of wolves made its way to the island. The wolves found a bountiful food source in the local moose and multiplied, reaching a peak population of about 50 animals in 1970.

Since then, the wolves and moose, fenced in by the waters of Lake Superior, have provided scientists with a fascinating study of the predator-prey relationship. In 2008 the island marked its 50th year of wolf-moose research and study. The study is a joint effort of the National Park Service and Michigan Technological University, and it has become the longest predator-prey study ever undertaken. In a large moose herd, wolves cull the sick, young, and old, preventing overpopulation. In fact, moose make up around 90 percent of wolves' diet. But the resulting moose herd—stronger and healthier—makes hunting more difficult, which, in turn reduces wolf breeding.

Populations of both animals have fluctuated dramatically over the decades. Today, the moose population is up from a decade ago, totaling some 1,050. Hikers have an excellent chance of spotting these 1,000-pound mammals, which often feed in ponds and lowlands or along inland lakeshores. Hidden Lake, across Tobin Harbor south of Lookout Louise, is an exceptionally good spot, since moose have a taste for its mineral licks. If you're lucky enough to come upon a moose, give it a very wide berth. Although they look

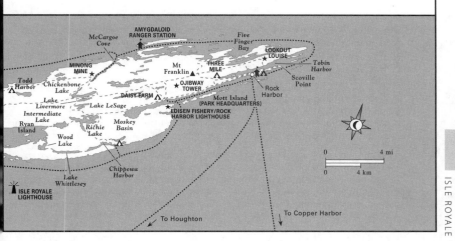

cartoonish and friendly, moose can be exceptionally dangerous if approached too closely. Cows safeguarding their calves and males behaving aggressively during the fall mating season are capable of inflicting lethal blows with their hooves.

For reasons not clearly understood, Isle Royale's wolf population plummeted in the 1990s. By 1998, just 14 wolves roamed the island in three packs. Biologists feared a lack of genetic diversity might be the critical factor that could cause the demise of the island's wolves. After a brief rebound between 2000 and 2008, the decline resumed. The winter 2017 count recorded only 2 wolves, and this low figure is cited as the primary reason for the increasing moose population. Whether the wolves will continue to survive remains one of the most compelling questions this living laboratory has yet to answer.

Backpackers rarely ever spot the shy and stealthy wolves, and the "wolf howls" often heard at night are most likely the haunting calls of loons. But the notion that even a very few wolves are out there, somewhere, and perhaps even watching from deep in the forest, is compelling enough for most, especially those lucky enough to spot a paw print along the trail.

Other Animals

Some of the other large mammals common in the northern Great Lakes region are notably absent from the island. Black bears never migrated to Isle Royale, and white-tailed deer introduced for hunting vanished early in the 20th century. Caribou and lynx, present in the 19th century, also disappeared. Instead, hikers may spot red foxes (which love to scavenge around campsites, so hang your pack), beavers, muskrats, hares, red squirrels, otters, and mink.

Bird watchers will enjoy scanning the water's surface for the common loon, which is indeed common here, along with the Canada goose, bufflehead, black duck, merganser, and mallard. Smaller birds frequenting the island include warblers, chickadees, thrushes, woodpeckers, and kingfishers.

None of Isle Royale's inland lakes can be reached by car or motorized boat, and many of them require serious effort to reach even on foot. This combination makes for great **fishing.** Sport fishing boats ply the Lake Superior waters around Isle Royale for lake

Moose vs. Wolf

Moose and wolves are the most noteworthy large mammals on Isle Royale. Neither species is indigenous to the island. Moose arrived around 1900 by swimming from the nearby Canadian mainland. Wolves made their appearance some 50 years later by walking across an ice bridge from Canada formed during the severe winter of 1948-1949. The resulting predator-prey relationship has been extensively studied ever since.

The island's isolation, the limited presence of humans, and limited quantifiable populations have created an ideal place for studying the relationship. Physical barriers prevent the island's animals from leaving easily, and effectively keep others at bay. So while the populations are by no means stagnant, their ups and downs can be tracked with relative ease and attributed to natural causes such as illness and hard winters. The majority of moose deaths, however, are caused by wolf predation.

An ongoing study of the wolf-moose relationship has confirmed that the two large animals are uniquely interdependent. Wolves are the only natural predator for the moose, and moose make up some 90 percent of the wolves' diets (the rest is beavers and snowshoe hares). The fates of the creatures are thus linked; a spike in one population or a drop in the other provides invaluable information to the researchers from Michigan Technological University who study the animals.

During the summer, researchers and volunteers head into the wild to study elements of the moose population by examining the carcasses, checking the impact of moose ticks, observing the moose as they forage, measuring the amount of available food, and collecting droppings for dietary analysis. The researchers also study the wolves, analyzing their droppings to gather DNA identifications for each of the predators on the island. There's no guarantee that they'll find every wolf, but since they tend to collect a large quantity of droppings, the list is fairly exhaustive.

Much of the work takes place in the winter, while the park is closed to visitors. From mid-January through early March, wolf and moose populations are measured through flyover observation. Researchers also estimate kill rates and perform studies on the carcasses.

Since 2010, the team conducting the survey has documented a decline in the impact of parasitic ticks on the moose population. This has led to an increase in the number of moose, which today stands at roughly 1,050. For their part, the wolf population in 2014 totaled about 10, split into two packs, plus one lone wolf wandering the island. Biologists speculate that inbreeding may account for the declining number of wolves. As the study continues, each year brings with it new and sometimes surprising information.

---

trout. But nearly all of the island's inland waters offer the ultimate fishing experience. Northern pike is considered a prime fish for its fighting spirit, and it can be found in almost any of the local lakes. Hungry hikers will be pleased to know that walleye, perch, and trout abound here too. Bring along a pack rod to fish from shore. Many lakes, like Feldtmann, Desor, Siskiwit, Richie, and Chickenbone, have trails leading directly to them. Other more remote lakes are open to fishing but require good backcountry skills to reach. No license is needed to fish Isle Royale's inland lakes, although Michigan regulations still apply. If you plan to drop a line in Lake Superior, you'll need a Michigan license, sold at the island's two camp stores.

A discussion of Isle Royale's animal life is not complete without mention of the island's insects. Like much of the Upper Peninsula, and many other wilderness areas, Isle Royale provides a fine home for **mosquitoes** and **blackflies,** especially in low-lying areas. From mid-June to mid-August, keep insect repellent with DEET close at hand. In general, insects are less of a problem on higher trails, which often catch a lake breeze.

ISLE ROYALE NATIONAL PARK

While many national parks struggle with their fates as islands of wilderness surrounded by a more developed world, Isle Royale represents the opposite scenario. It has the advantage of a much larger buffer zone protecting it from outside encroachment and influence. As a result, it's one of the most closely managed holdings in the national park system and presents some unique opportunities for conservation. Isle Royale is one of the few parks that regulates the number of visitors who pass through its gates. Though logistics have done a sufficient job of keeping numbers down thus far, the National Park Service could reduce the number further by cutting back on ferry service or on the number of campsites.

Limited access also allows the National Park Service to enforce rules more effectively. Dogs, for example, are not allowed on the island for fear they might bring rabies and other diseases to the island's wolf pack. The National Park Service also takes great pains to preserve the island's backcountry solitude, with a park brochure reminding hikers to "refrain from loud conversation," "avoid songfests," and "select equipment of subtle natural tones rather than conspicuous colorful gear."

Boat Tours

The **National Park Service** (906/482-0984, www.nps.gov/isro) shuttles visitors to various island attractions on its 25-passenger **MV Sandy.** Twice a week, the *Sandy* makes the short trip across the mouth of Moskey Basin to **Edisen Fishery.** The historic fishery of Peter and Laura Edisen has been restored to show what life was like at the commercial fisheries that once thrived on the island. From Edisen Fishery, it's a 0.25-mile walk to the stout and simple **Rock Harbor Lighthouse,** a white edifice built in 1855 to guide ships to Isle Royale's then-busy copper ports.

On Tuesday, Wednesday, and Friday evenings, the *Sandy* embarks on a sunset cruise to **Raspberry Island,** on the far eastern tip of the archipelago. The tour includes time to stroll along a boardwalk through a spruce bog as well as a loop around Scoville and Blake Points, a picturesque view of the Canadian shore, and a dramatic Lake Superior sunset.

Food and Accommodations

Those just looking for a quiet island stay and some pleasant day hikes can set up a base in comfort at the **Rock Harbor Lodge** (906/337-4993 or 866/644-2003, www.isleroyaleresort.com). Lodge rooms are basic

informational sign about Isle Royale National Park at Copper Harbor

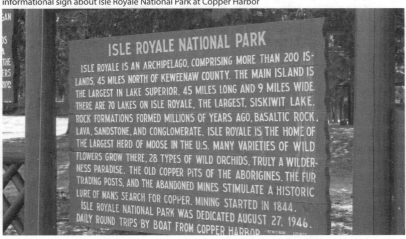

motel-style accommodations, but they are right at the water's edge with a glorious view of nearby islands and the open water of Lake Superior. This slice of civilization in the wilderness comes at a steep price; rates average $231-256. The dining room is open daily for breakfast, lunch, and dinner. Dinner offerings often include fresh lake trout from the restored Edisen Fishery. Guests also have use of an adjacent day lodge with a comfortable wood-burning fireplace. Nearby housekeeping cottages ($224-248) have small kitchens, one double bed, and two bunk beds. Reservations are a must.

The Rock Harbor Lodge dining room is open to nonguests, and for those fresh off the trails, its meals will taste like a gourmet feast. The Marina Store in Rock Harbor carries a good supply of food, camping supplies, fuel, and other essentials. There are two rustic cabins ($52) available at Windigo. The lack electricity and indoor plumbing, but they do offer basic shelter. There's also a well-equipped camp store, similar to Rock Harbor. Both also offer showers and laundry facilities.

If you want to see more of the island, ★ camping is the only way to do it. Rustic campsites are located throughout the island, with three types of sites available: individual tent sites for one to three tents, group sites for 7 to 10 people, and three-sided shelters that hold up to 6 people. You must first obtain a camping permit outlining your itinerary from the ranger station. Groups of six or less must obtain a small-party backcountry camping permit (free), and may use individual sites on a first come, first served basis.

Should you reach a site at the end of the day and find it full—this can happen, especially in August, and especially at sites a day's hike from Rock Harbor—the unwritten rules are that you double up. No one expects you to hike off into the dwindling light to the next campsite.

Groups of 7 to 10 must obtain a group camping permit ($25). Groups of this size must make reservations in advance and are required to use specially designated group campsites.

Come prepared. The camp stores, though well supplied, are not the places to outfit your trip. Carry a stove and fuel, since many sites do not permit fires and dead wood is limited. Bring a water filter, unless you plan to boil everything. Potable water is only available in Rock Harbor and Windigo, and chemical purifiers like halazone tablets will not kill the hydatid tapeworm found in Isle Royale waters.

Information

For general information on the park, camping, transportation options, and more, contact **Isle Royale National Park** (906/482-0984, www.nps.gov/isro).

Isle Royale was one of the first national parks to charge a park user fee, currently $7 pp per day. If you're traveling to the island by ferry or seaplane, the concessionaire will collect your fee. If you're traveling by private boat, you can pay at the ranger station at Windigo or Rock Harbor, or at the Houghton Visitors Center prior to your departure.

The National Park Service has long discussed charging admission fees to national parks as a way to compensate for shortfalls in federal funding. In the past, all gate fees were fed back into the federal government's general treasury, eliminating an incentive to levy a fee. With the new user-fee program, however, 80 percent of the monies gathered is spent at the collecting park. The remaining 20 percent is spent at national parks with priority maintenance projects. In Isle Royale's case, that means hundreds of thousands of dollars that will be spent maintaining trails and repairing or replacing docks.

Getting There

If getting there is half the fun, you'll be very excited by the time you arrive at Isle Royale. Travel to the island is not particularly convenient or cheap, which probably accounts for average visitor stays that are considerably longer than most other national park destinations. The average visit to Rocky Mountain

National Park is a few hours; to Isle Royale, three days, including day trippers who flow off the ferry, wander around the harbor for a few hours, and leave that afternoon.

Many, however, come to appreciate even the trip to and from Isle Royale, a mental decompression chamber of sorts that eases the passage between island wilderness and the civilized world.

Your options for travel to Isle Royale are seaplane, ferry, or personal boat.

FERRY

The National Park Service operates the largest ferry, the 165-foot *Ranger III,* which has been in service since 1958. It departs from Houghton twice a week, at 9am Tuesday and Friday, from late May to mid-September, for the six-hour passage to Rock Harbor. The one-way cost is $63 adults, $23 ages 6-12, free under age 6. Canoes and kayaks are an additional $22-50 if they're longer than 20 feet or weigh more than 90 pounds. Make reservations through the national park (906/482-0984, www.nps.gov/isro).

If you'd rather see more of the Keweenaw and spend less time on the ferry, drive another hour up the peninsula to Copper Harbor, where you can catch the *Isle Royale Queen IV* for a three-hour trip to Rock Harbor. It operates from mid-May through the end of September, with a varying schedule, adding additional departures as needed in July and August. The one-way cost is $65 adults, $33 under age 12. Canoes and kayaks are an additional $25. The *Isle Royale Queen IV* is highly reliable and has happily surprised weary backpackers by showing up to retrieve them on even the stormiest of days. But the ship richly deserves its nickname, "The Queasy." In heavy seas, its hull can rock and roll at a pretty good pitch. To check the schedule and make reservations, contact the **Isle Royale Line** (906/289-4437, www.isleroyale.com).

A third and fourth ferry run from Grand Portage, Minnesota. The 65-foot MV *Voyageur II* (outbound Mon., Wed., and Sat., inbound Tues., Thurs., and Sun.). Outbound departures are at 7:30am central daylight time outbound and at 8am inbound. On its way to Rock Harbor, it circumnavigates the island, offering drop-off and pickup service along the way. This makes for a slow but interesting trip. Rates start at $71 one way, but vary depending on your selected destination. *Voyageur II* can also carry canoes and kayaks for an additional $37 each way.

The Sea Hunter III departs at 8:30am central daylight time on Wednesday, Friday, and Saturday from Grand Portage to Windigo in two hours, then returns four hours later for those interested in simply a day trip. Reserve a spot through **Grand Portage-Isle Royale Transportation Line** (651/653-5872 or 888/746-2305 Nov.-Apr., 218/475-0024 or 218/475-0074 May-Oct., www.isleroyaleboats.com).

SEAPLANE

Seaplane service by **Isle Royale Seaplanes** (21125 Royce Road, Hancock, 906/483-4991, http://isleroyaleseaplanes.com, $320 pp round-trip, $220 pp one-way) in Hancock is the most expensive and usually the quickest way to the island, although the 35-minute flight can often be delayed by wind and fog. The plane, a Cessna 206 amphibious seaplane, flies Thursday to Tuesday and can carry up to four passengers. The plane cannot carry stove fuel, but you can purchase it on the island at the park store. Luggage is limited to 50 pounds per passenger.

PRIVATE BOAT

Arriving by private boat is popular in midsummer—perhaps a bit too popular for those who treasure the island's solitude and resent the whine of powerboat engines. The Rock Harbor and Windigo marinas offer docking and refueling for powerboats and sailboats; boats also are allowed to drop anchor in a secluded bay overnight and save the marina fee. Protected harbors are plentiful on the east end of the island, although most remain exposed to an east wind, but are nonexistent on the west end. Every boat arriving at the island must first stop at a ranger station in Windigo or Rock Harbor to obtain a permit and pay the park user fee.

Those with boats under 20 feet should not to attempt a Lake Superior crossing. Even if you have a larger vessel, consider the passage only if you possess strong navigation skills and a good marine radio. Lake Superior has many ocean-like characteristics, and storms can appear with little notice.

★ HIKING ISLE ROYALE
Day Hikes from Rock Harbor

Several day hikes are possible if you choose to "motel camp" in Rock Harbor. Don't miss **Scoville Point,** a 4.2-mile loop with interpretive signs that traces a rocky finger of land east of Rock Harbor. Another popular short hike (3.8 miles) is the loop to **Suzy's Cave,** formed by the wave action of a once much-deeper Lake Superior. **Lookout Louise,** north of Tobin Harbor, offers one of the island's most spectacular views, gazing over its ragged northeastern shoreline. If you have a canoe, it's a short paddle and then a two-mile hike. Without a canoe, it's a fine but lengthier hike along lovely Tobin Harbor and the eastern end of the Greenstone Ridge. You'll have to retrace your steps to return to Rock Harbor, making the trek a total of about 20 miles.

For another all-day hike, follow the Lake Superior shoreline to the Daisy Farm campground and the Ojibway Trail, which heads north and brings you to the **Ojibway Tower,** an air-monitoring station. The tower marks the highest spot on the eastern end of the island, and you can climb its steps (but not enter the tower room) for an unmatched view of the island's interior lakes and bays on both the north and south sides of the island. Travel back via the Greenstone Ridge and along Tobin Harbor for a varied 18-mile hike that will take you through blueberry patches, wildflower meadows, and serene shorelines. For a similar but shorter hike of about 10 miles, turn north at the Three Mile campground to

ascend **Mount Franklin,** another high point on the Greenstone Ridge.

Day Hikes from Windigo

If you'd prefer not to haul your possessions on your back, it's possible—but a little more difficult—to do day hikes out of Windigo. Because fewer trails exist here, most hikes will be of the out-and-back variety. The best loop option is to **Huginnin Cove,** a 9.7-mile route that passes through prime moose habitat before emerging onto the Lake Superior shore. There's a campground here if you choose to make it an overnighter. The east side of the trail passes an old mine, which was last active in 1892. Another excellent option is the **Feldtmann Lake Trail,** which winds along Washington Harbor before heading inland to one of the island's least visited lakes. You can hike the 17-mile route out and back in a day, but you'll enjoy your adventure more if you plan it as an overnight. Set up camp here and you'll likely be treated to moose sightings, unmatched fishing, and maybe the howl of a distant wolf. Plus, if you stay overnight, you'll have the time and energy for the short side trip to Lake Superior's pretty Rainbow Cove.

Longer Hikes

With 165 miles of trails, Isle Royale has far more outstanding hiking options than is possible to outline here. Consider a comprehensive guide like Jim DuFresne's excellent *Isle Royale National Park: Foot Trails and Water Routes* (4th ed.), published by The Mountaineers. If you prefer to avoid the busier areas of Windigo and Rock Harbor, consider arranging for the ***Voyageur II*** ferry (218/475-0024 or 218/475-0074) or the island's **water-taxi service** (906/337-4993) to drop you off and pick you up at another location.

In general, the **Greenstone Ridge** is the main route to traverse the island, a 42-mile trail of mostly high and dry terrain. It is also the most popular, though crowds are a relative thing on Isle Royale.

The park's second-longest, the 26-mile **Minong Ridge Trail** easily ranks as its most challenging. Traversing the north side of the island from near Windigo to McCargoe Cove, the rough and lightly used trail meanders over a rocky ridge and disappears through bogs. If you like surroundings that are primitive and peaceful, and don't get nervous about some poorly marked stretches, this trail is for you. Wildlife sightings, especially moose, are likely here. Though campgrounds are far apart on this trail, they're worth the effort. Little Todd Harbor and Todd Harbor are some of the nicest on the island.

Finally, the **Feldtmann Ridge Trail** loops along the southwestern shore, a well-marked but lightly used route of 22 miles. The trail offers outstanding variety, from the shoreline of Washington Harbor, through gentle bogs, up the high Feldtmann Ridge, and finally to the open wildflower meadows and waters of Siskiwit Bay.

PADDLING ISLE ROYALE

For paddlers, Isle Royale is a dream destination, a nook-and-cranny wilderness of rocky islands, secluded coves, and quiet bays interrupted only by the low call of a loon. First-time visitors can't do better than the **Five Fingers,** the collection of fjord-like harbors and rocky promontories on the east end of the island. Not only is it well protected (except from northeasters), it offers some of the finest and most characteristic Isle Royale scenery and solitude. Though Isle Royale is generally better suited to kayaks, open canoes can handle these waters in calm weather.

For kayaks, the entire island offers paddling opportunities, though some areas require long stretches of paddling with little

shoreline access. Note that open-water passages on Lake Superior should be attempted by experienced paddlers only, and are not at all recommended in an open boat like a canoe. Capsizing in Lake Superior is not merely an unfortunate experience; it's a life-threatening one. With water temperatures rarely exceeding the 40s, hypothermia can set in within a matter of minutes.

You can avoid open-water passages and still explore other areas of the island by making use of the *Voyageur II* **ferry** (218/475-0024 or 218/475-0074) or the island's **water taxi service** (906/337-4993), which will transport you and your boat to various docks on the northeastern half of the island.

Ferries can transport your boat, provided it is less than 20 feet long. You also can rent canoes, 14-foot fishing boats, and outboard motors at Windigo and Rock Harbor (906/337-4993). For Rock Harbor visitors, a wonderful day can be spent exploring Tobin Harbor, where rental canoes await.

Exploring the inland lakes is a remarkable experience on Isle Royale. Fishing is often superb, and moose often loiter near the shore, unaware of your presence. Plan your routes carefully to avoid grueling portages. Again, your best bet is to arrange for the water taxi or the *Voyageur II* ferry to drop you and your boat at a mid-island spot like Malone Bay, Chippewa Harbor, or McCargoe Cove. From there you'll have manageable, even easy portages to several lakes, including Siskiwit, Wood, Whittlesey, Intermediate, Richie, LeSage, Livermore, and Chickenbone. There's nothing quite like drifting across a wilderness lake in the middle of a wilderness island.

Marquette and the Lake Superior Shore

Home to the Upper Peninsula's largest city, the Lake Superior shore is deserving of a good portion of your time. Marquette is modern and cosmopolitan, especially for a city located in Michigan's most remote region. The presence

of Northern Michigan University makes it a college town, which means there's plenty to do, whether you're a fan of bars or live performances, college-level sports, or the arts and culture scene. If you're here for the great outdoors, you'll find plenty of it just over Marquette's doorstep: The rugged and undeveloped Huron Mountains lie to the west, while Presque Isle is truly one of the U.P.'s gems.

And while Lake Superior may not have the sandy beaches or be as swimmable as Lakes Michigan or Huron, it's almost impossible to be unmoved by the rough, wild shoreline. The rocky shoreline and its ocean-like appearance make the largest of the Great Lakes unquestionably the most awesome.

Munising and Grand Island are located on a picturesque bay that would rival any in the world for sheer beauty. Continue east and it only gets better, as the remarkable colors, cliffs, and rock formations of Pictured Rocks

National Lakeshore stretch out like an artistic masterpiece being unveiled. If you've never kayaked before, this is a good place to start. The national lakeshore is perfectly bookended on the opposite side by Grand Marais.

Don't forget to venture inland, where many of the U.P.'s renowned outdoor recreational activities await. Of particular interest is the Seney National Wildlife Refuge, which has 95,000 acres of wetlands, bog, and wilderness. Home to hundreds of species of birds and other animals, it also allows hiking and cycling, making it an ideal place to observe nature.

PLANNING YOUR TIME

You'll probably want to spend at least two or three days in Marquette. There's enough to do here to melt away any "wilderness fatigue." Marquette can also serve as an ideal launching pad for hub-and-spoke explorations of the surrounding areas. Set aside a day each

---

Previous: downtown Marquette; Pictured Rocks National Lakeshore. **Above:** a deer in Marquette.

Highlights

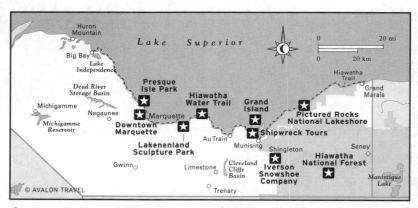

★ **Downtown Marquette:** Take a break from nature to enjoy the Upper Peninsula's most cosmopolitan city (page 185).

★ **Presque Isle Park:** Admire some of the area's most beautiful scenery by taking a drive, cycling, hiking, or skiing through this preserved park (page 186).

★ **Lakenenland Sculpture Park:** This quirky outdoor display of "junkyard art" is part artwork, part political commentary (page 187).

★ **Hiawatha Water Trail:** The 120-mile journey from Big Bay to Grand Marais is beautiful and adventurous (page 192).

★ **Grand Island:** Take a ferry 10 minutes off the shore of Munising and spend a day or a weekend exploring this isolated island (page 205).

★ **Hiawatha National Forest:** Several hundred acres of national forest provide endless recreational opportunities in every season (page 206).

★ **Shipwreck Tours:** Whether viewed from behind a scuba facemask or from a glass-hulled boat, the ruins of Lake Superior nautical lore are unforgettable (page 211).

★ **Pictured Rocks National Lakeshore:** These colorful, scenic rocks rank among the top tier of U.P. attractions. Kayaking is the best way to appreciate their grandeur (page 215).

★ **Iverson Snowshoe Company:** One of the very few manufacturers of snowshoes that still produce their wares by hand, Iverson offers fascinating factory tours (page 224).

Lake Superior

Sagola
69
95
Witch Lake
Michigamme Reservoir
95
Craig Lake State Park
Michigamme
▲ Mt. Arvon 1,979 ft

Huron Mountains
Rush Lake
Huron Mountain
Big Bay
Lake Independence

41
Dead River Storage Basin
Sugarloaf Mountain

Ishpeming
Negaunee
28
Warner Falls
35
DOWNTOWN MARQUETTE
SUGARLOAF MOUNTAIN
LITTLE PRESQUE ISLE STATE FOREST

0
10 mi
Eastern Time Zone
Central Time Zone

Gwinn
Escanaba River
New Swanzy
SAWYER INTERNATIONAL AIRPORT
553
Marquette
PRESQUE ISLE PARK
LAKENENLAND SCULPTURE PARK
★ OJIBWA CASINO

Rock
35
Kiva
41
Eben Junction
Trenary
67
Limestone
Cleveland Cliffs Basin
94
Au Train
28
HIAWATHA WATER TRAIL

Christmas
Munising
SHIPWRECK TOURS
Grand Island
GRAND ISLAND NATIONAL RECREATION AREA
PICTURED ROCKS

Shingleton
IVERSON SNOWSHOE COMPANY
94
Melstrand
H58
HIAWATHA NATIONAL FOREST
PICTURED ROCKS NATIONAL LAKESHORE

Hiawatha
28
Seney National Wildlife Refuge
Seney
To Sault Ste. Marie
77
Hiawatha Trail
Grand Marais

Blaney Park

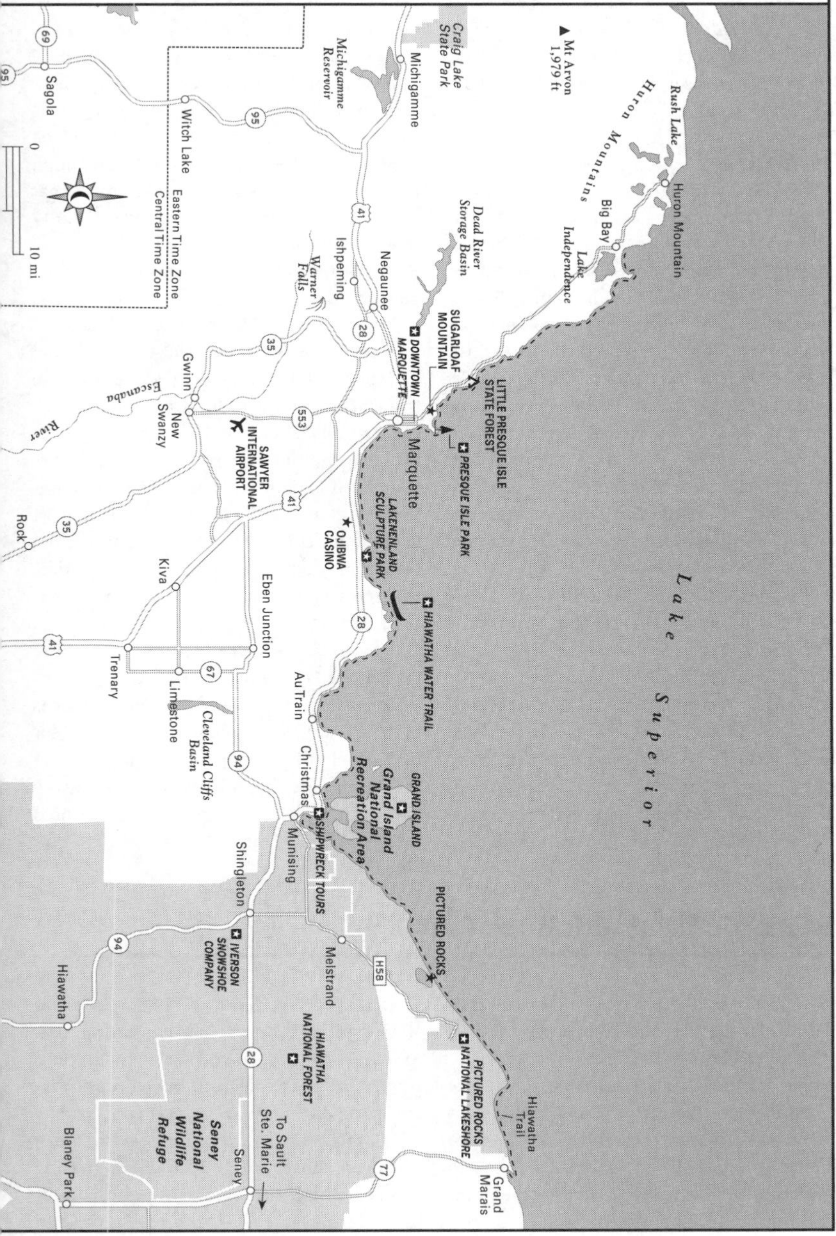

for Munising and Pictured Rocks, longer if you plan to explore the lakeshore by foot. Try to get out onto Lake Superior, whether by sea kayak, charter boat, or a tour. Two or three days will do just fine. Book a nice hotel, make some dinner reservations, and spend your days exploring.

HISTORY

Marquette and the Lake Superior shore weren't immune to the influence of trade and industry that shaped the rest of the Upper Peninsula. Indeed, its history is remarkably similar, albeit a bit tamer. French missionaries, including the city namesake, Jacques Marquette, explored the area in the mid-1600s. Fur trappers arrived several decades later, and the mines began operating in the mid-1800s. But it took more than mining to put the city on the map; a combination of industries gave Marquette its prosperity. Shipping, a stream of wealthy vacationers, and the mining of iron ore each contributed to the diverse local economy.

But not all of the Lake Superior shore was exploited, as the Huron Mountains remained largely untouched. Beginning around the 1880s, the Hurons became the wilderness retreat of choice for several millionaire industrialists. Cyrus McCormick, head of the lucrative farm implement company that would become International Harvester, amassed a huge wilderness estate around White Deer Lake, now part of the Ottawa National Forest's McCormick Tract Wilderness Area. Frederick Miller of Miller Brewing acquired his piece of wilderness at Craig Lake, now a wilderness state park. Dozens of others established "camps" at the Huron Mountain Club, an organization so exclusive that even Henry Ford was turned down for membership when he first applied. The members easily had enough clout to stop construction of a road that was to link L'Anse with Big Bay. County Road 550 unceremoniously ends just west of Big Bay—terminated by a gate and a security guardhouse.

Today, the 25,000-acre enclave is shared mostly by the descendants of those original members, who quietly protect and preserve this spectacular landholding. Though locals grumble about the lack of access to the property, no one can argue that the Huron Mountain Club has proved to be an exceptional steward of the land. It has kept away loggers, miners, and developers, leaving what some consider the most magnificent wilderness remaining in the state, perhaps in the entire Midwest.

The Pictured Rocks National Lakeshore joined the Huron Mountains as an exceptional specimen of nature in 1966 after areas of the Great Lakes shore were considered for inclusion in the national park system. The 43 miles of scenic shoreline between Munising and Grand Marais became the first national lakeshore in the United States.

Marquette and Vicinity

With just over 20,000 hardy year-round residents, Marquette ranks as the largest city in the Upper Peninsula. Tucked in a well-protected natural harbor midway across the U.P.'s northern shore, it grew and continues to thrive due largely to its central location, which has made it the U.P.'s center of commerce and government. Marquette also enjoys the status of being a central port for the iron industry.

Don't be deterred by the succession of strip malls and chain motels along U.S. 41—head toward downtown, which you'll find much more pleasant. Here you'll discover the city's rich architectural heritage, a U.S. Olympic Training Center, Northern Michigan University, and a beautiful setting along the high rocky Lake Superior shoreline. Marquette has never really promoted

Anatomy of a Murder

Lumberjack Tavern

Every small town has its share of interesting local lore, but the hamlet of Big Bay in the Huron Mountains can boast a special distinction. In 1952 attorney John Voelker, a former Marquette County prosecutor, received a call from Charlotte Peterson asking him to represent her husband, who had been charged with murder. A short time earlier, Army Lieutenant Coleman Petersen has been arrested and held after confronting and shooting bar owner Mike Chenoweth at the Lumberjack Tavern. The motive? Charlotte's credible allegation that Chenoweth had raped her at the bar during her husband's recent deployment. The case quickly became the talk of the town.

The fact of Petersen's guilt was not in dispute, yet Voelker agreed to take the case and used an unusual defense—a then-novel interpretation of the traditional insanity defense then called "irresistible impulse," which had not been used in Michigan since the late-nineteenth century. The tactic worked and resulted in the lieutenant's acquittal by mental disease of defect.

The unusual circumstances of the episode (a murder in an unlikely location, the unusual defense, and the heavy media attention) later inspired Voelker, who had a part-time vocation as a writer, to pen a novel on the incident, *Anatomy of a Murder,* written under the pen name Robert Traver and published in 1958. The next year saw a motion picture of the same name, directed by Hollywood legend Otto Preminger and starring Jimmy Stewart, Lee Remick, and Ben Gazzara. Both the book and the movie hew closely to the actual historical events, and their exceptional quality has led to their inclusion in many law school curricula for demonstrating a variety of legal strategies. The American Bar Association has ranked the movie as one of the 12 best trial films ever.

Today the **Lumberjack Tavern** (page 203) still operates and enjoys considerable notoriety due to its place in history. A local cottage industry capitalizing the town's fame has emerged in the form of souvenir shops and the like. Despite this small amount of commercialization, many visitors find the trip to the legendary bar a fun way to spend an afternoon.

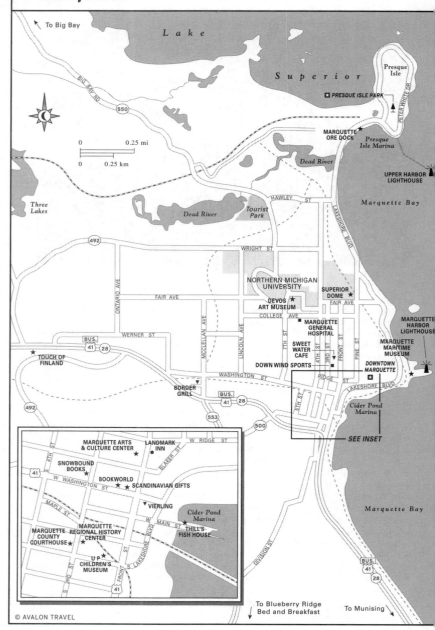

Marquette

To Big Bay

Lake

Superior

Presque Isle

PRESQUE ISLE PARK

Peter White Dr.

Presque Isle Marina

MARQUETTE ORE DOCK

Dead River

UPPER HARBOR LIGHTHOUSE

Marquette Bay

Three Lakes

Dead River

Tourist Park

HAWLEY ST

LAKESHORE BLVD

WRIGHT ST

492

ONTARIO AVE

FAIR AVE

NORTHERN MICHIGAN UNIVERSITY

SUPERIOR DOME

FAIR AVE

MARQUETTE HARBOR LIGHTHOUSE

DEVOS ART MUSEUM

COLLEGE AVE

MCCLELLAN AVE

LINCOLN AVE

MARQUETTE GENERAL HOSPITAL

7TH ST

4TH ST

3RD ST

FRONT ST

PINE ST

MARQUETTE MARITIME MUSEUM

WERNER ST

SWEET WATER CAFE

DOWN WIND SPORTS

DOWNTOWN MARQUETTE

BUS. 41 28

TOUCH OF FINLAND

WASHINGTON ST

RIDGE ST

LAKESHORE BLVD

492

BORDER GRILL

BUS. 41 28

5TH ST

Cider Pond Marina

553

500

SEE INSET

Marquette Bay

INSET:

MARQUETTE ARTS & CULTURE CENTER

LANDMARK INN

W RIDGE ST

4TH ST

BLAKER ST

41

SNOWBOUND BOOKS

BOOKWORLD

SCANDINAVIAN GIFTS

W WASHINGTON ST

MAPLE ST

VIERLING

Cider Pond Marina

MARQUETTE REGIONAL HISTORY CENTER

W MAIN ST

THILL'S FISH HOUSE

MARQUETTE COUNTY COURTHOUSE

3RD ST

FRONT ST

S LAKESHORE BLVD

U P CHILDREN'S MUSEUM

41

DIVISION ST

BUS. 41 28

To Blueberry Ridge Bed and Breakfast

To Munising

0   0.25 mi
0   0.25 km

550

© AVALON TRAVEL

itself as a tourist destination, but this may be to the visitor's benefit. Lodging and good restaurants are plentiful, the downtown and lakefront are ideal for strolling, and the U.P.'s natural attractions—rugged hills, waterfalls, wildlife, and wild rivers—all await barely outside the city limits, often without the crowds and typical tourist-trap blight.

SIGHTS
★ Downtown Marquette

Third Street, running north-south, and Washington Street, running east-west, represent Marquette's main cross streets, and where they meet is a good area to begin an exploration of downtown. This puts you in the heart of the shopping and historic district. Buildings like the 1902 **Marquette County Courthouse** (3rd St. and Baraga Ave.) and the 1927 **MFC First National Bank** (101 W. Washington St.) display the city's affinity for beaux arts architecture. Step inside the courthouse for a better look, and also to check out a display about Michigan Supreme Court Justice and author John Voelker, better known by his pen name, Robert Traver. An Ishpeming native, Traver wrote the popular novel *Anatomy of a Murder,* among other works. Based on a real murder in nearby Big

Bay, the book was made into a movie of the same name in 1959. Scenes from the film, starring Jimmy Stewart and George C. Scott, were filmed in the third-floor courtroom and in Big Bay. The **Marquette Regional History Center** (145 W. Spring St., 906/226-3571, www.marquettecohistory.org, 10am-5pm Mon.-Tues. and Thurs.-Fri., 10am-8pm Wed., 10am-3pm Sat., $7 adults, $6 seniors, $3 students, free under age 13) offers a walking tour brochure.

Downtown Marquette is home to distinctive shops worth a little browsing time. **Bookworld** (136 W. Washington St., 906/228-9490, www.bookworldstores.com, 10am-8pm Mon.-Sat., 9am-5pm Sun.) and **Snowbound Books** (118 N. 3rd St., 906/228-4448, www.snowboundbooks.com, 9:30am-6pm Mon.-Wed. and Fri., 9:30am-8pm Thurs., 9am-5pm Sat., 11am-3pm Sun.) offer a good selection of local and regional titles. Follow Main Street down to the waterfront, where **Thill's Fish House** (250 E. Main St., 906/226-9851, 8am-5:30pm Mon.-Fri., 9am-4pm Sat.) sells fresh catch and smoked whitefish from a little shop at the marina, in the shadow of the old wooden ore dock. Expect to pay around $10.50 per pound for whitefish and perch and

the Marquette County Courthouse

$15 per pound for walleye and other varieties, depending on market conditions.

The U.P.'s Scandinavian heritage looms large in Marquette. **Scandinavian Gifts** (1025 N. 3rd St., 906/225-1993, 10am-6pm Mon.-Fri., 10am-5pm Sat., 11am-4pm Sun.) showcases the sleek and simple lines of classic Scandinavian design in its selection of glassware and silver, plus lots of Norwegian sweaters too. Back on U.S. 41, **Touch of Finland** (2853 U.S. 41, 906/226-2567, www.touchoffinland.com, 9:30am-8pm Mon.-Fri., 9:30am-7pm Sat., 10:30am-6pm Sun.) has a bit of almost everything in its 4,000 square feet, including housewares, textiles, and a complete sauna department.

The old redbrick waterworks building now houses the **Marquette Maritime Museum** (300 Lakeshore Blvd., 906/226-2006, 11am-4pm Tues.-Sun. May 25-Oct., $7 adults, $3 under age 13). This worthwhile stop includes exhibits on everything from Native American birch-bark canoes to Great Lakes shipwrecks and lighthouses, an interactive display of a freighter's pilot house, and a working submarine periscope. Admission to the **Marquette Harbor Lighthouse** in available at an extra charge.

The **Marquette Regional History Center** (145 W. Spring St., 906/226-3571, www.marquettecohistory.org, 10am-5pm Mon.-Tues. and Thurs.-Fri., 10am-8pm Wed., 10am-3pm Sat., $7 adults, $6 seniors, $3 students, free under age 13) features excellent Native American exhibits as well as lots of mining and logging photographs and a large collection of old maps. There's an excellent bookstore as well.

If you're traveling with children, head for the **U.P. Children's Museum** (123 W. Baraga Ave., 906/226-3911, www.upchildrensmuseum.com, 10am-6pm Mon.-Wed., 10am-7:30pm Thurs., 10am-8pm Fri., 10am-6pm Sat., noon-5pm Sun., closed major holidays, $6, free under age 2), where they can climb into a tree habitat to learn about its root system, crawl into a replica wasp nest, or explore life in the aquifer under a pond.

The **Marquette Arts and Culture Center** (217 N. Front St., 906/228-0472, www.mqtcty.org, 10am-5pm Mon., 10am-9pm Tues. and Thurs., 10am-5pm Wed., 10am-5pm Fri.-Sat., free), located on the lower level of the **Peter White Public Library,** offers a gallery featuring the work of local artists that changes each month. You'll also find a museum shop offering many of the pieces for sale, as well as occasional informal concerts and plays.

For a unique type of Upper Peninsula experience, stop by Presque Isle Park to watch an ore carrier being loaded at the **Marquette Ore Dock,** located on Lakeshore Boulevard, shortly before the entrance to Presque Isle Park about four miles northeast of downtown. This behemoth structure, which extends almost 0.25 miles out into Lake Superior, is designed to interface with 600-foot-long ships as they're loaded with taconite pellets deposited by overhead railway cars. It's a noisy spectacle, and a pleasant reminder that a small part of the U.P.'s mining heritage still survives today. Check www.boatnerd.com for a schedule of vessel passages.

Where would you expect to find the world's largest wooden dome? In the heart of logging country, of course, and along Lake Superior, where hostile weather regularly foils outdoor sporting events. In 1991, Northern Michigan University completed the 8,000-seat **Superior Dome** (1401 Presque Isle Ave., 906/227-2850), affectionately known as the "Yooper Dome." Enclosing some five acres, the dome is fashioned from a framework of 781 huge fir beams, strong enough to withstand substantial amounts of snow. Along with hosting a variety of school sporting events and practices, the dome is open to the public for walking and running on weekday mornings. Call or stop by for specifics.

★ Presque Isle Park

A thumb of land thrust out into the big lake, **Presque Isle Park** (pronounced "presk ahyl," which translates from French as "almost an island" or "peninsula"), about four miles north of downtown off Lakeshore Boulevard, is a microcosm of the area's beauty: rocky red bluffs, tall pines, and lovely Lake Superior vistas. You can drive through the 323-acre park, but you'd do better to get out and stroll or ski along its many trails. Watch for albino white-tailed deer that survive in this protected setting. Near the park's entrance, there's a playground, a picnic area, tennis courts, and a marina. The park is the perfect spot to watch huge 600-foot-long freighters arrive at the towering **railroad ore dock.** Trains carrying pellets of taconite, an iron-clay mixture, from one of the nearby open-pit iron mines chug out onto the 70-foot-high elevated track and empty their loads into the hold below. Chutes transfer the taconite into the bellies of the ore freighters, which transport their cargo to the industrial centers of the southern Great Lakes.

DeVos Art Museum

Although it had its beginnings in the 1975 Lee Hall Gallery, the **DeVos Art Museum** (1401 Presque Isle Ave., 906/227-2235, http://art.nmu.edu, 10am-5pm Mon.-Wed., 10am-8pm Thurs., 10am-5pm Fri., 1pm-4pm Sat.-Sun., donation), part of Northern Michigan University's School of Art and Design, got a facelift with its 2005 reopening, complete with a new larger building, made possible by a grant from the DeVos Foundation of Grand Rapids. The museum's permanent collection, which represents work from numerous well-known artists, including Salvador Dalí, is displayed on a rotating basis, while other areas of the museum host temporary exhibits. You'll also enjoy the sculpture walk, where an inviting pathway snakes through one of the university's wooded areas.

Lighthouses

The **Marquette Harbor Lighthouse** (300 Lakeshore Blvd., 906/226-2006, http://mqt-maritimemuseum.com, 11am-4pm daily May 25-Oct., $7 adults, $3 under age 13) is one of Lake Superior's most attractive. The light and some of the land surrounding it was recently acquired by the Marquette Maritime Museum under a lease from the Coast Guard.

The lease will expire in 2032, so there's plenty of time to make it to the beautiful red light for a tour. As part of the lease agreement, all tours must be escorted by a member of the museum staff. Built in 1866 and expanded in 1906, the Marquette Harbor Lighthouse serves as an interpretive display and an extension of the museum.

To see another, slightly less scenic lighthouse, head to Presque Isle Park for a look at the **Presque Isle Upper Harbor Lighthouse.** The light is still guiding ships into the railroad ore docks nearby. **Granite Island Lighthouse** is located six miles offshore; it's a little more than 10 miles northeast of Marquette.

Stannard Rock Lighthouse is a little harder to get to, since it's located in Lake Superior, about 50 miles from Marquette's shoreline. Due to its considerable distance from land, charter services will usually only sail to the lighthouse in conjunction with a fishing trip. Two operators offering cruise are **Uncle Ducky Charters** (434 E. Prospect St., Marquette, 877/228-5447, www.paddling-michigan.com) and **Shelter Bay Charters** (E3394 Old M-28, Au Train, 906/892-8230, www.shelterbaycharterfishing.com).

★ Lakenenland Sculpture Park

Be sure to check out **Lakenenland Sculpture Park** (http://lakenenland.com), a free outdoor sculpture display located on M-28 about 15 miles east of Marquette. Artist Tom Lakenen specializes in "junkyard art" and has moved many of his creations to this site. Examples include rebar alligators, elephants, space aliens, and even political figures. Outdoor art exhibits are a rarity in much of the nation, and even rarer in Michigan's Upper Peninsula—seeing these intriguing sculptures in a forested rural setting makes for an interesting diversion.

Ishpeming and Negaunee

In many ways, these twin towns 15 miles west of Marquette represent the heart of the iron

The Art of Lakenenland

lumberjacks at Lakenenland

Nestled along M-28 about 15 miles east of Marquette is perhaps one of the Upper Peninsula's most unusual attractions. Lakenenland, the creation of local resident Tom Lakenen, is a large collection of junkyard art, in which discarded metal objects (steel girders, hot water heaters, oil drums) are repurposed into a vast array of colorful likenesses of dinosaurs, flying saucers, spiders, birds of prey, airplanes, and more. The 100 sculptures vary in size, but many are large, some as tall as 15 feet. The compelling exhibit can be viewed at any time and is free.

What motivated Lakenen to create this object of amazement? "It stated as a hobby. I was building these things and displaying them on my front lawn until the township told me I had to move them," explains Lakenen. At around them same time he bought the parcel of land on M-28 as an investment, and decided it would be the perfect home for his creations. But Lakenen did have another motivation—the all-too-frequent tourist traps that dot the landscape. "I wanted to do something with the land that families can visit and enjoy without having to spend a lot of money." There is secure box for those who wish to leave a donation, but Lakenen stresses that visitors should not feel obliged. The funds raised defray the cost of maintaining the site.

---

range. One of the Upper Peninsula's earliest iron mines, the Jackson Mine, opened here in 1847. The Empire and Tilden Mines, in nearby Palmer, continue to operate today, and represent the Upper Peninsula's last link to this part of its storied past.

Today, Ishpeming and Negaunee are tarnished versions of their former selves. The economy never recovered from the closing of most of the area's mines in the 1960s, and the once vital downtowns were further displaced by the commercial strips along U.S. 41, which passes just north of Ishpeming. But anyone who enjoys history will find these towns intriguing, with their vintage ornate storefronts, ramshackle antiques shops, and fenced-off cave-in areas, where the land has succumbed to decades of tunneling.

One of the finest museums in the Upper Peninsula, the state-run **Iron Industry Museum** (73 Forge Rd., Negaunee, 906/475-7857, www.michigan.gov/ironindustry-museum, 9:30am-4:30pm daily May-Oct., 9:30am-4pm Mon.-Fri., 9:30am-4pm 1st Sat. of each month Nov.-Apr., donation) is located along the Carp River off U.S. 41. The spot wasn't chosen for its scenery; it marks the site of one of the area's earliest iron forges, built in 1848. This small facility packs a lot of information and several expertly designed displays into a single exhibit hall. It tells the story of Michigan's $48 billion iron mining and smelting industry, which dwarfed the California gold rush ($955 million), Michigan's lucrative logging industry ($4.4 billion), and even Michigan's venerable copper mining ($9.6 billion). You'll learn how iron prompted the development of dozens of port towns and the giant ore freighters that now ply the Great Lakes. The Technology Timeline traces advancements in exploration, working conditions, and mining methods.

Few people think of Ishpeming as the center of the U.S. ski industry, but many of the large resorts in the Rockies can trace interest in the sport to Michigan. In 1887 residents of Northern Michigan, many of them Scandinavian immigrants, established the Ishpeming Ski Club, one of the oldest continuously operating clubs in the nation. In 1888 they organized the country's first ski jumping competition. Everett Kircher, visionary founder of Michigan's Boyne Mountain resort, invented the first successful snowmaking machine. As a result, Ishpeming was chosen as the site of the **U.S. National Ski Hall of Fame and Ski Museum** (610 Palms Ave., Ishpeming, 906/485-6323, www.skihall.com, 10am-5pm Mon.-Sat. year-round, donation), the sport's official hall of fame.

The museum, on U.S. 41 between 2nd and 3rd Streets, covers the sport from *way* back, beginning with a replica of a 4,000-year-old ski and pole found in Sweden. Most interesting are the displays of early ski equipment, including early poles, which "often doubled as weapons," an examination of the evolution of chairlifts, and an account of the skiing soldiers of the 10th Mountain Division, who played an important role in the mountains of Italy during World War II. The Hall of Fame plaques offer insightful short biographies of those who shaped the sport, from racers to resort owners.

ENTERTAINMENT
Ojibwa Casino

If you're looking for Marquette gaming, look no farther than the **Ojibwa Casino** (105 Acre Trail, 906/249-4200 or 800/560-9905, www.ojibwacasino.com) in Marquette. Table games include blackjack, roulette, craps, and poker, while more than 300 reel video and video poker machines play from a penny to $5. There are seven sites available at the Ojibwa Casino RV Park and free shuttle service to and from a number of chain hotels in the area. The Snack Bar serves up all sorts of food right on the casino floor, from soup, pizza, and burgers to shrimp and fish dinners, all at very reasonable prices. Be sure to check with the casino for Snack Bar specials.

FESTIVALS AND EVENTS

For more information on events in the area, contact the **Marquette County Convention and Visitors Bureau** (337 W. Washington St., Marquette, 906/228-7749 or 800/544-4321, www.travelmarquettemichigan.com).

U.P. 200

The **U.P. 200** (www.up200.org) is a sled-dog race held in mid-February that begins with a nighttime start in Marquette, heads to Grand Marais, and then returns to Marquette—a distance of 230 miles. At the checkpoints in Wetmore, Grand Marais, and again in Wetmore on the return leg, each participant is required to rest a minimum of five hours, making the race roughly a 36-hour event. An estimated 30,000 people watch the annual race, which has quickly grown into one of the U.P.'s most beloved spectator events. The start and finish are the big draws, but the race has prompted a weeklong calendar of activities, from broomball tournaments (hockey played with boots instead of skates, balls instead of pucks, and brooms instead of sticks) to fireworks. Serious mushers will be interested to know that the U.P. 200 is an Iditarod qualifying event.

Northern Michigan University

Hail Northern, we thy sons and daughters
Now bring thee tribute long deserved
Thou beacon light 'mid nature's grandeur
Through passing decades well preserved
Oh, may we labor with untiring zeal
That when these golden days have flown
We may with honor face the future
And match thy courage with our own.

Students at Northern Michigan University (NMU) are a rare and special breed. Not everyone can tolerate spending their winters in Marquette, on the frozen shores of Lake Superior, where the average daytime high temperature drops into the low 20s each January and where, in 1996, the lowest recorded temperature was a shockingly frigid -24°F. It's a place where class is more often canceled for cold than for snowfall. Michigan has other options for higher education: two Big Ten schools, the University of Michigan and Michigan State University, are located in the warmer climate of the Lower Peninsula. These students are here because they like it here.

Founded in 1899 with 32 students, NMU is the largest university in Michigan's Upper Peninsula, now with an enrollment of over 9,000, still quite small compared to some downstate schools. The school offers traditional education with 180 academic majors and 120 academic minors in such subjects as business, technology, education, and sociology. Northern Michigan takes special pride in its technology programs, which embraces the vision of providing a "learning environment that embraces technology to enhance student access, promote the development of independent learners, and encourage greater student faculty communication and collaboration." It was this vision that led the school to become the first state university in Michigan to become a "laptop campus," providing each of its students with a laptop computer and a standard set of software tools for use during the school year. The university upgrades students' computers every two years.

NMU's campus consists of more than 50 facilities located on the shores of Lake Superior. The most interesting of these is undoubtedly the Superior Dome, which has the distinction of being the world's largest wooden dome structure. A fascinating sight, the dome is 14 stories high with a diameter of 563 feet, and covers more than five acres. It's impressively built from Douglas fir,

Art Faire & Renaissance Festival

If you're the adventurous type, head over to Bancroft park in Ishpeming on the first Saturday of August to enjoy the **Art Faire & Renaissance Festival** (http://ishpemingrenfest.webs.com). The festival is a one-day event that features arts and crafts booths, food vendors, and engaging entertainment by singers, swordsmen, dancers, and musicians—all in the spirit of Renaissance. To get to Bancroft Park, take U.S. 41 west of Marquette and make a right turn when you get to Lakeshore Drive. Continue for 0.5 miles. Best of all, admission is free.

Hiawatha Traditional Music Festival

Summertime brings the **Hiawatha Traditional Music Festival** (906/226-8575, www.hiawathamusic.org) during the second-to-last full weekend of July. Featuring traditional music such as bluegrass, acoustic blues, folk, old time, and more, the Hiawatha is the only festival of its type and size in the U.P.

Pine Mountain Music Festival

The **Pine Mountain Music Festival** (906/482-1542, www.pmmf.org) runs during the final two weeks of June and is a celebration of opera, symphony, and chamber

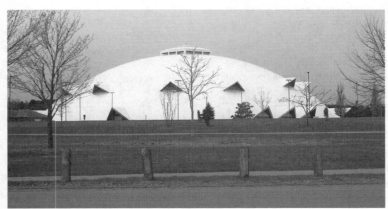

NMU's Superior Dome

a natural choice considering its location. Containing 781 beams and more than 100 *miles* of fir decking, the dome can withstand up to 60 pounds of snow per square foot. Inside, removable artificial turf (also the largest of its kind in the world) can host football, soccer, and field hockey. Beneath the turf are three basketball or volleyball courts, two tennis courts, and a 200-meter track.

The real action takes place at the Berry Events Center. An Olympic-size ice sheet, 200 by 100 feet, hosts ice hockey, the sport of choice here, where long winters and proximity to Canada make the sport popular. While NMU competes in NCAA Division II for most sports—basketball, football, and the like—hockey is a Division I sport, and is an experience that shouldn't be missed if you're in town.

There are other reasons to visit NMU's campus too. The school's drama department stages several theatrical productions each year, and the DeVos Art Museum offers scores of intriguing pieces by regional artists.

music that takes place at venues around the Upper Peninsula, usually in Marquette, Iron Mountain, and Houghton.

Harbor Fest

During the third week of August, Marquette plays host to its annual **Harbor Fest** (http://downtownmarquette.org), two days and nights of quality free music sponsored by the Marquette West Rotary. Representing different genres, the selection include bluegrass, classical, pop, and a series of "tribute bands"—groups that impersonate famous musical acts that most of the audience will remember: Chicago, James Brown, and Sly and the Family Stone, to name a few. Harbor Fest is held at Mattson Lower Harbor Park (Lakeshore Dr. and Pine St.) near the campus of Northern Michigan University.

Annual Marquette Blues Fest

During Labor Day weekend, Mattson Park is the site for the **Annual Marquette Blues Fest** (www.marquetteareabluessociety.com), three days of performances by both local and nationally known blues artists, which have included Johnny Rawls, Lurrie Bell, and Jeff Daniels with his Ben Daniels Band. Visit the website for the in the weeks prior to the next festival to view the lineup.

Art on the Rocks

Head to Presque Isle Park for the annual **Art on the Rocks** (http://marquetteartontherocks.com) held during the last weekend of July. The event is an art festival featuring a juried exhibition and sales.

North of the 45th Parallel

The name of the **North of the 45th Parallel** exhibition at NMU's **DeVos Art Museum** (1401 Presque Isle Ave., http://art.nmu.edu, 10am-5pm Mon.-Wed., noon-8pm Thurs., 10am-5pm Fri., 1pm-4pm Sat.-Sun. early June-early Aug., donation) explains its eligibility criterion: Only artists residing north of that line, which represents the midway point between the north pole and the equator, are permitted to display their work in the juried competition. The restriction is designated to emphasize the breadth of artists who call Northern Michigan home. The 45th parallel crosses Michigan around Gaylord, in the northern portion of the Lower Peninsula, and is often recognized as the dividing line between "up north" and "downstate."

International Food Festival

The **International Food Festival** happens each year for three days around the 4th of July and is held at Ellwood Mattson Lower Harbor Park (200 Lakeshore Blvd., Marquette). A tempting array of foods from the German, Asian, Mexican, and Cajun traditions are on offer. The event includes live entertainment and fireworks at dusk on July 4.

SUMMER SPORTS AND RECREATION
Hiking and Biking

The trail system in the greater Marquette area is complex and potentially confusing. Before setting out, a good first step is to visit www.travelmarquettemichigan.com for a series of interactive online maps of all the hiking and biking trails in the greater Marquette area. The entire Ishpeming-Negaunee area is part of the comprehensive **Range Mountain Bike Trail System,** with more than 25 miles of trails stretching from Teal Lake to Lake Sally, south of Suicide Bowl. Routes are detailed in the online maps.

As County Road 550 runs north out of Marquette toward Big Bay, you'll travel just six miles before the sign and parking area before **Sugar Loaf Mountain** lures you to pull over for a relatively easy 15-minute hike. A stairway makes for a gradual ascent up the rock, and you'll be rewarded with a sweeping view of Lake Superior to the north, the city of Marquette to the east, and the undulating landscape of the wild Huron Mountains stretching all the way to the western horizon.

There's great hiking and mountain biking in the surrounding terrain, much of it part of the **Little Presque Isle State Forest Recreation Area.** Several miles of trails wind around nearby Harlow Lake, up Hogsback Mountain, and along the Lake Superior shore. Parking is available in the unmarked lot on the west side of County Road 550; it's near an old gravel pit, about one mile north of the Sugar Loaf Mountain lot. The South Marquette Trails are part of the **Noquemanon Trail Network** (906/228-6182, www.noquetrails.org), ranked among *Bike* magazine's top 10 trails in 2005, and provide miles of hiking and biking. The Mount Marquette Loop is a five-mile trail, while the Carp River and Pioneer loops run a combined total of nine miles. The organization recently introduced a handy smartphone app (http://marquette.ifindtrail.com) featuring interactive maps of the whole trail network.

★ Hiawatha Water Trail

One of Lake Superior's greatest kayaking destinations, the **Hiawatha Water Trail** (www.hiawathawatertrail.org) passes along the shores of Marquette on the way from Big Bay to Grand Marais, a total of 120 miles. The most beautiful portion of the trail lies to the east, along Pictured Rocks National Lakeshore between Munising and Grand Marais, but getting there will take some hard paddling. Access points and campgrounds are available along the way; get a copy of the official

Hiawatha Water Trail Map at **Down Wind Sports** (514 N. 3rd St., Marquette, 906/226-7112, www.downwindsports.com).

Presque Isle is one of Marquette's most beautiful destinations, and visitors who only see it from land are missing out: This is the ultimate kayak trip. More than two miles of jagged shoreline is dotted with rugged crags, towering sandstone cliffs, rocks, and an undeveloped shore. Put in and take out at the Presque Isle Marina. For guided tours, contact **Uncle Ducky Outfitters** (434 E. Prospect St., 906/228-5447 or 877/228-5447, www.paddlingmichigan.com). The six-hour "Paddlers Choice" tour runs $154 pp. Uncle Ducky also offers guided tours of Marquette harbors, Presque Isle to Little Presque Isle, Huron Island, and Big Bay.

Golf

Marquette holds a few surprises for visitors searching out a round of golf. Try a visit to the new Greywalls course at the **Marquette Golf Club** (1075 Grove St., 906/225-0721, www.golfgreywalls.com, nonmembers $130 June-Sept., cheaper spring and fall, includes cart). Greywalls opened in 2005 to wide acclaim, earning high marks in *Golf Digest* and other magazines. The course's 18 holes are complemented by Marquette's natural terrain, featuring views of Lake Superior, rocky crags, and evergreen forests. Another 18 holes at the Heritage Course ($39, $26 for 9 holes) round out the semiprivate facility, the only 36-hole club in the Upper Peninsula.

Beaches

Lake Superior isn't exactly made for swimming; it's cold, the shoreline is often rocky, and the water is too deep in many places. Even though there are a few Lake Superior beaches in Marquette, not many people actually want to dive in. That said, you're still welcome to go for a dip if you're daring enough. Of course, there's more to do at a beach than swim: you can grill, sunbathe, play a game of volleyball, or toss a Frisbee. South Beach, just off Lake Street in Marquette, and McCarty's Cove on

Lakeshore Drive, are two of the city's most popular. Both are equipped with playground equipment and restrooms, and each offers pleasing views and sandy beaches perfect for an afternoon by the lake.

Off-Road Vehicles

For an off-road trail that's part of the state system, head south toward Gwinn. About five miles west of Gwinn, the **Bass Lake Motorcycle Trail** is open to vehicles less than 50 inches wide. The long loop, just under 25 miles, circles several lakes, including Bass, Crooked, Spring, and Pike. Take M-35 to Crooked Lake Road and head southwest to a parking area, which is near the Pike Lake and Bass Lake Campgrounds. The **Porterfield Lake Motorcycle Trail** is on the border of Marquette and Dickinson Counties, where more than 20 miles of trail split into several loops. Porterfield Lake Trail is eight miles southwest of Gwinn. Additionally, ORVs are allowed on all trails and forest roads on state land. Contact the **Michigan Department of Natural Resources** (DNR, www.michigan.gov/dnr) for more information.

Waterfalls

Among the most scenic of the Marquette region's waterfalls is **Warner Falls,** a 20-foot drop into the relatively still waters of the Warner Creek, which seems to be more a pond. Warner Falls is reasonably accessible: About eight miles west of Marquette, take M-35 south past Palmer and pull off less than one mile past the M-35/County Road 565 intersection. The falls are on the right and can easily be seen from the road.

The **Dead River Falls,** just west of Marquette, are beautiful but difficult to find and even harder to get to. Take U.S. 41 west of town to Wright Street and head north. Turn left at Forestville Road and drive to a powerhouse about 2.5 miles up. From there, park and take the gravel road to a clear trail on the left. Follow it down a steep hill, then turn right; stay on the path until you reach the falls.

For a map of additional falls in the area

and detailed instructions on how to get to them, contact the **Marquette County Convention and Visitors Bureau** (337 W. Washington St., 906/228-7749 or 800/544-4321, www.travelmarquettemichigan.com).

WINTER SPORTS AND RECREATION
Downhill Skiing

Marquette Mountain (4501 County Rd. 553, 906/225-1155, www.marquettemountain.com, lift tickets $30-47) gets a nod for its 600-foot vertical drop, one of the highest in the state. The 23 trails may not be exceptionally long, but they offer good variety, including bumps and tree runs. The half pipe and terrain park grow and improve every year. Located just three miles south of Marquette on County Road 553, it's popular all week long with college students and locals. Night skiing is offered Tuesday-Sunday in season, usually mid-November to early April. Rental equipment is available.

You'd hardly guess that the 300-acre **Al Quaal Recreation Area** (501 Poplar St., Ishpeming, 906/485-4565, www.noquettrails.org), on the north shore of Ishpeming's Teal Lake, is a city park. To get here, take Deer Lake Road north from U.S. 41. You can make a winter day of it, with a few downhill runs served by a rope tow, a 1.9-mile cross-country loop, an outdoor ice rink, and especially the 1,200-foot iced toboggan run where a small hourly fee includes a rental toboggan. The park is open daily, except the downhill runs, which are open on weekend afternoons only. Check the website for admission cost.

Ski and Snowshoe Trails

For cross-country skiing, continue south on County Road 553 to the **Blueberry Ridge Ski Trails** (free), 15 miles of groomed and tracked trails looping through the Escanaba River State Forest, including one lighted 1.7-mile circuit. Another option is the **Anderson Lake Pathway,** five miles south of Gwinn on County Road 557, with four hilly loops

ranging 2 to 4.3 miles in length. Both networks are open to mountain bikes in summer months.

Cross-country skiers looking for a challenge should head for the ominous-sounding **Suicide Bowl** trail network between Ishpeming and Negaunee. Groomed for skating and diagonal stride, it offers more than 18 miles of trails and a map dotted with phrases like "hairpin curve," "bad downhill," and "very difficult trail." The parking area is on Cliff Drive, south of Business M-28; follow it past downtown Ishpeming. This area is also the site of **Suicide Hill,** a ski jump used in international competitions.

Luge

If ski jumping isn't wild enough for you, you might want to try luge. Just south of Negaunee on M-35, **Lucy Hill** (www.negauneeluge.freehomepage.com, 765/586-5733) is operated by the Upper Peninsula Luge Club. The course meets International Luge Federation standards as an official luge track, dropping 300 feet with 29 turns. It's open to the public most weekend afternoons, with instruction and equipment available.

Snowmobiling

Marquette County has more land than any other county in Michigan, which means it has a lot of snowmobile trails. The main trail in and out of Marquette is **Trail 8,** pressing west toward Baraga along U.S. 41/M-28 and south to Gwinn. To get to Au Train or Munising, take **Trail 417,** which more or less follows M-28 east before dipping south a bit and rejoining with Trail 8. If you're heading up to Big Bay, take **Trail 310** out of town. For a detailed snowmobile trail map, contact the **Marquette County Convention and Visitors Bureau** (337 W. Washington St., 906/228-7749 or 800/544-4321, www.travelmarquettemichigan.com).

Additionally, snowmobiles are allowed to travel with the flow of traffic on the right side of all plowed roads in Marquette County—provided that they stay single-file and travel at a reasonable speed. For everyone's mutual safety, be careful, stop at intersections, and pay attention to all traffic. All snowmobiles are required to be registered and have a state trail permit, available through the **Michigan DNR** (www.michigan.gov/dnr) and at snowmobile shops throughout the state.

FOOD

For a city its size, Marquette has a very good selection of high-quality, locally owned restaurants. The ★ **Vierling Restaurant and Marquette Harbor Brewery** (119 S. Front St., 906/228-3533, http://thevierling.com, 11am-10pm Mon.-Sat., dinner entrées $18-39) stands out for its good food, century-old décor, and interesting views of the Marquette Harbor ore docks. Ask for a table near the large windows in back. The menu offers lot of variety, including vegetarian and Italian dishes and whitefish served five ways. Excellent breakfasts, soups, and sandwiches are available too. There is a microbrewery downstairs, featuring British-style ales and stouts.

For organic, natural food, you can't do better than the **Sweet Water Cafe** (517 N. 3rd St., 906/226-7009, www.sweetwatercafe.org, breakfast and lunch daily, dinner Wed.-Sun., dinner entrées $9-14). Locals give its tofu scramble and pancakes with whipped maple butter extra high marks. There are good smoothies too. Most menu items can be prepared gluten free. Locals will also point you to one of the locations of the no-frills **Border Grill** (1145 W. Washington St., 906/228-5228; 800 N. 3rd St., 906/228-0100, www.bordergrill.net, 11am-9pm daily, under $10) for savory Tex-Mex with fresh salsa.

ACCOMMODATIONS

The best spot in Marquette is easily the ★ **Landmark Inn** (230 N. Front St., 888/752-6362, www.thelandmarkinn.com, $179-259). Built in the 1930s as the Northland Hotel, it hosted such luminaries as Amelia Earhart and Abbott and Costello. After falling into disrepair and eventually closing in the 1980s, it has been beautifully restored and reopened as the Landmark. For not much more than you'd pay for a basic chain motel room, you get a taste of history, a touch of elegance, and a primo location, with Lake Superior on one side and downtown Marquette on the other.

South of Marquette, check into **Blueberry Ridge Bed-and-Breakfast** (18 Oakridge Dr., 906/249-9246, http://blueberryridgebedandbreakfastmqt.com, $100-140) for a quiet stay in the north woods. Many of the major hotel and motel franchises are represented in Marquette, especially along the U.S. 41/M-28 strip.

Camping

You can't pitch a tent at the **Little Presque Isle State Forest Campground** (906/228-6561, www.michigan.gov/dnr), north of Marquette on County Road 550, but the rustic cabins ($70)—no electricity, no running water, no roads all the way in—make for great camping, and they're available year-round. A 0.5-mile hike from the parking area will get you to your cabin, and once you're there, it's all hand-pumped water, wood-burning stoves, and vault toilets. There are 18 miles of hiking trails, along with miles of Lake Superior beach, fishing, and other recreational opportunities. Cabins sleep up to six, and reservations are required.

More traditional camping, either in a tent or at an RV site, can be found at **Marquette Tourist Park** (2145 Sugarloaf Rd., 906/228-0460, www.mqtcty.org, tent sites $18, with electricity $30, full hookup $35). The 40-acre in-town park has 110 rustic tent-only campsites; public restrooms, showers, and water and electrical hookups are also available. You'll also find fire rings, picnic tables, a ball field, and a playground. Advance reservations are strongly recommended. There are another 100 or so campsites at **Gitche Gumee RV Park** (2048 M-28 E., 866/447-8727, www.gitchegumeepark.com), which features amenities such as 70 cable TV channels, a movie theater, and a fudge factory.

There are four **state forest**

campgrounds in nearby Gwinn: Anderson Lake West (19 sites), Bass Lake (22 sites), North Horseshoe Lake (11 sites), and Pike Lake (10 sites), each accommodating tents and a few small trailers. There are no reservations and a few rustic amenities, including vault toilets and drinking water from a hand pump. Contact the **Michigan DNR Gwinn Field Office** (410 W. M-35, Gwinn, 906/346-9201, www.michigan.gov/dnr).

INFORMATION AND SERVICES

Get visit information from the friendly folks at the **Marquette County Convention and Visitors Bureau** (337 W. Washington St., 906/228-7749 or 800/544-4321, www.travelmarquettemichigan.com).

For local medical attention, **UP Health System Marquette** (580 W. College Ave., 906/228-9440, www.mgh.org) has a high-quality emergency room and trauma care center in the neighborhood of Northern Michigan University.

Marquette has plenty of banks and ATMs. Try the various **Wells Fargo** locations (101 W. Washington St., 906/228-1203; 1300 N. 3rd St., 906/228-1266; 6000 U.S. 41, 906/228-1258, www.wellsfargo.com), **River Valley State Bank** (1140 W. Washington St., 906/226-0300; 1101 3rd St., 906/226-0300, www.rivervalleybank.com), or **Northern Michigan Bank and Trust** (1502 W. Washington St., 906/228-7300, www.nmbank.com).

Note that Marquette and its surrounding areas are in the eastern time zone.

GETTING THERE AND AROUND
Car

Getting to Marquette by car is especially easy: U.S. 41 runs from the south and west; from the east, M-28 and U.S. 2 lead to U.S. 41, a better option than smaller roads such as M-553. U.S. 41 also runs through Ishpeming and Negaunee, west of Marquette. The three cities are beginning to blend into one long stretch of shops and services.

Air

If you're flying into town, **Sawyer International Airport** (MQT, 125 G Ave., Gwinn, 906/346-3308, www.sawyerairport.com) has scheduled flights from Detroit on **Delta Airlines** (800/221-1212, www.delta.com) and Chicago O'Hare on **American Eagle** (800/433-7300, www.aa.com).

You'll most likely want to rent a car; Sawyer has **Alamo** (800/462-5266, www.alamo.com), **Avis** (800/831-1212, www.avis.com), **Budget** (800/527-7000, www.budget.com), **Dollar** (800/800-3665, www.dollar.com), **Hertz** (800/800-3665, www.hertz.com), **National** (800/227-7368, www.nationalcar.com), and **Thrifty** (800/847-4389, www.thrifty.com). Bus service runs to Marquette and Gwinn on **Marq-Tran** (906/225-1112, www.marq-tran.com).

Boat

Marquette has two marinas: The **Cinder Pond Marina** (906/228-0469, www.michigan.gov/dnr) is located near Marquette's distinctive ore dock. There are 91 seasonal slips and 10 transient slips, as well as full amenities like electricity, showers, pump-out, gasoline, and day-use dockage. Cinder Pond Marina is open early May through late October, can be reached on radio channel 71, and is located at 46°31.56 N, 87°22.26 W. The Ellwood Matson Lower Harbor Park, a 22-acre open space with park benches, picnic tables, and a playground, stretches out to the west. The **Presque Isle Marina** (906/228-0464, www.michigan.gov/dnr) has 87 seasonal and 10 transient slips and is located at Presque Isle Park. Like Cinder Pond Marina, there are plenty of amenities. The marina is located at 46°34.20 N, 87°22.25 W. It's open early May through late October and can be reached on channel 9.

Bus

Bus service to Marquette is available on **Indian Trails** (989/725-5105 or 800/292-3831, www.indiantrails.com) on a route that stretches from Chicago to Calumet, stopping in Marquette as well as Escanaba, Houghton, and Hancock along the way.

The same public bus that shuttles visitors from Sawyer International Airport to Marquette runs a daily circuit around the area with regular stops in Marquette, Negaunee, Ishpeming, and Gwinn. **Marq-Tran** (906/225-1112, www.marq-tran.com) also offers door-to-door service for a small fee that increases with distance (though it won't be more than $5.60). Contact Marq-Tran for regular schedules and fees.

Taxi
For taxi service, call **Taxi Tycoon** (906/249-4428) or **Checker Transport** (906/226-7772, http://checkertransport.com).

Huron Mountains

Ask 10 people where the Huron Mountains begin and end, and you're likely to get 10 different answers. But everyone will agree that they fall within the vague boundaries of Lake Superior to the north and east and U.S. 41 to the south and west. It's over 1,000 square miles where the terrain rises to rugged hills and even mountains. Mount Arvon, about 15 miles due east of L'Anse, tops out at 1,979 feet, the highest point in the state.

On a map you'll see it's an intriguing parcel of real estate, virtually devoid of towns and roads. What the Huron Mountains do have, however, is peaks and valleys, white pine forests, hundreds of lakes, waterfalls that don't appear on maps, and the headwaters of several classic wilderness rivers, dazzling waterfalls, and total quiet—all in a place where animals far outnumber people. Even by U.P. standards, it's a rugged place. If the Huron Mountain Club should ever come up for sale, government officials would no doubt clamor to turn to it into a state or national park.

In the meantime, the rest of us have to be content simply knowing that such wonderful natural beauty is there and is lovingly protected. Although much of the Huron Mountains is inaccessible to the public, there are areas with public access that can be explored.

BIG BAY AREA
Many visitors approach the Huron Mountains from the east, where County Road 550 climbs 30 miles out of Marquette to the tiny town of **Big Bay** (pop. 260). Sited above Lake Independence and within minutes of Lake Superior, Big Bay is sandwiched between wilderness and inland sea. The town has swung from prosperity to near ghost town status more than once, first as a bustling logging outpost, then as one of Henry Ford's company towns, humming with busy sawmills. More recently, residents joke about how the local bank, wary of the town's volatile economy, was loath to loan money to town businesses—an overly conservative stance that proved to be the bank's undoing. While the town's 20 businesses were thriving, the bank closed down. Visitors now frequent Big Bay for its access to the Huron Mountains, Lake Superior harbor, Lake Independence fishing, and unique lodgings.

From Big Bay, the best way to venture into the backcountry is County Road 510, which branches off County Road 550 on the southeast edge of Big Bay and continues south to U.S. 41 west of Marquette. Another option is the Triple A Truck Trail, which branches off County Road 510. Both are usually well-maintained dirt and gravel roads, although wet or snowy weather can quickly render them impassable. Dozens of old logging roads and single-tracks branch off these main routes. To find your way around, you'll need either a topographic or the very good local map (sometimes called the "waterfall map") available for free from the **Marquette**

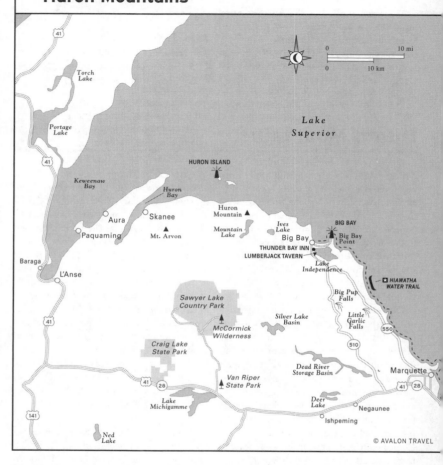

Huron Mountains

Torch Lake

Portage Lake

Keweenaw Bay

Aura

Skanee

Paquaming

Baraga

L'Anse

Mt. Arvon

Huron Bay

HURON ISLAND

Huron Mountain

Mountain Lake

Lake Superior

Ives Lake

Big Bay

BIG BAY

Big Bay Point

THUNDER BAY INN

LUMBERJACK TAVERN

Lake Independence

HIAWATHA WATER TRAIL

Big Pup Falls

Little Garlic Falls

Sawyer Lake Country Park

McCormick Wilderness

Silver Lake Basin

Craig Lake State Park

Van Riper State Park

Lake Michigamme

Dead River Storage Basin

Marquette

Deer Lake

Negaunee

Ishpeming

Ned Lake

© AVALON TRAVEL

County Convention and Visitors Bureau (906/228-7749 or 800/544-4321, www.travel-marquettemichigan.com).

SIGHTS
Craig Lake State Park
Craig Lake State Park is probably unlike any state park you've ever visited. The entrance is nearly seven miles down a rugged truck trail that often requires a 4WD vehicle and is periodically "improved" with sharp old mining rock that can inflict lethal wounds on

tires. Once you arrive at the Craig Lake parking area, you can access the 7,000-acre park on foot or, with a short portage, by canoe or kayak. No wheeled vehicles or boat motors are permitted anywhere within the park. The access road to the park is north from U.S. 41/M-28 about eight miles west of Champion.

McCormick Wilderness
Once the private wilderness retreat of Cyrus McCormick, whose father invented the reaping machine, the 27-square-mile **McCormick**

Wilderness was willed to the U.S. Forest Service by his family in 1967. Today it remains in pristine wilderness condition: remote, undeveloped, and largely unused. In other words, it's perfect for backcountry hiking and camping. No-trace camping is permitted throughout the wilderness area. For more information, contact the **Ottawa National Forest Ranger District** (4810 E. M-28, Kenton, 906/852-3500, www.fs.fed.us).

To access the McCormick Tract, follow U.S. 41/M-28 west from Marquette about 50 miles to Champion. Just after you cross the Peshekee River, follow the first paved road north. This is County Road 607, also called the Peshekee Grade or the Huron Bay Grade. In about 10 miles, you'll see a sign for Arfelin Lake; take the next road to the right and watch for a sign and a small parking area.

Once here, you'll be on your own to explore this rugged terrain of high hills, rivers, muskeg, and bedrock outcroppings. Don't expect marked and maintained hiking trails. This tract is wild, so with the exception of a well-worn path to White Deer Lake, where the McCormicks' lodge once stood, you'll be traveling cross-country. A compass and topographic map are absolute necessities. Wildlife sightings can be excellent as the state's largest moose herd roams here, which in turn has attracted predators like the elusive gray wolf. You're not likely to see a wolf, but you may be treated to one's hollow wail at your camp in the evening.

Moose

Van Riper State Park, just west of Champion on U.S. 41/M-28, is perhaps best known for its **Moose Information Center,** a kiosk that tells the story of the U.P.'s successful moose reintroduction program. Though moose were once common in the U.P., hunting and disease devastated the herd in past decades. Two "moose lifts" in the 1980s transported 59 of the giant mammals from Algonquin Provincial Park in Ontario to the lightly traveled wilderness along the Peshekee Grade near the McCormick Tract. It was quite a project:

wildlife biologists captured each moose, then airlifted them one by one in a sling, dangling beneath a helicopter, to a base camp where they were trucked 600 miles to the Huron Mountains.

Today, the region's moose population has climbed to 200 or 300. You may see them anywhere in this region, but your chances are best at dawn or dusk and in wet, swampy areas. The Marquette County Convention and Visitors Bureau publishes *Michigan Moose*, which offers help in locating occupied moose habitat and provides maps highlighting the moose viewing areas in Van Riper State Park, including the Peshekee Grade and Wolf Lake Road, east of Champion; Tahquamenon Falls State Park; and the Seney National Wildlife Refuge. You can pick up a copy at the **Michigan DNR office** (1990 U.S. 41 S.) in Marquette.

Mount Arvon

It's a tough drive to get to Michigan's highest peak, **Mount Arvon,** about 12 miles east of L'Anse, and the trip can be disappointing if you're expecting a dramatic view. It's hard to see the mountain from a distance, and when you reach the top, the forest is tall and dense. The only way to know you've reached the summit is a small blue sign stating, "You have reached Michigan's highest point." The roads are also in rough condition, which makes the 27-mile journey too burdensome for the casual traveler. For a map and directions, contact the **Baraga County Convention and Visitors Bureau** (755 E. Broad St., L'Anse, 906/524-7444 or 800/743-4908, www.baragacountytourism.org).

Lighthouses

The **Big Bay Point Lighthouse** is an above-average light. Located on a cliff at Big Bay Point, the two-story brick building and attached 60-foot-tall light have been converted into a charming bed-and-breakfast.

The 1868 **Huron Island Lighthouse,** located northwest of Big Bay and three miles off shore, is only accessible by private boat. The

Big Bay Point Lighthouse

island, part of the Huron National Wildlife Refuge, is open to the public during daylight hours. You can charter a sightseeing trip to the Huron Islands with **Uncle Ducky Charters** (434 E. Prospect St., Marquette, 877/228-5447, www.paddlingmichigan.com).

SUMMER SPORTS AND RECREATION
Hiking and Biking

Though it's situated right on busy U.S. 41, **Van Riper State Park** is worthy of mention. It has an amenity-rich modern campground on the eastern shore of Lake Michigamme that rarely fills up. Here you'll find a boat launch, great walleye fishing, and a fine swimming beach with unusually warm water and a sandy bottom. Many campers overlook the property on the north side of the road, the park's largest and most appealing acreage. It includes a rustic campground on the Peshekee River and four miles of hiking trails. Climb the Overlook Trail, a loop that ascends a rocky outcrop, for a great view of rolling forest land and Lake Michigamme. In addition, Van Riper is less than a dozen miles from the gated entrance to the McCormick Tract, so you can take advantage of modern comforts while spending your days in the rugged backcountry that begins just across the highway.

Visitors that make their way into **Craig Lake State Park** will be rewarded with the seclusion and backcountry hiking of Michigan's most remote state park. If you're going to make the journey to the park, you should take a vehicle with a high ground clearance for the seven-mile trek off paved roads, especially after a rainfall, when it's best to have a 4WD vehicle. The park has nearly 7,000 acres and two main trails that total more than 15 miles, half of which is part of the North Country Trail. Trails are rugged, often steep, and are frequently blocked by streams or other obstacles. There are six full lakes, several smaller ponds, and plenty of wildlife, including black bears, moose, and the more common deer. Adequate backcountry practices should be followed; make sure you go in well prepared. The access road to Craig Lake State Park is north from U.S. 41/M-28 about eight miles west of Champion. For backcountry preparation tips, maps, and directions, contact the **Michigan DNR** (906/339-4461, www.michigan.gov/dnr).

In the town of Big Bay, take the Big Bay Pathway, part of the Noquemanon Trail Network. Only one of the loops is for hiking and cycling, the relatively flat four-mile Hidden Grin Loop. The other three loops, totaling nearly six miles, are more appropriate for cross-country skiing in the winter. Take County Road 550 into Big Bay, then turn left on Dump Road and take it less than one mile to the trailhead, which is on the right.

The Commercial Forest Reserve Act gives property owners a tax break in exchange for allowing others access to their property, so trespassing isn't an issue as you explore most of the Huron Mountains. There are a wide array of possibilities for hiking and mountain-biking on old logging roads and various foot trails. Two spots worth exploring are **Gobbler's Knob,** a rock outcrop off County Road 510 that overlooks Lake Independence and Lake Superior, and the **Elliott Donnelley Wilderness Area,** off County Road 550, where a four-mile trail winds along the Little Garlic River and past Little Garlic Falls.

Keep in mind that the Huron Mountains can be a confusing place. It can be frustrating to drive down one dead-end logging road after another, or worse, to get hopelessly lost on one of hundreds of unmapped, unmarked trails. Before you head off into the woods, make sure you're equipped with a map, a compass, and a GPS unit, and that you're proficient in their use. Otherwise, it's best to find a local guide who can show you around on foot, mountain bike, or snowshoe.

Canoeing and Kayaking

In addition to its backcountry hiking trails, much of **Craig Lake State Park** is accessible by nonmotorized watercraft. There's a 0.25-mile portage from the parking lot to one of several boat landings on the lakes, though Crooked Lake is perhaps the most appealing, with lots of interesting bays and inlets. To reach it, paddle across the southeastern corner of Craig Lake and follow the 0.5-mile portage east. Be aware that many of the lakes are large enough to become rough during windy or stormy weather. You'll need a state park pass and a vehicle suitable for rough, unpaved roads. Contact the **Michigan DNR** (906/339-4461, www.michigan.gov/dnr) for more information.

Other large lakes in the area are suitable for canoeing or kayaking. A good example is Lake Independence in Big Bay; try taking the Iron River from the lake to Lake Superior. Closer to Marquette, the Dead River Storage Basin offers some nice paddling opportunities on the long, narrow surface. There are plenty of smaller lakes scattered throughout the Huron Mountains. Ask an outfitter for more information and advice. If you're looking for a good river, put in the Yellow Dog River at County Road 510 and take out five miles downriver at County Road 550 for an easy-to-middling white-water trip; this section is rated Class II-V.

Of course, experienced kayakers will want to spend some time paddling along the Lake Superior shoreline. Big Bay is the westernmost end of the **Hiawatha Water Trail** (www.hiawathawatertrail.org), more than 120 miles of Lake Superior shoreline that take paddlers all the way to Grand Marais to the east. There are at least 20 public access points and 23 water-accessible campsites along the way. Trail maps for the Hiawatha Water Trail are available for a fee at **Big Bay Outfitters and Anatomy of a Canoe** (308 Bensinger St., 906/345-9399, winter 906/250-2457). Big Bay and the shoreline between L'Anse and Marquette aren't as spectacular as Pictured Rocks to the east, but like most of the Great Lakes shoreline, you'd be hard-pressed to find a stretch that doesn't make a good place to get your paddle wet. Pay particular attention to the shore on either side of Big Bay Point, and be sure to check the weather reports, as Lake Superior can produce sudden storms.

Fishing

Big Bay's Lake Independence has a reputation as a good fishing hole. Anglers can visit the lake for walleye, yellow perch, and smallmouth bass; put in at the boat launch at **Perkins Park Campground,** just off Big Bay Road/County Road 550. For a more remote, secluded experience, head to Craig Lake, located a little north of U.S. 41/M-28 and a few miles west of Michigamme, where you'll find northern pike, smallmouth bass, and muskie.

As far as suitable rivers and streams go, you'll find them virtually everywhere. Try the Yellow Dog River for some decent trout. Head to the Little Garlic River, about 10 miles northwest of Marquette on Big Bay Road/ County Road 550, for steelhead.

Charters on Lake Superior, as well as inland lakes and rivers, can be arranged through a number of area companies, most of them in Marquette. **Uncle Ducky Charters** (434 E. Prospect St., Marquette, 877/228-5447, www. paddlingmichigan.com) is one of the best all-around charters, while **Rivers North Guide Service** (906/458-8125, www.riversnorth.net, half-day from $300, full-day $500) specializes in fly-fishing.

Beaches

Perkins Park Campground on the west side of Lake Independence has a nice, family friendly beach—and the water will be more comfortable than chilly Lake Superior too. Lake Michigamme, just off U.S. 41, has a pleasant swimming beach along the 0.5-mile frontage of Van Riper State Park. If it's late enough in the season and you don't mind Superior's bite, there's a small beach by the Big Bay Harbor of Refuge.

Off-Road Vehicles

For such a wide expanse of undeveloped land, there are disappointingly few trails marked for off-road vehicles. In fact, one of the only DNR trails for ATVs near the Huron Mountains is the Champion Trail, which runs south from Champion on U.S. 41/M-28 to Republic, a seven-mile ride.

Waterfalls

The waterfall map, which you can get from the **Marquette County Convention and Visitors Bureau** (337 W. Washington St., Marquette, 906/228-7749 or 800/544-4321, www.travelmarquettemichigan.com) will point you toward many of the region's falls. Some of the finest and most accessible

include **Little Garlic Falls, Hills Falls,** and **Big Pup Falls.** The latter two are on the beautiful Yellow Dog River, which splashes and tumbles over cliffs and through canyons from the Yellow Dog Plains north to Lake Independence. Pack a fly rod if you enjoy casting for trout; fishing can be great here. Little Garlic Falls is located on the Little Garlic River, 11 miles northwest of Marquette. Check the waterfall map for more detailed directions.

WINTER SPORTS AND RECREATION
Ski and Snowshoe Trails

The loops of the **Big Bay Pathway** are great for cross-country skiing once the snow falls. Meditation Loop is two miles long and suitable for beginners, while the Hidden Grin Loop, at four miles, is a longer intermediate-level loop. The other two paths, the three-mile Bear Mountain Loop and its one-mile Ridgeline Extension Loop, are more difficult.

The Saux Head Trails, like Big Bay Pathway part of the Noquemanon Trail Network, have about 7.5 miles of two-way groomed trails. The loops range from intermediate to advanced. Saux Head Trails are about 11 miles southeast of Big Bay. Take County Road 550 from Marquette, turn right on Saux Head Lake Road, and then turn left about one mile later. Parking areas are on the left. To ski or snowshoe any of these trails, you'll need a trail pass from the **Noquemanon Trail Network** (906/235-6861, www.noquetrails.org).

Snowmobiling

Trail 310 winds some 54 miles from Marquette west and north to Big Bay. From the other direction, **Trail 14** connects L'Anse and Big Bay over a distance of 56 miles. The two trails merge south of Big Bay via Alternate Trail 310; otherwise they meet up in Big Bay. The **Clowry-Big Bay Trail** (Trail 5) heads north into the Huron Mountains from Clowry, near Champion on U.S. 41/ M- 23, and joins Trail 14.

Snowmobiles are allowed on the plowed

surface of any of Marquette County's roads, provided you stay on the right-hand side and move with the flow of traffic. When operating a snowmobile on a public road, be especially careful, stop at all intersections, and watch for traffic. Stay off the state highways, and double-check the laws for riding on paved roads within individual towns and cities.

FOOD

★ **Thunder Bay Inn** (400 Bensinger St., 906/345-9220, www.thunderbayinn.net, lunch and dinner daily from 11am, $9-22) is known as the iconic hotel where scenes in the film *Anatomy of a Murder* were shot in 1959. The pub, added to the building for the filming of the movie, endures as a cornerstone of the community. The menu features classic American fare, plus homemade pizza and a number of Mexican specialties as well as a children's menu.

There are a few other dining choices in Big Bay. Lunch and breakfast are served at **Hungry Hollow Café** (County Rd. 550, 906/345-0075, www.cramsgeneralstore.com, 7am-2pm Mon.-Thurs., 7am-4pm Fri.-Sat., 8am-4pm Sun., under $10), part of Cram's General Store. Try the homemade pasties and soups. For dinner, go to the ★ **Lumberjack**

Tavern (202 Bensinger St., 906/345-9912, noon-2am daily, $9-20), where you'll find earnest, friendly people, great service, and good food. Many people come for the history, not the menu: In 1952, Mike Chenowith was murdered here, providing the inspiration for Judge John Voelker's bestselling novel *Anatomy of a Murder,* which was later made into an iconic motion picture of the same name directed by Otto Preminger.

ACCOMMODATIONS

There's a surprisingly good and varied choice of lodgings in tiny Big Bay. Probably the best known is the ★ **Thunder Bay Inn** (400 Bensinger St., 906/345-9220, www.thunderbayinn.net, May-Mar., $80-160), reopened in 2008 after new owners restored it to its former glory. Built in 1910, the hotel was purchased by Henry Ford during the 1920s as a place for him and his executives to stay when visiting his numerous U.P. sawmills. The inn offers a quiet, unhurried style of lodging characteristic of a bygone era—which means there are no TVs, radios, or telephones in the rooms. The rooms are simple but comfortable and very clean. Most rooms have a full bath. All have full or twin beds, except Room 201, which was occupied by Henry Ford and has a king bed.

Thunder Bay Inn

As a lighthouse, the ★ **Big Bay Point Lighthouse Bed-and-Breakfast** (3 Lighthouse Rd., 906/345-9957, www.bigbaylighthouse.com, $127-220) naturally occupies a dramatic position on a rocky point just a few miles from the town of Big Bay. The redbrick keeper's home, attached to the 1896 light, has been restored and fitted with seven very comfortable guest rooms, all except one with a private bath. Five rooms have Lake Superior views. The inn has extensive grounds, more than 43 acres and 0.5 miles of shoreline, set far back from busy roads. Guests can use the sauna, climb the light tower, or relax in the living room, where owners Linda and Jeff Gamble have collected lighthouse lore and history. Spa services are also available; reserve well in advance.

There are two budget choices in Big Bay, both in good locations. The **Big Bay Depot** (301 Bensinger Rd., 906/345-9350, $75, $285 weekly) occupies an old train depot overlooking Lake Independence. The five refurbished suites include full kitchens, two double beds, and lake views; pets are welcome. The independent **Picture Bay Motel** (8750 Big Bay Rd., 906/345-9820, $75-95) is neat as a pin. Two units have basic cooking facilities. Pets are welcome for an additional $5 per night.

Camping

Backcountry campers will find nearly unlimited options in the **Huron Mountains** and **McCormick Wilderness.** Respect private property rights, observe backcountry camping principles, and travel with a map, compass, GPS unit, and other essentials. If you're not experienced in the backcountry, it might be wise to plan your first trip by first stopping at **Downwind Sports** (514 N. 3rd St., Marquette, 906/226-7112, http://downwindsports.com) for information, maps and other essentials.

Straddling the highway, **Van Riper State Park** (851 County Rd. AKE, 906/339-4461, www.michigan.gov/dnr) offers easily accessible modern and rustic campsites, although it's within earshot of U.S. 41. The park also

rents out a cabin ($80) near the modern campground, which has a refrigerator-freezer, a toaster, a microwave, basic furniture, and sleeping space for six. Reserve well in advance.

At 7,000-acre **Craig Lake State Park** (906/339-4461, www.michigan.gov/dnr), you essentially get an organized campsite tucked in the backcountry wilderness. A rough seven-mile drive and a one- or two-mile hike brings you to many lovely and often empty campsites. Choose from sites that sit on beds of pine needles above the east shore of Craig Lake, or follow the portage trail east to sites on a small peninsula in Crooked Lake. Reservations are necessary for the campsites ($13) and for the rustic cabins on the northwestern shore of Craig Lake. It's best to reserve six months in advance. Originally built by Frederick Miller of Miller Brewing fame, these barebones cabins have bunks for your sleeping bag, some utilitarian furniture, and protection from the bugs and cold. The larger cabin ($86) includes a huge gathering room with a stone fireplace and sleeps 14. The other cabin ($65) sleeps six. Both have a water pump, firewood, and a rowboat.

INFORMATION AND SERVICES

For information about Big Bay and the Huron Mountains, contact the **Marquette County Convention and Visitors Bureau** (337 W. Washington St., Marquette, 906/228-7749 or 800/544-4321, www.travelmarquettemichigan.com), which has advice and trail maps for hiking and cross-country skiing.

Although there are no hospitals in Big Bay, there are two within 30 miles of the city. **The UP Health System Marquette Hospital** (580 W. College Ave., Marquette, 906/228-9440, www.mgh.org) has an emergency room and trauma center, or you can go to **UP Health System Bell Hospital** (901 Lakeshore Dr., Ishpeming, 906/486-4431, www.bellhospital.org), just south of U.S. 41. A third hospital is farther away in L'Anse; take Broad Street from U.S. 41 to Main Street and turn right to the **Baraga County Memorial**

Hospital (18341 U.S. 41, L'Anse, 906/524-3300, www.bcmh.org).

You'll want to do your banking in the bigger cities outside Big Bay and the Huron Mountains.

GETTING THERE AND AROUND
Car

The Huron Mountains aren't as easily accessible as the U.P.'s other areas; there are only two roads in. The best is Big Bay Road/County Road 550, which heads directly northwest from Marquette toward Big Bay. County Road 510 is an alternate and somewhat more meandering route. If you're planning on getting off the main roads, be warned that some of these smaller byways are little more than old logging roads. You'll want to have a 4WD vehicle, or at the very least, a vehicle with high clearance.

Air

The closest airport to the region is **Sawyer International Airport** (MQT, 125 G Ave., Gwinn, 906/346-3308, www.sawyerairport.com), which has scheduled flights from Detroit on **Delta Airlines** (800/221-1212, www.delta.com) and Chicago O'Hare on **American Eagle** (800/433-7300, www.aa.com). To rent a car, Sawyer has a bevy of rental services: **Alamo** (800/462-5266, www.alamo.com), **Avis** (800/831-1212, www.avis.com), **Budget** (800/527-7000, www.budget.com), **Dollar** (800/800-3665, www.dollar.com), **Hertz** (800/800-3665, www.hertz.com), **National** (800/227-7368, www.nationalcar.com), and **Thrifty** (800/847-4389, www.thrifty.com).

Boat

If you're boating to Big Bay, you can put in at the **Big Bay Harbor of Refuge** (906/345-9353, www.michigan.gov/dnr). With only six transient and four seasonal slips, space is limited, especially for day-use dockage. The Big Bay Harbor has the usual amenities: water, electricity, pump out, and gas, as well as restrooms, showers, and a picnic area. The harbor location is 46°49.45 N, 87°43.27 W.

Munising and Grand Island

When it comes to enticing visitors, nature dealt Munising a royal flush. The town of 2,700 curves around the belly of protected Munising Bay. The Grand Island National Recreation Area beckons just offshore. Pictured Rocks National Lakeshore begins at the edge of town and stretches over 40 miles. The Hiawatha National Forest encompasses the forests to the south and west.

M-28 leads to the heart of Munising, where you'll find most restaurants, independent motels, and the ferry dock for cruises to Pictured Rocks.

SIGHTS
★ Grand Island

Although it's just a 10-minute ferry ride from Munising, Lake Superior effectively isolates Grand Island. Part of the Hiawatha National Forest since 1989, the largely wooded 13,000-acre island (only 40 acres are privately owned) is a National Recreation Area. Roughly the size of Manhattan, it's available for hiking, beachcombing, mountain biking, and camping.

Don't miss the **historic cemetery** near Murray Bay, where you can absorb a little history. You can examine the gravestones of shipwreck victims and the island's first nonnative settlers. Grand Island had long been a summering ground for the Ojibwa people when Abraham Williams arrived in the 1840s to establish a trading post. He raised a family and died on the island in 1873 at the then-amazing age of 81. Today, only the descendants of Williams and their spouses can be buried here.

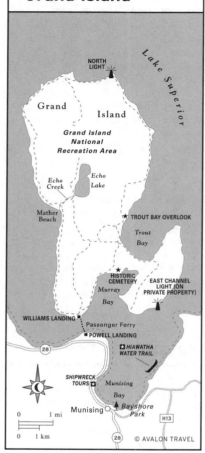

Grand Island

NORTH LIGHT

Lake Superior

Grand   Island

Grand Island National Recreation Area

Echo Creek   Echo Lake

Mather Beach

★ TROUT BAY OVERLOOK

Trout Bay

★ HISTORIC CEMETERY

EAST CHANNEL LIGHT (ON PRIVATE PROPERTY)

Murray Bay

WILLIAMS LANDING ■

■ Passenger Ferry
■ POWELL LANDING

🏕 HIAWATHA WATER TRAIL

SHIPWRECK TOURS 🏕

Munising Bay

Munising ○

🔺 Bayshore Park

0   1 mi
0   1 km

H13

28

© AVALON TRAVEL

Automobiles are not allowed on the island except with special permission or those owned by island landholders. Van tours now operate under special permit, bumping along a few dirt roads on the island's southern half. ATVs are allowed from October 1 to April 15, and mountain bikes are allowed anytime on all trails on public land. Dogs are allowed if leashed. Drinking water is not available on the island. The $2 daily user fee is collected by the ferry service. For more information, contact the Hiawatha National Forest's **Munising**

Ranger District (400 E. Munising Ave., 906/387-3700, www.fs.fed.us).

Altran Bus Service (906/387-4845, www.altranbus.com) offers two- to three-hour van tours of Grand Island (June-early Oct., $45 adults, $25 children). The tour makes six stops on the southern end of the island, including Echo Lake, the Trout Bay Overlook, and Mather Beach, an excellent swimming beach where Echo Creek empties into Lake Superior. Unless you have limited mobility, however, outdoors enthusiasts will likely grow frustrated with the amount of time spent inside a vehicle. Tours prices include the ferry fee but not the $2 recreation area user fee.

★ Hiawatha National Forest

A huge swath of the massive 860,000-acre Hiawatha National Forest sprawls out south of Munising, stretching all the way to Lake Michigan. It offers almost endless opportunities for hiking, mountain biking, and camping. Get information at the **Hiawatha National Forest Visitors Center** (400 E. Munising Ave., 906/387-3700, www.fs.fed.us), which shares a building and staff with the Pictured Rocks National Lakeshore.

Alger County Heritage Center

In Munising, a short way east of downtown on Washington Street, the **Alger County Heritage Center** (1496 Washington St., 906/387-4308, www.hsmichigan.org, noon-3pm Tues.-Sat., donation) keeps a fine collection of local historic artifacts that document the region's past. Visitors can peek at personal artifacts, Grand Island artifacts that include a log cabin from John Jacob Astor's American Fur Company, and Munising Woodenware.

Bayshore Park

At Munising's waterfront, the pleasant **Bayshore Park** provides a place for travelers to stretch their legs, enjoy a relaxing picnic, and admire the marina. In addition to the views of Grand Island just offshore and plenty of picnic tables, take time to visit the lovely Alger County Veterans Memorial Park, where the walkway bricks are engraved with names and messages honoring American soldiers; you can see artillery, a statue, and a monument.

Christmas

If you're driving into Munising from the west along M-28, you'll pass through Christmas, a small hardscrabble town that is most notable for Kewadin Casino and **Santa's Workshop** (E8035 St. Nicholas Ave., 906/387-2929, www. santas-workshop-christmas.com), a gift shop that capitalizes on the town's name by supplying Christmas decorations throughout the year. On the plus side, it offers visits with Santa (2pm-close Sun. Mar.-Nov., 2pm-close Sat.-Sun. Dec.). Store hours vary, so call ahead. You'll also be able to see what's supposedly the world's tallest Santa, the tallest Old Woman in the Shoe, and the largest concrete Frosty the Snowman.

KEWADIN CASINO

Thankfully, there's more in Christmas than a year-round gift shop and a huge Santa. The **Kewadin Casino** (N7761 Candy Cane Lane, 906/387-5475, www.kewadinchristmas.com) is located in Christmas, only a few miles west

Christmas in Michigan

A fun pastime on the Internet is to search for places with highly unusual names. Among these, the town of Christmas—located just west of Munising—surely deserves a place.

The Yuletide-themed town owes its name to a small footnote in its history. In 1938, an entrepreneur set up a small roadside factory in Au Train Township specializing in Christmas-themed items—ornaments, gifts, etc. Unfortunately, the building burned only two years later, forcing the business to close. But the locals had become so enamored with the place that the word *Christmas* was soon appropriated to the surrounding unincorporated area.

The name has attracted national attention. In 1966 the U.S Postal Service established the first post office in Christmas, and the town was chosen as the site of the First Day Cover for that year's Christmas stamp. Today, most businesses have Christmas themes, while streets sport cute monikers like Jingle Bell Lane, North Pole Street, and St. Nicholas Avenue. The town is otherwise unremarkable—consisting of a few stores, motels, and a recently added casino. But as you drive through Christmas, take some time to enjoy the sights, including the 35-foot-high Santa on M-28.

of Munising. With table games like blackjack, three- and four-card poker, and Let It Ride, in addition to slots, the Kewadin has some of the best U.P. gaming. Enjoy a bite to eat at Frosty's Bar and Grill, a moderately priced bistro.

Alger Underwater Preserve

When loggers were felling the vast stands of pine across the central Upper Peninsula in the 1800s, Munising grew into a busy port, with schooners carrying loads of timber to the growing cities of the southern Great Lakes and iron ore to an ever-growing number of factories. The narrow and shoal ridden passage between the mainland and Grand Island and along the Pictured Rocks shoreline was the ruin of many ships; their skeletons litter the lake floor here.

The **Alger Underwater Preserve** covers 113 square miles, from just west of Grand Island to Au Sable Point near the east end of Pictured Rocks National Lakeshore. Visit www.michiganpreserves.org to download "A Diver's Guide to Michigan Underwater Preserves" for invaluable advice on planning your expedition, including information on equipment and proper safety precautions. The Preserve is home to nearly a dozen ships, all well preserved in Lake Superior's cold

freshwater. Some wrecks, like the 19th-century *Bermuda* and the 145-foot *Smith Moore,* stand upright and nearly intact. Many of the dive sites in the preserve are marked with buoys to help ensure that they are protected from poachers. Under Michigan law, it's a felony to remove or disturb artifacts in any Great Lakes underwater preserve.

Lighthouses

Most of Grand Island's private property is on the thumb, including the unique **East Channel Light,** an 1867 wooden lighthouse made of hand-hewn timbers. Although the lighthouse has suffered from vandalism and neglect over the decades, recent years have proved more promising. In 1999 the Alger County Historical Society raised money to save the structure. To date, the timber sill and floor joists have been replaced, and the exterior walls have been strengthened. With the assistance of Northern Michigan University, restoration work is continuing. You can't visit the lighthouse by land because it's surrounded by private property, but you can view it at a distance from Sand Point on the mainland, near the western end of Pictured Rocks National Lakeshore.

On North Point, the **North Light** has

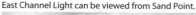

East Channel Light can be viewed from Sand Point.

just a 25-foot tower, but since it rises from a 175-foot cliff, it earns the honor of being the highest above sea level. The 1867 building is now a well-cared for private summer residence. Respect the owner's privacy and stay off the property. The two **Munising Range Lighthouses** were built in 1908 to help ships navigate the passage to the east and south of Grand Island; both are still operating today. The front tower is 58 feet tall, while the rear light is 33 feet tall. The lights and station building are not open to the public. The two **Grand Island Harbor Range Lights** serve the same purpose for the west passage.

SUMMER SPORTS AND RECREATION
Hiking and Biking Trails

A favorite spot in Hiawatha National Forest is the **Rock River Canyon Wilderness Area.** In this undisturbed corner of the national forest, about 12 miles west of Munising, the Rock River and Silver Creek have carved deep crevices in the sandstone, forming dark narrow canyons. Adding to the area's wild beauty is **Rock River Falls,** which pours 20 feet over a sandstone ledge. Though there are few developed hiking trails in the area, you can make your way along old logging roads and railroad grades. The canyons themselves require some scrambling for the adventurous. If you plan to explore the area, be sure to bring a compass and a topographic map, which are available from the visitors center.

To reach the wilderness area, take M-28 west from Munising. About five miles west of Au Train, watch for Rock River Road, also called County Road H-01, on the left. Follow it to Forest Road 2276 and turn right (west). Within four miles, you'll arrive at Forest Road 2293; turn south and travel 0.75 miles to a small parking area. A short trail leads down to the canyon and falls.

About 50 miles of trails crisscross Grand Island, mostly old roadbeds. If you're just visiting for a day, a mountain bike is the only way you'll have time to see the entire island; it's a 23-mile trip around the perimeter. It's

probably one of the best mountain bike routes in the U.P. for nontechnical riders, with wide grassy paths cutting through hardwood forests, passing under towering pines, snuggling up against Lake Superior shorelines, and providing spectacular views of wilderness bays and the distant Pictured Rocks.

Both hikers and bikers can reach **Murray Bay,** about two miles from the ferry dock at the southern end of the island. Murray Bay has a nice day-use area and a sand beach nestled in a grove of pines. There also are two campsites here, but the location near the ferry dock will limit your privacy.

North of Murray Bay, the island sprouts a tombolo, known as "the thumb," off its southeastern corner. This landmass wraps north and forms **Trout Bay,** a lovely spot ringed with honey-hued beaches and sandstone cliffs. Watch for the low profile of loons bobbing in calm waters. Trout Bay is home to the island's four other developed campsites, some of the most attractive you'll find.

Farther north, the island's most interesting trails follow the eastern and western shorelines. The **eastern shore** climbs high above lake level, offering occasional outstanding views of Pictured Rocks and the Grand Sable Dunes. The **western shore** provides ample opportunities to reach the fine sand beaches that line much of this side of the island. The island's interior trails are largely wooded and somewhat less interesting, unless you're hoping to spot a black bear. This shouldn't be too difficult as they're quite plentiful.

Canoeing and Kayaking

Paddlers will enjoy Trout Bay, which features some sea caves along its eastern shore and interesting paddling around the thumb. It's a full two-day journey around the entire island—a trip you'll remember and an outstanding way to experience this superlative parcel of the Upper Peninsula.

The **Hiawatha Water Trail** (www.michiganwatertrails.org) is another outstanding way to experience the Lake Superior shoreline in a sea kayak. Bookended by Big Bay to the west and Grand Marais to the east, the water trail stretches in either direction away from Munising and Grand Island. Get a map from **Northern Waters Adventures** (712 Munising Ave., 906/387-2323, www.northern-waters.com) in Munising. You can also rent sea or recreational kayaks from Northern Waters, as well as sign up for a guided day trip or overnight trip.

Fishing

Echo Lake is near the center of Grand Island. It offers great bass and northern pike fishing for anyone with a Michigan fishing license, but access can be a little tricky, since it is largely ringed with marshy grasses. You can also fish areas of Munising Bay such as Sand Point and the Anna River. Ice fishing is particularly good here too. The more remote northern end of the island is perhaps its most impressive part, with high cliffs, creeks, and untouched beaches. In recent years, peregrine falcons have nested nearby.

Golf

The **Pictured Rocks Golf and Country Club** (10240 County Rd. H-58, 906/387-3970, www.picturedrocksgolfcourse.com, $29 for 18 holes, cart $14) is an 18-hole, 6,246-yard course in Munising. With the exception of Munising's miniature **Eagle Falls Adventure Golf** (906/387-4653, http://eagle-fallsadventuregolf.com) on M-28 in Munising, Pictured Rocks is the county's only golf course, and it's a good one. The clubhouse has a restaurant and a well-stocked pro shop. Take M-28 to East Munising Avenue before continuing on Munising-Van Meer-Shingleton Road (County Rd. H-58) to the golf course.

Off-Road Vehicles

Even though there are no state ORV trails near Munising, there's still plenty of opportunity for off-roading, thanks to the vast stretch of **Hiawatha National Forest** (400 E. Munising Ave., 906/387-2512, www.fs.fed.us) that blankets the U.P. all the way down to St. Ignace. You can't ride on any road you chose,

however. Contact the U.S. Forest Service for a Motor Vehicle Usage Map, which details miles of forest roads open to ORVs. Bear in mind that there are patches of privately owned land scattered throughout the forest; respect private property and stay on federal forest roads.

Waterfalls

The Munising area sports an incredible density of waterfalls, which run the gambit from easy to difficult to reach. Among the latter, Rock River Falls in the Rock River Canyon Wilderness is especially worthwhile. The **Munising Visitors Bureau** (422 E. Munising Ave., 906/387-2138, www.munising.org) prints a helpful waterfall map that will direct you to all 17 waterfalls in Alger County. Nearby Pictured Rocks National Lakeshore also contains several notable falls.

The Tannery Creek spills over **Memorial Falls** and **Olson Falls,** just on the northeast edge of town. Follow County Road H-58 (Washington St.), leaving town to the northeast. Watch for a small wooden staircase on the right side of the road, across from the entrance to Sand Point and the National Park Service headquarters. If you've come by car, note that there's no parking alongside the road. Climb the stairs and follow the trail through a small canyon to Tannery Falls. To reach Memorial Falls, it's best to return to County Road H-58, turn right on Nestor Street, and follow the signs.

On the outskirts of town M-28 East leads to **Horseshoe Falls.** Next, turn east on Prospect Street and you'll see **Alger Falls,** which spills down along the highway. The impressive **Wagner Falls** is in the same area, just off M-94 near the junction with M-28. It's a well-marked spot, operated by the state park system as a scenic site. Though it feels secluded, 20-foot Wagner Falls is just a few minutes' walk from the parking area. Continue up the streamside trail past the main falls to the second cascade. About 20 miles west of Munising, you'll find picturesque **Laughing Whitefish Falls,** which enjoys protection as a state park scenic site. Water plunges 30 feet over hard dolomite rock ledges, then continues rolling and frothing twice that distance to the bottom of a gorge. To reach Laughing Whitefish Falls, follow M-94 west from Munising to Sundell, then go north on Dorsey Road for 2.5 miles.

Diving

Several factors combine to make the **Alger Underwater Preserve** one of the finest sport diving locations in the Midwest. This area features the wreckage of seven ships at depths from 12 to 105 feet, and the cold, pristine water keeps them from deteriorating. Many of them are in very shallow water, where visibility is excellent. Also, Grand Island moderates the cold water temperatures slightly, making diving a bit more comfortable. "It's one of the best wreck diving sites for beginners that I can imagine," notes Pete Lindquist, who operates a dive charter in Munising.

There are also preserves in Whitefish Point, Marquette, Keweenaw, and the Straits of Mackinac. The **Keweenaw Underwater Preserve** has several wrecks, but they're spread farther apart than in Alger, and they tend to be deeper, with some more than 200 feet down.

Go with **Abyss Dive Charters** (616/295-6542, www.abyssdivecharters.com) or **Great Lakes Divers** (989/916-9990, www.greatlakesdivers.com). You'll want to go in the warmer months and dive with scuba gear and a full wetsuit—these waters are cold, especially below the surface.

Just offshore from Munising High School, an **underwater museum** among dock ruins includes submarine signs that interpret large maritime artifacts. The Alger Underwater Preserve also attracts divers for its **sea caves** in about 20 feet of water, where sandstone cliffs have been eroded by wave action.

★ Shipwreck Tours

If you do just one thing in the Munising area, make it this fascinating two-hour tour. Pete Lindquist, an experienced local who also operates a dive charter, came up with the idea of installing viewing wells in the hulls of a couple of tour boats, so even nondivers could marvel at the area's shallow water shipwrecks.

The view through the 8- to 10-foot-long windows is truly remarkable. The boat glides directly over shipwrecks, some in as little as 28 feet of water. They fill the viewing windows like historic paintings, perfectly visible in the clear water and looking close enough to touch. On the *Bermuda,* you can easily make out deck lines, hatches, and even piles of iron ore lying on the deck. Weather permitting, the tour visits three shipwrecks dating from 1860 to 1926. Along the way, Lindquist's knowledgeable crew also shares history and points out features, including the wooden East Channel Light along the shore of Grand Island. Reservations are recommended. Contact **Grand Island Shipwreck Tours** (1204 Commercial St., 906/387-4477, www.shipwrecktours.com, $33 adults, $30 seniors, $12 ages 12-17) for schedules and to make reservations.

WINTER SPORTS AND RECREATION
Ski and Snowshoe Trails

Four miles south of Munising, in the Hiawatha National Forest, the **Valley Spur** (E8017 M-94, 906/387-4918, www.valleyspur.org, day pass $10, 3-day pass $25, free under age 19) ski trail system has some 27 miles of groomed trails ranging in difficulty from easy to expert. Loops range in length from one to seven miles. The Valley Spur lodge is open most weekends for warmth and a hot beverage. To get to Valley Spur, take M-94 south.

The Munising Ski Trail begins a few miles east of town and skirts close to the Superior shoreline in Pictured Rocks National Lakeshore. Most of the loops on the nearly 12-mile trail are rated for easy to intermediate skiing. Lengths vary from less than 1 mile to 2.5 miles. You'll want to be careful to stay on the trails too, as many sections are located along the tops of sheer cliffs. These make for beautiful sightseeing, but be sure to exercise caution. For more information, contact the

National Park Service (906/387-3700, www.nps.gov/piro).

Snowmobiling

Trail 417 leaves Marquette and takes you east to Au Train before hooking south to catch **Trail 8** (heading west, 8 will take you to Gwinn). Take Trail 8 east to follow the Pictured Rocks National Lakeshore all the way into Paradise and Whitefish Point. To get to Munising, head north on **Trails 7** or **419.** If you're interested in heading south, Trails 7 and 41 will take you there, connecting you to the miles upon miles of U.P. snowmobile trails. There are more than 300 miles of trails in Alger County alone, so you won't need to leave the county unless you want to. To get a state trail permit, contact the **Michigan DNR** (www.michigan.gov/dnr).

Ice Fishing

Many of the locations that provide good summertime fishing do just as well for ice fishing when the water freezes over. Try Anna River and the rest of Munising Bay, where you can break through the ice and angle for whitefish, lake trout, northern pike, and more.

Ice Sports

For winter recreation that's less conventional than skiing or snowmobiling, try **ice climbing** on Grand Island. Ice formations form on the sandstone cliffs on the east side of the island, and once the channel and bay begin to freeze over, ice climbers can tackle the 20- to 90-foot-high ice sheets. The **ice caves** just north of Eben Junction and west of Munising make for tamer recreation, but they're still impressive in their own way. Take snowmobile Trail 8 out of town to the caves that form when water seeping through the walls of Rock River Gorge freezes over.

FOOD

For a town on the edge of a national park that presumably gets a fair amount of tourist traffic, Munising has surprisingly little in the way of dining. Try **387 Restaurant & Beer Parlor** (400 Cedar St., 906/387-4067, http://387restaurant.com, 7am-10pm Sun.-Thurs., 7am-11pm Fri.-Sat., $9-17), on M-28 downtown, for fresh whitefish and lake trout, as well as grilled flatiron steak and smothered chicken. An extensive breakfast menu is also on offer. **Muldoon's Pasties** (1246 W. M-28, 906/387-5880, www.muldoonspasties.com, 9am-9pm daily, under $10) is the best spot in town for a fresh, authentic taste of the pasty, a potpie type meal that's a true U.P. classic.

If you're looking for a quick "grab and go" lunch between taking in all that Munising has to offer, check out **Johnny Dogs** (106 Lynn St., 906/387-1300, 11am-8pm daily, under $10). You'll find an unbelievable variety of the traditional hot dog, including the Piggy (pulled pork, barbeque sauce, and Monterrey jack cheese) and the Bacon Bleu (apple wood-smoked bacon and blue cheese with caramelized onions).

If Italian is on your mind, try **Main Street Pizza** (113 Maple St., 906/387-3993, 11am-11pm Mon.-Thurs., 11am-midnight Fri.-Sat., noon-11pm Sun., under $10) for a tempting array of pizza with various toppings, salads, and a few Mexican items.

If you're willing to take a little drive, one of the better restaurants in the Upper Peninsula is about 15 miles west of Munising in Au Train. Along the curve of Lake Superior's Au Train Bay on M-28, the ★ **Brownstone Inn** (E4635 W. M-28, Au Train, 906/892-8332, www.brownstoneup.com, 11am-9pm Mon.-Thurs., 11am-10pm Fri.-Sat., noon-9pm Sun., entrées $15-28) serves up original and ever-changing dishes, including delicious versions of the ubiquitous Lake Superior whitefish, Canadian salmon, extra jumbo gulf shrimp, and choice Angus steaks. There are good vegetarian options and an excellent Friday-night fish fry too.

ACCOMMODATIONS

The ★ **Sunset Motel on the Bay** (1315 E. Bay St., 906/387-4574, www.sunsetmotelonthebay.com, $169-249) has a great location right on Munising Bay at the east end of town. There are 15 rooms, and the motel's three suites have kitchenettes; each of the rooms faces the bay. It's a great find with great rates. Wireless Internet access is free, and pets are welcome. The downtown **Munising Motel** (332 E. Onota St., 906/387-3187, www.munisingmotel.net, $85-110) has 12 recently renovated rooms within walking distance of the city dock and Pictured Rocks Cruises. Another good option is the **Terrace Motel** (420 Prospect St., 906/387-2735, www.terracemotel.net, $45-100), close enough to downtown to easily access its restaurants and other amenities, but far enough to provide a secluded atmosphere.

Unlike most commercial strips, the one along M-28 on Munising's near east side is still within walking distance of downtown and the waterfront. It has some nice and tidy small motels like the **Superior Motel and Suites** (500 E. M-28, 906/387-1600, www.superior-motel.com, $120-160) and the **Pictured Rocks Inn and Suites** (420 M-28, 906/387-2493, $175-195), which offers a close-in location and an indoor pool. Two miles east of Munising, the **Alger Falls Motel** (E9427 M-28, 906/387-3536, www.algerfallsmotel.com, $125-135, cottage $139) has 16 rooms and a housekeeping cottage.

Camping

There are no reservations, fees, or permits required for camping on Grand Island. The island has two designated campgrounds, at **Murray Bay** (two sites) and **Trout Bay** (four sites), offering the relative luxury of pit toilets and fire rings. Backcountry camping is permitted throughout the island as long as you stay off the tombolo, off private property, and at least 100 feet away from lakes, streams, cliffs, trails, roads, and natural research areas. No ground fires are permitted. And remember, there is no drinking water anywhere on the island, so come prepared.

For ultimate convenience—and the luxury of seclusion—the Hiawatha National Forest's **Bay Furnace** (no reservations, $8) is a good choice. Just west of Munising and

north of M-28, it offers 50 rustic sites with a very nice setting next to Lake Superior and overlooking Grand Island. Some sites almost have their own private stretch of beach, and a short cross-country ski trail at the campground's north end gives campers a little extra breathing room.

Near the day-use area, you can examine the remains of the old charcoal furnace that at one time produced 20 tons of iron a day. During its heyday in the 1870s, as many as eight steamers at a time would line up at docks, bringing in wood to fuel the furnace and hauling away iron. Take M-28 west from Munising to Christmas and turn north at the Forest Service campground sign.

The Hiawatha National Forest has several other designated campgrounds nearby. Contact the **Hiawatha Visitors Center** (400 E. Munising Ave., 906/387-3700, www.fs.fed.us) for more information and directions.

Families gravitate to the **Wandering Wheels Campground** (906/387-3315, www.wanderingwheelscampground.net, rates vary) on M-28, three miles east of Munising, with 89 sites in a nice wooded setting. What you lose in wilderness you gain in kid-friendly amenities like an outdoor pool, basketball courts, and a recreation room.

INFORMATION AND SERVICES

You can get all of the visitor information you need from the **Munising Visitors Bureau** (422 E. Munising Ave., 906/387-2138, www.munising.org).

For immediate medical care, make your way to **Munising Memorial Hospital** (1500 Sand Point Rd., 906/387-4110, www.uphcn.org), a small community hospital located just north and east of town. Take East Munising Avenue where it splits from M-28 and follow it northeast to Washington Street; turn left and follow Washington to the hospital.

There aren't as many banks in Munising as in Marquette, but you shouldn't have trouble finding one if you urgently need cash. There's a **Wells Fargo** (419 E. M-28, 906/387-5371, www.wellsfargo.com); closer to the center of town is the main office of **Peoples State Bank of Munising** (100 E. Superior St., 906/387-2006, www.bankatpsb.com) and a branch of **First Merit Bank** (101 W. Munising Ave., 906/387-2610, www.firstmerit.com).

GETTING THERE AND AROUND
Car

To get to Munising by car, take M-28 from Marquette and points west. You'll pass through Au Train and Christmas along the way, and you'll be continuously rewarded with views of Lake Superior and Munising Bay, some of the more picturesque locations in the U.P. If you're coming from the east, M-28 merges with M-94, which heads north from Manistique and the Lake Michigan shore. It's more of a back road, but you can take Forest Highway 13 (H-13) north from Nahma Junction on U.S. 2.

Air

Munising's closest commercial airport is **Sawyer International Airport** (MQT, 125 G Ave., Gwinn, 906/346-3308, www.sawyerairport.com), just south of Marquette, a little less than an hour away, which has scheduled flights from Detroit on **Delta Airlines** (800/221-1212, www.delta.com) and Chicago O'Hare on **American Eagle** (800/433-7300, www.aa.com). There's no scheduled ground transportation from the airport, so you'll need to rent a car; try **Alamo** (800/462-5266, www.alamo.com), **Avis** (800/831-1212, www.avis.com), **Budget** (800/527-7000, www.budget.com), **Dollar** (800/800-3665, www.dollar.com), **Hertz** (800/800-3665, www.hertz.com), **National** (800/227-7368, www.nationalcar.com), or **Thrifty** (800/847-4389, www.thrifty.com).

Boat

Consider yourself fortunate if you're arriving in Munising by boat. You'll be able to sail past the Pictured Rocks National Lakeshore, an unbelievably scenic stretch of shoreline with plunging cliffs and, in places, very shallow waters. And then you'll sail past beautiful Grand Island into Munising Bay on your way to **Munising-Bayshore Marina** (906/387-3445, www.michigan.gov/dnr, mid-May-mid-Oct.). The marina's 9 seasonal and 10 transient slips have access to potable water, electricity, and restrooms. Nearby, there's a pleasant park with picnic tables and benches and plenty of lawn. Contact the harbormaster on channel 16 or 18. The marina is located at 46°24.52 N, 86°39.06 W.

The **Grand Island Ferry Service** (906/387-2600, http://grandislandup.com, daily Memorial Day-early Oct., $15 adults, $10 children, free under age 6) provides transit between Munising and Grand Island. There's a $5 additional charge for bicycles. Call for a current schedule. The ferry's departure point is about two miles west of downtown near Powell Point; follow M-28 west and watch for the signs. Even if you're planning just a day trip, you'd be wise to pack some warm clothing and a method for purifying water. Rough weather can cancel ferry service at any time. It's also easy to lose track of time and miss the last ferry. There is a ship-to-shore radio at Williams Landing in the event of an emergency. **Private boats** may be pulled ashore at Williams Landing and Trout Bay, and moored offshore in Murray Bay and Trout Bay.

Bus

Although there is no bus service to Munising, regional **Alger County Transit** (Altran, 906/387-4845, www.altranbus.com, $7) buses run between Munising and Marquette. Altran also provides dial-a-ride service for a fee. Call at least 24 hours in advance for reservations. You can also catch an Altran bus tour of Grand Island (June 15-Oct. 15, $27 adults, $12 children).

Pictured Rocks and Grand Marais

Lake Superior takes center stage at this national lakeshore, which is a mere 3 miles wide but stretches 40 miles along the magnificent lake from Munising to Grand Marais. Pictured Rocks derives its name from the sandstone bluffs that rise 200 feet directly from the water's surface, washed in shades of pink, red, and green from the mineral-rich water that seeps from the rock. These picturesque cliffs stretch for more than 15 miles, occasionally forming sculptures of crazy castle-like turrets, caves, and arches. The national lakeshore also features a lesser-known but equally spectacular stretch of shoreline called the Grand Sable Banks, where 200-foot sand dunes are hemmed by a 12-mile ribbon of sand and pebble beach. You'll also find lakes, forest trails, waterfalls, a lighthouse, and other historic attractions.

Pictured Rocks' season is short. Most of the park's 300,000 or so annual visitors come in July and August, when they're most likely to enjoy summer weather and daytime temperatures in the 70s. Visit in June and you'll share the park with fewer people, but the blackflies

and mosquitoes can be onerous. September may be the park's finest month, but it can be cold.

No matter when you go, pack plenty of warm clothing along with shorts. Even at the height of summer, evenings are almost always cool, dipping into the 50s. The giant refrigerator that is Lake Superior, where the water temperature rarely climbs out of the 40s, can put a chill in the air near the shoreline. In fact, a Lake Superior beach on a sweltering August afternoon may just be the most refreshing place on earth.

SIGHTS
★ Pictured Rocks National Lakeshore

Most people never lose their fascination with beautiful displays of nature. Hugging the Lake Superior coastline for 42 miles, **Pictured Rocks National Lakeshore** (906/387-3700, www.nps.gov/piro) is an archetypical example. Generations of writers, artists, and photographers have been inspired by the colorful hues of its escarpments. In 1820 the geologist

the sandstone cliffs of Pictured Rocks National Lakeshore

Pictured Rocks National Lakeshore

Henry Rowe Schoolcraft visited Picture Rocks and described it as having "some of the most sublime and commanding views of nature." In 1966 the U.S. Congress saw the need to protect this prized area and established Pictured Rocks National Lakeshore—the first such property in the nation—under the authority of the National Park Service.

For a full 15 miles, massive sandstone cliffs tower over the lake, some reaching heights of 200 feet. Because of the multidimensional geology of the area, the colors of various minerals combine with the groundwater to create streaks of red (from iron), yellow-brown (limonite), and pink-green (copper). Other physical features lie within the park's borders, including sand dunes and waterfalls, but for most visitors, the colorful cliffs are the main attraction. With a few exceptions, however, they can only be viewed from the water.

Mindful of this, local operators offer visitors of all abilities the opportunity to see and enjoy the cliffs. These include boat tours, sea kayaking, and hiking.

Pictured Rocks Cruises (906/387-2379, www.picturedrocks.com, Memorial Day-mid Oct., $38 adults, $10 ages 6-12, $1 under age 6) offers three-hour trips up the shoreline from Munising, sidling up practically close enough to touch the rock formations while giving you the perspective to comprehend the turreted shapes like Miners Castle. Though trips are offered up to seven times a day, plan for either the late afternoon or Sunset Cruises, when the sinking sun shows off the multicolored sandstone in its best light, providing the best conditions for photographs. The boats depart from the Munising City Pier.

Kayaking offers the skillful paddler-photographer the chance to get some truly remarkable shots from otherwise impossible angles.

MUNISING FALLS AREA

The highlight of this spot used to be the trail that led hikers behind the 50-foot **Munising Falls,** but erosion problems

MINERS CASTLE

For whatever reason, most people love to describe natural creations using the names of artificial objects. The sandstone cliffs five miles northeast of Munising Falls are known as **Miners Castle** for the turret-like shapes caused by wind and wave erosion. The nine-story-high rock formation is most impressive and ranks as one of the park's most popular attractions. Boardwalks and steps lead to two viewing platforms out on the rock, where you can peer down into the gloriously clear waters of Lake Superior. If that entices you to do a little beachcombing and wading, a nearby trail leads down some steps through the pines to the inviting **Miners Beach.**

To reach Miners Castle, follow County Road H-58 east from Munising to the well-marked turnoff for Miners Castle Road. Before you reach the Miners Castle formation itself, you'll see another sign on Miners Castle Road directing you to **Miners Falls.** It's a fairly easy one-mile walk to these pleasant falls, where Miners Creek tumbles 40 feet over a rocky escarpment.

CHAPEL BASIN AREA

Continuing northeast on County Road H-58, the next auto accessible route into the heart of the park is at Melstrand, where the gravel-and-dirt Chapel Road bumps six miles toward the shore and another park highlight, the Chapel Basin area. Park your car here, and you'll find plenty to entertain you during a long day hike or weekend: three waterfalls, a deep inland lake, Superior beaches, and a good loop hiking trail. **Chapel Falls** is the key attraction, as evidenced by the 1.5-mile paved pathway that leads to it.

If you turn left instead of right at Chapel Beach, you can make a 10-mile loop around **Chapel Basin.** Along the way, you'll pass **Grand Portal Point,** another significant Pictured Rocks landmark, before returning to the parking area. Don't leave Chapel Basin without a visit to **Mosquito Falls,** which is a bit farther inland off Chapel Road. The Mosquito River spills over a series of ledges,

Miners Falls

prompted its closure. It's still worth a stop, though, for the falls and the adjacent **interpretive center,** which offers a glimpse of the history of this peaceful area, home to a belching pig-iron furnace in the 1860s. Munising Falls also marks the west trailhead for the **Lakeshore Trail,** a 43-mile segment of the North Country Trail that spans seven states from New York to North Dakota. The Lakeshore Trail runs the length of the Pictured Rocks National Lakeshore. Predictably, it never strays far from the water's edge. The park's eastern trailhead lies near Sable Falls.

Past Munising Falls, the paved access road ends at **Sand Point,** home of the **National Lakeshore Headquarters** (N8391 Sand Point Rd., 906/387-2607, www.nps.gov/piro). While the headquarters houses offices and not visitor services, it displays some interesting Coast Guard and shipwreck artifacts on its grounds. Sand Point has a small beach and a boat ramp, a good spot to launch a small craft for exploring nearby Grand Island.

creating an accessible waterfall calm enough for wading and soaking fatigued hiking feet. A trail leads to various sections of the falls and links up with the Lakeshore Trail.

BEAVER LAKE

Located near the center of the park, 800-acre **Beaver Lake** is the largest inland lake in Pictured Rocks. Anglers are drawn to the lake and the tributaries that feed it, especially for trout. **Little Beaver Lake,** connected by a small channel, has a boat launch. Boats are limited to 10 hp or less, making this a pleasant waterway for paddlers. Little Beaver also has one of the park's three auto-accessible campgrounds, with eight sites available on a first come, first served basis. Be aware that wetlands cover much of the terrain between Beaver Lake and Lake Superior, so bugs can be a problem, especially in June and early July.

LIGHTHOUSE

It's a 1.5-mile walk along the Lakeshore Trail from the Hurricane River campground to the **Au Sable Light Station** at Au Sable Point. Built in 1874, the 87-foot brick light and its keepers did yeoman's duty for decades—warning ships away from the rock shoals that extend out for nearly a mile and create shallows of just 6 to 30 feet. Nonetheless, at least 10 steamers met their demise here. As you walk the trail from the campground, look for parts of the **shipwrecks** just offshore, which often poke out of the sandy bottom and are easily visible in the crystal-clear water. The light was automated in 1958.

Several recent restoration projects involved renovating the light keeper's quarters, rehabilitating the landscape, and installing a photovoltaic (solar-powered) system to power the site. **Tours** (906/387-3700, 11am-4:30pm Wed.-Sun. July-mid-Aug., $3, free under age 6) are offered.

GRAND SABLE DUNES

Just east of Au Sable Point, the **Log Slide Overlook** marks the site of a once busy logging operation. In the late 1800s, loggers used this high point—some 300 feet above Lake Superior—to send freshly cut logs down to the water's edge, where they were loaded onto Great Lakes schooners. Today, you can stand on a platform and simply marvel at the view, with the lighthouse to the left, the great dunes to the right, and the brilliant blue of the big lake filling the horizon.

Grand Marais

Though not part of Pictured Rocks National Lakeshore, the little town of Grand Marais marks the park's eastern boundary and is an excellent jumping-off point for a visit to the national lakeshore. This sleepy New England-like village is worth a visit for its simple windswept beauty. With an outstanding natural harbor, rare on Lake Superior's southern shore, Grand Marais was originally settled by fishermen. Loggers soon followed, when sawmills were built here in the 1860s and 1870s to handle the logging that went on just to the south.

Commercial fishing remains a key segment of the local economy, but it has become an increasingly difficult way to make a living. Today, tourism is what keeps the town ticking along. The downtown huddles around the harbor, which is a good spot for kayakers to play in the surf on a north-to-east wind. The few streets here offer some arts and crafts shops and a small number of clean, inexpensive motels and restaurants.

Follow the bay around to its western point to reach the pier. The adjacent Lake Superior shoreline offers a nice sand and pebble beach, which is closed if endangered piping plovers are nesting (Apr.-Aug.). Rock hounds should continue west along the beach, past the Woodland Park city campground, to reach a good spot for **hunting agates.**

Lake Superior State Forest

Traveling east from Beaver Basin, several dirt roads spiral south off County Road H-58 into the woods. These lead into the **Lake Superior State Forest,** part of the buffer zone protecting Pictured Rocks. Here you'll find plenty of inland lakes, hiking and biking trails, and rustic campgrounds. Many of these and are overlooked by the summer visitors to the national lakeshore. For more information on the state forest, contact the **Michigan DNR** (www.michigan.gov/dnr). Topographic maps ($4) of the area are available at the **Hiawatha Visitors Center** (400 E. Munising Ave., Munising, 906/387-3700, www.fs.fed.us).

FESTIVALS AND EVENTS
Annual Grand Marais Music and Arts Festival

The second weekend of August is the time slated for the **Annual Grand Marais Music and Arts Festival** (906/494-2447, www.grandmaraismichigan.com), a much anticipated event that showcases local artists, talented bands of various genres, and an array of food vendors. The festival is held at Woodland Park, near Braziel and Millen Streets.

SUMMER SPORTS AND RECREATION
Hiking and Biking

Two good hiking trails leave from the campground at Little Beaver Lake. The short and pleasant 0.7-mile **White Pine Trail** is a self-guided nature trail that circles through a 300-year-old pine forest. The five-mile **Beaver Basin Loop Trail** makes a lap around Little Beaver and Big Beaver Lakes, and then follows the Lake Superior shore past sea caves cut by the lake's pounding waves. Boardwalks skirt the wetlands before returning to the trailhead.

If you're in the mood for some exercise, the two-mile stretch of the **North Country Trail** from the Log Slide to the Au Sable Light Station is one of the park's most scenic hikes.

The **Grand Sable Banks and Dunes** (*grand sable* is French for "great sands") stretch for nearly five miles from the overlook, with glacial banks of gravel supporting the huge mounds of sand. They are magnificent when viewed from a distance, glowing gold and rising abruptly from the cobalt waters of Lake Superior. In many areas, especially near the overlook, the dunes are free of grasses and plants, so you can play around on them without fear of damaging fragile plant life or causing erosion.

Most people, however, choose to explore the dunes from the eastern end. Near the **Grand Sable Visitors Center** (E21090 County Rd. H-58, 906/494-2660, www.nps.gov/piro, 9am-5pm daily late May-Labor Day), a trail winds across the top of the dunes, where marram grass, beach pea, and sand cherry grow. Each plant binds to the sand and prevents shoreline erosion. Be careful to stay on the trail here. Interpretive signs discuss the plants' tenuous hold on the environment.

Canoeing and Kayaking

Paddlers can get the best view of Pictured Rock by **sea kayak.** This will allow you to avoid the rather touristy narration of the Pictured Rocks Cruise and really experience the true grandeur of this shoreline. Safety concerns cannot be overemphasized, however. Only experienced paddlers should venture out on their own, and only in a closed cockpit (not a canoe) after carefully monitoring weather conditions. Paddlers can get themselves into serious trouble at Pictured Rocks if caught in sudden summer squalls along the 15-mile rock wall without shelter. Having said that, sea kayaking along Pictured Rocks ranks as one of the finest paddles on the Great Lakes.

The stretch of Pictured Rocks and Lake Superior shoreline leading into Grand Marais is also the easternmost stretch of the **Hiawatha Water Trail** (www.hiawathawatertrail.org), which ends here, 120 miles from its starting point in Big Bay. If you're heading in the opposite direction, it's the beginning of a long and satisfying journey in a sea kayak.

If you're unsure of your abilities, hook up with **Northern Waters** (129 E. Munising Ave., Munising, 906/387-2323, www.northernwaters.com). The company offers outstanding day-long guided trips ($125 adults, $95 under age 17, minimum guest weight 75 pounds), ferrying guests and boats to a departure point at Miners Castle. Beginners are welcome, since the day includes some basic instruction and you'll be traveling in a tandem kayak with an experienced guide. Kayak rentals (and longer trips to Grand Island and Isle Royale) are also available.

Beaches

An icon near the **Twelvemile Beach** campground says it all. In indicating this is a permitted (but discouraged) beach area, it shows a swimmer not in the usual crawl position, but with water lapping at his ankles. In other words, the water here is bone-chilling cold. Swim if you dare, but wading is really more realistic—which is what keeps Twelvemile Beach the pristine, stunning ribbon of sand that it is. After all, if such a perfect beach boasted 75°F water, it would be overrun with Jet Skis and zinc oxide. Instead, it's a beach where you can stroll for hours with only the company of peregrine falcons, bald eagles, deer wandering down for a drink, and even the occasional black bear snorting around in the sand.

The Twelvemile Beach **campground** is easy to reach, just a short drive off County Road H-58 through a pretty birch forest. Many of the 37 campsites string out along a bluff over the beach. Arrive at midweek (or early on Saturday, often a turnover day) for one of the choice spots. Some are larger than the average house lot and undoubtedly have better views. Well-placed stairs allow campers and picnickers to reach the lake. The campground also has a nice **day use area** at its east end.

Just about five miles farther up the beach (or County Rd. H-58) lies the auto-accessible **Hurricane River campground,** where the Hurricane River empties into Lake Superior. This is also an exceptionally scenic campground, with 21 sites and a good location near the water and Au Sable Point.

Farther west, across County Road H-58 near the Grand Sable Visitors Center (E21090 County Rd. H-58), the sandy shores and often

warm waters of **Grand Sable Lake** are a wonderful spot for a swim or picnic.

Fishing

Fishing in the Pictured Rocks National Lakeshore—both in Lake Superior and the inland lakes and rivers—is a bit different from fishing elsewhere in the Upper Peninsula. Specifically, angling has been permitted by Congress for more than 40 years. It's not just an opportunity; it's your right. You'll be able to cast a line for a large selection of game fish, including walleye, northern pike, whitefish, smelt, smallmouth bass, coho salmon, and brook, rainbow, and lake trout. Try Lake Superior, Grand Sable Lake, Beaver Lake, and Little Beaver Lake for the greatest variety of fish. For rivers, it's best to try at Sable Creek, Hurricane River, Beaver Basin Streams, and Miners River, among others. Contact the staff at **Pictured Rocks National Lakeshore** (N8391 Sand Point Rd., 906/387-2607, www.nps.gov/piro) for guidelines, regulations, maps, and tips.

For fishing on state land near Grand Marais, try North and South Gemini Lakes for bass, bluegill, perch, and walleye. Ross Lake, two miles east, is a source for bass, bluegill, perch, and pike. And Canoe Lake, 2.5 miles south, offers perch and pike. Contact the **Michigan DNR** (906/452-6227, www.michigan.gov/dnr) for more info.

Off-Road Vehicles

East of Grand Marais, near Lake Superior between Blind Sucker Flooding and Muskallonge Lake, the first of two DNR ATV trails has an impressive 46 miles in three large loops. **Pine Ridge Trail** has parking at the intersection of County Road 416 and County Road 407; there's also access from Holland Lake Campground if you continue west on County Road 416. The **Two Heart Trail** actually connects to the Pine Ridge Trail, adding almost 34 miles, for a total of some 80 miles. Use the same trailhead parking as Pine Ridge, or you can get access to Two Heart from the Mouth of Two-Hearted River

Campground (gas is available here too) or Pike Lake Campground. The **Michigan DNR** (906/452-6227, www.michigan.gov/dnr) has more information and maps.

Waterfalls

Just inside the park's western boundary, a short trail leads to 50-foot **Munising Falls,** which spills into a narrow gorge before emptying into Lake Superior's Munising Bay. Head east to the Chapel Basin Area where, amid a pale birch forest some 1.5 miles from the parking area, a stream of frothing water drops like a horsetail 90 feet into a deep gorge and Chapel Lake below. Continue past the falls another 1.75 miles to reach Chapel Beach, where you'll find a backcountry campground. From here, you can turn right to Chapel Rock and follow the Lakeshore Trail 1.5 miles to **Spray Falls,** one of the least visited and loveliest waterfalls in the park, where Spray Creek drops over the sandstone cliffs right into Lake Superior.

The trail to **Sable Falls** leaves from the **Grand Sable Visitors Center** (E21090 County Rd. H-58, 906/494-2660, www.nps.gov/piro, 9am-5pm daily late May-Labor Day), a 0.5-mile walk largely composed of steps. As you work your way downhill, you'll be treated to several views of this exceptionally pretty falls, which drop in tiers through a narrow canyon and out to a rocky Lake Superior beach.

WINTER SPORTS AND RECREATION
Ski and Snowshoe Trails

The **Grand Marais Ski Trail** has several loops on the extreme east end of Pictured Rocks National Lakeshore, where County Road H-58/Au Sable Point Trail passes near Sable Falls and the Lake Superior shoreline. In fact, the E Trail loops close to the shore on an intermediate two-mile journey out and back. All of the loops here range from easy to intermediate, and vary in distance from less than 1 mile to nearly 2.5 miles, for a total of 10.4 miles. Parking is on either side of County

Road H-58, just west of William Hill Road. Be sure to watch for both car and snowmobile traffic when crossing the highway. For trail maps and additional information, the staff at **Pictured Rocks National Lakeshore** (N8391 Sand Point Rd., 906/387-2607, www.nps.gov/piro) are more than happy to help. You can jump on the North Country Trail as well.

Snowmobiling

There are more than enough snowmobile trails in the Pictured Rocks-Grand Marais region. The most important one is **Trail 8,** which cuts east-west from Munising to Sault Ste. Marie. At Pictured Rocks National Lakeshore, **Trail 89** bends away from Trail 8 and takes you north to the Superior shoreline. South of town, **Trails 443** and **43** connect to the rest of the U.P.'s snowmobile trails—south to St. Ignace and west to Escanaba, Ironwood, and the Keweenaw Peninsula. There's also a web of smaller trails that weaves around the city: Trails 88, 888, 9, and 492 will take you between the main trails and to other places in the region. Contact **Grand Marais Sno-Trails** (800/831-7292, www.sno-trails.net) for more information and a detailed map. And remember: According to the state, snowmobiles are allowed on the shoulders of plowed roads, and on any unplowed road. Follow the speed limits and drive with care.

FOOD

Grand Marais has a few good dining spots, both right downtown on County Road H-77. The **Grand Marais Tavern and Restaurant** (14260 Lake Ave., 906/494-2111, 11:30am-9pm Mon.-Wed., noon-11pm Thurs.-Sat., noon-9pm Sun., $7-14) is a great place to stop for lunch after hiking or time behind the wheel. There are great burgers, beer, and pizza, with a pleasant outdoor dining area overlooking Lake Superior.

Down the street, ★ **Lake Superior Brewing Company** (14283 Lake Ave., 906/494-2337, noon-2am daily, $10-15) does the microbrewery tradition proud, with homemade beers like Sandstone Pale Ale and Granite Brown, as well as sandwiches, soups, and great homemade pizzas. For a summer treat, stop in the retro **Superior Hotel** (Lake Ave. and Randolph St.), where a soda fountain still sells phosphates and penny candy.

ACCOMMODATIONS

The **Beach Park Motel** (21795 Randolph St., 906/494-2681, http://beachparkmotel.com, from $95, pets $10) has large rooms, each with a view of the water. A block east of County Road H-77 on Randolph Street, it's within walking distance to everything in town.

East of County Road H-77 on Wilson Street, **Voyageur's Motel** (21906 Wilson St., 906/494-2389, www.voyageursmotelmi. com, motel $105, 3-bedroom cottage $230, 2-night minimum) sits atop a ridge overlooking Grand Marais Harbor. Nice newer rooms, each with two queen beds, a mini fridge, and a coffee maker, plus a sauna-whirlpool facility, make this a good choice.

The historic **Superior Hotel** (14245 Lake Ave., 906/494-2539, www.grandmaraismichigan.com, $40, each additional person $5) is an old-fashioned hotel along the lines of a European-style hostel. Rooms are clean but very Spartan and do not include a TV or private bath. The rates, however, makes it an attractive option.

Still affordable, **Hilltop Cabins** (14176 Ellen St., 906/494-2331, www.hilltopcabins. net, $85-195) rents one- to three-bedroom cabins, each with a full living room, kitchen, and bath. Motel rooms with views of the bay are available, but the cozy cabins are much more desirable.

For more information and other lodging options, contact the **Grand Marais Chamber of Commerce** (906/494-2447, www.grandmaraismichigan.com).

Camping

Pictured Rocks has three auto-accessible campgrounds: Beaver Lake, Twelvemile Beach, and Hurricane River. Each is equipped with water and pit toilets. No reservations are accepted, and fees are $14-16. **Backcountry camping** is permitted only at designated hike-in sites, mostly along the Lakeshore Trail. Reservations (877/444-6777, www.recreation.gov) are required, and the website will issue you the required permit for $15 plus $5 pp per night. Most sites do not have water or toilets. Camping is also available in Munising, Grand Marais, and in Lake Superior State Forest, which borders Pictured Rocks to the south.

With an excellent location just outside the national lakeshore boundary, **Woodland Park** (906/494-2613, www.grandmaraismichigan.com, May 15-Oct. 15, $21-30) has more than 100 sites, all of which offer water and electricity. Opt for a more secluded one that requires you to get some exercise and walk up the beach a bit.

INFORMATION AND SERVICES

You'll find visitors centers at both ends of the national lakeshore. One is in Munising; the other is located inside the park at the Grand Sable Dunes, just a few miles from Grand Marais. Be sure to stop at one of these centers before beginning your visit. They have rangers on duty and excellent maps, displays, and historical information that will enhance your visit. Both also offer small but comprehensive bookstores. The **Munising Information Center** (400 E. Munising Ave., Munising, 906/387-3700, www.nps.gov/piro, 9am-5pm daily summer, 9am-4:30pm Mon.-Sat. mid-Sept.-Memorial Day), serving both the Pictured Rocks National Lakeshore and Hiawatha National Forest, is open year-round. The **Grand Sable Visitors Center** (E21090 County Rd. H-58, 906/494-2660, www.nps. gov/piro, 9am-5pm daily) is open from late May to Labor Day only. The **Munising Falls Visitors Center** (1505 Sand Point Rd., Munising, www.nps.gov/piro, 9am-5pm daily Memorial Day-mid September) is geared primarily to issuing backcountry permits and also has a bookstore.

The two closest hospitals are **Helen**

Newberry Joy Hospital (502 W. Harrie St., Newberry, 906/293-9200 or 800/743-3093, www.hnjh.org) in Newberry and **Munising Memorial Hospital** (1500 Sand Point Rd., Munising, 906/387-4110, www.munising-memorial.org) in Munising. To access either hospital, head south on M-77 until you get to M-28. For Helen Newberry Joy Hospital, turn left and follow M-28 to M-123; turn left again and travel north on M-123 to Harrie Street, then turn left to the hospital. For Munising Memorial Hospital, turn right onto M-28 from M-77, then turn right on Connors Road. Make a left at Munising/Shingleton Road, then another right at Washington Street to the hospital.

In Grand Marais, you can do banking at the **Peoples State Bank of Munising** (N14264 Lake St., Grand Marais, 906/494-2265, www.bankatpsb.com). You'll find more banking options in Newberry and Munising.

GETTING THERE AND AROUND
Car
The easiest route between Munising and Grand Marais will bring you well south of Pictured Rocks. Take M-28 east from Munising, then M-77 north to Grand Marais.

County Road H-58 offers closer access the area around the national lakeshore. From the Grand Marais end, you'll be able to get as far as the Kingston Lake Campground. From Munising and the west, you can get to the Little Beaver Lake Campground.

As a linear park, Pictured Rocks perennially struggles with auto accessibility versus invasiveness. There have been sporadic discussions for decades about a "Beaver Basin Rim Road" that would weave through the park nearer to Lake Superior, offering easier auto access to park attractions but undeniably changing the spirit and peacefulness of the largely road-free preserve.

Air
The closest commercial airport is **Chippewa County International Airport** (CIU, 5019 Airport Dr., Kincheloe, 906/495-5631, www.airciu.com), nearly 80 miles away, south of Sault Ste. Marie. **Delta Airlines** (800/221-1212, www.delta.com) offers scheduled flights from Detroit, and car rentals are available from **Avis** (906/495-5900, www.avis.com).

If you're traveling from other major cities, it may be easier to fly into **Sawyer International Airport** (MQT, 125 G Ave., Gwinn, 906/346-3308, www.sawyerairport.com) instead, about two hours' drive. Sawyer has scheduled flights from Detroit on Delta and Chicago O'Hare on American Eagle.

Boat
The **Burt Township Marina** (906/494-2613, 906/494-2381 off-season, www.michigan.gov/dnr, May 1-Oct. 15) in Grand Marais is the only natural harbor of refuge between Munising and Whitefish Point. You'll find a boat launch, fuel, electricity, water hookups, a pump-out station, and transient dockage. The marina is open seasonally and is located at 46°41.05 N, 85°58.15 W.

Bus
The **Altran Shuttle** (906/387-4845) is a county bus that makes regular runs (three times a week during the high season) to Munising Falls and Grand Marais and will drop off hikers at any point along County Road H-58. It's the perfect way for backpackers to enjoy the park without contributing to the growing vehicle problem. Call for schedules and rates or to make a reservation, at least one day in advance.

Seney and Vicinity

The train went up the track and out of sight, around one of the hills of burnt timber. Nick sat down on the bundle of canvas and bedding the baggage man had pitched out of the door of the baggage car. There was no town, nothing but the rails and the burnt over country. The thirteen saloons that had once lined the one street of Seney had not left a trace.

Ernest Hemingway,
"Big Two-Hearted River"

Applied to the small town of Seney, Hemingway's quote may be a bit of an exaggeration. Seney is still there, a small dot on the map at the crossroads of M-77 and M-28. But by the time Hemingway's protagonist, Nick Adams, was exploring the central U.P., the town of Seney was indeed just a shadow of its former self.

"Hell town in the Pine," loggers once called it, the new center of a logging trade that had crept northward into the U.P. after depleting the lucrative stands of red and white pine in the northern Lower Peninsula. Seney was the center of the action in the 1880s, both in and out of the woods. Situated along a railroad siding and the shores of the Fox River—used to transport the logs—the city became an important transit point. Besides logging, the local economy thrived on drinking, gambling, and womanizing. Seney didn't lack for local color: legendary characters included P. K. "Snap Jaw" Small, who entertained barroom crowds by biting the heads off live toads and birds, and "Protestant" Bob McGuire, who sharpened his thumbnails into miniature bowie knives. Seney was sensationalized in the national press, in a manner similar to Tombstone, Arizona, and other towns of the Wild West.

Seney never had the huge fertile forests so common elsewhere in Michigan. Glaciers scrubbed this swath of the central U.P. flat, creating a patchwork of rivers, wetlands, and rocky, sandy soil. The red and white pines that did grow here were leveled in just a few short years. Soon loggers were settling for the less valuable hardwoods and small conifers, burning the scrub as they went. Shortly after the turn of the century they moved on, leaving behind the now barren land and vast "stump prairies."

Optimistic farmers followed the quickly departed loggers. They burned the brush and went to great lengths to drain the wetlands, digging miles of 20-foot ditches. Their hopes were quickly dashed by the area's poor soil and short growing season. Soon, they too departed, but the fires had a more lasting effect, deeply scarring the fragile soil.

These days humans are finally trying to help instead of harm this beleaguered land. The immense Seney National Wildlife Refuge now manages and protects 150 square miles immediately west of M-77, restoring the wetlands with an intricate series of dikes and control ponds that began as a 1930s Civilian Conservation Corps project. Today, the refuge is an important sanctuary and nesting place for a rich variety of waterfowl.

The area's rivers remain a wonderful resource as well. The Fox, Manistique, and Driggs all snake through this area, along with countless creeks and lesser branches. Henry Ford, Calvin Coolidge, and Ernest Hemingway all fished these legendary trout waters, as anglers do today. Here too Hemingway used a bit of literary license: it was really the Fox that he so eloquently chronicled in his Nick Adams stories. He merely borrowed the more romantic sounding name of the Big Two-Hearted River, which in fact flows just east of here.

SIGHTS
★ Iverson Snowshoe Company

Aluminum snowshoes now dominate the sport, but for beauty and tradition, they simply can't match white ash and rawhide snowshoes. In Shingleton, 25 miles west of Seney on M-28, Anita Hulse and her two sons operate this wonderful factory, where workers hand-shape strips of local ash into classic snowshoe frames.

Visitors are welcome at **Iverson Snowshoe Company** (E9664 M-28, Wetmore, 906/452-6370, www.iversonssnowshoes.com, 8am-4pm Mon.-Fri.), one of just two wooden snowshoe manufacturers left in the country. You can watch workers shave and saw strips of ash, steam them, bend them around a form, and send them to a drying kiln overnight. Finished frames are laced with gummy strips of rawhide or newer-style neoprene. All of this happens in a small building, where visitors practically lean over the shoulders of the workers.

Iverson manufactures about 11,000 snowshoes a year, about a third of which go to L.L.Bean. Other customers include REI, the Norwegian army, park rangers, and utility workers. Iverson also makes rustic chairs and tables, to order only. It's best to call ahead if you're interested in a tour; groups of more than five or six should definitely call.

Seney National Wildlife Refuge

The **Seney National Wildlife Refuge** (1674 Refuge Entrance Rd., 906/586-9851, www.fws.gov/refuge/seney) occupies a huge swath of land west of M-77 and south of M-28. At 95,000 acres, it's intensely managed by the U.S. Fish and Wildlife Service, part of the U.S. Department of the Interior, with dikes and control structures used to artificially raise and lower the water levels within a network of 21 major pools, simulating a natural wetlands cycle.

The system impounds more than 7,000 acres of water in these pools, and natural wetlands sprawl beyond that. While humans on foot or bicycle can access much of this preserve via an extensive network of maintenance roads, the refuge offers plenty of seclusion for its inhabitants. More than 200 species of birds and nearly 50 species of mammals have been recorded here, including bald eagles, trumpeter swans, loons, and on rare occasions, even moose or wolves. Whether you're an experienced bird-watcher or just a casual observer, Seney is a wonderful place to see a fascinating array of wildlife.

Start your visit at the excellent **National Wildlife Refuge Visitors Center** (M-77, www.fws.gov/refuge/seney, 9am-5pm daily

Seney National Wildlife Refuge

May 15–Oct. 20), five miles south of the town of Seney on M-77. A 15-minute audiovisual program, informative displays, and printed materials will provide a good overview of what you can expect to see in the refuge. Some of the handouts will increase your chances of spotting birdlife, pinpointing things like eagle nests and ponds frequented by loons. Sightings are often best in the early morning and evening.

The **Pine Ridge Nature Trail** departs from the visitors center and allows for a quick 1.4-mile foray into wetland habitat. The self-guided trail circles a pool, and a stretch of boardwalk spans a marshy area.

The one-way **Marshland Wildlife Drive** also departs from the visitors center and makes a seven-mile auto-accessible loop through the refuge, with several interpretive signs placed along the way. The route includes three observation decks equipped with spotting scopes. You can borrow binoculars from the visitors center. An eagle's nest is visible from the road, as are several pools frequented by herons and swans. Trumpeter swans were hand-raised and released here and are now seen regularly. Tundra swans also migrate through in spring and fall. An adjacent three-mile **fishing loop** accesses a fishing platform and is also open to autos.

Strangmoor Bog

One of Seney's most unusual features, **Strangmoor Bog** lies deep in the wetlands near the refuge's western boundary, and unfortunately is not easily accessible to visitors. Strangmoors, or string bogs, are finger-like bogs alternating with sand ridges that are remnants of ancient beaches. They are typically found only in arctic and subarctic regions, and Seney's bog is one of the southernmost examples in North America.

SUMMER SPORTS AND RECREATION
Hiking and Biking

Unfortunately, most visitors to Seney never get out of their cars and venture beyond the Marshland Drive. A bicycle is really the best way to experience Seney. Bikes are welcome on more than 100 miles of gravel and dirt maintenance roads, which are closed to motorized traffic except refuge vehicles. You won't find any exciting or technical rides, as the land is flat, a bicycle allows you to cover far more ground than you could hiking and is quiet enough not to frighten the wildlife. There's also something magical about spinning down a gravel road amid all the chirping, twittering, and honking, with nothing but waving grasses and glinting ponds surrounding you for miles.

Easy terrain, easy access, and well-marked trails make Seney a great choice for families or less active cyclists. You will want a mountain bike or hybrid bike, since the gravel can be tough on skinny tires. No off-road riding is permitted in the refuge.

There are three main access points for the refuge. One is at the Visitor Center on M-77, where trails sprout off the Marshland Drive. This area is the most heavily visited, but trails here weave between many different pools, so the ride is interesting, and waterfowl sightings can be particularly good. Note that Loops 1 and 2 are part of the Marshland Drive and are open to motor vehicles.

A second access point is about three miles south of the visitors center, near the Grace Lutheran Church. Turn west at the sign for the Northern Hardwoods cross-country ski area, referred to as Smith Farm by locals. You'll soon reach a small parking area and a gate across the road. The trail begins just a few hundred yards west. This is a more lightly visited area of the refuge. From here, Loop 5 makes a 12.2-mile circle, including a stretch that runs parallel to the Driggs River.

If you stay on the trail that follows the Driggs, rather than swinging back east to complete Loop 5, after about nine miles you'll emerge onto M-28 west of the town of Seney. This is the third access point, called Driggs River Road. It's a well-defined road for the first 1.5 miles south of M-28 until it arrives at the refuge boundary.

Canoeing and Kayaking

Paddling is an excellent way to explore the western reaches of the refuge, and it happens that the Manistique is an easily navigable canoeing river, with a sand bottom and just enough twists and turns to keep things interesting. It can be popular at the height of summer, so it's best to go off-season or early in the day for optimal solitude and wildlife watching. Put in at the roadside park on M-77, one mile south of Germfask, or arrange a trip through Northland Outfitters. If you have your own boat, you can opt for the lightly traveled Driggs or Creighton Rivers. Both cross M-28 west of Seney. Paddling is not permitted on any refuge pools or marshes.

Northland Outfitters (906/586-9801, www.northoutfitters.com) is located on M-77 in Germfask, just south of the refuge entrance. The company rents mountain bikes, camping gear, canoes, and kayaks, and offers paddling trips on the Manistique.

Fishing

The refuge allows some fishing within its boundaries. Pick up information on its special regulations at the visitors center. Perch and northern pike are most common. Fishing can be quite good on area rivers, especially for bass, northern pike, and walleye. You'll need to move to the upper reaches if you're after trout.

The Fox River

In 1919, Ernest Hemingway stepped off a train in Seney, asked for directions to a good trout stream, and was directed up an old railroad grade to the east branch of the Fox River. Where truth meets fiction we'll never know, but Hemingway's U.P. travels resulted in "Big Two-Hearted River," his Nick Adams tale about fishing what was really the Fox. Consequently, the Fox has always carried a special cachet in the U.P. and among trout fishing enthusiasts.

Of course, Michigan has dozens of superb **trout fishing** streams, but most anglers seem to agree that the Fox belongs on the A-list.

According to Jerry Dennis, author of several Michigan fishing books, it has produced some gargantuan brook trout. "The Fox even today has a reputation for brook trout of a size rarely encountered elsewhere in the United States. Fish 15 to 20 inches long are taken with fair regularity," he writes. The east branch still is considered the river's prime stretch, partly because it's more difficult to reach. To get here, you can hike in from M-77 north of Seney, where it flows just west of the road. A state forest campground eight miles up M-77 from Seney offers public access. Many locals simply cast near the bridge at Seney, where the main river flows under M-28. Because of the Fox's allure, the DNR is considering instituting special fishing regulations. Check with authorities before heading out.

The **Fox River Pathway** was no doubt prompted by perennial interest in Hemingway's narrative. The route stretches 27 miles north from Seney to just shy of Pictured Rocks National Lakeshore, and by U.P. standards, it's somewhat bland. Its most appealing stretch—especially for anglers looking for fishing access—is the southern end, where the trail parallels the main river for 10 miles. Farther north, it follows the Little Fox and the west branch. Heading north, the trail traverses the Kingston Plains, where loggers left behind stump prairies. Markers along this route offer information about the area's logging history.

Because it passes through a good deal of cutover land, the trail can be extremely hot and dry. If you plan to hike it, be sure to carry a water purification system. You'll find rustic campgrounds at both trailheads, and just one along the route, about six miles from the southern end.

For hikers, another much shorter option is the trail that heads north from the Fox River Pathway's northern terminus at the Kingston Lake Campground. Not considered part of the pathway, this trail winds through pines and hardwoods in the Lake Superior State Forest for four miles before spilling out onto a particularly deserted and delightful stretch of Twelvemile Beach on Lake Superior, inside Pictured Rocks National Lakeshore.

WINTER SPORTS AND RECREATION
Ski and Snowshoe Trails

It seems that as soon as the snow falls, the wildlife refuge is open for cross-country skiing and snowshoeing. The largely flat trails are groomed from mid-December through mid-March and make for a pleasant way to pass an afternoon. The trailhead for six different skiing loops is located just off Robinson Road west of M-77. Stop by the visitors center for maps and more information. Half of the trails are easy and suitable for beginners. The others will present a bit of a challenge, but given the relatively flat terrain, experienced skiers shouldn't have any problems. Loops range from less than one mile to two miles in length. You can snowshoe anywhere in the refuge except on the groomed ski trails.

Snowmobiling

The best part about snowmobiling in Seney is its proximity to the trails that spread across the Grand Marais region north of town. The **Seney Trail** (Trail 43) cuts diagonally through Seney before connecting to the remaining miles of the Upper Peninsula's trails. Unplowed roads and the shoulders of plowed roads are open to snowmobiles as well.

FOOD AND ACCOMMODATIONS

If you're hungry, stop at any of the smattering of restaurants that have gathered along M-28 as you approach town from either direction.

There is lodging in Seney, but you'll find better choices elsewhere. Newberry, Manistique, Munising, and Grand Marais are all within 30 minutes' drive. If you'd like to stay in town, try a room at the affordable **Fox River Motel** (906/499-3332, www.foxrivermotel.com, $55-80 summer, $60-85 winter) downtown at the corner of M-77 and M-28. Wi-Fi is included.

Camping

There are plenty of campgrounds to choose from, even if none of them are in the refuge, where no overnight camping is allowed. Still, there are a few places to go nearby. The **East Branch Fox River State Forest Campground** (906/341-2355, www.michigan.gov/dnr, $13) has 19 sites for tents or small trailers. Take M-77 north of Seney about seven miles. To get to the **Fox River State Forest Campground** (906/341-2355, www.michigan.gov/dnr, $13), take County Road 450 northwest of Seney to the seven rustic campsites for tents and small trailers only. Both of these campgrounds work on a first come, first served basis.

You'll find small and rustic **Mead Creek Campground** (906/341-2355, www.michigan.gov/dnr, $13) just off County Road 436 about 15 miles west of M-77 near Germfask. Mead Creek has nine sites with vault toilets and water from a hand pump, and is first come, first served.

For more camping options, ask at the **National Wildlife Refuge Visitors Center** (M-77, www.fws.gov/refuge/seney, 8am-4:30pm daily May 15-Oct. 20).

INFORMATION AND SERVICES

Visitor information for the **Seney National Wildlife Refuge** can be obtained from the **U.S. Fish and Wildlife Service** (1674 Refuge Entrance Rd., 906/586-9851, www.fws.gov/refuge/seney). When you first arrive, stop by the visitors center to view an orientation slide show, exhibits, and obtain information. The center is located on M-77 a few miles north of Germfask.

For medical care or the hospital, head east along M-28 to Newberry and the **Helen Newberry Joy Hospital** (502 W. Harrie St., Newberry, 906/293-9200 or 800/743-3093, www.hnjh.org). Take M-28 to M-123 and turn left; take another left on Harrie Street to the hospital.

GETTING THERE AND AROUND

Car

Getting to Seney by car is simple. The town is at the intersection of M-77, the north-south highway that runs between U.S. 2 and Grand Marais, and M-28, the main artery that cuts east-west through the middle of the peninsula. Seney is 40 miles from Manistique, 35 miles from Munising, and 25 miles from Grand Marais.

Air

Unfortunately, Seney is a fairly long drive from either **Chippewa County International Airport** (CIU, 5019 Airport Dr., Kincheloe, 906/495-2522, www.airciu. com), south of Sault Ste. Marie, or **Sawyer International Airport** (MQT, 125 G Ave., Gwinn, 906/346-3308, www.sawyerairport. com), near Marquette. Both airports have plenty of car rental options, and it's easy to get to Seney via M-28. Driving time from either airport is about 1.5 hours.

Public Transportation

Currently there is no public transportation serving Seney.

Whitefish Bay to the Lake Huron Shore

On the northwestern tip of the bay, Whitefish Point boasts the oldest active lighthouse on Lake Superior, but it's probably better known for its proximity to Tahquamenon Falls, the largest and arguably most beautiful waterfall in the

Upper Peninsula. Whitefish Bay is also the place to go for Lake Superior swimming, since the water tends to be warmer here than in Marquette. The pleasantly named community of Paradise, just to the south, will probably be your base of operations.

The quickest way to Sault Ste. Marie from the west is to take M-28 to I-75, but then you'll miss out on the drive along Whitefish Bay, where Lake Superior narrows and becomes the St. Mary's River. To enjoy this beautiful scenery, take a leisurely ride along the Lake Shore Drive/Whitefish Bay Scenic Byway.

You'll no doubt want to spend time at Sault Ste. Marie, watching the big ships make their way through the locks or strolling along quaint Portage Avenue. Don't forget to cross into Canada and visit the other Sault Ste. Marie. You'll love what America's friendly northern neighbor has to offer.

Les Cheneaux and Drummond Island are perfect for pure relaxation. These quiet isles are close to both Sault Ste. Marie and busy Mackinac Island but feel like they're hundreds of miles away. Get out on the water and explore the channels and islands.

PLANNING YOUR TIME

Sault Ste. Marie is the largest city in the eastern U.P and is certainly worth a day of your time. In fact, you can easily spend the entire afternoon at the locks. Work in a trip to Tahquamenon Falls and a visit to Les Cheneaux, and most visitors will want to spend about two or three days in the region. Serious hikers, bikers, or boaters should plan on a longer stay, since there are plenty of outdoor attractions—state parks galore, Hiawatha National Forest, and the placid waters of Lake Huron. If you have time, head out to Drummond Island for some secluded hiking.

HISTORY

The Ojibwa people were the first settlers of the area, migrating here in the 1500s. They

---

Previous: Tahquamenon River; Soo Locks. **Above:** Crisp Point Light.

Look for ★ to find recommended
sights, activities, dining, and lodging.

Highlights

★ **Lake Superior Nature Sanctuary:**
This remote sanctuary is home to several endangered and rare species (page 235).

★ **Great Lakes Shipwreck Museum:** This museum commemorates ships that succumbed to the lakes and honors those who were lost while sailing them (page 235).

★ **Tahquamenon Falls State Park:** This *grand dame* of Upper Peninsula waterfalls is unquestionably one of the most photographed and widely loved landmarks in the entire state (page 236).

★ **Soo Locks:** Watching giant freighters

navigate the locks is an engaging way to spend a few hours (page 247).

★ **Drummond Island:** Snowmobile trails, hiking paths, and unmatched golf courses are only a few of the reasons to head to this relaxing out-of-the-way destination (page 256).

★ **Les Cheneaux:** Located only 30 miles from the Bridge, these 36 islands are worth a visit for their sightseeing and seclusion (page 258).

★ **Great Lakes Boat Building School:** Tour this pillar of the boating community and you'll be both amazed and inspired at the skills and dedication of the students and staff (page 259).

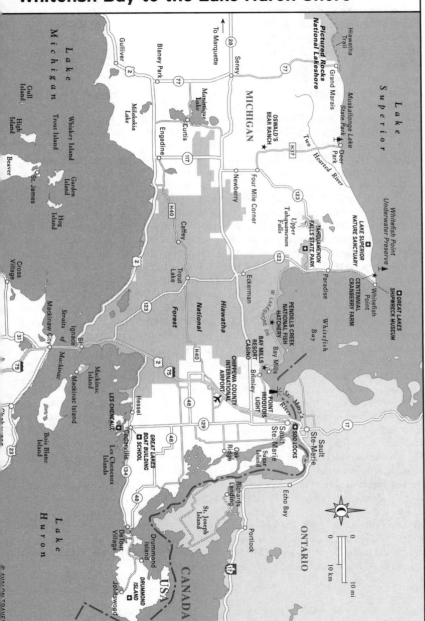

discovered a rich supply of whitefish in the area's turbulent waters and established a permanent settlement at the edge of the rapids, making this one of the oldest continuously settled areas in the Midwest. *Addik-kim-maig*, the Ojibwa name for whitefish, means "deer of the waters," a reference to the fish's importance as a food source. The Ojibwa lived off the river's riches here for more than 300 years, but in a sad and often repeated tale, the arrival of Europeans put an end to the Ojibwa way of life and took away this important fishing ground. The combination of warring Iroquois—forced west by immigrants taking over their homelands—and new European settlement at the Soo eventually drove the Ojibwa out of the region.

The French also lived off the area's riches for many years, establishing a major fur trading post here in the mid-1600s, then a Jesuit mission. By the early 1800s, Michigan's northern reaches were thoroughly settled, and people were discovering the bounty of the area's natural resources—copper, iron, lumber, and grain—all ringing the shores of Lake Superior.

The only problem was the rapids. For decades, ship cargo had to be unloaded by hand, portaged around the rapids by horses and mules pulling carts, then reloaded onto another vessel. In 1839, the American Fur Company built a short railroad line, which eased the job, but transport remained backbreaking and exceedingly slow. Great Lakes shipping was booming on the lower Great Lakes, but the resources of the Lake Superior region remained underutilized, its cargo backed up by the rapids.

Eastern industrialists then began lobbying for government funded locks as a solution. But the portaging business had become the lifeblood of Sault Ste. Marie's economy, and the community opposed such a project. Locals managed to stave off the inevitable until 1852, when President Millard Fillmore signed a bill authorizing construction of the first lock at Sault Ste. Marie.

In 1855, the State Lock opened, which was actually a pair of locks, each 350 feet long. They were an instant success. In their first year, they facilitated the transit of nearly 12,000 tons of iron ore. Within a decade, the annual figure soared to more than 120,000 tons. By World War I, the nation's hunger for iron and copper, coupled with the opening of vast iron mines in Minnesota's Mesabi Range, made the Soo Locks the busiest shipping canal in the world. Even today, the freight transported each year across Lake Superior and through the Soo Locks exceeds that of the Panama and Suez Canals combined.

Soon after the completion of the State Lock, the burgeoning commercial traffic made it clear that more locks were needed. The 515-foot Weitzel Lock opened in 1881. Since then, several additional locks have been built to handle both the increased traffic and the ever-expanding size of Great Lakes freighters. Today, three American locks are in operation (a fourth, the Sabin Lock, has been place in "caretaker" status and is no longer used), including the 1,200-foot Poe Lock, built in 1968 to accommodate the huge transport ships now common on the Great Lakes. There is also one lock operating on the Canadian side of the strait.

The oldest city in Michigan, Sault Ste. Marie is inseparable from the locks that shaped its past and continue to define it today. This linchpin of Great Lakes commerce, and of the local economy has experienced little growth in recent years. The Ojibwa-owned Kewadin Casino and a prison complex south of town rank as the area's largest employers, along with some state government administrative jobs and Lake Superior State University. Tourism, however, remains the economic lifeblood of the area, with many visitors coming specifically to see the parade of goods that continuously passes through town via a miracle of nautical engineering.

Paradise and Vicinity

"The searchers all say they'd have made Whitefish Bay if they put 15 more miles behind her…" Singer-songwriter Gordon Lightfoot immortalized the ill-fated ore carrier *Edmund Fitzgerald* for the masses, but locals here need no reminders. During a fierce November squall in 1975, the huge ore carrier vanished, taking the lives of all 29 hands, just 20 miles from **Whitefish Point** and the safety of **Whitefish Bay.**

On Lake Superior, the largest and fiercest of the Great Lakes, northwest storms can build over 200 miles of cold, open water. They unleash their full fury on an 80-mile stretch of water from Grand Marais to Whitefish Point, earning the area its nickname, "Graveyard of the Great Lakes." Not surprisingly, Whitefish Point has long served as a beacon for mariners, a narrow finger of land reaching toward Canada and forming Whitefish Bay, one of the few safe havens on this unpredictable inland sea.

SIGHTS
★ Lake Superior Nature Sanctuary

The Lake Superior Nature Sanctuary is wild and undeveloped, even by Upper Peninsula standards. The 369-acre plot of land on the Lake Superior shoreline is filled with endangered, threatened, and rare plant species in addition to common Upper Peninsula wildlife: bears, deer, and coyotes. The land is preserved by the **Michigan Nature Association** (866/223-2231, www.michigannature.org), which recommends guided visits and organizes field trips to the sanctuary. It's difficult to get to, and only foot traffic is allowed within the sanctuary. If you decide to make a visit, plan on it being a full day affair.

★ Great Lakes Shipwreck Museum

To commemorate the many ships that failed to round that point of safety, Whitefish Point is now the appropriate home of the **Great Lakes Shipwreck Museum** (18335 N. Whitefish Point Rd., 888/492-3747, www.shipwreckmuseum.com, 10am-6pm daily May-Oct., $13 adults, $9 children and students, free under age 6, $38 families). With dim lighting and appropriately haunting music, this fine compact museum traces the history of Great Lakes commerce and the disasters that sometimes accompanied it. Several shipwrecks are chronicled here, each with a scale model, photos or drawings, artifacts from the wreck, and a description of how and why the ship went down. Most compelling is the *Edmund Fitzgerald* display, complete with a life preserver and the ship's bell, recovered in a 1995 expedition led by museum founder Tom Farnquist, an accomplished diver and underwater photographer.

Housed in the former Coast Guard station, the museum, which occupies a complex of buildings, also includes the restored light keeper's home, a theater showing an excellent short film about the *Fitzgerald* dive, and an interesting gift shop with nautical charts, prints, books, and more. To reach the museum, take M-123 to Paradise and follow Whitefish Point Road 11 miles north. This absorbing museum makes Whitefish Point a most worthwhile destination.

Whitefish Point Underwater Preserve

For experienced divers, the **Whitefish Point Underwater Preserve** (www.michiganpreserves.org) offers a fantastic array of wrecks—18 steamers and schooners are littered all around the point. Check the website for a complete list, but be aware that the *Edmund Fitzgerald* is not among them. Good visibility is a hallmark of this 376-acre preserve. Most wrecks lie between 40

The Memory and Mystery of the *Edmund Fitzgerald*

In early November 1975, the 729-foot lake carrier *Edmund Fitzgerald* departed Superior, Wisconsin, loaded with 26,000 tons of taconite pellets, bound for the port of Detroit and nearby steel mills. Launched in 1958, the *Fitzgerald* had a long and profitable record as flagship of the Columbia Line of the Oglebay Norton Corp., with whom Northwestern Mutual Life Insurance, the ship's owner, had contracted. This was to be one of the last trips across Lake Superior before the shipping lanes and Soo Locks shut down for the season.

The *Fitzgerald* had rounded the Keweenaw Peninsula when, at dusk on November 10, one of the worst storms in 30 years screamed across Lake Superior. Winds howled at 90 miles an hour, whipping the immense lake into 30-foot swells. The *Fitzgerald* was prepared for bad weather from the northeast, as Superior was notorious for its November gales. Like the captain of the 767-foot *Arthur M. Anderson* traveling nearby, the captain of the *Fitzgerald* had chosen to follow a more protected route across the lake, some 20 to 40 miles farther north than usual.

Just 10 miles apart, the two captains had been in intermittent visual and radio contact, discussing the perilous weather, which had dangerously shifted from northeast to northwest. At 7:10pm, the *Fitzgerald* captain radioed, "We are holding our own." Then abruptly at 7:15, radio contact was lost. Turning to his radar, the captain of the Anderson was shocked to see the *Fitzgerald* completely vanished from the screen. The massive lake carrier and all 29 hands disappeared without transmitting a distress call.

When the storm cleared, the *Edmund Fitzgerald* was found in 530 feet of water, just 17 miles from the shelter of Whitefish Bay. The wreck lay at the bottom severed in two pieces some 170 feet apart. Debris was scattered over three acres, evidence of the force with which the massive hull hit bottom. Many believe the *Fitzgerald* sank bow first, which means nearly 200 feet of the ship would have towered over the water's surface at impact.

But after more than 35 years, an exhaustive Coast Guard investigation, and several dives to the site, crucial questions about the incident will most likely never be answered. Of the many theories put forth, the Coast Guard postulates that the ship took on water through leaking hatches, then developed a list and was swamped by the storm's huge waves. Others believe that, outside the normal shipping lane, the vessel scraped bottom on uncharted shoals. Still others believe the warm taconite pellets weakened the structure of the ship, causing it to snap in two when caught between two particularly enormous waves. It's also possible that elements from each of these theories contributed to the ship's demise.

Each November the victims of the disaster, along with those of other maritime tragedies, are remembered at Mariners Church in Detroit during the Great Lakes Memorial Service. Mariners is referenced by folk singer Gordon Lightfoot in his iconic song "The Wreck of the Edmund Fitzgerald" as "the Maritime Sailors Cathedral."

The ship was named after the Chairman of Northwestern Mutual, which commissioned it as an investment in 1957. At its 1958 christening, Fitzgerald's wife experienced difficulty breaking the champagne bottle, ultimately having to make three attempts—considered a harbinger of bad luck in nautical lore.

and 270 feet deep and are located in areas unprotected by harbors. Only very experienced divers and boaters should dive here. Contact the **Paradise Area Tourism Council** (906/492-3927, www.paradisemi.org) for information on area dive services.

★ Tahquamenon Falls State Park

West of Newberry, the headwaters of the Tahquamenon River bubble up from underground and begin a gentle roll through stands of pine and vast wetlands. Rambling and twisting northeast through Luce County, the river grows wider and more majestic by

Tahquamenon Falls State Park

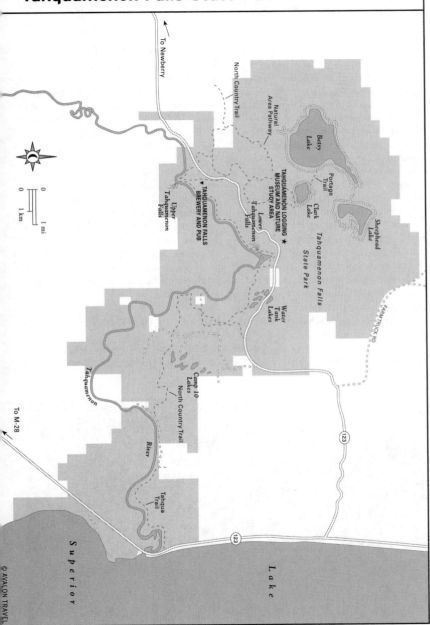

To Newberry

North Country Trail

Natural Area Pathway

Betsy Lake

Portage Trail

Clark Lake

Sheephead Lake

TAHQUAMENON LOGGING MUSEUM AND NATURE STUDY AREA ★

Upper Tahquamenon Falls

▲ TAHQUAMENON FALLS BREWERY AND PUB

Lower Tahquamenon Falls

Tahquamenon Falls State Park

Water Tank Lakes

FARM TRUCK RD

Tahquamenon

Camp 10 Lakes

North Country Trail

123

River

Tahqua Trail

To M-28

123

Superior

Lake

0   1 mi
0   1 km

© AVALON TRAVEL

the time it enters **Tahquamenon Falls State Park** (41382 M-123, 906/492-3415, www.michigan.gov/dnr). Then, with the roar of a freight train and the power of a fire hose, it suddenly plummets over a 50-foot drop, creating a golden fountain of water 200 feet wide.

As many as 50,000 gallons of water per second gush over the Upper Tahquamenon, making it the second-largest waterfall by volume east of the Mississippi, eclipsed only by Niagara. Adding to Tahquamenon's majesty are its distinctive colors: bronze headwaters from the tannic acid of decaying cedars and hemlocks that line its banks, and bright white foam from the water's high salt content.

Accessing Tahquamenon Falls is easy, since both the Upper Falls and Lower Falls lie within Tahquamenon Falls State Park, which provides short well-marked paths to prime viewing sites. At the **Upper Tahquamenon Falls,** follow the trail to the right and down the 74 steps to an observation deck, which will bring you so close you'll feel the fall's thundering power and its cool mist on your face, which on a hot summer day is wonderfully refreshing. The deck offers a stunning view of both the placid waters above and the furious frothing below.

Four miles downstream, the **Lower Tahquamenon Falls** plunge over a series of cascades. The best vantage point is from a small island in mid-river. A state park concessionaire rents out canoes and rowboats to make the short crossing.

Tahquamenon Logging Museum and Nature Study Area

Just north of Newberry, the **Tahquamenon Logging Museum and Nature Study Area** (41382 W. M-123, 906/293-3700, http://tahquamenonloggingmuseum.org, $5 adults, $2 children, free under age 6) presents an overview of the region's logging history. Antique mining equipment, old logs of impressive size, and photos, maps, and other artifacts are all housed in original rustic Civilian Conservation Corps buildings. The phrase "Nature Study Area" refers to the trail and boardwalk that can take you into the Tahquamenon Forest and along the Tahquamenon River. This walk offers an exceptional opportunity to view nature in its most pristine form. Take M-123 north of Newberry to the museum.

Luce County Historical Museum

Another of Newberry's history museums, the **Luce County Historical Museum** (411 W.

Tahquamenon Falls

Harrie St., 906/293-8417, 1pm-4pm Wed.-Fri. mid-June-Labor Day, by appointment in fall, free) doesn't just retell area history; it *is* history. The 1894 building is listed on the National Register of Historic Places and has served as both the jail and the sheriff's home. Today, it houses historic artifacts, an original jail cell, an old-fashioned schoolroom, a courtroom, and scores of other items of interest.

Oswald's Bear Ranch

It's true: There are wild black bears in the Upper Peninsula. Bumping into them on a camping excursion can be a frightening experience, but seeing them at **Oswald's Bear Ranch** (13814 County Rd. 407, 906/293-3147, 9:30am-5pm daily Memorial Day-Labor Day, 9:30am-4pm Sept., $20 per car or motorcycle, $10 individuals, free for active military), not so much. Twenty-nine live black bears roam four habitats here, safe for visitors to observe in a natural setting. This is one of the United States' largest bear ranches and once held the largest captive black bear in the world. Tyson Bear, who died in 2000, weighed 880 pounds. You can observe the bears on a walking tour. North of Newberry, take M-123 to County Road 407 and head west to the ranch.

Lighthouses

Whitefish Point Light (18335 N. Whitefish Point Rd.) first beamed a warning in 1849, and has done so ever since, making it the oldest operating light station on Lake Superior. Marking the Bay's entry, the Whitefish Point Light is a utilitarian-looking 80-foot steel structure. Though it looks relatively modern, the current tower actually dates to 1902. The beefy design was considered an extraordinary engineering experiment at the time, but one deemed necessary to withstand the gales that frequently batter this exposed landscape. The light was automated in 1970. Guided tours of the lighthouse are available individually for $5, but are only $4 when purchased in conjunction with admission to the adjacent Great Lakes Shipwreck Museum.

If you're an especially passionate lighthouse buff, you'll find a truly obscure one to add to the list. The 58-foot **Crisp Point Light** sits on a tiny arc of land 14 miles west of Whitefish Point, on an isolated, unbroken stretch of Lake Superior shoreline. Though an automated light took over duty decades ago, the handsome 1904 tower and adjacent home still stand. The tower was recently painted, the beginning of some much needed preservation work. You'll need a map or the *DeLorme*

Whitefish Point Light

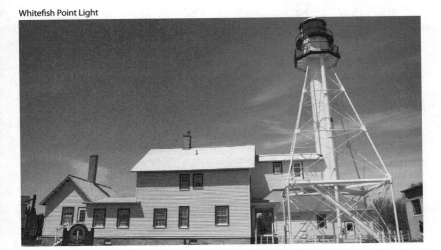

Gazetteer to find the light; a 4WD vehicle will also be helpful. Don't attempt the last couple of miles if the ground is wet and muddy. The light is about nine miles east of the mouth of the Two-Hearted River. Reach it from the west on County Road 412, or from the east via the Farm Truck Road truck trail off M-123. The lighthouse is open for tours (http://crisp-pointlighthouse.org), but hours vary with the availability of volunteers; check the website for current hours.

FESTIVALS AND EVENTS
Wild Blueberry Festival

Traverse City has its Cherry Festival, and Paradise, not to be undone, has its very own **Wild Blueberry Festival** (www.wildblue-berryfestival.org). Observed during the third weekend of August, the annual event celebrates the area's heritage as a place where wild blueberries once grew in great abundance. The festival is held right off M-123 in the heart of Paradise and features arts and crafts vendors (where the exhibitors are required to be the actual artists), plenty of music, including the Blueberry Jamboree, held during the evenings, and, of course, blueberry pie eating contests, blueberry pie sales, and more.

SUMMER SPORTS AND RECREATION
Hiking and Biking

Wedged on a 0.25-mile strip of land between Lake Superior and Muskallonge Lake, **Muskallonge Lake State Park** (30042 County Rd. 407, Newberry, 906/658-3338, www.michigan.gov/dnr) occupies the site of the old Deer Park township. It was once home to a sawmill, a hotel, and no doubt a saloon or two. Today, a couple of fishing resorts represent the only commerce in this remote area, about 18 miles east of Grand Marais. The North Country National Scenic Trail passes through here, and there are a few feeder trails letting you connect to and hike a section of the historic path.

The trails at **Pretty Lakes Quiet Area**

(906/293-3293) also connect to the North Country Trail. The five beautiful lakes are connected by a short trail. Take M-123 to County Road 407 north of Newberry and go left on County Road 416 to the campground. There's another short 1.25-mile trail at nearby **Bodi Lake State Forest Campground** (906/293-3293). M-123 connects with County Road 500 near Tahquamenon Falls State Park; take County Road 550 north to County Road 437 and follow it to Bodi Lake.

The dominance of Tahquamenon Falls themselves makes it easy to overlook the balance of the 40,000-acre **Tahquamenon Falls State Park** (41382 W. M-123, 906/492-3415, www.michigan.gov/dnr), Michigan's second largest. In sharp contrast to the often frenzied crowds at the falls—over 500,000 visitors per year, the most of any U.P. state park—the vast majority of the parkland remains peaceful and is etched with 25 miles of little-used **hiking trails.** From the Upper Falls, the **Giant Pines Loop** passes through a stand of white pines before crossing M-123. Once on the north side of the highway, you can link up with the **Clark Lake Loop,** a 5.6-mile hike that traces the southern shoreline of the shallow lake. Another worthwhile option is the **Tahquamenon River Trail,** which begins on the north side of the Tahquamenon River at the Lower Falls. For four miles it hugs the river's edge until it ends at the Upper Falls.

Canoeing and Kayaking

The **Two Hearted River,** clean and clear and usually quite mellow, is well suited for canoeing. In spring, however, rapid snowmelt can cause it to produce a serious amount of white water. A state designated wilderness river, the Two-Hearted winds through pine and hardwood forest; the only signs of civilization you're likely to see are a handful of cottages at the river's mouth. There are several low banks and sandbars, so picnic spots are easy to find. The Two-Hearted is also a widely regarded blue-ribbon trout stream, so be prepared for plenty of anglers when the season opens in April.

Put in at the High Bridge State Forest Campground on County Road 407 for a 23-mile trip to the mouth. You'll find two state forest campgrounds and other camping sites along the route.

It's possible to paddle nearly all 94 miles of the **Tahquamenon River.** A popular put-in is off County Road 415 north of McMillan, but you'll start off through several miles of bug-infested wetlands. A better choice is about 10 miles downstream, off County Road 405 at Dollarville, where you'll also avoid portaging around the Dollarville Dam. Beyond Newberry, you'll be treated to a trip with nice natural feel, since no roads come anywhere near the river. Watch the banks for bears, deer, and other wildlife. Naturally, you'll have to portage around the falls, but then you can follow the river to its mouth without any other interruptions.

Fishing

Water is the draw at **Muskallonge Lake State Park** (30042 County Rd. 407, 906/658-3338, www.michigan.gov/dnr). The park's two miles of Lake Superior frontage are wonderfully secluded, with low grass-covered dunes stretching off to the east and west and no visible development in either direction. Muskallonge Lake is stocked by the DNR and produces good fishing opportunities for northern pike, walleye, smallmouth bass, and perch. Because the lake is relatively shallow, it warms up enough for comfortable swimming—a rarity in the U.P. that explains this park's somewhat surprising popularity in summer. A modern campground offers several sites overlooking the water. Sites are usually available even in summer, but you can always reserve one by phone or online.

The final 16 miles of the Tahquamenon River wind through the park, emptying into Whitefish Bay at its eastern end. Fishing for muskie and walleye is usually quite good in the pools below the Lower Falls. Also consider joining the fleet of runabouts and anglers in waders near the mouth of the river, where trout often school.

Bird-Watching

A vital resting spot for migratory birds crossing Lake Superior, Whitefish Point is a bird-watcher's dream. Beginning with the hawk migration in April, and continuing through late fall, the point attracts an amazing variety of birds. Eagles, loons by the thousands, songbirds, waterbirds, owls, and unusual species like arctic loons and arctic terns all pass through, some 300 species in all. Even if you're not a bird enthusiast, plan to spend some time at this remarkable site, where you can wander the sand beaches, watch the birds, and keep an eye out for the big lake freighters that pass quite close to shore as they round the point. Bring along binoculars and an extra jacket. For more information, contact the **Whitefish Point Bird Observatory** (6914 N. Whitefish Point Rd., 517/580-7364, www.wpbo.org), staffed by the Michigan Audubon Society.

Golf

For golfing in the area, head to **Newberry Country Club** (5073 M-123, 906/293-8422, www.newberrycountryclub.com, $38 for 9 holes, $50 for 18 holes peak season, includes cart), a challenging 18-hole championship course at the corner of M-28 and M-123. The Newberry Country Club has been around for more than 80 years—not as long as some clubs up here, but it's not new either—and offers a driving range, a pro shop, and a bar and restaurant. Contact the country club to ask about packages, special rates, and events.

Off-Road Vehicles

Choices are limited for off-road vehicle trails in the Whitefish Point area. Some DNR trails aren't too far away, but you'll need to head west or south to find them. You can, however, ride on any state forest road that hasn't been specifically marked as off-limits, so you'll find a few trails nearby. Try Lake Superior State Park or many of the roads in the nearby Hiawatha National Forest. Contact the **Sault Ste. Marie Ranger District** (4000 I-75 Business Spur, Sault Ste. Marie, 906/635-5311, www.fs.fed.us) for motor vehicle usage maps.

Waterfalls

For another look at Tahquamenon River and Falls, you may want to plan a day for the **Toonerville Trolley and Riverboat** (906/876-2311 or 888/778-7246, www.train-andboattours.com, mid-June-Labor Day, $47 adults, $43 over age 61, $25 ages 4-15, free under age 4). It's much more appealing than the slightly pedestrian name suggests and is a good way to experience a remote stretch of the river. Departing from Soo Junction near Newberry (watch for a sign on M-28), a narrow gauge train crawls its way five miles along an old logging route, through a roadless spruce and maple forest, tamarack lowlands, and peat bogs. In about half an hour, the train sighs to a stop deep in the woods at the Tahquamenon River's banks, where you'll transfer to a large tour boat and cruise downstream nearly two hours toward the falls. Just as the river begins to roil and boil, the boat docks on the river's south shore, and guests walk the last 0.5 miles to the falls. It's an entertaining 6.5 hour trip that has been in operation since long before a state park provided easy access to the falls. The original tour operator, who was the grandfather of current owner Kris Stewart, used a Model T truck with train wheels to reach the river. You can choose just the train trip to the riverbank and back (1.75 hours, $15 adults, $14 over age 61, $8 ages 4-15, free under age 4). Trains leave at 10:30am; reservations are recommended.

WINTER SPORTS AND RECREATION
Ski and Snowshoe Trails

The exciting thing about Paradise is that it feels very much like a paradise, even when it's buried under several feet of snow. Cross-country skiers will find a couple of well-groomed loops just off M-123 about a mile west of town. Paradise Pathway's loops range 1.5 to 3 miles long. Contact the **Paradise Area Tourism Council** (906/492-3927, www.paradisemi.org) for more information.

Nearby, **Tahquamenon Falls State Park** (41382 W. M-123, 906/492-3415, www.michigan.gov/dnr) has several miles of groomed ski trails, and countless more if you're interested in backcountry skiing. The River Trail leaves the parking area and runs about four miles to the ranger station. This trail isn't a loop, so you'll have to backtrack. There's also the one-mile-long Nature Trail. The Giant Pines Loop is 3.5 miles and closest to the parking area; farther away are the Wilderness Loop, at 7.4 miles, and the 5.6-mile Clark Lake Loop. A number of these loops and trails connect to the North Country Trail, so you have an additional 4,400 miles of trails available.

In Newberry, try the **Canada Lake Pathway** (906/293-3293) for 14 miles of groomed ski trails near Natalie State Forest Campground, southeast of Newberry.

Snowmobiling

If you want to snowmobile up to the very end of Whitefish Point, take **Trail 453,** which will eventually get you there, although there's a network of trails that you'll need to navigate first. If you're heading east from Grand Marais, **Trail 8** will get you to Paradise before it curves south and east to Sault Ste. Marie. Several miles before Paradise, however, Trail 8 intersects with **Trails 452** and **451,** which head north and hit 453 and continue to the tip of Whitefish Point. Heading down to Newberry, take **Trail 49.**

FOOD

If you want to cut loose, head to **Timber Charlie's** (101 Newberry Ave., 906/293-3363, www.timbercharlies.com, 8am-7pm daily, $10-15), a family-friendly place that serves basic fare. Try selections of Mexican, Italian, seafood, steak, and burgers; there's also a full bar.

In Paradise, you can't do much better than the ★ **Tahquamenon Falls Brewery and Pub** (906/492-3300, 9am-10pm daily, $9-21), a microbrewery and restaurant with great food and a relaxed brewpub atmosphere. Best of all, it's just steps away from the viewing area for the Upper Falls. Selections of steak, fresh fish, hefty burgers, and other sandwiches give way to that Yooper classic, the pasty. If you haven't stopped for one at a roadside diner, you'll want to get one here.

ACCOMMODATIONS

There are some nice hotels in and around Paradise and Newberry, but for more selection, including plenty of chains, it's worth the drive to Sault Ste. Marie. One of the best hotels up here is the **Paradise Inn** (8359 N. Whitefish Point Rd., 906/492-3940, $110-138), at the junction of M-123 and Whitefish Point Road. Two of the 36 rooms at this modest but well-kept motel are suites with jetted tubs. Continental breakfast and guest laundry are available as well.

Another excellent option is the **Magnuson Grand Hotel Lakefront** (8112 N. M-123, 906/492-3770, http://magnusongrandlake-front.com, $162-189). Although a bit pricey, the waterfront views, indoor pool, and superb breakfast makes this a great place for travelers desiring something a bit more upscale.

There are additional lodging options in Newberry. For a historic feel, try the elegant, intimate bed-and-breakfast **The MacLeod House** (6211 County Rd. 441, 906/293-3841, www.superiorsights.com, $75-105).

Camping

About 11 miles east of Grand Marais on County Road H-58 is the **Blind Sucker River** campground, a deceptively terrible name for such an appealing place to camp. There are three state forest campgrounds in this area: along the Blind Sucker River, along the Blind Sucker Flooding, and near Lake Superior. If you choose to camp along the Superior shore, be prepared for cold nights, even in August.

Even more attractive may be the state forest's **Pretty Lakes Quiet Area,** about eight miles to the southeast. Here you'll find five

small clear lakes, ringed with sand and linked together by short portages. There are canoe campsites on Beaverhouse, Camp Eight, and Long Lakes, along with an 18-site rustic campground near the approach road at Pretty Lake. No motors are allowed on Pretty, Brush, Beaverhouse, or Long Lakes. This is indeed a pretty, secluded spot where you'll listen to loons and other wildlife rather than the whine of powerboats and automobiles. To reach it, it's easiest to stay on County Road H-58, which becomes County Road H-37/County Road 407 when it swings south at Muskallonge Lake State Park. About five miles south, turn west on County Road 416 and follow it 2.5 miles to the campground. If you have a good map, you can also follow County Road 416 from the Blind Sucker area.

There are dozens of other lakes and campsites in the Lake Superior State Forest. Pick up a good topographic map and contact **Lake Superior State Forest** (906/293-5131, www.michigan.gov/dnr) for more information.

INFORMATION AND SERVICES

For tourism and visitor information for the area, contact the friendly people at the **Newberry Area Tourism Association** (906/293-5562 or 800/831-7292, www.new-berrytourism.com) or the **Paradise Area Tourism Council** (906/492-3927, www.par-adisemi.org).

Since the stretch of land between Grand Marais and Sault Ste. Marie is relatively secluded, most essential services are located in the bigger cities west and east of Whitefish Point. Although Newberry is small, with just 1,550 people, there's a good community hospital, the **Helen Newberry Joy Hospital** (502 W. Harrie St., Newberry, 906/293-9200 or 800/743-3093, www.hnjh.org). Take M-123 into Newberry and continue west on Harris Street to the hospital. The hospital also offers weekly clinic services in Paradise, with a physician or nurse practitioner visiting the **Paradise Community Health Center** (1414 N. M-123, Paradise, 906/492-3881) each Thursday.

Most of the area's easily accessible banks are located in Newberry. The **Tahquamenon Area Credit Union** (www.tacumi.com) has branches in Newberry (7693 M-123, 906/293-5117 or 800/575-5117), Engadine, Rudyard, and Pickford. Other banks in Newberry include **mBank** (414 Newberry Ave., 906/293-5165, www.bankmbank.com) and **First National Bank of St. Ignace** (1014 S. Newberry Ave., 906/293-5160, www.fnbsi.com).

GETTING THERE AND AROUND
Car

If you're driving from Grand Marais, the quickest and easiest route is south on M-77 to M-28 east until you reach M-123. Left onto M-123 takes you through Tahquamenon Falls State Park into Paradise. The trip should take 1.5 hours. The other option is more time-consuming, but it hugs Lake Superior and is more scenic than the alternate stretch of flat, uninspired scenery along M-28. It's about a two-hour drive if you head east out of Grand Marais on the Grand Marais Truck Trail, which bends south after Muskallonge Lake State Park as County Road 407. Continuing south, follow the leftward bend to the east, then turn left on M-123 and follow it to Paradise. Past Paradise, M-123 continues south until it reconnects with M-28 east of Newberry.

From Sault Ste. Marie, take I-75 south to M-28 and head west until you come to M-123; proceed north.

Air

The closest airport to Paradise, Tahquamenon Falls, and the rest of Whitefish Point is **Chippewa County International Airport** (CIU, 5019 Airport Dr., Kincheloe, 906/495-5631 or 800/225-2525, www.airciu.com), south of Sault Ste. Marie, which offers two daily flights from Detroit on Delta Airlines. You'll need to rent a car if you fly in because there's no public transportation to Paradise. Car rentals at the airport are by **Avis** (906/495-5900, www.avis.com). The drive to Paradise takes a little more than an hour via M-80 toward I-75 (follow the signs) and take I-75 north to M-28. Take M-28 west for 30 miles before you hit M-123, which will take you north to Whitefish Point.

Boat

The small **Whitefish Point State Dock** (906/492-3415, www.michigan.gov/dnr), near the tip of Whitefish Point at 46°45.32 N, 84°57.52 W, has only a handful of slips and limited amenities, but it's one of only two harbors between Grand Marais and Sault Ste. Marie. The other is **Little Lake State Dock** (906/658-3372, www.michigan.gov/dnr), about halfway between Grand Marais and Paradise at 46°43.06 N, 85°21.48 W and with even fewer amenities than Whitefish Point.

Sault Ste. Marie

At the foot of Whitefish Bay, mighty Lake Superior narrows to form the St. Mary's River, the waterway that links it to Lakes Huron, Michigan, and their counterparts to the south. Because Lake Superior is 21 feet higher than the other lakes, the St. Mary's River is a series of falls and rapids near Sault Ste. Marie. "Sault," pronounced "soo" and often used as a nickname for the city, means "Falling Water," a name bestowed by early French explorers.

Sault Ste. Marie is the U.P.'s second-largest city, with a population of 14,000. This historic place is well worth a visit, especially to view the boat traffic through the famous Soo Locks, which link Lakes Superior and Huron. But don't overlook the area to the south and

east, where the lovely blue-green waters of Lake Huron wrap around the end of the peninsula, a scalloped shoreline of quiet bays and a scattering of isolated and picturesque islands.

SIGHTS
Curtis Lewis Memorial Highway

The twisting, scenic **Curtis Lewis Memorial Highway,** also called Lake Shore Drive, follows the curve of Lake Superior's Whitefish Bay from M-123 east 20 miles or so to Sault Ste. Marie. It's almost an attraction in itself, passing through the eastern unit of the Hiawatha National Forest and offering views

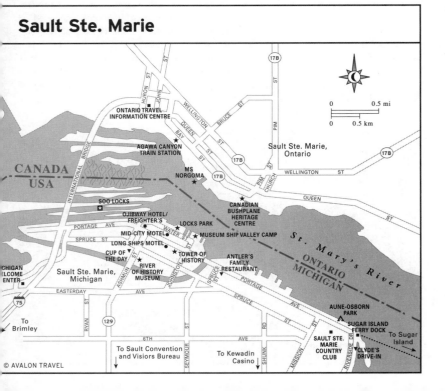

Sault Ste. Marie

© AVALON TRAVEL

of the far end of Lake Superior and a few other worthwhile stops.

Mission Hill Overlook is the kind of road where every view is better than the last. As the highway curves south, watch for the turn-off to the west marking this terrific overlook. Drive up the sand and gravel road for grand sweeping views of the river and bay, Ontario's Laurentian Mountains, the cityscape of Sault Ste. Marie, freighters that look like toy ships, the Point Iroquois light, and, just below, Spectacle Lake.

Four miles west of tiny Dollar Settlement, the federally run **Pendills Creek National Fish Hatchery** (21990 W. Trout Lane, 906/437-5231, www.fws.gov, Mon.-Fri., call for hours, fee) raises thousands of lake trout that grow up to tempt anglers in Lakes Superior, Michigan, and Huron. Visitors can wander around the tanks to peer down at the hundreds of wriggling trout fry and the breeder trout that weigh in at 15 pounds or more. The raceways are covered to keep birds and other predators at bay. Outdoor areas are also accessible on weekends.

Just beyond the Bay View campground, the **Big Pine Picnic Grounds,** a day-use area in the Hiawatha National Forest, is a wonderful spot to take a break. It offers a pleasant shaded area under a canopy of huge white pines and a pretty sand and pebble beach along Whitefish Bay.

Continuing east, don't miss the chance to climb the tower at the **Point Iroquois Light** (906/437-5272, hours vary, generally 9am-5pm daily May 15-Oct. 15), where Whitefish Bay narrows into the St. Mary's River. Since 1855 a beacon here has helped guide ships through this extremely difficult passage, where reefs lurk near the Canadian shore and the rock walls of Point Iroquois threaten on the U.S. side. In 1870, the original wooden light tower was replaced with the present one, a classic white-painted brick structure. A keeper's home was added in 1902.

With fewer and fewer lighthouses open to the public, it's fun to climb the iron spiral staircase for a freighter captain's view of the river, the bay, and the continuous shipping traffic. Stop in the adjacent light keeper's home, where the local historical society has restored some rooms to illustrate the life of a light keeper; other rooms feature displays and old photos. The lighthouse and adjacent beach are now part of the Hiawatha National Forest, which should help ensure its continued preservation.

The Soo Locks Boat Tour takes passengers through the American and Canadian locks.

The History of the Soo Locks

The St. Mary's Rapids have been an impediment to transportation for as long as people have lived in the area. Faced with a 20-foot drop on the way from Lake Superior to Lake Huron, the indigenous Ojibwa people would take their canoes out of the water and portage around the rapids. Early European settlers did the same until the fur trade and an increased European presence demanded ships too large to portage. They solved the problem by having two sets of ships, one on the Lake Superior side and one on the Lake Huron side. After reaching the Lake Superior Rapids, good would be unloaded and transported to ships waiting on the Lake Huron side. This proved to be a workable but inefficient solution.

The Northwest Fur Company built the first locks in the 1790s on the Canadian side of the river. Though small, at 38 feet, and they remained in use until being destroyed in the War of 1812, forcing a return to the old system.

The next locks weren't built until 1853-1855, when the Fairbanks Scale Company agreed to construct two locks in exchange for 250,000 acres of public land, which the company hoped to exploit for mining. The two 350-foot locks were turned over to state control upon completion. In 1881 demand for newer and larger facilities prompted a transfer to the United States Army Corps of Engineers, which continues to operate and maintain the locks today.

The locks are an amazing feat of engineering, consuming and enormous amount of power and requiring regular maintenance. To meet the challenge, the U.S. Hydroelectric Power Plant just south of the locks is part of the overall facility. The plant generates more than 150 million kilowatt-hours of electricity each year, with the locks receiving first priority. Any remaining electricity is distributed to Sault Ste. Marie, Michigan, and surrounding eastern U.P. communities.

Of the four locks—the Davis Lock, Sabin Lock, MacArthur Lock, and Poe Lock—the Poe Lock is the largest, and along with the MacArthur Lock sees the most use. Each is capable of handling large ships; the Poe Lock is 1,200 feet long and can take ships with up to 72,000 tons of cargo. Operations are quick, with each lock able to drain and fill in a matter of minutes. Some 10,000 ships pass through the locks each year despite their annual winter closure. During winter the Army Corps works on maintenance and repairs.

You can watch the daily operations of the Soo Locks from the visitors center, which lets you get fairly close to the massive freighters as they make their way along the St. Mary's River. You'll also find several informative displays about the history and operation of the locks. Try a trip through the locks with Soo Locks Boat Tours. On the last Friday in June, the Army Corps of Engineers host its **annual open house, known as "Engineer's Day"** (www.saultstemarie.com/soo-locks-engineers-day), which allows the public to see facilities that are normally off-limits.

★ Soo Locks

Nearly every visitor to the Soo makes a pilgrimage to the locks, right in the heart of downtown Sault Ste. Marie at the end of Ashmun Street (Business I-75). The city has smartly dressed up this area with lovely **Locks Park.** Blue freighter signs mark the **Locks Park Walkway,** which wanders along Water Street and is dotted with interpretive plaques that explain the city's heritage and other objects of historical interest. These include a former U.S. Weather Bureau Building, a Japanese torii (ceremonial gateway) and an obelisk commemorating the 1905 dedication of the Soo locks.

In the heart of this rather formal park, the U.S. Army Corps of Engineers manages the locks and a **visitors center** (906/253-9290, www.saultstemarie.com, 9am-9pm daily mid-May-mid-Oct.) next to a raised **viewing platform** that lets you see the locks in action. Start at the visitors center to get some background on how the locks work. A moving model shows how the locks raise and lower ships by opening and closing the gates of a lock chamber and allowing water to rush in or out. No pumps are required; the locks are gravity-fed, which means the water simply seeks its own level. Other displays explain the construction of the locks. A knowledgeable staff with a PA system, along with video cameras upriver, notify you about approaching vessels. In summer months, you can usually count on a ship coming through about once an hour. You can also call the visitors center to get the day's shipping schedule, but times can change depending on weather conditions and other factors.

It's easy to while away an hour or two watching the ships as they crawl through the locks with seemingly just inches to spare. Summer evenings are especially pleasant, when you'll likely have the platform to yourself to watch the illuminated ships. If you're lucky, you might see a "saltie," an oceangoing vessel that's likely hauling grain to foreign ports. Overall, the three most common Great Lakes shipments are iron ore for steelmaking; limestone, which is a purifying agent for steelmaking and also used in construction and papermaking; and coal for power plants.

The locks and viewing platform are open through the Great Lakes shipping season, March 25 to January 15. Those are the official dates when the locks terminate operations for winter maintenance. Ice buildup on Lake Superior often affects the length of the shipping season as well.

After viewing the locks, you can "lock through" yourself on the extremely popular **Soo Locks Boat Tour** (800/432-6301, www.soolocks.com, early May-mid-Oct., $29 adults, $12 ages 5-12). The two-hour trip takes you through both the American and Canadian locks and travels along both cities' waterfronts. Also offered are lunch, dinner, and various special cruises to see lighthouses, Fourth of July fireworks, etc. At busy times, you'll be in the midst of freighter traffic, dwarfed by their enormous steel hulls. The large passenger boats have both heated and open deck areas. Boats depart as early as 9am from two docks on Portage Avenue.

Museums

After you've watched the big Great Lakes boats, the **Museum Ship Valley Camp** (501 Water St., 906/632-3658 or 888/744-7867, www.saulthistoricsites.com, 9am-6pm Mon.-Sat., 10am-5pm Sun. mid-May-mid-Oct., longer hours July-Aug., $14 adults, $9 ages 6-16) gives you a chance to see what it was like to live and work aboard a giant steamer. This 550-foot steamship logged more than one million miles on the Great Lakes hauling ore, coal, and stone from 1907 to the mid-1970s. Now it's permanently docked five blocks east of the Soo Locks. Visitors can tour the pilothouse, engine room, main deck, crew quarters, coal bunker, and more. The ship has a number of aquariums and maritime displays, some better than others. The most popular is a display on the sinking of the *Edmund Fitzgerald,* including two tattered lifeboats found empty and drifting on the lake. All in all, it's well worth a couple of hours. Make sure to stop at the museum shop, housed in a separate building next to the parking lot. It has an excellent selection of maritime books and videos.

Like most observation towers, the **Tower of History** (326 Portage Ave., 906/632-3658, www.saulthistoricsites.com, 9:30am-5:30pm Mon.-Sat., 10am-5pm Sun. mid May-mid Oct., $7 adults, $3.50 ages 6-16), four blocks east of the Soo Locks, is an ugly blight on the landscape: a 21 story stark concrete monolith, but with a wonderful 360-degree view of the twin Soo locks, the St. Mary's River, Lake Superior, and forests rolling off in the distance. Rather than being stuck behind windows, you get to enjoy the views from an open-air deck. Bring a jacket, as it can get chilly. The tower also includes a few small exhibit areas and a theater showing documentary videos. Luckily, there is an elevator to the top. Interestingly, the tower was originally built as a bell tower for the neighboring church. Intended as part of a larger church complex, financial difficulties caused the project to be abandoned. In 1980 the tower was donated to Sault Historic Sites.

The **River of History Museum** (531

Ashmun St., 906/632-1999, www.riverofhistory.com, 11am-5pm Mon.-Sat. mid May-mid Oct., $7 adults, $3.50 ages 5-17) uses the St. Mary's River as the framework for telling the story of the region's history. Life-size dioramas depict things like Native Americans spear fishing in the rapids and a French fur trapper's cabin (the French were the first European settlers in the region). The museum incorporates lots of sound in its displays: dripping ice from melting glaciers, roaring rapids, Ojibwa elders passing down legends. One hopes this relatively new museum will keep building on this idea.

The Museum Ship Valley Camp, Tower of History, and River of History Museum can all be visited by purchasing a **combination ticket** (www.saulthistoricsites.com, $25.25 adults, $12 ages 5-17), providing a significant savings off the individual admission prices.

Lighthouses

Soo Locks Boat Tours (1157 E. Portage Ave. and 515 E. Portage Ave., 906/632-2512 or 800/432-6301, www.soolocks.com) offers the option of extending their popular locks tour with the **St. Mary's River Lighthouse Cruise** ($65 pp, free under age 4). After riding through the Soo Locks, you'll get a short tour of the St. Mary's River and a float-by of a number of picturesque lighthouses. See the unoccupied but intact keeper's residence at **Cedar Point** and the remains of the original light on **Round Island.** You'll cross into Canadian waters (there's no need for a passport) and see the **Gros Cap Reefs Lighthouse** and the **Point Louise Range Lights.** Morning departures include a continental breakfast and coffee, and box lunches are available with advance reservations. During the trip, you'll be able to see the **Point Iroquois Lighthouse** from the boat, but this one is worth going out of your way to visit on land.

Sault Ste. Marie, Ontario

Just across the International Bridge lies the Soo's sister city in Ontario, also named Sault Ste. Marie. With a population of 75,000, it's the larger of the two cities, with a more diversified economy, which includes a huge steel plant and a paper company. Aside from these industries, Sault Ste. Marie, Ontario, also has a great deal to offer visitors. Downtown, a lovely **boardwalk** rambles along the river for about a mile, beginning at the bridge and extending east past fishing platforms, shops, and the MS *Norgoma,* the last passenger cruise ship built for the Great Lakes, now a museum. On Wednesday and Saturday, there's a farmers market near the tented pavilion.

One of the most advertised and popular visitor attractions is the **Agawa Canyon Train Tour** (129 Bay St., 705/946-7300 or 800/242-9287, www.agawacanyontourtrain.com, once daily early June-mid-Oct., Sat.-Sun. Jan.-Mar., C$91 adults, C$81 over age 59, C$46 under age 19, free), a full-day (8am-6pm) round-trip through the scenic wooded gorge of the Agawa Canyon. The tour includes a two-hour stopover in the canyon, where you can hike to lookouts, visit waterfalls, wander along the river, or just enjoy the grassy picnic area. The train trip is even more popular (and slightly more expensive) in the fall color season, which usually runs mid-September to mid-October, and in winter, when it is known as the Snow Train (the two-hour layover is eliminated during the winter trip). Tours depart at 8am from the station; reservations are recommended.

As in Alaska, bush planes are an integral part of life in the wilds of the Canadian north. A small plane with pontoons can get you where no land vehicle can, since almost any remote lake can serve as a landing strip. The **Canadian Bushplane Heritage Centre** (50 Pim St., 705/945-6242 or 877/287-4752, www.bushplane.com, 9am-6pm daily mid-May-mid-Oct., 10am-4pm daily mid-Oct.-mid-May, C$12 adults, C$11 seniors, C$7 students, C$3 children), near Pim and Bay Streets on the waterfront, chronicles the history of Canada's bush planes, which began with the Ontario Air Service in the 1920s and was established to fight forest fires. Even if you're not an aviation buff, you'll enjoy this unique museum, housed in the Air Service's old waterfront hangar.

You can reach Ontario via the three-mile-long **International Bridge** (934 Bridge Plaza, 906/635-5255 U.S., 705/942-4345 Canada, www.saultbridge.com, toll $3.50/C$4.60 one-way). You can exchange money and pick up maps and other useful area information at the **Ontario Travel Information Centre** (705/945-6941, www.ontariotravel.net) at the foot of the bridge. Documentation required to enter Canada is proof of citizenship, typically a passport. To reenter the United States after visiting Canada you need either a valid passport or an Enhanced Drivers License issued by one of the states that participates in the Western Hemisphere Travel Initiative (WHTI).

ENTERTAINMENT
Bay Mills Resort and Casino
Bay Mills Casino (11386 W. Lakeshore Dr., Brimley, 877/229-6455 or 888/422-9645, www.baymillscasinos.com) offers the usual gaming standbys—blackjack, roulette, craps, three-card poker, Texas hold 'em, and more. It also has something that few other U.P. casinos provide: free alcoholic drinks while actively gaming. If that's not enough to bring you to their doors, there are more than 1,000 slot and video poker machines and Royal Ascot video horse racing. You'll also find several varied dining options. Black Bay Grille and Games is located right on the waterfront, Sacy's Restaurant offers a fine dining environment, and there are also two lounges and a café. Bring your clubs for a round of golf (you can also rent some from the pro shop), or stay the night in the hotel, with 140-plus rooms.

Brimley's other casino, **Kings Club Casino** (12140 W. Lakeshore Dr., Brimley, 10am-midnight Sun. and Wed.-Thurs., 10am-2am Fri.-Sat.), is actually part of the Bay Mills Resort. Shuttle service is offered between the two casinos. Unlike may gaming venues, Kings Club is not open 24 hours. Kings Club is one story and has more than 280 slot and video poker machines. That's a far cry from the casino's beginning, when Kings Club was the first Native American-operated blackjack casino in the country and the first in Michigan to offer slots and keno.

FESTIVALS AND EVENTS
International 500 Snowmobile Race
The **International 500 Snowmobile Race** (www.i-500.com) has been held in Sault Ste. Marie since 1969. Forty years ago, the I-500 was conceived as a snowmobiling version of the Indianapolis 500. The 500 miles are handled by a team of drivers, although someone will occasionally go it alone, on a one-mile iced track, while Sno-Cross races are held concurrently at the same venue. Races are usually held in early February, after several warm-up events.

International Bridge Walk
The **International Bridge Walk** is held each summer on the last Saturday of June as a symbol of friendship between two cities and two nations. It's similar to the annual Labor Day walk across the Mackinac Bridge, except that the 2.8-mile walk is about half the distance, and you actually get to stroll into Canada. Be sure to bring your passport or Enhanced Drivers License.

SUMMER SPORTS AND RECREATION
Hiking and Biking
West of town, the **Algonquin Pathway** has more than nine miles of trails for hiking and biking and, in the winter, cross-country skiing. Two miles of the path are lighted. Take I-75 to 3-Mile Road and head west, turn right on 20th Street and left on 16th Avenue to the trailhead. Another good spot is the **Pine Bowl Pathway,** 19 miles southwest of Sault Ste. Marie. Pine Bowl has nearly eight miles of trails and rolling terrain. To get here, take I-75 south to the Kinross/Tone Road exit and head east on Tone Road, then turn right onto Wilson Road.

You'll be able to find some good trails at a number of area campgrounds. **Monocle Lake Campground** (Forest Rd. 3699, 906/635-5311), in Hiawatha National Forest 21 miles west of Sault Ste. Marie and near the Point Iroquois Light, has an inviting two-mile loop accessible from its day-use parking lot. A viewing platform overlooks an active beaver pond before the trail heads uphill to another overlook, which has views to the St. Mary's River and beyond, before returning to the parking lot.

At **Soldier Lake Campground** (Forest Rd. 3138, 906/635-5311), in Hiawatha National Forest 30 miles west of the city, there's a footpath that winds its way around the 15-acre lake and a spur that connects to the North Country Trail. Slightly farther out, 38 miles west of Sault Ste. Marie and a few miles south of M-28 in Hiawatha National Forest, **Three Lakes Campground** (Forest Rd. 3142) has an easy one-mile loop around Walker Lake.

Fishing

Sault Ste. Marie is uniquely positioned for some of the Upper Peninsula's finest fishing. With Lake Superior above and Huron below, the Soo sits on the wide ribbon of the St. Mary's River that links the two and offers the chance to snag walleye, perch, pike, trout, salmon, and, of course, whitefish. Contact the **Sault Ste. Marie Convention and Visitors Bureau** (225 E. Portage Ave., 906/632-3366 or 800/647-2858, www.saultstemarie.com) for more detailed information and a peak fishing guide.

For inland lake fishing, try a visit to **Monocle Lake,** a 172-acre inland lake with walleye, smallmouth bass, pike, and perch. The lake is 40 to 45 feet deep and has two reefs near Hiawatha National Forest's **Monocle Lake Campground** (Forest Rd. 3699, 906/635-5311). There's a boat launch between the campground and the day-use area. **Soldier Lake Campground** (Forest Rd. 3138, 906/635-5311) is on the shores of a much smaller 15-acre lake in Hiawatha National Forest, with bass and perch for the catching. Consider **Lake George** and **Munuscong Lake** as well.

Captain Harold Bailey runs **Blue Heron Fishing Charters** (11589 E. Village Rd., 906/635-5134 or 906/632-1775, www.blue-heronfishingcharters.com, Apr.-Nov., day trip $300, $55 per additional person). His qualifications are stellar: He's a local fisherman with more than 40 years' experience on the St. Mary's River and surrounding waters.

trail marker on the North Country Trail near Soldier Lake Campground

Captain Bailey will provide all the equipment you need, or bring your own, but you'll be responsible for bringing your lunch and, more importantly, a Michigan fishing license. An Ontario license, although not totally necessary, is also a good idea. **River Cove Fishing Charters** (2841 Riverside Dr., 906/632-7075, www.rivercove.com, half-day $280, full-day $390, night $250) offers charters as well as night fishing for walleye. Bait and all equipment are provided.

Boating

In addition to fishing charters, **River Cove** (2871 Riverside Dr., 906/632-7075, www.rivercove.com) can take up to five passengers on a scenic boat cruise. Choose from Soo Harbor and the north end of Sugar Island ($250), Neebish Island Cut/St. Joseph Island Iron Bridge ($275), and a sunset Soo Harbor cruise ($250). Rates may vary depending on fuel costs. You can get scenic dinner cruises from **Soo Locks Boat Tours** (1157 E. Portage Ave. and 515 E. Portage Ave., 906/632-6301 or 800/432-6301, www.soolocks.com, 5:50pm Fri.-Wed., $58 adults, $35 ages 3-12), departing from Dock 1. After the dinner buffet and dessert, you'll experience what it's like to travel through the impressive Soo Locks.

Golf

The 18 holes at the **Sault Ste. Marie Country Club** (1520 Riverside Dr., 906/632-7812, http://saultstemariecc.com, $20 for 9 holes, $39 for 18 holes, includes cart) are among the choicest of the Upper Peninsula, and some of the oldest as well. The course opened more than 100 years ago and was expanded into an 18-hole course in the 1980s. Visit the pro shop or have an evening dinner at Fairway's Restaurant and Lounge, located in the clubhouse. Take Portage Avenue east out of the city to the country club.

There are another 18 holes at **Tanglewood Marsh** (2600 W. 16th Ave., 906/635-0617 or 906/635-7651, www.tanglewoodmarsh.com, $19 for 9 holes, $34 for 18 holes, includes cart). Take I-75 to exit 392 and head west on 3-Mile

Road. Turn right on 20th Street and left on Oak Street, then curve right on 16th Avenue to the clubhouse.

Brimley has one of the U.P.'s top-rated golf courses at Brimley's **Wild Bluff Golf Course** (11335 W. Lakeshore Dr., 906/248-5860 or 888/422-9645, www.wildbluff.com, $40 for 9 holes, $70 for 18 holes, includes cart), which is part of the Bay Mills Resort. The 18-hole championship course received an impressive 4.5 stars from *Golf Digest,* and it's easy to see why. A fine pro shop and an elegant player's lounge complete the golf experience.

Bird-Watching

Like Whitefish Point, the Sault Ste. Marie area is a popular spot for bird-watching. Among the best places to scout for avian life is **Sugar Island,** the large island east of Sault Ste. Marie between Michigan and Ontario. The 15-mile-long island and the St. Mary's River both attract migratory birds, particularly snowy and great gray owls. Both the Little Traverse Conservatory and the Osburn Preserve, which is owned by the University of Michigan Biological Station, help conserve and preserve the island's wildlife and make the southern part of the island a great place for bird-watching. Look for spruce grouse, black terns, sedge wrens, and long-eared owls.

Beaches

One of the finest beaches in the area is on the edge of **Monocle Lake** (906/635-5311, www.fs.fed.us) in Hiawatha National Forest, 20 miles west of Sault Ste. Marie on Lake Shore Drive. The large lake makes for some great swimming, certainly better than chilly Lake Superior. This swimming area is easily accessible from the day-use parking area and is equipped with grills and picnic tables. To get here, take the Whitefish Bay National Scenic Byway (Lake Shore Dr.) as it follows the shoreline west of St. Ignace to Forest Road 3699. If you're determined to swim in Lake Superior, head over to **Brimley State Park** (9200 W. 6-Mile Rd., 906/248-3422, www.michigan.gov/dnr) on the shores of Whitefish Bay. The water here tends to be among Lake Superior's warmest.

Off-Road Vehicles

Off-road trails are scarce in this area. The only one in Chippewa County is the 29-mile **Kinross Motorcycle Trail,** about 20 miles south of Sault Ste. Marie near Kinross and the Chippewa County International Airport. As its name implies, the trail is open only to motorcycles. The trail's three main loops all extend from a central parking area. Take Tone Road east from I-75 to Wilson Road and turn right to the parking area. Although there are no other designated trails in the county, all state forest roads are open to off-road vehicles unless specifically marked otherwise. More than 2,000 miles of roads in the Hiawatha National Forest are open to ATV/ORV use. For motor vehicle usage maps and more information, contact the **Sault Ste. Marie Ranger District** (4000 I-75 Business Spur, 906/635-5311, www.fs.fed.us).

WINTER SPORTS AND RECREATION
Ski and Snowshoe Trails

On the west side of the city, the trails at the **Algonquin Pathway** offer cross-country skiers a series of loops that total nine miles, with the longest two-mile loop illuminated for night skiing. To get here, take I-75 to 3-Mile Road, then head west to 20th Street and turn right. Take 20th Street to the intersection with 16th Avenue.

The **Pine Bowl Pathway** is about 20 miles southwest of the city and has nearly eight miles of groomed trails. To get to Pine Bowl from Sault Ste. Marie, head south on I-75 to the Kinross/Tone Road exit (exit 378) and take Tone Road east to Wilson Road; turn right on Wilson to the pathway.

Downhill Skiing

You could go to **Sault Seal Recreation Area** (2601 Minneapolis St., 906/635-6961, www.saultcity.com, 3pm-9pm Tues.-Fri., noon-9pm Sat.-Sun., adults $10, children $6) for

some downhill skiing, but the big draw here is tubing, with seven downhill runs. If you're looking for better skiing, head elsewhere in the U.P., or consider crossing the border into Canada for the **Searchmont Resort** (103 Searchmont Resort Rd., Searchmont, 705/781-2340 or 800/663-2546, www.searchmont.com) in Ontario. Either option will require several hours of driving.

Snowmobiling

The main drags into and out of Sault Ste. Marie by snowmobile are **Trail 8,** which heads west and north to Whitefish Point, Manistique, and Marquette, and **Trail 49,** which drops south toward Les Cheneaux before connecting to the rest of the Upper Peninsula's network of trails. In the city itself, Trails 8, 49, and others (449 and 497) run parallel to many of the streets. After crossing Power Canal near the Soo Locks, you must stay on the trail or risk a fine.

FOOD

Start your day at **Cup of the Day** (406 Ashmun St., 906/635-7272, www.cupoftheday.com, 7:15am-5pm Mon. and Fri., 7:15am-6pm Tues.-Thurs., 8:15am-3pm Sat., under $10) for good coffee drinks, a juice bar, and sandwiches and salads at lunchtime. In the Ojibway Hotel, ★ **Freighters** (240 Portage Ave., 906/632-4211, www.ojibwayhotel.com, breakfast 8am-11am Mon.-Fri., 8am-noon Sat., 8am-1pm Sun., lunch 11am-2pm Mon.-Sat., noon-2pm Sun., dinner 2pm-10pm Mon., Wed., and Fri.-Sat., 2pm-9pm Tues. and Sun., $14-29) offers a wall of glass overlooking the locks and a very nice menu featuring steaks and seafood, with an emphasis on local fish. This is also a great spot for breakfast.

For an old fashioned "service at your car" burger place, cruise on over to ★ **Clyde's Drive-In** (1425 Riverside Dr., 906/632-2581, 9am-10pm daily, under $10), at the Sugar Island ferry dock, for the great grilled hamburgers they've been making since 1949. Inside, seating and a menu of other fried items are also available. **Antler's Family**

Restaurant (804 E. Portage Ave., 906/253-1728, www.saultantlers.com, from 11am daily, $8-26) serves up burgers, ribs, fresh fish, steaks, and Mexican-style dishes in a setting with more than 300 game head mounts. Don't go when you have a headache—they have a strange habit of setting off sirens and whistles for no particular reason. Kids will naturally love this place.

ACCOMMODATIONS

Now part of the Ramada chain, the rather plush ★ **Ojibway Hotel** (240 W. Portage Ave., 906/632-4100 or 800/654-2929, www.ojibwayhotel.com, $149-225) has the nicest accommodations in town and the best location, overlooking the St. Mary's River and the locks. For the very best view, ask for an upper level room facing north. The elegant 1928 building has been beautifully restored, with large rooms, an indoor pool, a whirlpool, and the enjoyable Freighters restaurant. Ask about packages for a better deal.

For the same good location but for less money, try the ★ **Long Ships Motel** (427 W. Portage Ave., 906/632-2422 or 888/690-2422, www.longshipsmotel.com, $70-95), a clean and comfortable independent motel with a fine spot across from Locks Park. A little farther east but still within walking distance of the river and downtown is the **Mid-City Motel** (304 E. Portage Ave., 906/632-6832, $55-70).

Much of Sault Ste. Marie's lodging is gradually transitioning to chain establishments, which tends to boost the number of available beds (good for tourism), but sacrifices the charm and uniqueness of the old mom-and-pop independents. Currently the Soo area has the highest concentration of chains in the eastern U.P., as it is the region's largest city and most popular tourist draw. Most, however, are not within walking distance of the locks.

Camping

Right in Sault Ste. Marie, there's a modern 65 site municipal campground at **Aune-Osborn Park** (1225 Riverside Dr., 906/632-3268, www.sault-sainte-marie.mi.us) on the St. Mary's River near the Sugar Island ferry dock. Just east of Brimley, **Brimley State Park** (906/248-3422, www.michigan.gov/dnr) offers about a mile of sandy Lake Superior beach and a large modern campground. It's a good choice for anyone looking for an easy place to set up camp to enjoy the Soo and other nearby attractions. Although it's just a campground, Brimley is a popular park, so consider making reservations if you're aiming for a summer weekend. For a little more seclusion, head farther west to the **Hiawatha National Forest** (906/635-5311, www.fs.fed.us). Within 30 minutes' drive of the Soo, you can find pretty and private tent sites next to the Lake Superior shore at Bay View, or near the great fishing point at Monocle Lake. Reservations are not possible.

INFORMATION AND SERVICES

For more information on the Sault Ste. Marie area, contact the **Sault Ste. Marie Convention and Visitors Bureau** (536 Ashmun St., 906/632-3366 or 800/647-2858, www.saultstemarie.com). For regional information and maps, stop by the **Michigan Welcome Center** (943 Portage Ave. W., 906/632-8242, 8am-4:30am daily) near the International Bridge.

When you plan to **cross the border** to enter or leave the United States, make sure you have a passport, a passport card, or another travel document that's compatible with the Western Hemisphere Travel Initiative (this can include an Enhanced Drivers License, U.S. military ID with military travel orders, or a Native American Tribal Photo ID). For a complete list of acceptable documents, visit the U.S. Department of State's travel website (http://travel.state.gov), but for most visitors it's as simple as a passport and, for foreign visitors, a passport from your country of citizenship along with a visa or visa waiver. You'll be stopped at the border crossing and asked to show your documents, followed by a few simple questions. Make sure you're prepared and respond truthfully and respectfully. Refrain from making any kind of humorous remark to the customs agents. They're instructed to take everything a traveler says seriously.

There are a few situations when things can get a bit more complicated. Be prepared to declare all goods, particularly items purchased or left abroad (gifts) and any firearms you're carrying. You'll be required to pay duty on larger amounts of certain items: wine and liquor (more than 40 ounces), beer (more than 23 cans or bottles), and cigarettes (more than 200). If you're traveling with children and are not their parent or legal guardian, you'll need to have a letter from their parents or guardian giving their permission to leave the United States and enter Canada with their child. If the child is a naturalized U.S. citizen you'll also need her or his U.S. Certificate of Citizenship. Make certain a contact phone number is included. For more information, contact **U.S. Customs and Border Protection** (906/632-7221, www.cbp.gov) or **Canada Border Services Agency** (204/983-3500, www.cbsa-asfc.gc.ca).

Medical care in Sault Ste. Marie is readily available. For more than a century, **War Memorial Hospital** (500 Osborn Blvd., 906/635-4460, www.warmemorialhospital.org) has been providing the eastern Upper Peninsula with quality health care. To get there, take Ashmun Street to Spruce Street and head west to the hospital.

You won't have a problem finding banks or ATMs in Sault Ste. Marie. Two large national institutions are located on Ashmun Street, just south of Portage Avenue: **Huntington Bank** (511 Ashmun St., 906/635-5251, www.huntington.com) and **PNC Bank** (3398 I-75 Business Spur., 906/635-1112, www.pnc.com). There are several other banks near the Soo's waterfront, including **First Merit Bank** (501 Court St., 906/632-6888, www.firstmerit.com) and **Central Savings Bank** (511 Bingham Ave., 906/635-6250, www.centralsavings-bank.com).

GETTING THERE AND AROUND

Car

If you're coming north over the Mackinac Bridge from the Lower Peninsula, Sault Ste. Marie is a short, easy 45-minute drive on I-75. If you're going to Portage Avenue and downtown, get off at exit 394 and turn left onto Easterday Avenue. Take the next right, onto Eureka Street, which quickly becomes Portage Avenue and takes you along the riverfront to the locks. There's a very helpful visitor information center as soon as you turn onto Eureka Street. Stop here for maps, brochures, and additional information.

Exit 394 is the last before the border crossing. If you don't get off here, you'll soon find yourself on the International Bridge crossing into Canada. Make sure you have your passport or other travel documents. If you're entering the United States from Canada, King's Highway 17 (the Trans-Canada Highway) will get you to the International Bridge.

If you're arriving from the western Upper Peninsula, take M-28 to I-75, then follow I-75 north to Sault Ste. Marie.

Air

The closest commercial airport is **Chippewa County International Airport** (CIU, 5019 Airport Dr., Kincheloe, 906/495-5631 or 800/225-2525, www.airciu.com) in Kinross, about 20 miles south of Sault Ste. Marie. Scheduled flights run daily from Detroit on Delta Airlines, and car rentals are available from **Avis** (906/495-5900, www.avis.com).

Boat

There are two marinas in Sault Ste. Marie: the **Charles T. Harvey Marina** (2442 Riverside Dr., 906/632-6741, www.michigan.gov/dnr), located on the lower St. Mary's River with more than 30 boat slips and the usual amenities: electricity, water, showers, and pump-out service. It is located at 46°28.15 N, 84°18.00 W. The harbormaster can be reached on channel 9.

The **George Kemp Marina** (485 E. Water

St., 906/635-7670, www.michigan.gov/dnr). is in downtown Sault Ste. Marie. It has more than 50 slips with electricity, water, showers, and pump-out service. Kemp Marina is located at 46°29.57 N, 84°20.21 W. The harbormaster can be reached on channel 9.

Bus and Shuttle

To get to Sault Ste. Marie on public transportation from elsewhere in the United States, **Indian Trails** (989/725-5105 or 800/292-3831, www.indiantrails.com) has regular service to the Sault. Call for current schedules and rates, or use the convenient fare finder tool on the website. You can also access the **Mackinaw Shuttle** (888/349-8294, www.mackinawshuttle.com) if you're already in Northern Michigan.

The Huron Shore

East of I-75, the Upper Peninsula narrows into a series of smaller peninsulas, points, and islands in Lake Huron. The area has a simple, pretty, and tranquil feel, the kind of place where casual cycling, beachcombing, and picnicking set the pace for a summer day. While there's plenty to explore for the casual time-rich visitor, there are few true destinations. In fact, the whole area is often overlooked by guidebooks, which suits the locals and summer cottage owners just fine. So don't get too excited about sightseeing; just pack a lunch, put on a pair of comfortable shoes, and while away the day along a rocky shoreline.

SIGHTS
DeTour Village

DeTour Village marks the end of the road and the end of the Upper Peninsula mainland. This small village has long served an important navigational role for ships heading up and down the St. Mary's River. Many ships squeeze through DeTour Passage, the narrow waterway between the point and Drummond Island. They make a turn, or detour, to chart a course from the St. Mary's River to the Straits of Mackinac. DeTour Village is a very old community that has guided ships with its navigational light since 1848. It remains a pleasant place to watch the ship traffic from public parks and gardens along M-134.

Nearby Lime Island marks the centerpiece of the **Island Explorer Water Trail,** a boating route that travels from Lime to Mackinac Island along a linked network of islands. For more information, contact the **DeTour Area Chamber of Commerce** (625 N. Ontario St., 906/297-5987). You can also stay at cabins and cottages on state forest land on Lime Island. For more information on rates and availability, contact the **Sault Ste. Marie Forest Management Unit** (906/635-5281, www. michigan.gov/dnr).

★ Drummond Island

Here's a trivia question: What's the largest U.S. island in the Great Lakes? Probably few would guess Drummond, a quiet, low key type of place. Some 65 percent of Drummond Island is state-owned land. The rest is owned mostly by summer residents, who swell the island's population to about 5,000 in July and August—but you'd never know it. Life on this idyllic island is geared toward fishing, so most residents cluster along the shorelines, although these cloistered places can rarely be seen from the island's few roads.

With rocky shorelines, inland lakes, marshy lowlands, hardwood forests, and open meadows, Drummond Island boasts remarkably diverse animal and plant habitats. More than 24 different kinds of orchids grow wild on the island. Loons, bobcats, moose, and a pack of wolves all roam here along with more common species.

Drummond and its neighboring islands are actually above-ground deposits of limestone, part of the Niagara escarpment that stretches

Drummond Island

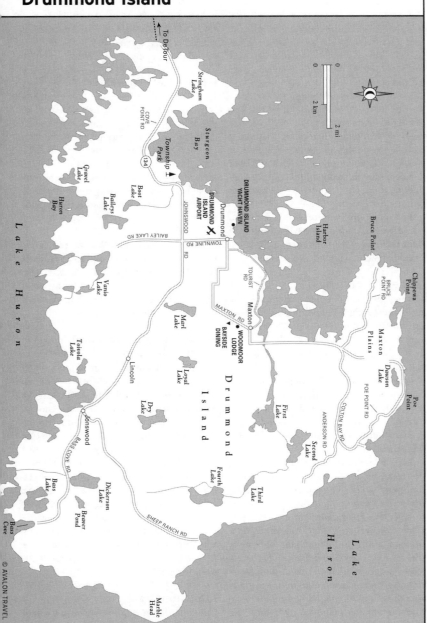

© AVALON TRAVEL

from Door County, Wisconsin, and across northern Lake Michigan. In an area called the Maxton Plains at the island's north end, this slab of limestone bedrock lies near the surface, covered by just a thin layer of alkaline soil. This unusual combination supports one of the world's foremost examples of alvar grassland, a rare mix of Arctic tundra and Great Plains plants, including Hill's thistle, false pennyroyal, and prairie dropseed. The Nature Conservancy owns more than 800 acres of the Maxton Plains. The preserve is open to the public, so you can explore this moon-like landscape where large boulders of conglomerate flecked with red jasper, called puddingstone, punctuate the barren expanses of limestone bedrock.

For more information on Drummond Island, call the **Drummond Island Tourism Association** (906/493-5245 or 800/737-8666, www.drummondislandchamber.com).

★ Les Cheneaux

"The Snows," everyone calls them, though the real name for these islands is Les Cheneaux (lay shen-O), French for "The Channels." And there are channels aplenty. Like shards of glass, 36 long and narrow islands lie splintered just off the U.P.'s southeastern shore, forming a maze of calm channels and protected bays in northern Lake Huron. Not surprisingly, it's a delight for boaters. Tall sailboats, small runabouts, classic cabin cruisers, and simple canoes all share these waters, as they have for more than a century.

Les Cheneaux first attracted boaters in the 1880s for the area's renowned fishing. Early enthusiasts came here from nearby Mackinac Island, already a popular vacation getaway for the wealthy. At first, these resort dwellers from Mackinac arrived on daylong excursions. Before long, they built their own cottages to revel in the solitude not found in the other Great Lakes resort areas. Because its summer guests were predominantly wealthy industrialists from southern Michigan, Indiana, Illinois, and Iowa, Les Cheneaux maintained a tactful, understated

style. Cottages were elegant but not ostentatious. Boats were sleek but not showy.

The islands of Les Cheneaux still maintain that genteel simple air. If you're the kind of person who doesn't want or need to be entertained, you'll enjoy this charming area, free of crass commercialism. Nautical pastimes rule here, but in proper Les Cheneaux style, they rarely take the form of a powerboat or a screaming Jet Ski. Boating here is best exemplified by the amazing array of classic wooden craft you'll see puttering and purring through the channels. The nation's first (and now oldest) Chris Craft franchise was founded in Hessel in 1926. Many of those early boats survive today thanks to the area's crystal-clear water, the short boating season, and careful maintenance, which all help preserve the tender wooden hulls.

"Life is Better with Water," proclaims the website of the **Les Cheneaux Islands Area Tourist Association** (670 W. M-134, Cedarville, 888/364-7526, http://lescheneaux. org). For detailed information about this idyllic place, a visit here is a must.

Harbor Island National Wildlife Refuge

About 1.5 miles off the shore of Drummond Island, the comparatively small **Harbor Island National Wildlife Refuge** is far enough to be remote, but still close enough that it isn't hard to get to. You can access the 695-acre island by private boat. Some popular recreational activities include offshore fishing and hunting. There's also a small swimming beach. Wildlife includes foxes, snowshoe hares, grouse, and sparrows. During the winter the refuge has been known to welcome timber wolves from Ontario's nearby St. Joseph Island. The refuge is managed by **Seney National Wildlife Refuge** (1674 Refuge Entrance Rd., Seney, 906/586-9851, www.fws.gov).

Lighthouses

Lighthouse lovers won't want to miss a tour of **DeTour Reef Light Station,** over 80 feet tall and listed on the National Register of Historic Places. Stationed between Drummond Island and the village of DeTour, the 1931 light underwent extensive restoration and reopened for tours in 2005. It's a bold, boxy lighthouse, with sharp lines that seem suited to the job of warning ships of the dangerous reef below the surface. The **DeTour Reef Light Preservation Society** (906/493-6303 June-Aug., 616/874-9458 Jan.-May, www.drlps.com) arranges tours of the lighthouse (Sat. in summer, advance reservations required, $100 nonmembers, $80 members). The two-hour tour, limited to six people, begins with a boat ride to the light, then climbs a 20-foot ladder and continues through the lighthouse and to the top of the watch room.

★ Great Lakes Boat Building School

It might seem almost natural, given the strong boating tradition of the Les Cheneaux area, that the community is home to a highly regarded school devoted to boat construction. Housed in a handsome boathouse-style building, the **Great Lakes Boat Building School** (485 S. Meridian St., Cedarville, 906/484-1081, www.glbbs.org) teaches students in their choice of a one- or two-year program in traditional wooden boat construction. Those continuing to the second year take on the project of assembling a yacht, including the interior and all mechanical systems. This fascinating school offers free public tours (10am and 2pm Mon.-Fri. year-round), an excellent way to learn about the area's nautical traditions. The 1.5-hour tour is led by a senior faculty member and offers visitors the opportunity to see students at work. The guide is able to answer questions, which tend to be rather numerous.

ENTERTAINMENT
Kewadin Casino

The eastern U.P. seems to have a high density of casinos. There are gaming parlors in St. Ignace, Sault Ste. Marie, Christmas, Brimley, and elsewhere, all within a couple of hours of Les Cheneaux and Drummond Island. But that hasn't stopped the small **Kewadin Casino** (3395 N. 3-Mile Rd., Hessel, 906/484-2903) from opening in Hessel. Gaming is limited to slots and some blackjack. There are no hotel rooms, and a deli is the best among the casino's few amenities.

a wooden boat built at the Great Lakes Boat Building School

Photographing Wildlife

If you're traveling the Upper Peninsula at a more leisurely pace and have an interest in photography, you may want to dedicate a day or more to testing your skills in the field—and possibly be rewarded with a few compelling wildlife images. The Upper Peninsula is home to many four-legged subjects, including moose, elk, and white-tailed deer. Look to the sky to snap a shot of a migratory bird of prey; bald eagles, hawks, and ospreys all abound.

What you'll need: Obtaining a quality image requires two essentials: the proper gear and a good deal of patience. Since wildlife shots are normally taken from a considerable distance, a good SLR camera equipped with a telephoto lens of at least 300 mm is a must. To avoid blurred images from camera shake, a tripod or some object on which to steady the camera and lens is also something you should include.

Where to go: Some of the best locations include the Seney National Wildlife Refuge near Seney, the Refuge's Whitefish Point unit, and within the Hiawatha National Forest.

What to do: Arrive at your intended viewing destination at an early hour—at daybreak if possible—and choose a spot close to where your intended subject is most likely to appear (near tall trees for birds of prey, alongside an inland lake or pond for moose or waterfowl). When setting up your equipment, set your aperture and shutter speed in advance. Take frequent meter readings to guard against images that are either blown out or too dark. Finally, do your absolute best to remain quiet and remain alert. Good luck!

FESTIVALS AND EVENTS

During the second weekend of August, Hessel is home to the **Les Cheneaux Islands Antique Wooden Boat Show** (906/484-2821, http://lciboatshow.com, $7 adults, free under age 12) believed to be the largest such show in the country, featuring more than 100 wooden-hulled vessels. Wooden boat owners and aficionados from around the country show up in the small U.P. town to celebrate wooden boats of all types. The boat show takes place in conjunction with **The Festival of Arts,** so even if you're not interested in wooden boats, there's plenty to do; browse the vendor booths in search of handmade crafts and artwork. For information, contact the **Les Cheneaux Historical Association** (906/484-2821, www.lchistorical.org).

SUMMER SPORTS AND RECREATION
Hiking and Biking

A mountain bike is a fun way to explore Drummond Island, since M-134 dissolves into a variety of double-tracks and, eventually, single-track roads. Don't expect technical riding, as the island is quite flat. When you venture into state land, you'll likely end up sharing some of the designated DNR trails with ATVs, which can be both irritating and potentially dangerous. But with 76 miles of trail, you're sure to find stretches with little or no traffic. For specific trails, ask about **Marble Head View Point** as well as **Warners Cove** and **Gravel Lake** on the south shore. Trail information is available from the **Drummond Island Tourism Association** (906/493-5245 or 800/737-8666, www.drummondislandchamber.com).

An eastern Upper Peninsula road biking map is available from the Michigan Department of Transportation or from the **Les Cheneaux Tourist Association** (670 W. M-134, Cedarville, 888/364-7526, www.lescheneaux.org). The map highlights major biking roads in the area, including Hessel, Cedarville, DeTour, and other cities. It also offers advice on traffic levels, shoulder width, and other issues of concern to bikers. For mountain bikers, there are plenty of double-tracks, trails, and back roads. You can get detailed information from the visitors center on the island, located at the corner of M-134 and Townline Road.

Canoeing and Kayaking

A canoe or kayak is a great way to explore the waters of Les Cheneaux. The fjord-like bays and 150 miles of ragged shoreline make this a magical place to paddle. One of the best routes to take is the **North Lake Huron Paddle Trail,** which extends for some 75 miles from DeTour nearly to St. Ignace, passing among the islands of Les Cheneaux on the way. It's best to get a guide while paddling the islands, since the ins and outs of the waterways make it easy to get lost. For kayak tours, rentals, and advice, pay a visit to **Woods and Waters Ecotours** (20 Pickford Ave., 906/484-4157, www.woodswaterecotours.com), an outfitter and guide company in Hessel. Guided day trips of the North Lake Huron Paddle Trail are offered, as well as half-day, full-day, and sunset kayak trips. Custom tours can also be arranged.

Fishing

Anglers aren't going to spend much time in Les Cheneaux before the channels start calling. It's easy to see why. This is a place unlike any other. Book a fishing charter with **Island Charters** (117 N. Greenwood Dr., Cedarville, 906/235-3825, http://islandchartersmi.com, half-day $450, full-day $800, tours available). You can also arrange for a half-day or full-day expedition with **Dreamseaker Charters and Tours** (888/634-3419, www.dreamseaker. com, half-day $600).

One of the popular spots for inland fishing is **Munuscong River State Forest** (906/635-5281, www.michigan.gov/dnr), where you can cast at the river for walleye, pike, bass, and perch, or head one mile east to Lake Munuscong for more fishing. For additional fishing spots and information about fishing seasons, contact the **Les Cheneaux Islands Tourist Association** (670 W. M-134, Cedarville, 888/364-7526, www.lescheneaux. org).

Boating

The best way to see Les Cheneaux, of course, is to get out on the water. Aside from the pretty wooded islands, part of the fun is eyeing the beautiful old boathouses that dot the shorelines, especially on Marquette Island. If you have your own craft, you'll find launches in Hessel and Cedarville, the only two towns in the area. Though the waters are protected and normally quite safe, be sure to bring a chart, or at least a map provided by local businesses. The various bays, channels, and points can be rather confusing. Many cottages rent boats or include them in their rates.

Golf

For such a mellow place as Drummond Island, you might be surprised to run across **The Rock** (33494 S. Maxton Rd., 906/493-1000 or 800/999-6343, www.drummondisland. com/golf, $59-69 for 18 holes), a spectacular designer golf course completed in 1990. The first-rate course makes fine use of the natural environment, its holes weaving through woods and limestone outcroppings. In 2008 The Rock earned a four-star rating from *Golf Digest* as part of the magazine's "Best Places to Play." Contact The Rock for specials and packages.

The nine-hole **Les Cheneaux Club Golf Club** (1407 Golf Links Rd., 906/484-3606, www.lescheneauxgolfclub.com, $15 for 9 holes, $21 for 18 holes, $7-14 pp gas-powered cart) in Cedarville is the oldest still playable and continuously played links in Michigan. It was first played in May 1898 on natural forest, sand, water, and rock. In Hessel, try the **Hessel Ridge Golf Course** (2061 N. 3-Mile Rd., 888/660-9166, www.hesselridge.com, $22 for 9 holes, $38 for 18 holes, includes cart, reduced rates after 3pm). The 18-hole, 6,415-yard course is located on a ridge overlooking Hessel, with tree-lined boundaries, well-manicured greens, and beautiful views.

Off-Road Vehicles

Three off-road trails are maintained within the Les Cheneaux area. The farthest west is

Bay City Lake Trail, a short distance north of Hessel. The 50-inch trails here consist of three loops that total nearly eight miles around Bay City Lake. To get here, take 3-Mile Road north of Hessel to Bay City Lake Road, just past Hessel Ridge Golf Course, and turn left to the parking area. The 8.4-mile **Birch Hill Trail** is for motorcycle use only, and is located east of Cedarville. Take M-134 to Prentiss Bay Road and continue north to the parking area. Nearby, the **Foreman Lake Trail** has several additional miles of trails. Continue north on Prentiss Bay Road, turn right on Traynor Road, and then right again on Springer Road. Closer to DeTour, **Cranberry Lake Trail** runs for eight miles from M-48 to Caribou Lake. This trail is for vehicles less than 50 inches wide, and there's parking at the trailheads on M-48, just north of M-134, and on M-134 itself, near the turnoff for DeTour Campground.

Drummond Island, with its vast stretches of state-owned land, is an ideal place to take ATVs. There are more than 65 miles of trails, many of them looped and much of them through old-growth boreal forests. Pay special attention to the island's northern shore, which has plenty of stunning Lake Huron views. Also, with the exception of M-134 between the ferry and Channel Road, all of Drummond Island's roads, paved and unpaved, are ATV friendly. Ask for a full-color map from the **Drummond Island Tourism Association** (906/493-2565 or 800/737-8666, www.drummondislandchamber.com) or local businesses. But it doesn't stop there; Drummond Island is also home to **Turtle Ridge Off-Road Terrain Challenge Park** (906/493-1000, www.turtleridgeorv.com, $30 per day, multiple-day discounts), which has rock crawls, hill climbs, mud, and more.

WINTER SPORTS AND RECREATION
Ski and Snowshoe Trails

On Drummond Island, cross-country ski trails include 4.5 miles at the **Rainbow Trail,** a groomed, mostly flat trail on Maxton Cross Road. No snowshoeing is allowed at the Rainbow Trail. The **Drummond Island Resort and Conference Center** (http://drummondisland.com) has 15 miles of groomed trails for cross-country skiing. Skis are available for resort guests to use for free.

Visitors interested in snowshoeing can head to a section of trails specifically set aside by Drummond Island Resort, and there are two miles of snowshoe trails available on the Island Heritage Trail at Drummond Island Township Park. Additionally, all 76 miles of the island's designated DNR trails are accessible by snowshoe. Contact the **Drummond Island Tourism Association** (906/493-2565 or 800/737-8666, www.drummondisland-chamber.com) for additional information.

Back on the mainland, skiers can try the five groomed miles at the **Peek-A-Boo Hill Cross Country Ski Trail,** maintained by the Les Cheneaux Nordic Ski Club. To get to the trail, take Blindline Road north of M-129, then go west on State Avenue to the Les Cheneaux Community Schools' running track, where you'll find the trailhead. The **Search Bay Backcountry Ski Trail** is a good option, located five miles west of Hessel. The two 1.5-mile loops make a figure eight. They're groomed and easy to ski, taking you out onto the small peninsula of St. Martin's Point. The trailhead is accessible south of M-134.

Snowmobiling

Drummond Island Resort and Convention Center is a good place to start when snowmobiling on the island. It's a good place to gain access to Drummond Island's astonishing 100 miles of groomed snowmobile trails. As for rentals, **Drummond Island Resort** rents snowmobiles ($199-225 per day) and requires a $500 damage deposit. Free snowmobile maps are available from local businesses and the tourism association.

The trails in Les Cheneaux connect with the hundreds of miles of trails that crisscross the Upper Peninsula. **Trail 47** extends from DeTour and will take you to **Trail 2** near St. Ignace, making stops in Cedarville and

Hessel along the way. **Trail 491** splits north from 47, taking you to Pickford, while **Trail 49** will take you north to Kinross and Sault Ste. Marie. Additionally, you can operate your snowmobile on all unplowed roads in Mackinac County, as well as on the far right side of paved roads and the unpaved portions of highways. Obey traffic laws and speed limits, and be careful.

FOOD

For such a small town, Cedarville actually has a nice selection of restaurants. ★ **Cattail Cove Restaurant and Lounge** (22 Hodeck St., 906/484-2995, noon-11pm Mon.-Thurs., noon-midnight Fri.-Sat., 9am-10pm Sun., $10-23) is a good example. It's no surprise to see fresh local fish on the menu, since the restaurant owns its own fish market; try a Great Lakes catch while you're in the area. You can get good char-grilled prime rib too. The outdoor deck overlooks Cedarville Bay, making it the perfect place for a cocktail or two in good weather.

If you're in the mood for some Italian, head over to **Ang-Gio's** (232 W. M-134, 906/484-3301, 8am-9:30pm daily, $8-17) for some tasty pizza. Another spot for Italian food in Cedarville is **Fired Up!** (33 Hodeck St., 906/484-3473, 11am-8pm Mon.-Sat., $12-19), where you'll find delicious stromboli and bruschetta sandwiches and pasta dishes such as linguine and penne plus traditional spaghetti and meatballs. Hungry yet?

In DeTour, stop by **Fisher's Restaurant** (168 Ontario St., 906/297-2801, www.fishersrestaurant.net, 9am-4pm Tues.-Thurs., 9am-7pm Fri.-Sun., $10-15) for good food, great service, and a worthwhile lunch buffet. Another favorite is ★ **Mainsail Restaurant and Saloon** (410 N. Ontario St., 906/297-2141, www.mainsailrestaurant.com, 9am-10pm daily, $13-21), a casual restaurant that serves three hearty meals daily. Examples include steak, shrimp, fresh fish, salads, and burgers—solid American food plus a few burritos. Stop by the saloon for draft beer and mixed drinks. As an added bonus,

Mainsail is home to the original blueprints for the *Edmund Fitzgerald,* the freighter that met with tragedy and was immortalized by Gordon Lightfoot.

Drummond Island has a fair handful of restaurants too. The **Port of Call Restaurant** (30420 E. Johnswood Rd./M-134, 906/493-5507, www.drummondislandfudge.com, 10am-8pm Mon., 10am-8pm Wed.-Sat., 10am-4pm Sun. mid-Apr.-late Nov., $15-25) is an establishment that prides itself in offering a selection of international items that aren't usually found in U.P. restaurants. Traditional breakfast items like eggs Benedict and bagel sandwiches give way to Belgian waffles, Greek gyro omelets, and European bakehouse breads like Russian pumpernickel and Jewish rye. Lunch and dinner menus feature Asian vegetable noodle soup, Greek gyros, English fish-and-chips, and pierogi with Polish sausage. You'll find plenty of traditional, Midwestern American food too. Port of Call features an impressive wine selection.

At the Drummond Island Resort and Conference Center, try **Pins Bar & Grill** (33494 S. Maxton Rd., 906/493-1000 or 800/999-6343, www.drummondisland.com, 8am-9pm daily, $18), where you'll find burgers, pizza, wings—and bowling.

ACCOMMODATIONS

On Drummond Island, stay in luxury at ★ **Woodmoor Lodge** (33494 S. Maxton Rd., 906/493-1000 or 800/999-6343, www.drummondisland.com, $119-155), a grandiose retreat with a handsome log lodge. Guests have access to all Drummond Island Resort facilities, including an outdoor pool, tennis courts, bowling, and even sporting clays. You can also rent some Frank Lloyd Wright-style cottages, many overlooking Potagannissing Bay.

Another good lodging choice is ★ **Drummond Island Yacht Haven** (33185 S. Water St., 906/493-5232, www.diyachthaven.com, $68-292 nightly, $700-1,390 weekly), with large cabins overlooking island-studded Potagannissing Bay. The larger three bedroom cabins have limestone fireplaces. The property also offers sandy beaches, boat rentals, and other amenities. Contact the **Drummond Island Tourism Association** (906/493-5245 or 800/737-8666, www.drummondislandchamber.com) for more choices.

Along the Lake Huron shore near Cedarville, the **Spring Lodge Cottages** (916 Park Ave., Cedarville, 906/484-2282 or 800/480-2282, www.springlodge.com, $600-1,250 weekly) have a wonderful location in the heart of Les Cheneaux, right on the Snows Channel. Large and well-kept grounds house cottages, most overlooking the water. Boat rentals are available on-site.

For nicer-than-average motel rooms and an indoor pool, try the **Cedarville Lodge** (M-134, Cedarville, 906/484-2266, http://cedarvillelodge.net, $119-140). Another affordable choice is the **Islands Inn Motel** (90 E. M-134, 906/484-2293, www.islandsinnmotel.com, $78-88). The **Les Cheneaux Motel** (769 M-134, 906/484-2581, www.lescheneaux.com, $69-81) offers superb rates and includes a kitchenette in each unit.

Camping

Drummond Island's best camping is at **Township Park** (no reservations, $10, $12.25 with electricity), just north of M-134, not far from the ferry dock. This rustic campground (no showers) has pretty sites tucked in the woods on Potagannissing Bay. There's a sand beach and a boat launch.

Camp along the Lake Huron shore and under the pines in a former state park now managed by the **Lake Superior State Forest** (906/293-5131, www.michigan.gov/dnr). The marked beach and picnic area is on M-134, six miles west of DeTour Village. For more seclusion, boaters should head for **Government Island,** the only publicly owned island in Les Cheneaux. Once a Coast Guard station, it's now part of the **Hiawatha National Forest** (906/643-7900, www.fs.fed.us). Outhouses

and picnic tables are available at a couple of primitive sites on the northeastern and southern ends of the small island; no-trace camping is permitted anywhere on the island.

INFORMATION AND SERVICES

There are a few sources for helpful visitor information. Among the finest are **Les Cheneaux Islands Tourist Association** (670 W. M-134, Cedarville, 888/364-7526, www.lescheneaux.org) and the **Drummond Island Tourism Association** (906/493-5245 or 800/737-8666, www.drummondislandchamber.com).

The nearest hospital is St. Ignace's **Mackinac Straits Hospital** (1140 N. State St. St., St. Ignace, 906/643-8585, www.mackinacstraitshealth.org), about 30 minutes' drive from Cedarville and an hour from DeTour. Take M-134 to I-75, then head south, exiting at the I-75 Business Loop (exit 348). Continue south for about two miles and look for the hospital on the right just after you pass the Mackinac County Airport. Another option is **War Memorial Hospital** (500 Osborn Blvd., Sault Ste. Marie, 906/635-4460, www.warmemorialhospital.org), a bit farther away.

Most of the area's banks are in Cedarville, where you'll find a **Central Savings Bank** (143 W. M-134, 906/484-2036, www.centralsavingsbank.com), on M-134 as you pass through town; **First National Bank of St. Ignace** (192 S. Meridian St., 906/484-2262, www.fnbsi.com); and the **Soo Co-Op Credit Union** (90 Beach St., 906/484-2073, www.socoop.com) downtown.

In DeTour, go to the **Central Savings Bank** (109 Elizabeth St., 906/297-3061, www.centralsavingsbank.com) near the Drummond Island Ferry dock. While on the island, go to **Detour Drummond Community Credit Union** (34857 S. Townline Rd., 906/493-5763, www.ddccu.com).

GETTING THERE AND AROUND

Car

One of the Huron Shore's draws is its convenient accessibility. If you're taking the Bridge up from the Lower Peninsula, Cedarville is a short 30-minute drive up I-75 and along M-134. It's another 30 minutes along M-134 to DeTour and Drummond Island. From Sault Ste. Marie, head south on I-75 and catch M-134 or take M-129 straight down. M-129 is a shorter distance, but the interstate is fast and convenient and won't add much time to your drive.

The one-mile-long auto crossing is managed by the **Drummond Island Ferry** (906/235-3170, $14 per vehicle, plus $2 pp) for a 10-minute trip across the St. Mary's River. Ferry service is offered year-round. Fares and schedules can change without notice; see www.diyachthaven.com for current schedules and additional pricing for trailers, snowmobiles, camper units, and other details. Additional information can be obtained from the **Drummond Island Tourism Association** (906/493-5245 or 800/737-8666, www.drummondislandchamber.com).

Air

Most air passengers to the eastern U.P. fly into **Chippewa County International Airport** (CIU, 5019 Airport Dr., Kincheloe, 906/495-5631 or 800/225-2525, www.airciu.com), which has scheduled flights from Detroit on Delta Airlines and rental cars from **Avis** (906/495-5900, www.avis.com). Driving time to DeTour from Chippewa County Airport is 1 to 1.5 hours.

About 90 minutes' drive from DeTour, **Pellston Regional Airport** (PLN, U.S. 31, Pellston, 231/539-8441), south of Mackinaw City in the Lower Peninsula, has scheduled flights from Detroit on Delta Airlines. Car rental is offered through **Avis** (213/539-8302, www.avis.com), **Budget** (231/539-8160, www.budget.com) and **Hertz** (231/539-3131, www.hertz.com).

Boat

Les Cheneaux's 36 islands, sheltered channels, and bays make this a boater's dream. If you're one of the fortunate ones boating here, you'll want to head to the **Hessel/Clark Township Marina** (906/484-3917 or 906/484-2672, www.michigan.gov/dnr, late May-early Sept.), which has 30 transient slips and a boatload of amenities. Along with the expected water, electricity, pump-out, and showers, Hessel Marina is close to marine-repair supplies, a fish-cleaning station, and a laundry. The marina is located at 46°00.05 N, 84°25.30 W. Use radio channel 9.

Farther east, you can go to **DeTour State Dock** (906/297-5947, www.michigan.gov/dnr, mid-May-late Sept.), with basic amenities and a harbormaster on duty. Use radio channel 16, then switch to 71. It's located at 45°59.43 N, 83°53.50 W. For other marinas, consider **Cedarville Marine** (906/484-2815, www.cedarvillemarine.com) in Cedarville or Hessel's **E. J. Mertaugh Boat Works** (906/484-2434, www.ejmertaughboatworks.com). Additionally, there are a number of private marinas on Drummond Island. Contact the **Drummond Island Tourism Association** (906/493-5245 or 800/737-8666, www.drummondislandchamber.com) for more information.

Public Transportation

There is no regularly scheduled public transportation to Les Cheneaux, so you'll need your own vehicle.

Background

The Landscape

GEOLOGY AND GEOGRAPHY

Michigan is easily one of America's most geographically peculiar states. Split in two, it consists of two enormous peninsulas, each surrounded on three sides by the Great Lakes. For many, the image of the mitten-shaped Lower Peninsula represents the state as a whole, but the Upper Peninsula deserves recognition in its own right. In geographic size, it's large enough to hold the combined area of New Jersey, Connecticut, Rhode Island, and Delaware—all within its scalloped borders.

A combination of cataclysmic volcanic eruptions and soupy tropical seas initially formed what we call Michigan. In the northeastern part of the state, near Lake Superior and northern Lake Huron, volcanoes erupting billions of years ago laid down thick layers of basalt, which later tilted and faulted, forming the area's rugged, rocky topography of ancient mountain ranges and steep sawtooth shorelines.

Much later, a series of powerful glaciers carved out the Michigan landscape, most recently just 12,000 years ago. Four separate ice sheets scraped across the region, scouring out depressions that became lakes, lowlands, and ragged shorelines. When the ice melted and the glaciers retreated, the meltwater filled the vast basins and created the modern Great Lakes.

Michigan's Upper Peninsula comprises two distinct land regions, the Superior Uplands and the Northern Highlands. The Superior Uplands spans the western two thirds of the Upper Peninsula, the region formed by the ancient volcanic activity. It presents a landscape of dramatic beauty, characterized by rugged basalt cliffs and thick boreal forests of fir, spruce, and birch—all part of the vast Canadian Shield that dips down from the Canadian arctic, across portions of the northern Great Lakes region, and back up the west side of Hudson Bay in a giant horseshoe. Much of the region rises more than 1,000 feet above sea level, including the state's highest point, Mount Arvon—which tops out at 1,979 feet. The Superior Uplands are also the location of some of the nation's richest sources of minerals, most notably copper and iron ore. Most of the known deposits have been depleted by aggressive mining during the 20th century.

South and east of the Superior Uplands lie the Northern Highlands, covering the eastern Upper Peninsula and extending down into the northern half of the Lower Peninsula. Here basalt bedrock gives way to sandstone and limestone, and boreal forests segue into pine and hardwoods. Once heavily logged for its vast and valuable stands of white and red pine, the Northern Highlands today are prized for the recreation opportunities provided by its woods, water, and wildlife.

The western Upper Peninsula borders northeastern Wisconsin and stretches east for 334 miles between Lakes Superior and Michigan. It reaches a third Great Lake, Huron, where it terminates at Drummond Island. Also recognized as part of the U.P. is Isle Royale, a 45-mile-long archipelago in Lake Superior, and Michigan's only national park It is one of the remotest and least visited properties in the national park system.

Although the U.P.'s landmass covers more than 16,000 square miles, water shapes the peninsula's character—its 1,700 miles of shoreline are on three of the Great Lakes and account for more than half of Michigan's total of 3,288 (second only to Alaska among U.S.

---

states). In addition, the U.P. includes more than 4,000 inland lakes, 12,000 miles of rivers, and over 300 named waterfalls. It boasts 11 federally designated Wild and Scenic Rivers and is home to America's first National Lakeshore, Pictured Rocks.

The Great Lakes State, Water Wonderland, Land of Hiawatha—many of these Michigan nicknames most accurately apply to the Upper Peninsula. However, the area north of the bridge is often simply known as God's Country.

CLIMATE

Weather patterns in the U.P. can be unpredictable, as the presence of the Great Lakes exerts considerable influence. Temperatures can be surprisingly moderate, since the lakes tend to cool the hot air of summer and warm the cold winds of winter. Average afternoon highs during July and August are in the 70s (except near the shores). From December through February, they drop into the low 20s, and can often get much colder.

Although the area has four well-defined seasons, temperatures can vary widely. You can enjoy springlike skiing conditions in February or experience temperatures in the single digits at Thanksgiving. In summer you may swelter on a hike through the woods, but soon feel the need to don a jacket when visiting a Lake Superior beach. None of this should deter you from visiting the Upper Peninsula—just make sure you're prepared for all the possibilities.

The Lake Effect

The Great Lakes often act like large insulators—slow to warm up, slow to cool down—and can have a dramatic effect on snowfall. Dry winter air travels over the Great Lakes as prevailing westerly winds, absorbing moisture. When this air hits land, it dumps its precipitation in the form of **lake-effect snow.** This phenomenon most often affects the Superior Highlands, which explains why many of the U.P.'s successful ski resorts are clustered near Iron Mountain along the western edge of the peninsula.

The prevailing western breezes also affect Great Lakes water temperatures, most noticeably on Lake Michigan. During summer, the winds warm surface waters that blow east toward Lake Michigan beaches in the northwestern Lower Peninsula. While the lake is rarely warm enough for swimming on the Wisconsin side, it can be exceedingly pleasant in the Lower Peninsula and at least tolerable in the U.P., as evidenced by the hundreds of popular swimming beaches lining the west side of the state.

Lake Superior is altogether different. Water temperatures in this northern lake rarely climb out of the 40s, save for the occasional shallow bay. "No one's ever drowned in Lake Superior," the saying goes. "They all die of hypothermia first."

Freshwater freezes more quickly than saltwater, and the Great Lakes often ice over several miles out from shore. The commercial shipping season shuts down from January 15 to March 25, but persistent ice can hamper it for much longer. During the especially severe winter of 2013-2014, ice clogged the Straits of Mackinac well into April, making it difficult for Mackinac Island to prepare for the upcoming tourism season. Ice floes on Lake Superior persisted well into May.

Commercial ships can regularly cut through ice up to a foot thick, but thicker ice requires the Coast Guard's *Mackinaw,* a 240-foot heavily reinforced ship specifically designed for ramming a passage through ice. The *Mackinaw* can "back and ram" its way through walls of ice as massive as 10 feet.

A Few Words About Winter

The Upper Peninsula's winter is long and cold. Snow and cold temperatures are virtually constant from Thanksgiving to Easter. In an average season, the U.P. receives some 160 inches of snow.

This, however, represents an average. U.P. snows are legendary, especially in the Keweenaw Peninsula, where 300-inch winters are not unusual. In summer, curious pierlike devices can be seen sprouting from front

What's So Great About These Lakes?

By any standard, the Great Lakes are enormously impressive. Carved away by receding glaciers several thousand years ago, the five lakes are beautiful, useful, recreational—and massive. The combined lakes (Superior, Michigan, Huron, Erie, and Ontario) cover more than 94,000 square miles and hold an estimated 6 *quadrillion* gallons of water, nearly one-fifth of the Earth's freshwater and enough to cover the 48 contiguous states to a depth of nearly 10 feet. Here are some more interesting facts about the lakes you'll encounter in the U.P.

Measured by surface area, **Lake Superior** is the largest body of freshwater in the world, at 31,700 square miles, roughly the size of Maine. Its shoreline stretches an amazing 1,826 miles, farther than the distance from Houghton to Miami. Superior is also the deepest of the Great Lakes (1,332 feet at its deepest point), but if measured by volume, there are two lakes that are larger: Lake Tanganyika in East Africa and Lake Baikal in Siberia. However, Lake Superior is large enough to hold each of the other Great Lakes, as well as all the water from Lake Erie an additional three times. The lake holds 3 quadrillion gallons of water (the numeral 3 followed by 15 zeros), accounting for a full 10 percent of the world's freshwater. More than half the water from the Great Lakes is contained in Superior, which is enough to submerge North and South America to a depth of one foot.

The second largest, and the only one entirely within the United States, **Lake Michigan** is 307 miles long and 118 miles wide, and holds just shy of 1,180 cubic miles of water. With an average depth of 279 feet, Lake Michigan is 925 feet deep at its deepest point. Its surface area is 22,300 square miles, and it has more than 1,600 miles of shoreline. Technically Lake Michigan and Lake Huron are hydrologically inseparable, which means they have the same surface elevation and are not separated by a river. The Straits of Mackinac connect the two lakes.

Lake Huron is the third largest of the Great Lakes by volume, holding some 849 cubic miles of water, but the second largest by surface area at 23,010 square miles. Manitoulin Island is the largest island in a freshwater lake in the world, with an area of more than 1,000 square miles. The island also has more than 100 lakes of its own, including Manitou Lake, the world's largest lake on an island in a lake. And if the collective perimeters of the lake's 30,000 islands were added to its mainland coastline, Lake Huron could boast the longest shoreline of any of the Great Lakes.

doors and leading to sidewalks on Keweenaw homes, usually a few feet off the ground. These serve as a guide for show shoveling. The accepted standard is not to do so until at least 24 inches are on the ground. Ladders nailed to roofs are there for a specific reason as well. When accumulated snows threaten to collapse the roofs, the ladders provide a foothold from which to clear it.

It's important to be aware of the **wind chill factor,** the effect of the cold temperatures combined with biting winds. When it's 5°F outside, a 15-mph wind will make it feel like -25°F. Not only is this exceedingly uncomfortable, it also elevates the risk for frostbite or hypothermia. Owing to its importance, weather forecasts usually warn about the wind chill factor. Remember to take into consideration both the actual temperature and the wind chill when dressing for the outdoors.

Despite this, many people welcome the Upper Peninsula's winter, as it accounts for a huge portion of the state's tourism revenue. Few other areas in the Midwest can offer as reliable a season for skiing, snowboarding, snowmobiling, ice fishing, and snowshoeing.

ENVIRONMENTAL ISSUES

The Upper Peninsula's primary environmental concern is the safeguarding of the area's prized natural resources. Thankfully, citizens have traditionally been more than willing to step in and oppose those who would abuse the land. Throughout history, there have been various threats to the region's ecosystem, beginning with the fur trade, followed by mining and logging, and more recently by asbestos dumping, nuclear waste, and water-use issues. Metallic sulfide mining, a potentially lucrative economic opportunity but controversial, since it can cause severe environmental damage, is now being permitted in a limited number of Upper Peninsula locations. Whether it will continue is still undetermined.

In sum, the Upper Peninsula is still a relatively wild place but may not stay that way. The Upper Peninsula Environmental Coalition and similar organizations continue to work diligently to keep this land the natural paradise it is today.

PRESERVATION

Beginning in the 1920s, as the mining and timber industries began their declines, modern concepts of land and resource preservation became a priority, beginning with the establishment of the Ottawa and Hiawatha National Forests in the late 1920s. In 1931 Isle Royale became part of the National Park System. The 1940s saw the addition of the Porcupine Mountain and Tahquamenon Falls State Parks. Still more land would follow, including the Pictured Rocks National Lakeshore in 1966. The recent history of the Upper Peninsula tells the story of a region that been exploited for its resources gradually becoming a natural domain protected from the excesses of industry.

Plants and Animals

TREES

There's a reason the **white pine** is Michigan's state tree. Vast stands of the magnificent trees once covered the northern portions of the state, making Michigan the nation's leading lumber center. Pines from the Great Lakes State rebuilt much of Chicago after the Great Fire and supplied a hungry nation as it expanded westward across the treeless plains.

Today, a few tracts of these magnificent species remain—scraping the sky with towers of virgin white pine, red pine, hemlock, and cedar. Much of the U.P.'s original prime logging land is now second-growth pines, with many now reaching considerable heights. Today's logging operations still clear-cut, but in much smaller sections, and are increasingly shifting to selective cutting methods.

ANIMALS
Mammals

Though it's called the Wolverine State, only meager evidence exists of wolverines ever having lived in Michigan, even in the Upper Peninsula. One possible explanation as to how the state obtained its name can be attributed

to early fur traders, who may have brought wolverine pelts to the numerous trading posts in the Upper Peninsula. In February 2004, however, a wolverine was sighted and

Michigan State Symbols

- · State tree: white pine
- · State bird: American robin
- · State fish: brook trout
- · State flower: apple blossom
- · State gem: Isle Royale greenstone
- · State stone: Petoskey stone
- · State reptile: painted turtle
- · State fossil: mastodon
- · State soil: Kalkaska Sand
- · State wildflower: dwarf lake iris
- · State game mammal: white-tailed deer

photographed in Huron County, at the tip of the thumb in the Lower Peninsula. It was the first confirmed sighting in some 200 years and was a shock to state Department of Natural Resources biologists.

With an estimated 85 percent of its area forested, the U.P. harbors a considerable number of gray and red foxes, skunks, squirrels, beavers, minks, muskrats, and other small mammals. The entire state has a large, and often problematic, population of white-tailed deer. Of all the large mammals, this is the one you'll see most frequently—and often not until one leaps out in front of your car. The U.P. is also home to more uncommon mammals: a healthy number of black bears, 200 to 300 wolves, moose, bobcats, and cougars.

Birds

Some 300 varieties of birds live in the state, including such notable species as bald eagles, peregrine falcons, hawks, loons, swans, herons, and dozens of songbirds. Hunting for game birds such as ducks, geese, grouse, and pheasant is popular. Michigan lies on a major migratory pathway, offering excellent bird-watching during both spring and fall. Of special note is the hawk migration, as thousands fly between Canada and the southern Lower Peninsula.

Aquatic Life

An abundance of fish thrive in both the Great Lakes and inland waters. Sportfishing remains popular on the Great Lakes, especially for chinook salmon, coho, steelhead, lake trout, and brown trout. Commercial fishing has decreased dramatically over the last few decades, due to overfishing and the accidental introduction of the lamprey eel and zebra mussel to the Great Lakes.

On inland waters, the walleye and yellow perch are prized for flavor, while the muskie and northern pike are considered a top sport fish. Bass, trout, and pan fish can also be found in inland waters. Michigan has several blue-ribbon streams (www.trailstotrout.com), especially in the eastern U.P.

Reintroduction and Management Programs

Two of the Upper Peninsula's mammals are testimonies to the effectiveness of reintroduction and management programs. The **gray wolf** is believed to have been present in each of Michigan's counties at some point, but by 1910 they were relegated to just the Upper Peninsula. Before their reappearance in the 1990s, Michigan's last wolf pups were born in the mid-1950s near Pictured Rocks. Wolves were first protected in 1965, and were listed as endangered in 1973. Despite this, four of the animals were relocated to the U.P. from Minnesota in 1974, only to be killed. Today the wolves are thriving. In 1991 a pair of wolves produced the first pups born in the state's mainland in more than four decades. That population, estimated at about 20 animals in 1992, is believed to have descended from animals that wandered to the U.P. from Minnesota, Wisconsin, or Ontario. In 2009, the wolf was removed from Michigan's list of threatened species.

In the 1980s, **moose** were reintroduced to a remote area south of the U.P.'s Huron Mountains, with officials releasing a total of 61 moose from Ontario in two separate operations. Most interesting was the method of reintroduction: Wildlife biologists airlifted the moose one by one in a sling dangling beneath a helicopter to a base camp, from where they were trucked 600 miles to the Huron Mountains. Van Riper State Park in Michigamme has an interesting display with photos of the famous "moose lifts." The reintroduction worked, though not as well as hoped. The moose population failed to meet the project goal of 1,000 animals by 2000. Today, several hundred moose roam the western U.P., and their population continues to grow.

The programs of wolf and moose management in the Upper Peninsula don't involve Isle Royale, which is under the direct control of the National Park Service. A separate and ongoing study of the predator-prey relationship between the species on the island has been conducted for more than 55 years, the longest continuous study of its kind anywhere. Although island populations rise and fall periodically, a variety of factors have affected the populations of both animals in recent years.

According to the study's 2016-2017 Annual Report, the moose population has spiked to some 1,500, while the number of wolves has declined to only two.

History

MICHIGAN'S NATIVE PEOPLES

Buried under layers of glacial ice until about 10,000 years ago, the land that is now Michigan was inhospitable to many of the indigenous people that thrived in much of the Midwest, such as the Paleo and Archaic Indians. Some of the first signs of Michigan civilization can be found in the Upper Peninsula's Keweenaw Peninsula, where the Copper Culture people of about 5000-500 BCE left evidence of their skill as prehistoric miners, devising ways to extract copper from bedrock and fashioning it into tools. Some archaeologists believe these people may have been the very first toolmakers anywhere.

The **Algonquin** people migrated to the Great Lakes region from the region of the St. Lawrence River later, most likely after 1000 CE. The Algonquians were divided into three tribes: the **Ottawa** (or Odawa), the **Ojibwa** (or Chippewa), and the **Potawatomi.** Together, they called themselves the **Anishinabe,** or "First People." They named their new land "Michi Gami," meaning "Large Lake." In and around that lake they found the state's abundant wildlife, including white-tailed deer, abundant fish, moose, elk, and black bears, as well as rich natural resources that nourished them for centuries before the arrival of the Europeans.

The three groups coexisted peacefully, each moving to a different area. The Ottawa settled around the Straits of Mackinac, Sault Ste. Marie, and the Leelanau Peninsula; the Ojibwa moved west, along the shores of Lake Superior; and the Potawatomi headed south, to the southern half of the Lower Peninsula.

They communicated regularly, and their peaceable relationship proved valuable when invaders came to their lands. Together, they successfully fought off the warring Iroquois who came from the east in the 1600s, and they presented themselves as a strong, unified people when Europeans arrived.

THE FRENCH

Étienne Brûlé, the first European to arrive in what is now Michigan in 1615, was more interested in exploiting the land than conserving it. Brûlé was sent by Samuel de Champlain, lieutenant governor of New France, who hoped to find copper and a shortcut to the Far East. Brûlé sent back reports recounting the land's untamed beauty and previously unknown flora and fauna.

Other opportunists soon followed. Some were after the region's rich supply of furs, others after the people of what they viewed as a godless land. Among the most famous of these early explorers was the Roman Catholic missionary Jacques Marquette, who established the state's first permanent settlement, at Sault Ste. Marie in 1668, and a second outpost at the straits of Michilimackinac in 1671. The arrival of the French coureurs de bois, a loose term referring to unlicensed traders, provided a sharp contrast to the priests and ruling class. Rugged individualists, they lived among the Native Americans, respected their customs, and hunted and trapped the region's rich stores of game.

Marquette's 17th-century writings attracted more settlers, mostly fur traders, including John Jacob Astor. By the early 1800s, Astor's American Fur Company,

Two States in One

Is it a case of simple sibling rivalry or a marriage of irreconcilable differences? The relationship between the Upper and Lower Peninsulas of Michigan is a paradox. While the two Michigans are physically linked by a five-mile-long bridge, culturally they remain a world apart. Many Lower Peninsula residents dismiss the Upper Peninsula as a collection of bug-infested backwoods filled with yokels. U.P. residents (who proudly call themselves "Yoopers") find these generalizations insulting, especially when those very same Lower Peninsula people seem to enjoy the U.P.'s woods, wildlife, and beaches while on vacation.

The fact the two are joined as a single state is an accident of history. The Michigan Territory wound up with the Upper Peninsula as compensation pursuant to an agreement struck with Ohio in 1837. Both Michigan and Ohio had fought over the "Toledo Strip," a valuable port on Lake Erie. For Michigan to earn admission to the Union, Congress demanded that the Michigan Territory relinquish all rights to the Toledo Strip in exchange for a "barren wasteland"—the western two-thirds of the Upper Peninsula. What at the time seemed unfortunate for Michigan, however, proved to be a boon when priceless quantities of iron ore and copper were discovered just a few years later. Much of the rivalry is good-natured. U.P. residents like to joke about blowing up the Mackinac Bridge and are given to displaying bumper stickers portraying a giant U.P. with a tiny Lower Peninsula dangling from its eastern end. Yet there is a kernel of seriousness to the squabble. Upper Peninsula residents feel they pay taxes to a distant state capital but receive very little in return, save for government-protected land and wildlife programs. From time to time, residents launch pseudo-serious drives to declare sovereignty from the rest of Michigan and create the state of Superior. As a musical group from Ishpeming, Da Yoopers, satirically sings, "Dear Mr. Governor, you better turn us loose / We asked you for some rest stops, instead you sent us moose / The honeymoon is over, the declaration's written / We'll take what's above the bridge, and you can keep the mitten."

headquartered on Mackinac Island, had made him the wealthiest man in the United States.

THE BRITISH

As European colonization continued, the area's peacefulness was shattered. The lucrative fur trade attracted the British traders who, by the late 1600s, began traveling from New York and across Lake Huron, finally arriving in St. Ignace. They began bartering their goods for pelts and, from the French point of view, interfered with the established trade and threatened the alliances they had made with the indigenous people. Before long, growing animosity between the British and French peaked, resulting in the French and Indian Wars in the mid-1700s.

The war effectively ended the 150-year French era, and in 1759 ushered in British rule. Occasional skirmishes among the French, British, and Native Americans continued, especially around the Straits of Mackinac. In one of region's more exciting historical moments, a group of Ojibwa successfully raided the British-run Fort Michilimackinac in 1763 as part of Pontiac's Rebellion. Today, museums and historic state parks in the area chronicle the events.

The British ruled the colony with an iron fist. While the French had treated the Native Americans with a certain amount of respect, the British allied themselves with tribes that were traditional enemies of those indigenous to the area. After Pontiac's Rebellion, the Native Americans negotiated slightly better terms for their relationships with the ruling British, who made peaceable changes to some of their policies. The British actively discouraged settlement of the state's interior to protect their rich fur empire. In 1783, the Treaty of Paris gave the lands to the newly independent United States.

STATEHOOD FOR MICHIGAN

In 1825 New York's Erie Canal opened, which connected Albany on the Hudson River to Buffalo on Lake Erie. This new water route enabled more and more people to move westward and settle in the Michigan Territory. From 1820 to 1830, the population more than tripled to just over 31,000. In 1837 the burgeoning territory was awarded statehood, making Michigan the 26th state admitted to the Union. For the first 10 years of its existence, Detroit served as the new state's capital. In 1847, as mandated by the state's original constitution, the seat of government moved to Lansing, primarily for reasons of security; locating the capital farther from the international frontier would make it safer from potential British attacks.

The Upper Peninsula, however, was almost left out of the new state. Due to poor surveying at the time, a feud ignited between Ohio and the Territory of Michigan over a 468-square-mile section of land known as the Toledo Strip. The Toledo War—a bit of a misnomer, as there was virtually no physical fighting—ensued, which remained unresolved until 1836, when Congress awarded the strip to Ohio and gave Michigan the western three-quarters of the Upper Peninsula in compensation, which otherwise would likely have gone to Wisconsin. The deal also paved the way for Michigan's admission to the Union. All this seemed little consolation to Michigan, until the seemingly worthless frontier of the Upper Peninsula began to yield its bounty of minerals during the subsequent copper and iron booms.

By 1840 more than 200,000 people had migrated to Michigan. Early industries revolved around farming and agriculture, with lumber becoming a hugely successful enterprise by the latter part of the century. Altogether, more than 160 billion board feet of pine were cut and hauled from Michigan's north woods by the 1890s—enough to build 10 million six-room houses. While the southern part of the state grew increasingly civilized, the north woods and the Upper Peninsula became filled with wild and rollicking logging camps.

INDIAN REMOVAL ACT

In one of the most heartbreaking chapters in American history, President Andrew Jackson signed the Indian Removal Act in 1830, giving the U.S. government permission to "trade" Native American lands east of the Mississippi for unspecified lands out west. The federal government claimed it was for the protection of the Native Americans, correctly predicting that settlers would continue to surge into their homelands in the name of frontier expansion.

The Native Americans obviously had no interest in leaving areas that had been their homelands for centuries. For unknown reasons, indigenous people in Northern Michigan and Wisconsin were largely ignored by the federal Indian Bureau at first; most likely it was because the federal government found their lands undesirable at the time. Their experience contrasts with the Potawatomi, who lived on choice farmland in southern Michigan and were forcibly removed.

Sadly, the federal government's persecution of the Native Americans did eventually reach Northern Michigan. By the mid-1800s, treaties had "legally" confiscated much of their land in both the Upper and Lower Peninsulas and established many of the reservations that exist today.

The government of the new State of Michigan, however, did treat the indigenous people with a modicum of decency. In 1850, Native Americans were given the right to vote and even to run for office in counties where the population was predominantly indigenous, a concession then unheard of elsewhere.

THE COPPER RUSH

In 1840, state geologist Douglass Houghton confirmed the presence of copper in the Upper Peninsula's Keweenaw Peninsula. These were vast deposits of pure native copper, much of it near the surface. The federal government acquired the western half of the U.P.—along with its mineral rights—from the Ojibwa in 1842, just as prospectors began flooding toward the wild and remote Keweenaw. The young United States had an insatiable appetite for the metal, first for new industrial machinery, later for Civil War munitions, and eventually for electrical wiring and other innovations. Houghton's discovery proved to be of incalculable value.

The copper rush began almost overnight, first with prospectors, then with large mining enterprises swarming the Keweenaw. Lucky prospectors secured deck space on Great Lakes vessels and sailed up Lakes Huron and Michigan, then along the southern shore of Lake Superior. At the same time, hundreds of others straggled through the roadless wilderness, trudging overland through northern Wisconsin by snowshoe, or following rivers through thick forests to reach the fabled riches. It was the nation's first mineral rush.

The burgeoning copper industry employed thousands of immigrant laborers, built cities, made millionaires, and made possible extravagant luxuries like opera houses and mansions, many still standing today in Calumet and Laurium. Before it was over, King Copper had generated more than $9.6 billion in wealth—some 10 times more than the more famous California gold rush.

The entire nation turned to Northern Michigan for its copper. During much of the 19th century, the Keweenaw Peninsula produced 75 percent of all U.S. copper; during the Civil War, it produced 90 percent. More than 400 mining companies operated in the Keweenaw during copper's heyday. The demand for labor drew immigrants from more than 30 countries, most notably the British Isles and Scandinavia. With multiple cultures sharing the same mine shafts and communities, Copper Country served as one of the nation's first examples of ethnic diversity.

But by the mid-20th century virtually all the larger mines had closed due to depletion and poor economic conditions, leaving behind tattered homes and empty streets. Soon after, newer mines emerged in the southwestern United States and South America, which proved more productive and cost-effective. Today, lumber and tourism stand as the primary economic pillars of the Upper Peninsula.

Economy and Government

ECONOMY

For almost two centuries, Michigan has been a microcosm of the country's great industrial transition. As the state's primary industries—metals, logging, and (in the Lower Peninsula) automobile manufacturing—have slowly declined, Michigan has been forced to confront a rocky road of economic instability that shows no signs of ending.

Unfortunately, the severity of this downturn has been much more pronounced in the Upper Peninsula. When the mines closed, many U.P. communities were left without new sources of jobs and income, leaving them a shell of their former selves. Driving through Escanaba's historic downtown, for example, it's almost impossible not realize the city is a just shadow of what it once was, and that its streets are an echo of more prosperous times.

Many of the small former mining towns are beginning to show significant wear around the edges, which contributes to their unassuming small-town charm. At the same time, residents of the U.P. are not the sort of people to surrender during tough times, whether it's a particularly bitter winter or a permanently rough economy. In any case, the reason most people come to the U.P. is precisely because of its decidedly "unmetropolitan" atmosphere.

Logging and Mining

The Upper Peninsula's economy was long based on logging and mining. Great fortunes were made in logging in the late 1800s, as

Michigan's vast stands of virgin timber produced enough wood to lay an inch-thick plank across the entire state with enough left over to cover Rhode Island.

It's difficult to gain an appreciation of the riches harvested from Michigan's copper and iron mines, each of which dwarfed the gold rush in California. Michigan produced more than $9.6 billion worth of **copper** and a staggering $48 billion worth of **iron,** in contrast to just $955 million produced from the gold rush. The riches and the miners disappeared as the most accessible deposits were exhausted and global economics began to play a role.

Tourism

The gradual decline in the mining and timber industries was followed by the rise of tourism, which emerged as the U.P.'s economic salvation. Mackinac Island has long had a reputation as one of America's prime vacation spots, even before the iconic Grand Hotel was built. Today, the entire U.P. subsists on tourism, successfully marketing its natural resources and recreational opportunities as its most attractive assets. In 2005, Sherman's Travel cited the "majestic wildlife, unspoiled rivers, waterfalls, and dense forests" as just one of the reasons for putting the Upper Peninsula on its list of Top 10 Summer Destinations, an honor it shared with London, the Hamptons on Long Island, and the Greek Islands.

Shipping

Just as tractor-trailers rumble down the nation's highways, commercial ships transport commodities across the Great Lakes. Officially designated as the nation's "Fourth Seacoast" by Congress in 1970, the Great Lakes serve as a vital transportation artery for much of the nation's commerce.

With its hundreds of miles of Great Lakes shoreline and deepwater ports, Michigan's Upper Peninsula is a key player in the Great Lakes transportation network. In addition, the Soo Locks that link Lakes Superior and Huron at Sault Ste. Marie rank among the largest and busiest lock systems in the world.

Iron ore forms the foundation of the Great Lakes trade. In Upper Peninsula ports like Escanaba and Marquette, huge lake carriers, some as long as 1,000 feet, load iron ore from nearby mines, then transport it to steelmaking centers in the southern Great Lakes, which supply industrial manufacturers, including the nation's auto industry. The Great Lakes fleet hauls up to 125 million tons of cargo each year, including more than 58 million tons of iron ore—nearly twice the "float" of any other commodity. Shipping is a highly economical method of transporting heavy and bulky commodities such as ore.

Great Lakes shipping is affected by global competition. Each year, increasing levels of durable goods ranging from refrigerators to automobiles regularly arrive in the U.S. from overseas, which translates to a decrease in domestic steel production, which in turn reduces the need for iron ore shipments. Secondly, other transportation networks, such as trains and trucks, compete with shipping for certain commodities. Overall however, shipping has proved to be a stable industry, with total cargo shipments remaining high even over the last decade.

GOVERNMENT

During the early 20th century, Michigan was traditionally a stronghold of the Republican party. Beginning with the Great Depression, however, a competitive two-party political system emerged, as the Democratic Party made major inroads throughout the state.

Since then, the Detroit area, many rural areas of the Lower Peninsula, and much of the Upper Peninsula have proved influential in determining the direction of presidential elections. Democratic candidates carried Michigan in every presidential election from 1992 to 2012, but in the most recent presidential race in 2016, Michigan went Republican.

But all this talk of Republicans and Democrats seems rather passé when compared to the Upper Peninsula's relatively recent and occasionally serious talks of seceding from Michigan to form its own autonomous state. It would be called Superior, clearly a reference to Lake Superior. Little has come from these efforts, and it's likely nothing ever will, considering the Upper Peninsula accounts for just three percent of Michigan's total population of 10 million. The movement was most popular back in the 1960s and 1970s, and occasionally lives on today in half-joking comments and a few satirical bumper stickers.

People and Culture

The residents of Michigan's Upper Peninsula today reflect a diversity of backgrounds due to the region's multilayered history. The French "empire builders" were the first Europeans to arrive, and in due time the British replaced the French. Early American settlers included large and diverse groups from western New York and New England. During the 19th century, immigrants from Europe came seeking a better life, particularly Finns, Swedes, Italians, and Cornish people who worked in the Upper Peninsula mines and lumber camps. Many of today's residents are directly descended from these pioneers.

Today, Upper Peninsula residents number around 311,000, slightly more than 3 percent of Michigan's approximately 9.8 million citizens, ranking Michigan as the nation's ninth most populous state. According to the U.S. Census Bureau, the U.P.'s five largest cities contain about 20 percent of its people: Marquette's population is 20,780, Sault Ste. Marie's 14,000, Escanaba's 12,300, Menominee's 8,400, and Iron Mountain's 7,800.

NATIVE AMERICANS

In most books of Michigan history, the land's first inhabitants are given little more than a cursory nod, a line or two that identifies the approximately 100,000 early Native Americans as belonging to the tribes of the "Three Fires," the **Ojibwa, Ottawa,** and **Potawatomi.** The three tribes collectively called themselves the Anishinabe, or "First People." Another tribe with a significant presence in the Upper Peninsula during the 1700s was the **Menominee,** who lived in northern Wisconsin and parts of the U.P.

Today, Michigan is home to one of the largest Native American populations in the country, estimated at 50,000, many of them in the Upper Peninsula. Arriving at a precise figure is impossible, since the label "Native American" can be defined in one of several ways: politically (tribal membership), ethnically (genealogy), or culturally (personal identification). Depending on the method used, Michigan may have the largest Native American population east of the Mississippi. Today, only a small percentage of these people live on reservations.

There are a number of reservations scattered throughout the peninsula, including federally recognized tribes in Brimley, Wilson, Baraga, Watersmeet, Manistee, L'Anse, Ontonagon, and Sault Ste. Marie, home of the Sault Ste. Marie Tribe of Chippewa Indians, the largest federally recognized tribe in the Great Lakes area. Of these, five are authorized to operate their own police agencies and courts, which exercise exclusive jurisdiction over certain laws involving Native Americans and events that occur within their reservations. Tribal courts have broad powers in matters involving child welfare and in a variety of civil matters involving tribe members and nonmembers when the activities in question occur within their jurisdiction. In addition, Native American tribal councils throughout the state provide a variety of outreach services, economic development initiatives, and cultural activities.

Most reservations have cultural centers with museums or displays open to the public. Many communities also host powwows (native dance ceremonies) and festivals. Check with local convention and visitors bureaus, or inquire at tribal headquarters, which are prominent and well-marked buildings on most reservations.

THE IMMIGRANTS

Traveling Michigan's numerous rivers as early as the 1600s, the French fur traders, missionaries, and voyageurs were the area's first European settlers, establishing posts in far-flung areas across the state. Most of these immigrants, however, didn't arrive until more than a century later, traveling from abroad in great waves during the early 1800s. Still more settlers came in the 1830s and over the next two decades, in response to widespread famines in Europe.

The Lower Peninsula is home to descendants of immigrants from many foreign lands, including Holland, Germany, Canada, various African nations, India, and the Middle East. By contrast, the ethnic makeup of Upper Peninsula residents is markedly different. The iron and copper mines lured immigrants from Sweden, Finland, Italy, and England's Cornwall with promises of steady work and decent wages. **Swedes** and **Finns** in particular took to the U.P., possibly due to the resemblance of the area's woods and rushing rivers to their native Scandinavia.

Significant Scandinavian influences remain in the U.P., including active Finnish- and Swedish-speaking communities. Finnish names, foods, and the ubiquitous sauna can be found throughout the Keweenaw Peninsula. The community of Hancock today remains largely Finnish, reflected even in its street names. Some 16 percent of the Upper Peninsula population is Finnish, with the northwest Upper Peninsula containing the largest population of Finnish Americans in the United States. Finnish influences can also be found in Marquette, while Escanaba reflects a noticeable Swedish character.

Arts and Entertainment

HISTORICAL MUSEUMS

Not surprisingly, many of the peninsula's museums cover the lore and legends of the Great Lakes and the state's maritime industry. Paradise, located near the eastern U.P.'s Whitefish Point, is home to the **Great Lakes Shipwreck Museum,** which includes artifacts from 13 shipwrecks, including an exhibit that features the bell from the *Edmund Fitzgerald*, the Great Lakes ore carrier that mysteriously sank in 1975, and whose memory was immortalized in a song by folk singer Gordon Lightfoot. The museum does an excellent job of telling the haunting tale of the hundreds of ships that met their demise in the area's frigid, turbulent waters. Also in the U.P., the **National Ski Hall of Fame** in Ishpeming chronicles the downhill and cross-country versions of the sport, while neighboring Negaunee is home to the **Michigan Iron Industry Museum,** an excellent state-run facility on the site of one of the state's first iron forges.

ENTERTAINMENT

Due at least in part to its rural character, the Upper Peninsula lacks much of the cultural entertainment common to more populated areas in terms of theater, music, dance, and nightlife. However, several towns host summertime music festivals, the largest of which is the Pine Mountain Music Festival, as well as opera, symphony, and chamber music. These happen at various locations across the peninsula each summer. You'll be able to find theatrical productions and musical performances in the peninsula's college towns, particularly at Northern Michigan University in Marquette. Another popular venue is the Calumet Theatre in Calumet, which offers a variety of entrainment options during the summer months.

Festivals and Events

The Upper Peninsula offers a wide range of events held annually. While many are listed in the destination chapters, these are the most popular:

Ft. Mackinac Memorial Day Observance
Ft. Mackinac on Mackinac Island, early morning on Memorial Day

· Soldiers march from the fort to the nearby cemetery to perform a short ceremony.

Ft. Wilkins Memorial Day Program
Ft. Wilkins near Copper Harbor, Memorial Day

· This event celebrates the fort's history while honoring all service members who have died for our nation.

Baraga County Lake Trout Festival
L'Anse, second weekend in June

· This is a classic small town summer festival, complete with a pie eating contest, a beach volleyball tournament, and, of course, the Keweenaw Classic Fishing Tournament.

Mackinac Island Lilac Festival
Mackinac Island, 10 days in mid-June

· This charming festival celebrates life on the island, including a 10k run, concerts, wine tastings, the Grande Parade, and much more.

Annual Antiques on the Bay Classic and Antique Car Show
Downtown St. Ignace, third weekend in June

· This urbane affair displays elegant machines from the golden age of the automobile.

Les Cheneaux Boat Fest
Hessel, second weekend in August

· This show offers a rare glimpse at an array of classic nautical beauties.

Native American Gaming

Gaming is a form of entertainment that the U.P. excels in. As sovereign lands, reservations often are able to offer high-stakes gambling that is not legally allowed elsewhere in the state (except in Detroit). Michigan's first Native American casino opened near Sault Ste. Marie in 1984. The Bay Mills Blackjack Casino originally had just 15 blackjack tables and one dice table in a 2,400-square-foot room located in the tribal center. Visitors promptly showed their love of gambling, pouring tens of millions of dollars into casino coffers, initiating a gaming tradition that has escalated ever since.

Several Native American casinos operate in Michigan, including many in the Upper Peninsula. They range from small, simple gambling halls to sumptuous showplaces; most are open 24 hours a day, seven days a week, and have become enormous tourism draws. The Vegas Kewadin complex in Sault Ste. Marie has added an interesting art gallery, which displays paintings, jewelry, and crafts by Native Americans. Not surprisingly, more and more Native American communities, many of which struggle economically near the poverty level, are seeking to open their own casinos.

By the early 1990s, the state government decided to enter the picture. In 1993 the state legislature passed and Governor John Engler signed the Tribal State Gaming Compact, giving the state eight percent of net income derived from games of chance. Contributions to state coffers total hundreds of millions of dollars. While providing the state government with an easy source of funds, the success of Native American gaming has also provided tribal governments with greater power and influence.

While the pros and cons of gambling remain a matter of political and ethical debate, there's no arguing the positive spinoffs that gaming provides to the reservations' overall economies. Within these communities, revenue from gambling has provided jobs while funding schools, health care facilities, cultural centers, and other essential needs. Additionally, the gaming industry has yielded economic benefits outside Native American communities by creating jobs in the building trades and the tourism industry. By all appearances, Michigan residents and visitors will never lose their desire to pursue Lady Luck.

Essentials

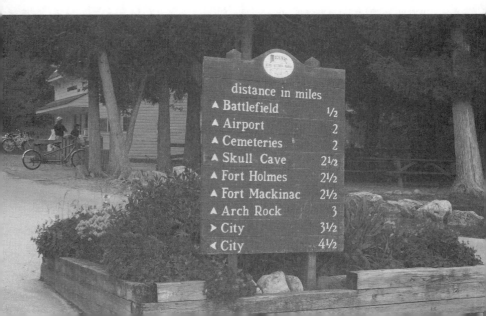

Transportation

GETTING THERE

Car

The only route to the Upper Peninsula from the Lower Peninsula by car or bus is via the Mackinac Bridge on I-75—an exhilarating experience for most but deathly frightening for some. Since 2015 the toll is $4 per passenger car, with no increases currently planned. From Wisconsin, U.S. 41 runs north of Green Bay into Menominee, while U.S. 141/U.S. 8 enters Michigan near Norway and Iron Mountain. Moving west, U.S. 45 connects with U.S. 2 at Watersmeet, and both U.S. 51 from the south and U.S. 2 from the west meet in Ironwood.

Travelers coming from Canada may take King's Highway 17 (the Trans-Canada Highway) to Sault Ste. Marie, Ontario, and cross the St. Mary's River via the International Bridge into the United States. Passenger cars are currently charged a toll of $3.50 (C$4.60). See www.michigan.gov/iba for the latest information. Currency exchange rates are available at www.xe.com/ucc.

Bus

Indian Trails (800/292-3831, www.indiantrails.com), a Michigan-based company, runs regularly scheduled bus routes throughout Michigan, including the Upper Peninsula. Main routes go between Calumet and Milwaukee via Marquette and to St. Ignace and Ironwood via Escanaba.

Air

Detroit Metropolitan Airport (DTW, 800/642-1978) is the area hub for **Delta Airlines** (888/750-3284, www.delta.com), allowing you fly to Detroit from anywhere in the United States and overseas, connecting to several of the Upper Peninsula's commercial airports, including Escanaba, Marquette, Pellston/Mackinac Island, and Sault Ste. Marie. Houghton is only accessible via Chicago.

Flights from Detroit are rather limited, with only one or two arrivals and departures per day at regional airports. The major airports for U.P. destinations are:

- **Pellston Regional Airport (PLN):** U.S. 31, Pellston, 231/539-8441, www.pellstonairport.com

- **Chippewa County International Airport (CIU):** 119 Airport Dr., Kincheloe, 906/495-2522, www.airciu.com

- **Delta County Airport (ESC):** 3300 Airport Rd., Escanaba, 906/786-4902, www.deltacountymi.org

- **Sawyer International Airport (MQT):** 225 Airport Ave., Gwinn, 906/346-3308, www.sawyerairport.com

- **Houghton County Memorial Airport (CMX):** 23810 Airpark Blvd., Calumet, 906/482-3970, www.houghtoncounty.org

Boat

Surrounded by hundreds of miles of shoreline, Michigan's Upper Peninsula is easy to access via the Great Lakes, and visitors who do will find a high concentration of marinas. The Parks and Recreation Division of the state Department of Natural Resources (DNR) has established a network of protected **public mooring facilities** along the Great Lakes, a "marine highway" that ensures that boaters are never far from a safe harbor. More facilities are being added every year, with the ultimate goal of assuring that a boater is never

---

Driving Distances and Times

From Chicago to:

- Escanaba: 315 miles, 6.5 hours
- Houghton: 421 miles, 9.5 hours
- Ironwood: 403 miles, 7.75 hours
- Marquette: 386 miles, 8.25 hours
- Sault Ste. Marie: 509 miles, 7.75 hours
- St. Ignace: 458 miles, 7 hours

From Detroit to:

- Escanaba: 435 miles, 8.25 hours
- Houghton: 554 miles, 11.5 hours
- Ironwood: 694 miles, 13 hours
- Marquette: 456 miles, 9 hours
- Sault Ste. Marie: 345 miles, 5.25 hours
- St. Ignace: 295 miles, 4.5 hours

From Grand Rapids to:

- Escanaba: 393 miles, 8 hours
- Houghton: 513 miles, 11.5 hours
- Ironwood: 585 miles, 10.5 hours
- Marquette: 415 miles, 8.75 hours
- Sault Ste. Marie: 304 miles, 5 hours
- St. Ignace: 254 miles, 4.25 hours

From Milwaukee to:

- Escanaba: 295 miles, 5 hours
- Houghton: 332 miles, 5 hours
- Ironwood: 320 miles, 6.5 hours
- Marquette: 296 miles, 6.75 hours
- Sault Ste. Marie: 417 miles, 9.75 hours
- St. Ignace: 366 miles, 8.75 hours

more than 15 shoreline miles from a protected public mooring. Mooring fees vary. For more information or a free *Michigan Harbors Guide*, contact the **DNR Parks and Recreation**

Division (P.O. Box 30257, Lansing, MI 48909, 517/373-9900, www.michigan.gov/dnr).

GETTING AROUND
Car

Roads in the Upper Peninsula are plentiful, and most major arteries are in good condition. Along with interstate and federal highways, the state is honeycombed with numerous state highways, marked on road maps by a number surrounded by a circle or oval. On road signs, however, state highways are identified by their official insignia, which is the number of the road centered within a white diamond. In conversation, they are described with an "M," as in, "Follow M-28 west to Marquette." County roads are marked with squares on most road maps, and may be designated "CR."

Two routes traverse the peninsula from east to west: M-28 is the northern route, passing through Marquette; U.S. 2 is the southern route, passing through Escanaba. If you're traveling the eastern end of the U.P. all the way to Ironwood, M-28 is usually faster. Several state and federal highways running north-south link M-28 and U.S. 2. These include, from east to west, I-75, M-123, M-77, U.S. 41, U.S. 145, and U.S. 45, among others.

When planning a route in the Upper Peninsula, consult your map legend regarding road surfaces. Roads you might assume are paved may be gravel or dirt, which can make for very slow going. All state and federal highways are paved and well maintained, as are most county and secondary roads. For construction updates, see www.michigan.gov/roadwork, or call the Michigan Department of Transportation's road construction hotline (800/641-6368).

The speed limit on interstate highways in Michigan is 70 mph, unless otherwise posted. Most four-lane highways and many two-lane highways now have limits of 65 mph. Complete and current information regarding Michigan speed limits can be found by visiting www.michigan.gov/speedlimits.

For first-time visitors to Michigan, one of the most confusing aspects of driving

ESSENTIALS
TRANSPORTATION

the state's major roads is a type of turn only found here: the Michigan left. Ordinarily, direct lefts turns are prohibited at intersections where a Michigan left is in place. Instead, to turn left onto an intersecting road, it's necessary to continue past the intersection and make a U-turn at the median crossover, double back to your intended street, and finally turn right. To turn left onto a major crossing road, turn right, then make a U-turn at the median and continue on your way. According to the Department of Transportation, these turns serve to relieve congestion and reduce both the number and the severity of crashes. Crashes at intersections with a Michigan left have dropped 30 to 60 percent overall, enough to make one wonder why other states haven't adopted the idea. Since these turns are usually installed at high-traffic intersections (and can only be used when at least one of the roads is a divided highway), there are relatively few in the Upper Peninsula, but they are present in some of the larger cities, particularly along U.S. 41/M-28 near Marquette.

There's a long-standing joke about Michigan roads that goes: "Michigan has four seasons: winter, winter, winter, and road construction." While certainly an exaggeration, the quip does refer to a perennial problem caused by the state's weather: temperatures swing from below freezing to a thaw and then back to freezing, while heavy snowfalls mean heavy snowplows, sand, and salt. All this stress causes road surfaces to deteriorate quickly, forcing the Michigan Department of Transportation (MDOT) to work constantly from Easter through Thanksgiving to correct the problem.

WINTER DRIVING

Michigan roads are generally well maintained in winter, plowed free of snow and then salted or sanded. While salt is more effective at melting, sand is less destructive to the pavement and the environment. During or immediately after a storm, however, difficult or even dangerous conditions can occur as road crews strive to keep up with conditions. County and city crews prioritize their attention by well-established protocols; first preference goes to federal and state highways, major thoroughfares, and roads to schools and hospitals, followed by less vital routes. Minor roads are handled differently, especially in the Upper Peninsula. A sign reading "Seasonal Road: Not Maintained in Winter" indicates that the route is neither plowed nor patrolled. To check winter driving conditions before you travel, call the AAA road conditions number (800/337-1334).

If you're unfamiliar with driving in snow, exercise special caution; allow ample extra room between you and the car in front, and remember that stopping distances can be considerably longer. If your car isn't equipped with antilock brakes, tap your brake pedal lightly in rapid succession to come to a stop. Do not stomp on them, or you'll lose control of your vehicle. If your car does have ABS antilock brakes, apply steady pressure, and the system's computer will do the work. A 4WD vehicle will provide better traction but not greater stopping ability.

Chains and studded snow tires are not permitted on Michigan roads. For winter, many residents do switch to snow tires, which have a heavier tread. If you have a rear-wheel-drive car, adding weight to the back end can greatly improve traction. Bags of sand or water-softener salt work well, with sand also useful in getting a vehicle unstuck.

Bear in mind that ice is considerably more dangerous than snow, since it limits traction and stopping ability even more. Be especially aware of black ice, meaning pavement that looks wet but is actually covered with of glaze of ice. Watch for icy roads as rain turns to snow (called "freezing rain"), especially on bridges, which freeze first due to the cold air circulating above and below the road. Ice also forms after a number of cars travel over a snowy surface, compressing it into a slick, hard pack. This often happens on heavily traveled federal and state highways. On four-lane roads, the lesser-used left lane usually looks snowier but may actually be less dangerous.

Equip your vehicle with a shovel, sand (kitty litter works even better), and boots in case you get stuck. Throw the sand or kitty litter under the front tires for a front-wheel-drive car, the rear tires on a rear-wheel drive. Keep the tires straight and *slowly* apply the gas—doing so excessively will only make the problem worse. Gently rocking the car forward and back, especially if you have someone who can push, works best.

Keep a flashlight, flares, blankets, and extra clothing in your vehicle in case you have to spend the night in your car. It could save your life. In rural areas, help may not always arrive promptly. If you see a car stuck on a snow bank or in a ditch, be a Good Samaritan and offer the stranded driver a push or a ride to town.

DRIVING AND DEER

Well over one million deer inhabit Michigan, posing a significant threat to drivers. Several thousand collisions between deer and motor vehicles occur each year, some of them fatal. In the U.P. alone, some 2,700 deer-vehicle accidents are reported annually, while many more go unreported. Deer behave erratically and will dart in front of your car with absolutely no warning, suddenly emerging from the woods or a roadside ditch. Be particularly alert at dawn and dusk, when they tend to be most active, and especially during firearm hunting season in November. Yellow and black "leaping deer" signs warn motorists of roadways where crossings are common, but they can appear absolutely anywhere.

If you see deer by the side of the road, slow down and prepare to stop. If you see a deer cross ahead of you, be especially cautious. Where there's one deer, there are usually several. If you do hit a deer, notify the nearest law enforcement office immediately.

CAR RENTALS

Rental cars are available at most commercial airports around the peninsula. In the U.P.'s larger cities, you'll have access to the major companies like **National** (800/227-7368), **Budget** (800/527-0700), **Hertz** (800/654-3131), **Dollar** (800/800-3665), and **Avis** (800/831-2847). Quality local operators are mentioned in the *Getting There and Around* sections. It is strongly recommended that you reserve a car in advance, as small locations have limited inventory. If you plan to do any exploring in the Upper Peninsula, ask about the rental company's policies regarding off-road driving. Many forbid you to leave pavement, which can curtail your access to many U.P. sights.

BORDER CROSSINGS

Due to heightened national security after 9/11, the traditionally lax rules at Canadian-U.S. border crossings have become more stringent. Since 2009 a passport or equivalent travel document is required; see the U.S. Department of State's travel website (http://travel.state.gov) for a complete list of acceptable documents. Each vehicle is stopped at the customs checkpoint, where all of the passengers will have to present proper ID and answer a few questions, including questions about citizenship and the reason for visiting. If you're traveling with a minor for whom you aren't the parent or legal guardian, you'll need a signed letter from the parent or legal guardian that grants permission for the child to leave the country and that includes a contact phone number. Pets require proof of proper vaccinations; any plants will be confiscated.

All foreign visitors, including Canadians, must have a passport to enter the United States. Visit www.usa.gov/visitors/arriving.shtml for current information and requirements.

For visitors arriving by car, the bridge connecting Michigan's Upper Peninsula to Ontario is the International Bridge from Sault Ste. Marie to Sault Ste. Marie ($3.50/C$4.60

for a passenger car). If arriving by boat, visitors must check in at the nearest customs station immediately upon arrival.

Any goods purchased abroad must be declared, and the proper duty must be paid on certain items, including alcohol and cigarettes beyond personal-use limits. Bringing firearms across the border for lawful sporting purposes, such as hunting, requires declaring the weapon at customs and having the necessary paperwork in hand. Failure to declare a weapon may result in arrest.

Recreation

NATIONAL PARKS AND FORESTS

Michigan's Upper Peninsula is home to two national forests and a national lakeshore: The **Ottawa National Forest** in the western Upper Peninsula covers 982,895 acres; the **Hiawatha National Forest** in the eastern U.P. adds another 860,000 acres; and **Pictured Rocks National Lakeshore** extends along 42 miles of Lake Superior shore. **Seney National Wildlife Refuge** occupies 95,000 acres of cutover logging land in the eastern Upper Peninsula, while **Isle Royale National Park** is virtually a world of its own, a 45-mile-long wilderness surrounded by the waters of Lake Superior.

In the Upper Peninsula, most parks, except a few key attractions such as noteworthy waterfalls and beaches, are notably secluded, yet they offer a remarkable quantity and quality of activities for anyone interested in the outdoors. **Hiking** trails tend to be little used. **Campsites** are more secluded, more rustic, and are also lightly used. **Mountain biking** is permitted on most federal forest lands, although forbidden in state or national parks. Inland lakes can be difficult to reach with a boat trailer, so they tend to be ideal for those looking for a quiet **paddling** experience.

Contact the national forest headquarters to receive information on hiking, camping, paddling, and other activities: **Ottawa National Forest** (E6248 U.S. 2, Ironwood, 906/932-1330, www.fs.fed.us/r9/ottawa); **Hiawatha National Forest, Escanaba** (2727 North Lincoln Rd., Escanaba, 906/786-4062, www.fs.fed.us/r9/forests/hiawatha).

STATE FORESTS

Like national forests, state forests are hidden gems for anyone seeking a quiet corner of woods or water. Much of the state's forestland was actually acquired by default, picked up during the Depression when property owners were unable to pay their taxes. Their loss was certainly the public's gain. Much of the property is exceptional, consisting of rivers, waterfalls, lakes, beaches, and forest. Collectively, state forestland in the U.P. amounts to 3.9 million acres, the largest such holding in any state east of the Rocky Mountains.

To receive maps and information on Upper Peninsula state forest camping, hiking, and more, visit the **Michigan Department of Natural Resources (DNR)** website (www.michigan.gov/dnr) or contact **Copper Country State Forest, Baraga** (906/353-6651), **Escanaba River State Forest, Escanaba** (906/786-2351), and **Lake Superior State Forest, Newberry** (906/293-5131).

STATE PARKS

You'll see it scores of times in this guide: Michigan's Upper Peninsula has an outstanding state park system. They are well planned, well maintained, and showcase some of the state's most diverse and beautiful land. Some state parks were clearly set aside for public access, such as the state park beaches along the Lake Michigan shore, while others preserve historic sites and natural jewels like the Porcupine Mountains or Mackinac Island.

The U.P. has 21 state parks and nearly 60 state forest campgrounds. The **DNR Parks**

"Take Nothing but Pictures—Leave Nothing but Footprints..."

"And kill nothing but time." Although the precise authorship of this quote is disputed, it's generally attributed to the Baltimore Grotto (local chapter) of the National Speleological Society, a national organization dedicated to exploration and conservation of caves in the United States. The saying, or at least the first part of it, is often displayed in state parks and forests throughout Michigan to emphasize the most essential responsibility of any visitor—the obligation to leave the environment as undisturbed as possible, and to allow future visitors to experience nature unsullied.

Today's conservation movement reflects a tradition of thought that goes back to the late-19th century when future president Theodore Roosevelt noticed the threat posed to natural resources in the western United States by timber and hunting interests. The experience inspired Roosevelt to take proactive steps toward conservation after he assumed office. As president, he created the National Forest Service, proclaimed 51 bird reserves and 4 game preserves, and signed legislation creating the first national parks.

As First Lady of the United States, Lady Bird Johnson took a strong interest in protecting and enhancing the environment by promoting the Highway Beautification Act of 1965, which limited roadside billboards and promoted planting of flowers along roadways. In 1970 President Richard Nixon signed legislation establishing the Environmental Protection Agency to enforce a series of new laws limiting pollution.

But for today's visitor, honoring the motto of the Baltimore Grotto is simple. Make certain that your stopover includes removing refuse—paper, trash, and plastic gags. Respect native plants and animals. Be a friend to the earth.

and Recreation Division (517/373-9900, www.michigan.gov/dnr) publishes a handy *State Parks Guide* that includes a map, a short profile of each park, and a chart listing each park's amenities. You can get much of the same information from the website.

Since 2010 Michigan no longer charges daily entry fees for state parks. In lieu of this, the state has introduced the **Passport Perks** program, where any driver with a car licensed in Michigan can purchase an annual pass for $11 ($31 for nonresidents), regardless of the number of passengers in the vehicle. The annual pass, issued in the form of a sticker placed on either the license plate or on the inside passenger-side windshield, is valid for all Michigan state parks. Participation in Passport Perks also allows the user to access discounts at businesses located near the parks. Recreation passports can be purchased at any state park or forest, and can also be obtained at any Michigan Secretary of State office. For more information, visit www.michigan.gov/passportperks.

Camping requires an additional fee. Rates range from $13 to $31 per night depending on the specific location selected, time of year, and whether the campsite is rustic or more modern, with flush toilets, showers, and electricity. Some parks also rent "mini cabins," tiny shelters that offer a roof and walls to protect you from the elements, but little more, for around $40 per night. These book up fast, so be sure to reserve well ahead. A few parks, including Porcupine Mountain Wilderness State Park and Craig Lake State Park, rent out rustic cabins equipped with bunks and a stove or other cooking facility for $25-65 per night. They're great if you have a group or if you're visiting when the bugs are particularly fierce. These are extremely popular; calling to reserve as early as January is advised.

For a $2 fee, you can make a camping reservation at any park in advance by calling 800/447-2757 or reserving online at www.midnrreservations.com. You can request a specific site, but it will not be guaranteed. Camping reservations are strongly recommended in summer months at many state parks. This guide indicates if a park is particularly popular.

HIKING

With its bevy of national and state parks, national and state forests, national lakeshores, and private land accessible for public use, Michigan's Upper Peninsula has almost unlimited offerings for hikers. Where you go depends on your taste. This guide provides you with a number of ideas.

For backpackers, Isle Royale National Park in Lake Superior is an outstanding choice, free of roads and other development. Rustic campsites along the way allow you to walk across the 45-mile-long island, and water taxi services can get you back to your starting point. Slightly less remote, Porcupine Mountains Wilderness State Park in the western Upper Peninsula also offers great backpacking in a rugged backcountry environment that's uncommon in state parks.

Michigan also has hundreds of miles of linear hiking trails, such as the Bay de Noc to Grand Island Trail, which bisects the U.P. And for those really looking for an adventure, the **North Country National Scenic Trail** (www.nps.gov/noco) traverses the Upper Peninsula as part of a national trail that, when complete, will stretch from North Dakota to New York. Many long segments of the trail crossing national forest land are already open to hikers in Michigan. Check with national forest officials for more information.

BICYCLING

With its rolling topography, miles of shorelines, and ample country roads, Michigan's Upper Peninsula makes for a great bicycling destination. Some favorite areas for road cycling include the quiet roads near Les Cheneaux and through the temperate Garden Peninsula. Check with local visitors bureaus for suggested routes.

Michigan leads the nation in its number of rails-to-trails sites, with 55 old railroad beds converted into multiuse trails. Some, like the Bill Nichols trail in the Keweenaw Peninsula, are very rough. The term refers to a dormant railroad path with the rails removed, while everything else was left as-is, sometimes including railroad ties and sharp old mining rock. Some of these more primitive trails are appropriate only for snowmobiles and all-terrain vehicles, although most, especially the Bill Nichols venue, are great for mountain bikes, passing through wonderful wilderness terrain.

Unlike much of the Midwest, Michigan

is kind to mountain bikers. Good technical mountain biking can be found in many state and national forests. You'll find more miles than you could ever ride. Off-road riding in places like the Keweenaw and the Huron Mountains is the best between the Rockies and the Appalachians, and Michigan adds an extra perk—some stunning Great Lakes views.

SKIING

Each winter the upper Great Lakes produce a number of lake-effect snows, which fall onto some of the Midwest's hilliest terrain. That convenient marriage has made the Upper Peninsula the top ski destination in the Midwest. Strictly speaking, while the area isn't truly mountainous, the resorts do an admirable job of working creatively with the terrain, carving out 600-foot vertical drops and runs that wind through the pines or offer spectacular views of the Great Lakes.

Though downhill ski areas can be found throughout the peninsula, most are concentrated in the western U.P. from Ironwood to the Porcupine Mountains.

Cross-country skiers have even more to choose from. Though they don't all offer lodging, there are several privately run cross-country trail systems in the U.P. Many of the downhill resorts, such as Big Powderhorn Mountain in Bessemer, also have notable cross-country trails. The national lakeshores and many state parks groom trails for skiing, and the state and national forests offer virtually limitless opportunity for backcountry skiing.

For information on both downhill and cross-country skiing, contact **Pure Michigan** (800/644-2489, www.michigan.org/skiing).

GOLF

The U.P. has plenty of top-tier courses, many which feature a diverse terrain of hills and water views that make for an extraordinary golfing experience. Drummond Island, Mackinac Island, and Marquette are home to some of the U.P.'s finest golf courses. Here you'll find award-winners like The Rock at the Drummond Island Resort and Conference Center, The Jewel at the Grand Hotel on Mackinac Island, and Greywalls at the Marquette Golf Club. You'll also find plenty of well-kept and challenging courses elsewhere on the peninsula. For more information, consult the destination chapters or contact **Pure Michigan** (800/644-2489, www.michigan.org/golf).

BOATING AND FISHING

Michigan leads the nation in boat registrations with an astonishing 940,000. There are also an estimated 200,000 to 300,000 legally unregistered boats in the state, meaning there are well over a million watercraft in the state. Michigan boaters cruise from port to port on the Great Lakes, sail along scenic shoreline like Pictured Rocks and along island chains, water ski on thousands of inland lakes, paddle white-water rivers and quiet waters, and fish just about everywhere.

Small watercraft such as day sailors, fishing boats, and canoes are readily available to rent in many U.P. communities. Contact the local chamber of commerce or visitors bureau in the area you plan to visit for more information. For larger sailboats or powerboats, contact the **Michigan Charter Boat Association** (800/622-2971, www.micharterboats.com). The Pure Michigan website (www.michigan.org) also has an interactive travel planner that can provide you with a list of charter operations in a given region.

If you'll be hauling your own boat by trailer, the **Michigan DNR** (517/373-9900, www.michigan.gov/dnr) publishes a list of public launch sites. If you'll be arriving by water, see the *Getting There* section earlier in this chapter for information on Great Lakes public mooring facilities. A Coast Guard-approved lifejacket—known as a PFD, or personal flotation device—is required for each person on any kind of boat.

Michigan's Upper Peninsula is a paddler's dream. You can **canoe** or run white water down several nationally designated Wild and Scenic Rivers, **surf** waves along

Lake Michigan's shoreline, or **sea kayak** along Pictured Rocks or Isle Royale National Park. For a more peaceful experience, the Sturgeon River is a favorite. The U.P. also has several notable white-water rivers, including the beautiful Presque Isle River and the Ontonagon. For more information on paddling destinations and liveries, contact the **Michigan Association of Paddle Sports Providers** (www.michigancanoe.com).

Fishing has long been exceedingly popular in Michigan. It comes in all seasons and styles, from fly-fishing along a pristine stream to relaxing in an ice-fishing shanty while watching a football game. The quantity of blue-ribbon trout streams is unrivaled anywhere east of Montana. The Fox, the Chocolay, the Carp—you'll find most of the best streams in the eastern U.P.

"Deep-sea" charters on the Great Lakes go after the big chinook salmon, coho, and lake trout. Lake Michigan's Bay de Noc arguably offers the finest walleye fishing in the state, if not all the Great Lakes. Inland, literally thousands of lakes harbor walleye, northern pike, muskie, bass, and pan fish. Some of the most popular spots are the Manistique Lakes chain and huge Lake Gogebic.

The ultimate level of solitude can be found in the dozens of small lakes in the Ottawa and Hiawatha National Forests, which are peaceful, harder to get to, and lightly used. As a result, these waterways teem with fish. Some, like the Sylvania Wilderness, have special fishing regulations, so check with authorities. All Michigan waters require a valid Michigan fishing license. For specific fishing information, contact the **DNR Fisheries Division** (517/373-1204, www.michigan.gov/dnr).

HUNTING

With its abundance of wildlife, forests, and undeveloped land, Michigan's long history of hunting continues as strongly today as it ever has. And when most people think about hunting in Michigan, white-tailed deer tend to be the first creature that comes to mind. There are some 325,000 deer in the Upper Peninsula.

Of these, hunters take several thousand each year; in 2015, hunters killed some 20,000 deer.

While the sentiment and sympathies of many people tend toward the deer, this annual culling of the herd helps prevent much larger problems, chief among them being deer-vehicle accidents and fatalities. When the statewide deer population peaked in the 1980s at about two million animals, signs of distress were seen in the herd. Animals were perilously underweight and in some places as many as 6 of 10 fawns died. Some 125,000 animals starved to death during a single hard winter. Deer-vehicle accidents increased to 40,000 each year, killing an average of 5 people and injuring an additional 1,500 annually. Crop damage appeared and threatened significant economic damage as the urban and suburban deer population grew. Fencing, trapping, and birth control have proved far less effective in controlling the population than recreational hunting, which is the most efficient means of balancing the population and encouraging healthy cohabitation with human interests and the economy.

The DNR has spent many years trying to strike a balance between scientific herd management and other considerations to maintain a healthy deer population, working with hunters and members of the agricultural industry to develop a mutually beneficial situation. The ideal herd size is around 1.5 million animals, with a buck population of approximately 35 percent. Michigan's hunting rules and regulations change frequently as management needs vary. Special hunting seasons are declared and canceled as needed, and specific rules balance the number of antlerless and antlered deer that can be taken by each hunter. There are a number of general regulations, in addition to season-specific rules that often change from season to season.

Hunting Licenses

No one can hunt in Michigan without the proper license. For state residents, this is a fairly easy and inexpensive process, costing $15 each for a firearm or archery license to take one buck during each season. Nonresidents will have to pay considerably more, $151 each for firearm and archery seasons. It's a much steeper price, but given the abundance of deer and the quality of Michigan hunting, it's worth it. To apply for a license, residents need a valid driver's license or a State of Michigan ID card. Nonresidents need to obtain a MDNR Sport card, a type of Michigan ID allowing you to hunt, fish, and trap in the state. The cost is only $1, and it can be ordered online (www.mdnr-elicense.com). Both residents and nonresidents born on or after January 1, 1960, must either present a hunter safety certificate or a previous hunting license, or must sign their license in the presence of a license agent. Hunters are required to carry the signed license and ID whenever they're hunting.

What type of license you get depends on how you like to hunt, and when or where you do it. Buck hunting regulations are different in the U.P. than in the rest of the state and vary depending on the type of license purchased, so take your time and make sure you're buying exactly what you intend. Note that any deer that has at least one antler extending three or more inches above its skull is considered "antlered." Any deer without antlers or with the longest antler extending less than three inches above the skull is considered "antlerless."

You can buy a separate license for both archery and firearm season, which will limit you to only one antlered deer in the U.P. for all seasons combined. You can also use the archery license to tag an antlerless deer during archery season. The Michigan DNR also sells combination deer hunting licenses, which consist of a regular and a restricted license. In the Upper Peninsula, both the restricted and regular license have antler point restrictions. With the restricted license, hunters can take a deer that has at least one antler with four or more antler points, each at least one inch in length. The regular license can be used on deer with at least one antler with three or more antler points, each at least one inch in

length. Both the regular and combination license can be used for antlerless deer in the U.P.

Deer are not the only animals hunted in the Upper Peninsula. Hunters can go after both black bear and elk, although there is a lottery system and drawing for each of these animals. There are also drawing systems for wild turkey, antlerless deer, reserved waterfowl, and special deer hunts. Rabbits and hares, crows, pheasant, quail, grouse, and squirrels can also be hunted in Michigan. Fur harvesters and trappers can hunt foxes, coyotes, badgers, beavers, bobcats, muskrat, mink, and more.

Public and Private Land

The Upper Peninsula has seemingly endless acres of public land accessible to hunters. Contact the Michigan DNR for a comprehensive list of locations. In addition to public land, the state has purchased public hunting rights to selected tracts of privately owned land, as well as more than two million acres of commercial forests statewide. Hunters can also ask permission to hunt on private land. A verbal agreement from the landowner is all that's necessary. A few tips for asking: Get permission well in advance, and approach the door alone or with one other person. Be certain to leave your firearm behind. If you can't visit the landowner, write a letter or email asking to meet in person or make arrangements by phone. Provide your name and contact information, the dates and times you'd like to hunt, and exactly where on the land you'd prefer to hunt. Ask if there are any prohibited areas, and respect any additional requests from the landowner, including party size limits, ORV limits, and safety zones. Leave the property exactly as you found it or better. And always thank the landowner when finished.

Hunting Safety

It goes without saying that firearms and bows are deadly, so carry and use them with utmost care. As a means of cutting down on hunting accidents, the state has a clothing requirement that is strictly enforced: "You may not hunt with any device or trap with any firearm, on any lands during daylight hunting hours from August 15-April 30, unless you wear a hat, cap, vest, jacket, or rain gear of highly visible orange color, commonly referred to as Hunter Orange." The Hunter Orange garment must be the outermost garment and visible from all sides. Camouflage items that have at least 50 percent or more of the surface in Hunter Orange are legal. There are a few exceptions. The requirements don't apply to archery deer hunters except when hunting during the youth firearm season and the November firearm deer season. Waterfowl, crow, wild turkey, and archery bear hunters are also exempt.

This information explains only the highlights of Michigan's complex hunting regulations. For complete information, visit www.michigan.gov/dnr and click "Hunting and Trapping" on the left side. From this page you can also request a print copy of all Michigan Hunting and Trapping guidelines.

BEACHES

The beaches of the Upper Peninsula have a completely different mood than most of the Lower Peninsula's sandy destinations. Often wild and windswept, rocky and remote these coastlines remind you that you are definitely in "the Other Michigan." Striped cliffs rise directly from Lake Superior at **Pictured Rocks National Lakeshore;** nearby, the **Grand Sable Dunes** and **Twelvemile Beach** provide enough sand to thrill even the most devoted beachcomber. You probably won't see many people along Twelvemile Beach, but you may catch a glimpse of a deer, or even a black bear, headed to the water's edge for a drink. While perfect for long, sandy walks, only a hardy few actually swim in Lake Superior, as the water temperatures rarely climb out of the 40s.

The U.P. shares its southern shore with Lake Michigan, a winding border filled with secluded bays and inlets. A favorite of anglers, it also offers some good beaches—if you know where to look. Public access is a bit more difficult. Some of the best spots are along U.S. 2 from Naubinway to the Straits of Mackinac, where rest stops and county parks point you toward nice sandy beaches hidden behind the pines. You'll find another good sandy stretch along Green Bay between Menominee and Escanaba, where **J. W. Wells State Park** and several county parks offer inviting beaches.

DIVING

A century ago, the Great Lakes were the highways of their era—the fastest and most efficient mode of transport. Commodities like lumber, copper, and iron ore were hauled from the forests and mines to Great Lakes ports; passengers traveled on steamships from urban areas around the southern Great Lakes to imbibe the fresh cool air of northern resorts.

Of course, the Great Lakes were also known for shallow reefs and violent storms, which led to hundreds of shipwrecks. Additionally, the fresh cold waters—also free of barnacles and worms—kept those shipwrecks from decaying. Today many sit on the lake floor, undisturbed and virtually unchanged.

A century later, these freshwater time capsules are an unending source of delight for divers. Michigan has set aside nine areas where shipwrecks were particularly prevalent as **underwater preserves,** protecting their historic significance and mapping and marking them for divers. Together they cover 1,900 square miles of Great Lakes bottomland—an area roughly the size of Delaware. Off the shores of the Upper Peninsula, underwater preserves are located off the Keweenaw Peninsula and at Marquette, Munising, and Whitefish Point on Lake Superior as well as around the Straits of Mackinac in Lake Huron.

Most of the popular dive sites are marked with buoys in summer by volunteers of the Michigan Underwater Preserve Council. All the preserves are served by dive charters. For more information, request the booklet that describes each preserve and provides a list of dive charters and other services from the

(560 North State St., St. Ignace, MI 49781, 800/970-8717, www.michiganpreserves. org). You can also contact the chamber of commerce or visitors bureau near the preserve you want to visit and consult the appropriate chapters in this guide.

Food and Accommodations

FOOD AND DRINK

Throughout the Upper Peninsula, many Main Street cafés and bakeries serve up the pasty, a potpie creation of beef, potatoes, onions, rutabagas, and other vegetables. (Pronounce it PASS-tee, not PACE-tee.) Brought to the U.P. by Cornish miners, the pasty made for a hearty and filling meal that was easy to transport deep into the mine and warm up later with their candles. The same concept works well today if you're headed from town to your campfire.

Another Michigan food well worth tasting is its abundant fresh fish, from brook trout to Great Lakes whitefish. In Great Lakes ports, you'll often be able to find a commercial fishery operating a small retail store, usually down by the docks. They often sell both fresh catch and smoked fish. The latter is absolutely superb with a bottle of wine and a Great Lakes sunset.

Wine and Beer

While wineries in the Upper Peninsula are not plentiful, there are some standouts. **Threefold Vine Winery** (5856 NN Rd., Garden, 906/644-7089) in the Garden Peninsula is an example. Due to its fortuitous location, which offers mild winters and temperate weather, the locale is excellent for growing grapes. Another worthwhile destination is **Northern Sun Winery** (983 10th Rd., Bark River, 906/399-9212, www.northernsunwinery.com).

Instead, beer is the craft beverage of choice, at which a number of microbreweries across the peninsula excel. Among the best are the **Keweenaw Brewing Company** (408 Shelden Ave., Houghton, 906/482-5596, www.keweenawbrewing.com), the **Library Bar and Restaurant** (62 North Isle Royale St., Houghton, 906/487-5882, www.library-brewpub.com), and **Hereford and Hops Steakhouse and Brewpub** (624 Ludington St., Escanaba, 906/789-1945, www.herefordandhops.com).

LODGING OPTIONS

Michigan's Upper Peninsula is well served by most of the moderately priced national chains, but lacks the higher-end hotel groups such as Hilton or Westin. If you prefer staying in a chain establishment, pick up a copy of its national directory or consult its website to find current locations, rates, and services

---

Pasties

Prepare your favorite pie-crust recipe, making enough for four nine-inch pans. Then mix together:

- 2 pounds cooked pork and/or beef, cut into half-inch cubes

- 2 cups onion, diced

- 1 cup rutabaga, diced

- 1 cup potatoes, diced

- Salt and pepper to taste

Roll pastry out and cut four circles, using a nine-inch plate as a pattern. On one-half of the dough, layer meat, then onion, rutabaga, potatoes, and more meat. Fold pastry in half, then roll and crimp edges tightly together. Prick with a fork three times. Bake on a cookie sheet for one hour at 400°F. Makes four large pasties.

---

for its properties in Michigan. There's nothing inherently wrong with chains, but there are plenty of alternatives. All Michigan lodgings charge a 6 percent "use tax," similar to a sales tax. Many counties also have additional room taxes, ranging 2 to 5 percent, to fund their visitors bureaus and other tourism-related services.

Camping

Camping in Michigan's Upper Peninsula can run a wide gamut. You can park an RV next to a pool with a waterslide, or you can pitch a tent in backcountry so remote you could go weeks without seeing another soul. With tens of thousands of campsites in the state, you'll have no problem finding the option best for you.

This guide lists many campgrounds, admittedly omitting highly developed RV-type properties. Many of the state park campgrounds are included since they are almost universally good and often the best option in a particular area. Some can get busy in summer months, however. You can reserve ahead of time and even request a specific site, although it's not guaranteed, by calling 800/447-2757 or visiting www.midnrreservations.com.

State and national forests also tend to have excellent camping facilities, generally more rustic but located in appealing isolated places. A directory of Upper Peninsula campgrounds is available from the **Michigan DNR** (517/373-9900, www.michigan.gov/dnr). Backcountry camping is also permitted in many forests and on commercial lands owned by paper and mining companies.

For a complete list of private campgrounds, view a free *Michigan Campground Directory* at the **Association of RV Parks and Campgrounds of Michigan** website (9700 Hwy. 37 S., Buckley, MI 49620, 231/269-2267, www.michcampgrounds.com) or order a print copy for $3. You can also order a free *RV and Campsite Guide* from the **Michigan Association of Recreational Vehicles and Campgrounds** (2222 Association Dr., Okemos, MI 48864, 517/349-8881, www.marvac.org).

For help in selecting public or private campgrounds geared to your tastes and destination, check out the interactive Travel Planner on the **Pure Michigan** website (www.michigan.org).

Independent Motels

The combination of interstate highways and chain motels proved fatal to hundreds of independently owned motels in the last few decades as Americans proved their love for efficiency and predictability. Recently, however, the pendulum seems to be swinging the other way—interesting inns and distinctive lodges seem to be appearing in the most unlikely of places.

Many of these are traditional old mom-and-pop motels reminiscent of the 1960s—places with a neon vacancy sign and lawn chairs out front, the kind of places now romanticized along Route 66.

The good news is that they never really left the Upper Peninsula. Too out-of-the-way to attract the big chains, many U.P. towns still have several independent motels. They're still not fancy, and in some cases can appear tired and unappealing. But on the other hand, many mom-and-pop motels are clean, tidy, and remarkably inexpensive, and sometimes offer perks most national chains don't—allowing pets, for example. Additionally, they're often pedestrian-friendly, located in town or along a waterfront, rather than stranded out along a highway. Be aware that some do not accept credit cards, but if they don't, they will almost always take a personal check. Many are listed in this guide, and you may discover many more. Don't be afraid to try.

Bed-and-Breakfasts

The Upper Peninsula has dozens of bed-and-breakfast inns. Some are the traditional old-fashioned variety—a spare room or two in someone's quaint old farmhouse—but those have become the exception rather than the norm. Today's B&Bs run the gamut from large inns with amenities like pools and tennis courts to renovated lighthouses and other quaint historic buildings. For a Michigan bed-and-breakfast directory, contact the **Michigan Lake to Lake Bed and Breakfast Association** (888/575-1610, www.laketolake.com).

Ski and Golf Resorts

Several of the U.P.'s ski resorts double as golf resorts in summer, ringed with lodging that ranges from motel-style rooms to condo units and townhouses with kitchens, which allow you to save money by eating in. Many also offer a number of other amenities, such as pools, game rooms, and fitness centers, so they can be a particularly good choice for families with active kids. While golf resorts tend to be pricey, ski resorts that don't have the summer golf draw can be great bargains. For information on golf resorts and ski resorts with lodging open in the off-season, consult **Pure Michigan** (800/644-2489, www.michigan.org).

Health and Safety

HAZARDS
Contaminated Water

Even the most pristine Michigan waters may be tainted with *Giardia lamblia,* a microscopic organism most commonly transmitted in the feces of beavers, moose, and other mammals. It is present in many lakes and streams in the Upper Peninsula. **Giardiasis** can result in severe stomach cramps, vomiting, and diarrhea. As one Isle Royale ranger says, "It won't kill you, but it may make you wish you were dead." Neither chemical treatment with halazone nor a water filter will make water safe from giardia; the safe alternative is a water purifier capable of filtering down to 0.4 microns or less. Boiling is also effective, but make certain to get the water to a full rolling boil for five minutes. Isle Royale water may also be infected with the **hydatid tapeworm,** also requiring purifying or boiling.

Mosquitoes and Blackflies

Michigan's Upper Peninsula has its share of insects. The first hatch of **mosquitoes** usually occurs in early June, depending on local weather conditions. Their bite causes little or no pain but will leave a small lump and an itchy reaction. Be aware that some mosquitoes can carry communicable diseases. Malaria is nonexistent this far north, but mosquito-borne diseases such as West Nile virus have recently made national headlines, so it's best to take measures against bites. Mosquitoes can persist all summer but tend to be less of a problem as the season wears on, especially if conditions are dry. Mosquitoes are most common in low-lying wet areas and woods. Unfortunately, this accounts for a vast portion of the U.P. They tend to be most active at dusk. The best way to avoid them is to stay in a breeze and wear pants and long sleeves. While many people will endorse repellent as an effective measure, with those containing DEET the best, studies have linked it to several health risks. If you choose to use repellent, be sure to wash your hands carefully before eating and read the label warnings, especially before applying it to small children.

Blackflies can be an equally bothersome travel companion. They pose less of a health risk than mosquitoes but have a far more painful bite—somewhere between a mosquito bite and a bee sting on the pain scale. Blackflies resemble houseflies, only larger. They tend to be worst in the deep woods and during the early summer. U.P. blackflies can be the stuff of legend; anyone planning time in the backcountry should carry the strongest repellent available and to pack a head net. Even if you're not in the backcountry, blackflies can make their presence known. If you come prepared, they're more irritating than problematic.

Ticks

Wood ticks and **deer ticks** are found in U.P. woods and grasslands. The larger wood tick, which is about 0.25 inches long, can attach itself to the skin and suck the blood of its victim. Despite this ominous sounding fact, the insect is relatively harmless. If you find a wood tick on you, your companion, or your pet, grasp it as close to the head as possible and yank. Don't leave a piece of the insect embedded, which can lead to infection. Ticks prefer warm areas of the body (human or canine)—the scalp, neck, armpits, or genitals. Check under your dog's collar and around its ears.

Deer ticks are considerably more dangerous. They may transmit **Lyme disease,** a potentially debilitating condition. Lyme disease shows up as a temporary red rash that often resembles a ring, which slowly expands outward. Other symptoms as the disease progresses include sore joints, fatigue, and nausea. If left untreated, it can lead to arthritis and severe neurological and cardiac problems. Caught early, antibiotics can treat it effectively.

Additionally, deer ticks are tiny—often hardly larger than the head of a pin. Like wood ticks, they burrow into the skin, especially in warm places. After hiking, check yourself and your hiking partners carefully. If it's large enough, grasp the tick and pull it like you would a wood tick, or use tweezers. If you've been in a tick infested area, watch for a rash within the next week, and have anything suspicious looked at promptly by a doctor. Your best defense against ticks is to wear long pants and long sleeves and to spray yourself liberally with an effective repellent, such as those containing DEET.

Dogs are also highly susceptible to Lyme disease. Check your dog carefully and thoroughly for deer ticks by slowly running your fingers or a comb through her coat to get a look at the skin—a task that requires considerable patience from both you and your dog. Again, ears, necks, bellies, and genitals are areas most preferred by ticks. Signs that your dog may have acquired Lyme disease include nausea, fatigue, and lameness that may come and go from different joints. If you see potential symptoms, take your pet to a veterinarian immediately. Like humans, dogs respond well to antibiotics if the disease is caught early enough.

There is a canine vaccine for Lyme disease, but veterinarians express divided opinions on its effectiveness. There are some very good tick repellent sprays on the market intended for dogs.

Black Bears

When it comes to bigger animals, deer are by far the greatest danger, as they cause thousands of accidents each year on Michigan roads. But **black bears** certainly seem more frightening, especially when you're deep in the woods. Black bears are found throughout Northern Michigan, with the Upper Peninsula having an especially large population. They usually live in areas of heavy forest, but will routinely wander into open spaces, especially for berries and other food sources. They're beautiful animals, and you should consider yourself lucky if you observe one.

Black bears are generally shy creatures that would prefer to have nothing to do with you. If they hear you coming down the trail, they'll likely run the other way. If you happen to see one before it sees you, make sure you've left it an escape route, then clap, yell, or bang pans. Give especially wide berth to a mother with cubs. There are very few documented cases of black bear aggression against humans, and theories vary on what to do if you should ever find yourself in such a situation. Most behaviorists believe that, unlike grizzlies, black bears will be intimidated by dominant behavior such as shouting and waving your arms.

The worst problems occur when bears are lured into populated areas by human carelessness. It's always sad to see a bear relocated away from its home territory, but it happens frequently in campgrounds when humans don't properly store food or dispose of garbage. If you're car camping, keep all foodstuffs right

in your car (with the doors and windows closed and locked!). If you're tent camping, keep everything in airtight storage containers if possible, and suspend the containers on a line between two trees, high enough off the ground and far enough apart to be out of a bear's reach. Latched coolers placed under a picnic table are insufficient to keep bears out.

Clean pans and utensils right away, dumping the water well away from camp, and store them with the food. Never, ever keep any food (even gum) in your tent. Bears have an extremely good sense of smell and may be tempted to join you. Some say cosmetics also can attract them, so play it safe and store all soap and toothpaste with the food. It's also a good idea to leave your tent unzipped during the day while you're gone. Bears are curious, and if they want to look inside your tent, they'll make their own entrance if they can't find one.

If you're at a campground, deposit garbage in the animal-proof refuse containers provided. If you're backcountry camping, pack it out. Never, ever attempt to feed a bear, no matter how "tame" it may seem.

EMERGENCIES

All of Michigan's Upper Peninsula is tied into the 911 emergency system. Dial 911 for free from any telephone (including pay phones) to reach an operator who can quickly dispatch local police, fire, or ambulance services. This service also works from cellular phones. Be aware, however, that cell towers can be few and far between in rural areas. Much of the Upper Peninsula remains without reliable cellular or digital wireless service, but this can vary from carrier to carrier.

Hospitals

Every major city in the sparsely populated Upper Peninsula has a hospital, so you likely won't be too far away from quality medical care, unless you're deep in the woods.

Major hospitals include **Mackinac Straits Hospital** (220 Burdette St., St. Ignace, 906/643-8585, www.mackinacstraitshealth.org), **Marquette General Health System** (580 W., College Ave., Marquette, 906/228-9440, www.mgh.org), and **War Memorial Hospital** (500 Osborn Blvd., Sault St. Marie, 906/635-4460, www.warmemorialhospital.org).

right
ESSENTIALS
INFORMATION AND SERVICES

Information and Services

VISITOR INFORMATION

For general information on traveling in Michigan, your best source is the state-run **Pure Michigan** (800/644-2489, www.michigan.org, 9am-5pm Mon.-Fri.). Your call is answered by a real person who can send or fax brochures and consult a vast database to field your questions about festivals, lodgings, and a myriad of other topics. It's a much more helpful service than many tourism hotlines.

You may find it even more convenient to visit the state tourism database at **www.michigan.org.** This is a comprehensive website with an interactive menu that provides specific information tailored to the parameters you set. Tell it you want to go charter fishing on Lake Superior in fall, and it will

display a list of appropriate charters; click on each for a detailed description, rates, and directions. Currently the site has categories for accommodations, attractions, camping, charter boats, communities, events, golf, restaurants, shopping, and skiing.

For information specific to the Upper Peninsula, contact the **Upper Peninsula Travel and Recreation Association** (P.O. Box 400, Iron Mountain, 906/774-5480 or 800/562-7134, www.uptravel.com).

The Michigan Department of Transportation operates seven **Welcome Centers** throughout the state. These facilities are stocked with travel literature and staffed with "travel counselors" who are quite knowledgeable about the state in general and their

region in particular. The Welcome Centers are open year-round.

You'll find Welcome Centers at major gateways to the peninsula and at a few other "interior" locations. They're marked on the state highway map and with signs on the nearest highway. Hours vary.

MAPS

Michigan's official state road map is one of the few maps of the state that doesn't parcel the Upper Peninsula into frustrating and impossible to follow pieces. You can pick one up at a Michigan Welcome Center or request one from Pure Michigan.

For more detail, the DeLorme *Michigan Atlas and Gazetteer* provides great detail, with the state portrayed in 102 large scale maps. Though the 15-inch-long format is unwieldy for hikers, it's a great resource for planning your trip, and even identifies lighthouses, historic sites, waterfalls, industrial tours, and other points of interest. You can find it at many Midwestern bookstores for $19.95, or contact **DeLorme** (800/561-5105, www.delorme.com).

If you'll be exploring the backcountry; you're best off with an official topographic map produced by the U.S. Geological Survey. Michigan's national forests and lakeshores have topographic maps for sale at their visitors centers and ranger stations. Outside federal lands, you may find them (or other good detailed maps) in local outfitter shops, but don't assume it will. If you can, buy one ahead of time at an outfitter or map specialty store that carries topographic maps. If they don't have the one you need, they can help you look up its

number and should be able to order it for you. You also can contact the **U.S. Geological Survey** (800/872-6277, www.usgs.gov) for a free map index and order form.

TIME AND MONEY

The Upper Peninsula is located in the eastern time zone, with the exception of the four Upper Peninsula counties that border Wisconsin. Gogebic, Iron, Dickinson, and Menominee Counties are in the central time zone.

Visa and MasterCard are accepted throughout the peninsula, except in some of the smallest towns. ATMs also are becoming more and more prevalent, tied into the national Cirrus network. That said, there still are a number of mom-and-pop motels that accept only cash or checks. You might be surprised at how many small establishments are willing to take an out-of-town check, which they may prefer over credit cards. Cash is required at self-registration campgrounds. Never count on getting by with only plastic.

If you're traveling to or from Canada, you'll find currency exchanges at the border and at nearby banks in both countries. In the past, Canadian and U.S. money was accepted interchangeably in border areas, especially coins. In recent years, however, exchange rates have changed dramatically; plan to exchange currencies when traveling in either direction.

If you're a U.S. resident with Canadian currency left over at the end of a trip, it's best to have bills, not coins. Most American banks (especially away from border areas) will exchange only paper money.

Resources

Suggested Reading

ATLASES

DeLorme. *Michigan Atlas and Gazetteer.* Yarmouth, ME: DeLorme, 2012. Covering everything from major highways and byways to the back roads, this is one of the most detailed atlases you can find. Topographical maps and GPS grids are included (www.delorme.com).

Sportsman's Connection. *Northern Michigan All-Outdoors Atlas and Field Guide.* Superior, WI: Sportsman's Connection, 2008. Detailed maps, supplemental information, and helpful advice make this a must-have atlas for anyone who wants to spend any amount of time in Michigan's outdoors.

FICTION

Harrison, Jim. *True North.* New York: Grove, 2004. Best known as the author of *Legends of the Fall,* Michigan native Harrison tells the story of a wealthy, dysfunctional family with the Upper Peninsula's harsh landscape as the backdrop. A tragedy, the book can be shocking and dark, but filled with beauty.

Hemingway, Ernest. *The Nick Adams Stories.* New York: Scribner, 1981. Hemingway's semiautobiographical account tells the story of Nick Adams as his life progresses from soldier to veteran, writer, and parent.

Monson, Ander. *Other Electricities: Stories.* Louisville, KY: Sarabande, 2005. Raised in the U.P., Monson presents a melancholic vision of his native peninsula through this critically acclaimed collection of stories and lists.

Traver, Robert. *Anatomy of a Murder.* New York: St. Martin's Griffin; 25th Anniversary Edition, 2005. This popular historical novel was written under a pseudonym by state Supreme Court justice John Voelker about a love-triangle murder that took place at the Lumberjack Tavern in Big Bay. The gripping novel was made into a feature-length movie in 1959, filmed on location in Marquette and Big Bay, by legendary director Otto Preminger. Highly recommended.

GENERAL INTEREST

Emerick, Lon L. *The Superior Peninsula: Seasons in the Upper Peninsula of Michigan.* Skandia, MI: North Country Publishing, 1996. A collection of essays about and "love letters" to the big lake and its peninsula, categorized by season.

Peterson, Carolyn C. *A View From the Wolf's Eye.* Calumet, MI: Copper Island Printing, 2008. The personal account of a woman who worked on Isle Royale with her husband for 37 summers conducting the ongoing study of the moose-wolf relationship while raising a family. An intimate account of nature from the perspective of one of its custodians.

Peterson, Rolf O. *The Wolves of Isle Royale: A Broken Balance.* Ann Arbor, MI: University of Michigan Press, 2007. Internationally known wolf researcher Peterson has compiled a firsthand account of Isle Royale National Park's ongoing wolf study. A delightful, informative book, it's filled with personal stories and powerful images.

Stonehouse, Frederick. *The Wreck of the Edmund Fitzgerald.* Gwinn, MI: Avery Color Studios, 2006. A thorough and thoughtful analysis of one of the most tragic disasters to occur on the Great Lakes. While offering no firm opinion as to the cause of the tragedy, the author discusses the events leading up to this famous shipwreck and the various theories of what caused its demise.

Traver, Robert. *Trout Magic.* New York: Touchstone, 1989. Personal reflections on the pleasures and solitude of trout fishing from accomplished author Robert Traver, better known as Justice John Voelker.

NATURAL HISTORY

Gostomski, Ted, et al. *Island Life: An Isle Royale Nature Guide.* Hancock, MI: Book Concern Printers, 2007. A comprehensive reference to the flora and fauna of Isle Royale in small paperback form. Excellent companion for a fishing or camping trip.

Grady, Wayne. *The Great Lakes: The Natural History of a Changing Region.* Vancouver: Greystone, 2011. A wonderfully illustrated natural history of the lakes with fascinating information on their formation as well as their present-day ecology and biology. Part written history, part photographic record, this book would be a beautiful and informative addition to any coffee table.

Kershaw, Linda. *Trees of Michigan: Including Tall Shrubs.* Auburn, WA: Lone Pine Publishing, 2006. This is *the* guide for tree identification in Michigan. Nearly 300 species of trees are referenced here, with color photographs and illustrations of the bark,

leaves, flowers, and overall shape of each tree. Tips are included for distinguishing among similar species.

Tekiela, Stan. *Birds of Michigan Field Guide.* Cambridge, MI: Adventure Publications, 2004. In this handy pocket-size guide, the author separates the wheat from the chaff, providing 112 concise yet informative summaries of the most common of Michigan's 800 bird species. Written in nontechnical language with vibrant, pleasing images.

OUTDOOR RECREATION

DuFresne, Jim. *Isle Royale National Park: Foot Trails and Water Routes,* 4th ed. Petoskey, MI: Michigantrailmaps.com, 2011. The definitive guide to Isle Royale, filled with practical information about campsites, portages, fishing spots, and more. Small enough to carry along, and an indispensable resource.

DuFresne, Jim. *Porcupine Mountains Wilderness State Park: A Backcountry Guide for Hikers, Backpackers, Campers, and Winter Visitors.* San Diego: Thunder Bay Press, 2009. An indispensable guide to this mammoth wild and beautiful park, with extensive coverage of the park's trail system for both day hikers and backpackers.

Hansen, Eric. *Hiking Michigan's Upper Peninsula.* Guilford, CT: FalconGuides, 2005. Hansen set out to hike and map 50 of the Upper Peninsula's finest trails, many of them little-known gems. His work is magnificently displayed in this book through compelling images.

Hillstrom, Kevin, and Laurie Collier Hillstrom. *Paddling Michigan.* Guilford, CT: FalconGuides, 2001. This extensive paddling guide predominantly covers routes and rivers in the Upper Peninsula but does include some Lower Peninsula waterways.

Suggested Viewing and Listening

MOVIES

Anatomy of a Murder, 1959. Based on the novel by Michigan Supreme Court justice and Ishpeming native John Voelker, this movie is based on an actual 1952 murder case in which Voelker, then a private attorney, was defense counsel, and filmed in Big Bay and Marquette. The film stars Jimmy Stewart and George C. Scott and was directed by Otto Preminger.

Escanaba in da Moonlight, 2001. Starring, written, and directed by Jeff Daniels, this offbeat comedy has taken some heat for its portrayal of the residents of Escanaba, yet some people claim it's spot on. With a quirky plot and a good deal of off-color humor, this film isn't for everyone.

Somewhere in Time, 1980. While not a classic, this film has acquired a cult following and a reputation as a timeless love story. Its stars, Jane Seymour and Christopher Reeve, are overshadowed only by the magnificent Grand Hotel and the Mackinac Island setting.

MUSIC

Stevens, Sufjan. *Greetings from Michigan: The Great Lakes State,* 2003. When Michigan native Sufjan Stevens released his Indie ode to Michigan, people took note. Pay special attention to songs set in the Upper Peninsula. Includes "For the Widows in Paradise, For the Fatherless in Ypsilanti," "The Upper Peninsula," "Tahquamenon Falls," "Sleeping Bear, Sault Saint Marie," and "Oh God, Where Are You Now? (In Pickerel Lake? Pigeon? Marquette? Mackinaw?)."

Lightfoot, Gordon. "The Wreck of the *Edmund Fitzgerald,*" 1976. From the album *Summertime Dream,* Gordon Lightfoot's folk retelling of the tragic sinking of the *Edmund Fitzgerald* during a Lake Superior storm immortalized the event in popular memory.

Internet Resources

STATEWIDE INFORMATION

Travel Michigan
www.michigan.org
Michigan's official travel website is an integral part of the state's Pure Michigan tourism campaign. It's the most visited state tourism site in the United States, and is frequently updated.

Upper Peninsula Travel and Recreation Association
www.uptravel.com
Upper Peninsula-specific tourism information and numerous helpful links. Request the free travel planner.

OUTDOOR RECREATION AND CAMPING

Michigan Department of Natural Resources
www.michigan.gov/dnr
The site for state park info, campground reservations, and information on all sorts of outdoor recreation, including fishing, hunting, and snowmobile registration.

Michigan Interactive
www.fishweb.com

A great resource for all sorts of outdoor activities in Michigan, including interactive maps for fishing, hiking, and snowmobile and off-road vehicle trails.

National Park Service
www.nps.gov
Official one-stop shopping for all of the national parks and lakeshores in Michigan—Isle Royale, Keweenaw, and Pictured Rocks—plus Sleeping Bear Dunes in the Lower Peninsula as well as the North Country National Scenic Trail.

U.S. Forest Service
www.fs.fed.us
A site that provides valuable information about both the Hiawatha and Ottawa National Forests.

TRANSPORTATION
Michigan Department of Transportation
www.michigan.gov/mdot
The best, most up-to-date source for information on major road construction projects and various public transportation options.

WEATHER
Weather Michigan
www.weathermichigan.com
An easy-to-use collection of Michigan-related weather links, all in one place.

Visitor Information

Bays de Noc Convention and Visitors Bureau
230 Ludington St.
Escanaba, MI 49829
906/789-7862
800/533-4386
www.visitescanaba.com

Delta County Area Chamber of Commerce
230 Ludington St.
Escanaba, MI 49829
906/786-2192
888/335-8264
www.deltami.org

Drummond Island Tourism Association
P.O. Box 200
Drummond Island, MI 49726
906/493-5245
800/737-8666
www.drummondislandchamber.com

Ironwood Tourism and Lodging Council
P.O. Box 706
Ironwood, MI 49938
906/932-4850
www.ironwoodtourismcouncil.com

Keweenaw Convention and Visitors Bureau
56638 Calumet Ave.
Calumet, MI 49913
906/337-4579
800/338-7982
www.keweenaw.info

Les Cheneaux Tourist Association
P.O. Box 10
680 W. Hwy. 134
Cedarville, MI 49719
888/364-7526
www.lescheneaux.org

Mackinac Island Tourism Bureau
7274 Main St.
Mackinac Island, MI 49757
906/847-3783
www.mackinacisland.org

Mackinaw Area Visitors Bureau
10800 W. U.S. 23
Mackinaw City, MI 49701
231/436-5664
800/666-0160
www.mackinawcity.com

Manistique Tourism Council
P.O. Box 37
Manistique, MI 49854
906/341-2410
www.visitmanistique.com

**Marinette/Menominee Area
Chamber of Commerce**
601 Marinette Ave.
Marinette, WI 54143
715/735-6681
www.mandmchamber.com

**Marquette County Convention and
Visitors Bureau**
337 W. Washington St.
Marquette, MI 49855
906/228-7749
800/544-4321
www.travelmarquettemichigan.com

Newberry Area Tourism Association
P.O. Box 308
Newberry, MI 49868
906/293-5562
800/831-7292
www.newberrytourism.com

Paradise Area Chamber of Commerce
5370 N. Hwy. 123
Paradise, MI 49768
906/492-3219
www.paradisemichigan.org

**Sault Ste. Marie Convention
and Visitors Bureau**
1808 Ashmun St.
Sault Ste. Marie, MI 49783
906/632-3366
800/647-2858
www.saultstemarie.com

St. Ignace Visitors Bureau
6 Spring St.
St. Ignace, MI 49781
800/338-6600
www.stignace.com

**Tourism Association of
the Dickinson County Area**
333 S. Stephenson Ave., Suite 202
Iron Mountain, MI 49801
800/236-2447
www.ironmountain.org

**Western U.P. Convention
and Visitors Bureau**
405 N. Lake St.
Ironwood, MI 49938
906/932-4850
800/522-5657
www.explorewesternup.com

Index

List of Maps

Photo Credits

MOON NATIONAL PARKS

ACADIA NATIONAL PARK
HILARY NANGLE

ARCHES & CANYONLANDS NATIONAL PARKS
W.C. McRAE & JUDY JEWELL

BANFF NATIONAL PARK
ANDREW HEMPSTEAD

DEATH VALLEY NATIONAL PARK
JENNA BLOUGH

GLACIER NATIONAL PARK
BECKY LOMAX

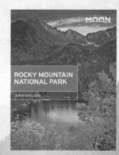

GRAND CANYON
KATHLEEN BRYANT

GREAT SMOKY MOUNTAINS NATIONAL PARK
JASON FRYE

MOUNT RUSHMORE & THE BLACK HILLS
Including the Badlands
LAURAL A. BIDWELL

ROCKY MOUNTAIN NATIONAL PARK
ERIN ENGLISH

In these books:

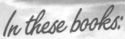

- Full coverage of gateway cities and towns
- Itineraries from one day to multiple weeks
- Advice on where to stay (or camp) in and around the parks

More Guides & Getaways

CHICAGO
REBECCA HOLLAND

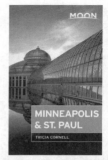

MINNEAPOLIS & ST. PAUL
TRICIA CORNELL

75 GREAT HIKES
MINNEAPOLIS & ST. PAUL

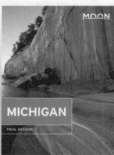

MICHIGAN
PAUL VACHON

MICHIGAN'S UPPER PENINSULA
PAUL VACHON

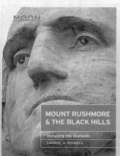

MOUNT RUSHMORE & THE BLACK HILLS
Including the Badlands
LAURAL A. BIDWELL

ROUTE 66
Road Trip
MIDPOINT CAFE
CANDACY TAYLOR

WISCONSIN
THOMAS HUHTI

WISCONSIN'S DOOR COUNTY
THOMAS HUHTI